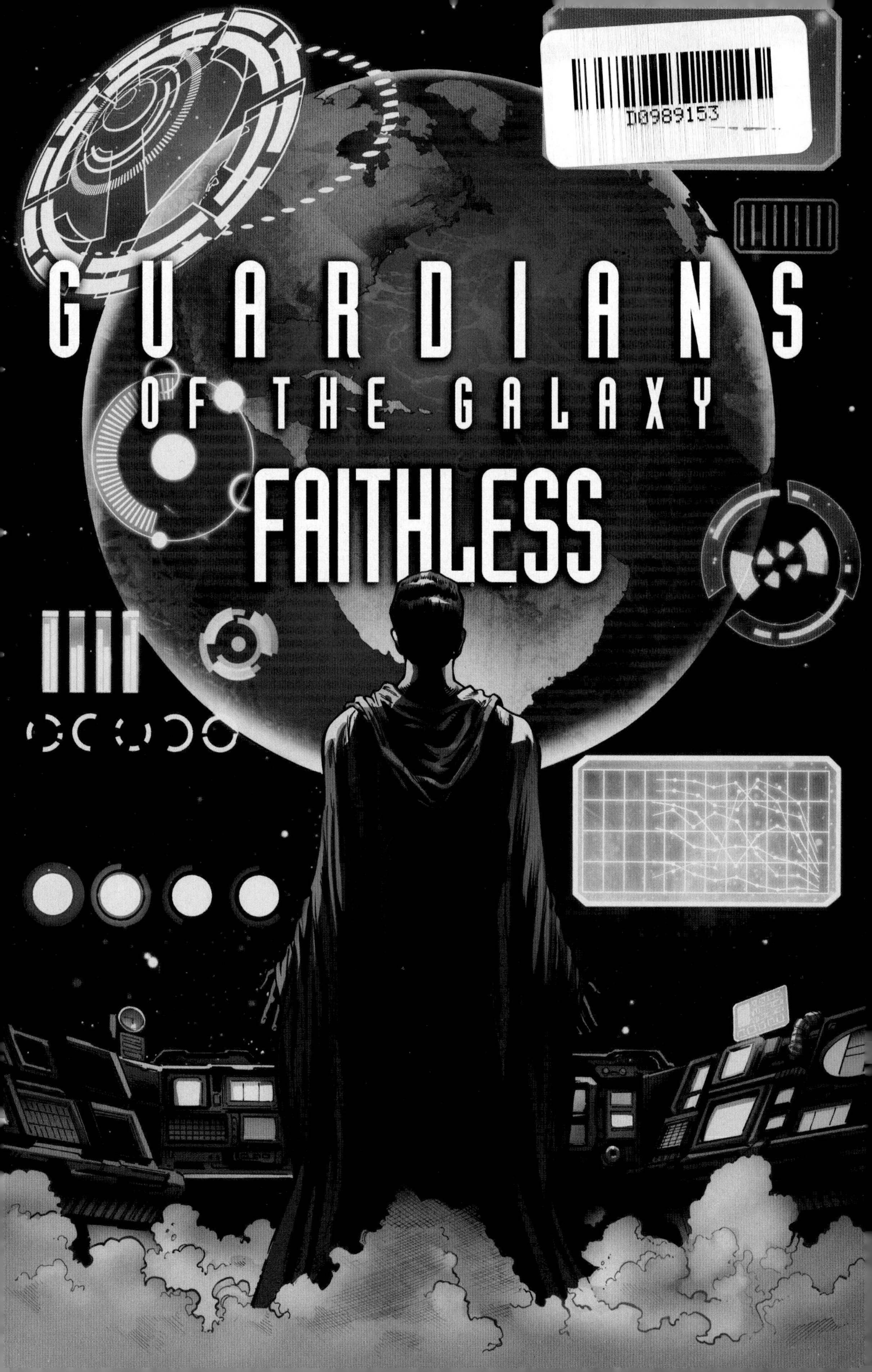
GUARDIANS
OF THE GALAXY
FAITHLESS

The galaxy's greatest warriors gathered to hear the reading of
Thanos' last will and testament — only to be attacked by the Black Order
as they sought to recover the Mad Titan's body!

The Black Order opened up a black hole and cast several heroes —
including the Starjammers, Quasar, Cosmo, the Silver Surfer, Darkhawk,
Adam Warlock and many others — into the abyss.

Luckily, a group of heroes escaped and re-formed the Guardians of the Galaxy.

But what happened to the many who weren't so lucky…?

collection editor JENNIFER GRÜNWALD
assistant managing editor MAIA LOY
assistant editor CAITLIN O'CONNELL
editor, special projects MARK D. BEAZLEY

vp production & special projects JEFF YOUNGQUIST
book designers SALENA MAHINA & ADAM DEL RE
svp print, sales & marketing DAVID GABRIEL
editor in chief C.B. CEBULSKI

GUARDIANS OF THE GALAXY VOL. 2: FAITHLESS. Contains material originally published in magazine form as GUARDIANS OF THE GALAXY (2019) #7-12 and GUARDIANS OF THE GALAXY ANNUAL (2019) #1. First printing 2019. ISBN 978-1-302-91589-6. Published by MARVEL WORLDWIDE, INC., a subsidiary of MARVEL ENTERTAINMENT, LLC. OFFICE OF PUBLICATION: 1290 Avenue of the Americas, New York, NY 10104. © 2019 MARVEL No similarity between any of the names, characters, persons, and/or institutions in this magazine with those of any living or dead person or institution is intended, and any such similarity which may exist is purely coincidental. **Printed in the U.S.A.** KEVIN FEIGE, Chief Creative Officer; DAN BUCKLEY, President, Marvel Entertainment; JOHN NEE, Publisher; JOE QUESADA, EVP & Creative Director; TOM BREVOORT, SVP of Publishing; DAVID BOGART, Associate Publisher & SVP of Talent Affairs; Publishing & Partnership; DAVID GABRIEL, VP of Print & Digital Publishing; JEFF YOUNGQUIST, VP of Production & Special Projects; DAN CARR, Executive Director of Publishing Technology; ALEX MORALES, Director of Publishing Operations; DAN EDINGTON, Managing Editor; SUSAN CRESPI, Production Manager; STAN LEE, Chairman Emeritus. For information regarding advertising in Marvel Comics or on Marvel.com, please contact Vit DeBellis, Custom Solutions & Integrated Advertising Manager, at vdebellis@marvel.com. For Marvel subscription inquiries, please call 888-511-5480. **Manufactured between 12/27/2019 and 1/28/2020 by LSC COMMUNICATIONS INC., KENDALLVILLE, IN, USA.**

10 9 8 7 6 5 4 3 2 1

"FAITHLESS"

ANNUAL #1

DONNY CATES, AL EWING, TINI HOWARD, ZAC THOMPSON & LONNIE NADLER
writers

JOHN McCREA, YILDIRAY CINAR, IBRAHIM MOUSTAFA & FILIPE ANDRADE
artists

MIKE SPICER, RAIN BEREDO & JAY DAVID RAMOS
color artists

GIUSEPPE CAMUNCOLI & JEAN-FRANÇOIS BEAULIEU
cover art

#7-12

DONNY CATES   CORY SMITH
writer   penciler

CORY SMITH [#7-8] & VICTOR OLAZABA [#9-12]
inkers

DAVID CURIEL
color artist

GEOFF SHAW & DAVID CURIEL; DYLAN BURNETT &
ANTONIO FABELA; ARIEL OLIVETTI & ANTONIO FABELA;
AND TRADD MOORE & DAVE STEWART
flashback artists, #12

DAVID MARQUEZ & DEAN WHITE [#7]; MIKE HENDERSON &
DEAN WHITE [#8]; PATCH ZIRCHER & DEAN WHITE [#9-10]
AND GEOFF SHAW & DEAN WHITE [#11-12]
cover art

Jessamine County Public Library
600 South Main Street
Nicholasville, KY 40356
859-885-3523

LAUREN AMARO
assistant editor

DARREN SHAN
editor

ANNUAL #1

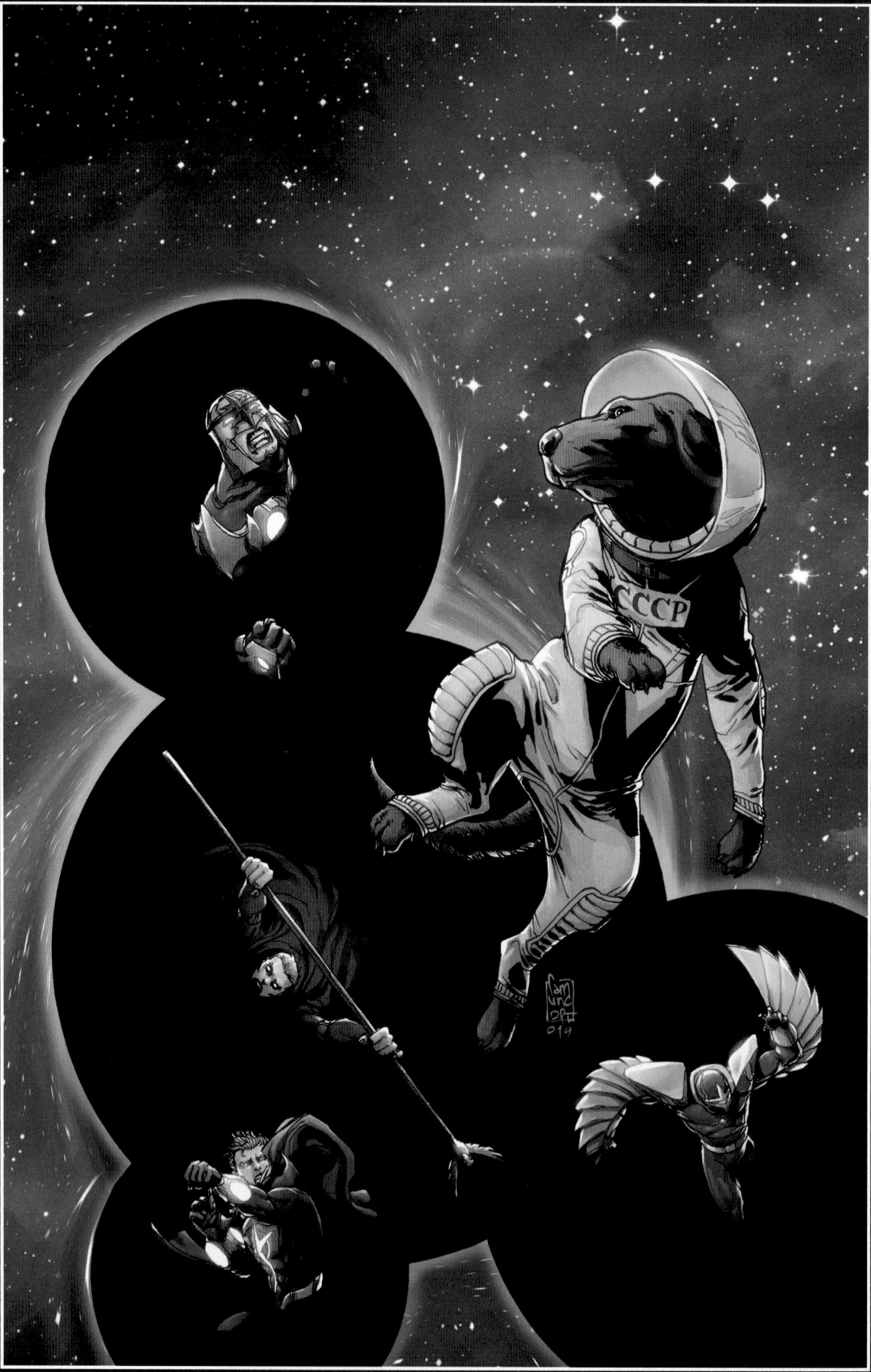

CCCP

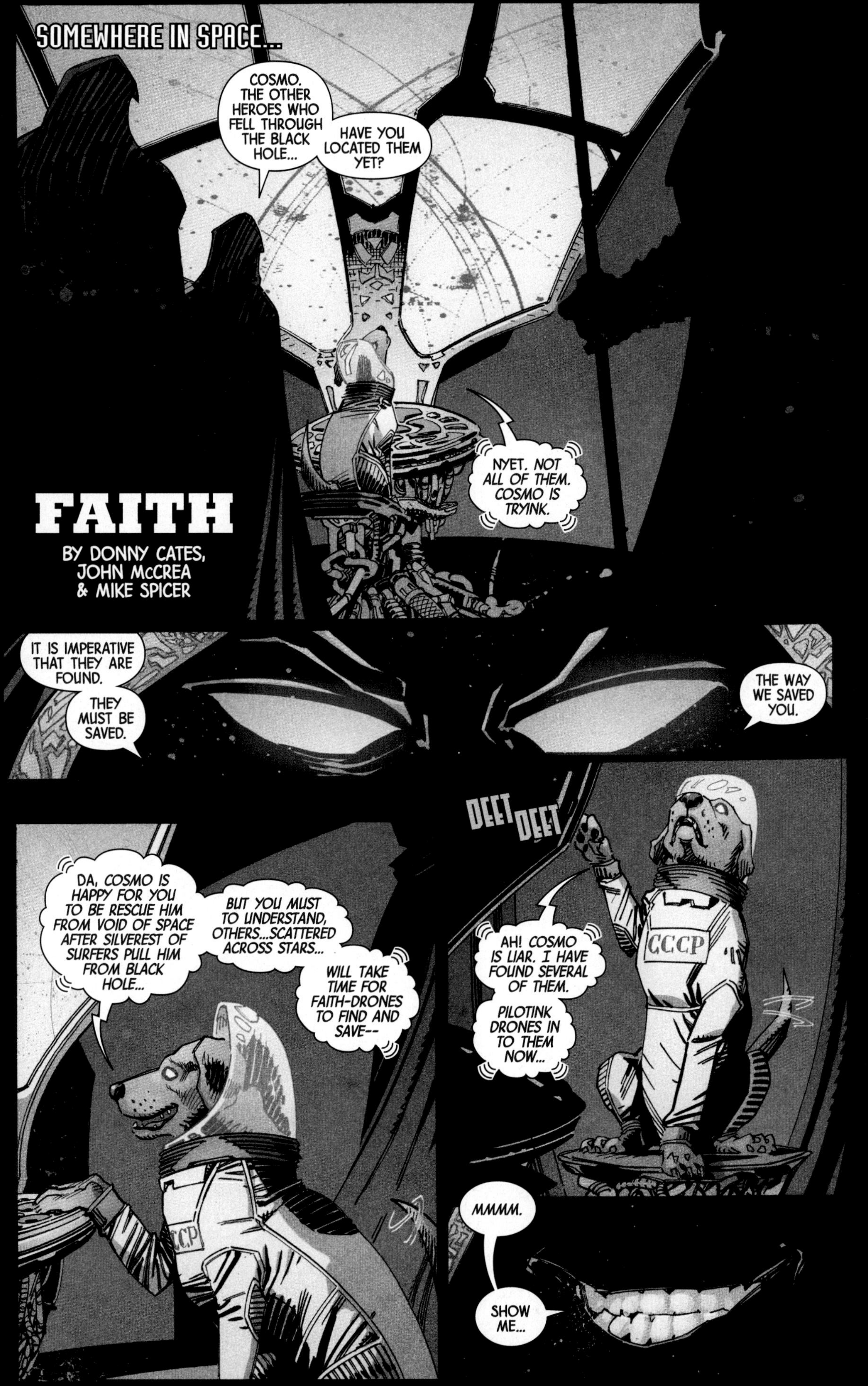
SOMEWHERE IN SPACE...
COSMO. THE OTHER HEROES WHO FELL THROUGH THE BLACK HOLE...
HAVE YOU LOCATED THEM YET?
NYET. NOT ALL OF THEM. COSMO IS TRYINK.
FAITH
BY DONNY CATES, JOHN McCREA & MIKE SPICER
IT IS IMPERATIVE THAT THEY ARE FOUND.
THEY MUST BE SAVED.
THE WAY WE SAVED YOU.
DA, COSMO IS HAPPY FOR YOU TO BE RESCUE HIM FROM VOID OF SPACE AFTER SILVEREST OF SURFERS PULL HIM FROM BLACK HOLE...
BUT YOU MUST TO UNDERSTAND, OTHERS...SCATTERED ACROSS STARS...
WILL TAKE TIME FOR FAITH-DRONES TO FIND AND SAVE--
DEET DEET
AH! COSMO IS LIAR. I HAVE FOUND SEVERAL OF THEM.
PILOTINK DRONES IN TO THEM NOW...
CCCP
MMMM.
SHOW ME...

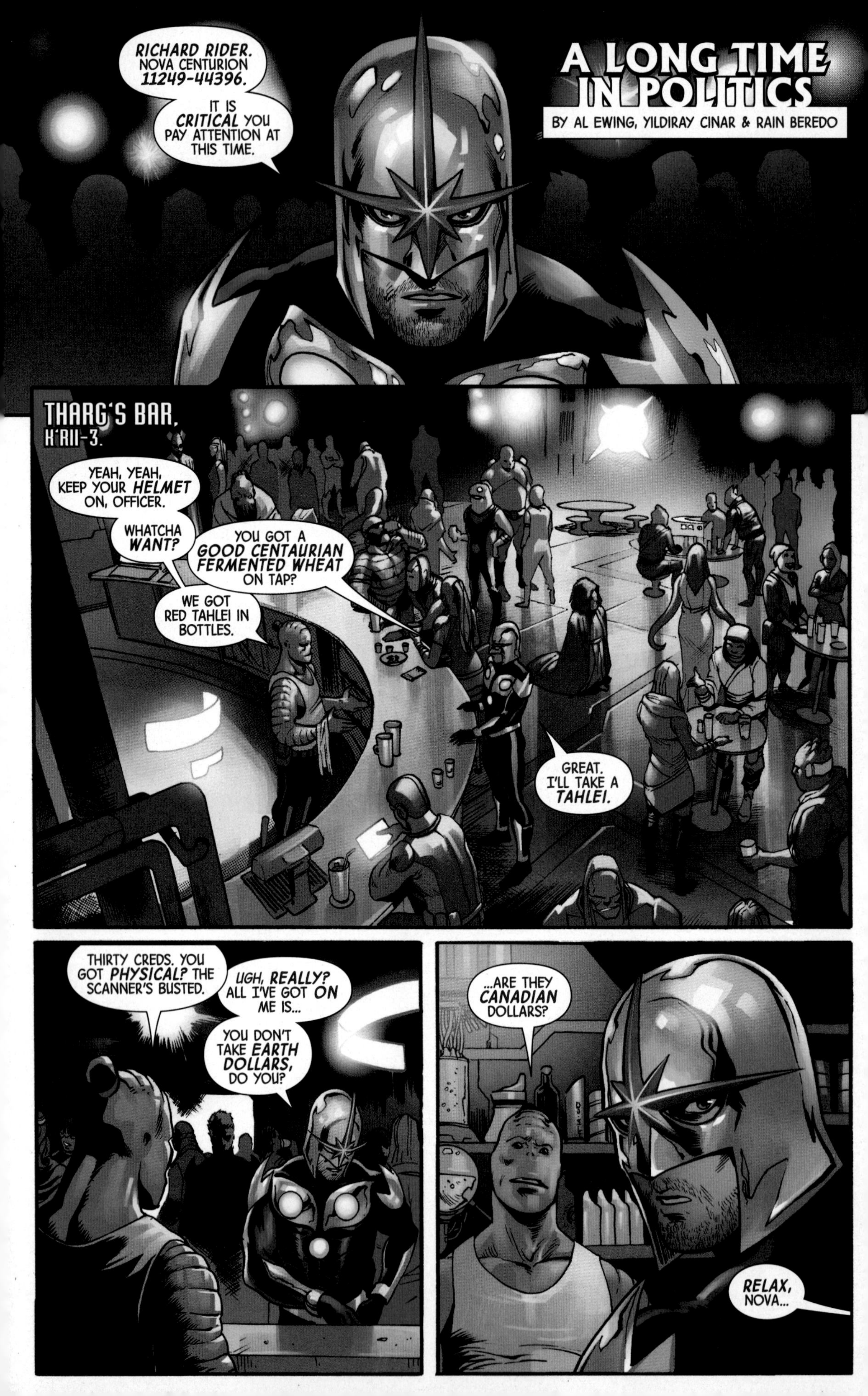
RICHARD RIDER. NOVA CENTURION 11249-44396.
IT IS CRITICAL YOU PAY ATTENTION AT THIS TIME.
A LONG TIME IN POLITICS
BY AL EWING, YILDIRAY CINAR & RAIN BEREDO
THARG'S BAR, K'RII-3.
YEAH, YEAH, KEEP YOUR HELMET ON, OFFICER.
WHATCHA WANT?
YOU GOT A GOOD CENTAURIAN FERMENTED WHEAT ON TAP?
WE GOT RED TAHLEI IN BOTTLES.
GREAT. I'LL TAKE A TAHLEI.
THIRTY CREDS. YOU GOT PHYSICAL? THE SCANNER'S BUSTED.
UGH, REALLY? ALL I'VE GOT ON ME IS...
YOU DON'T TAKE EARTH DOLLARS, DO YOU?
...ARE THEY CANADIAN DOLLARS?
RELAX, NOVA...

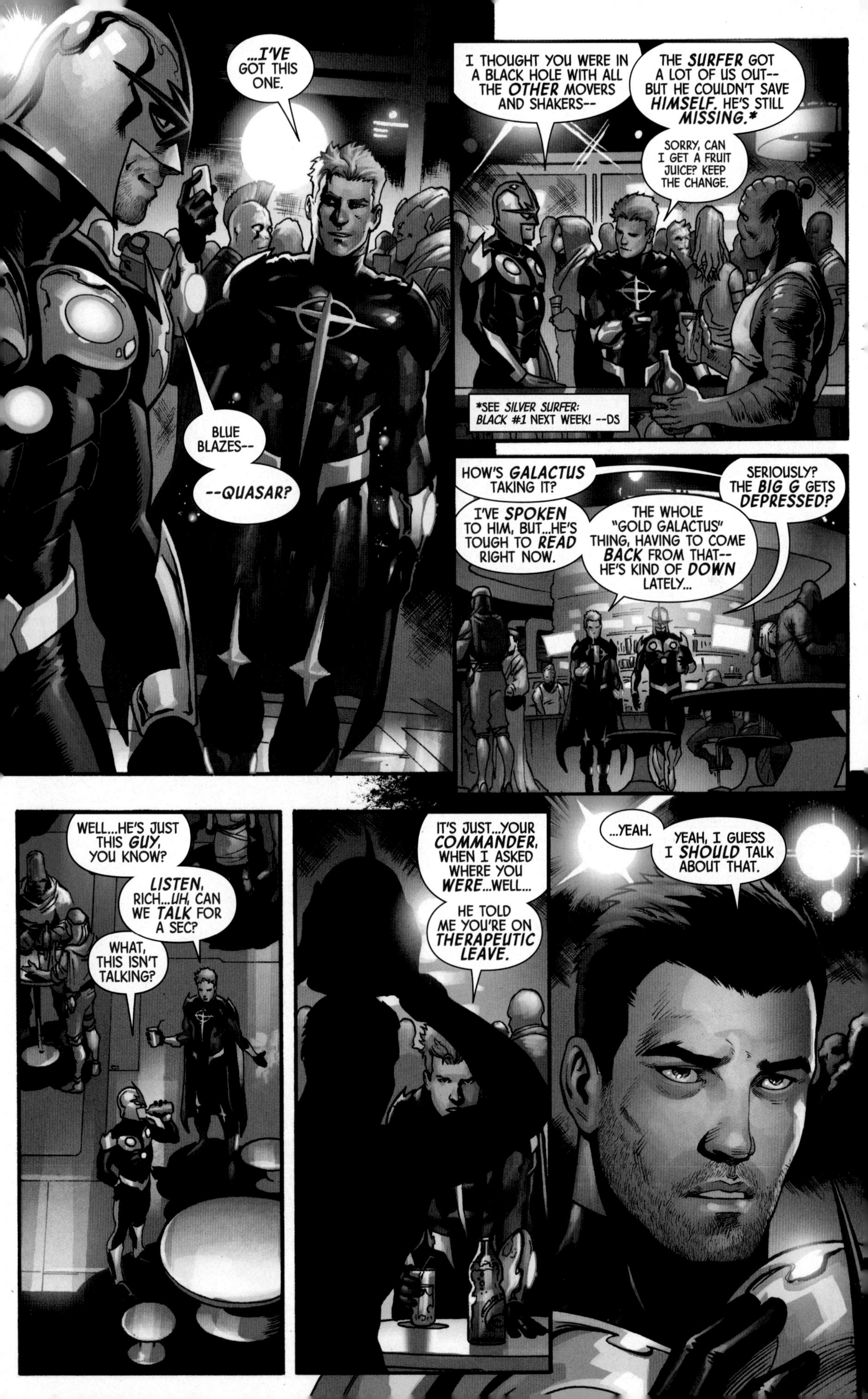
...I'VE GOT THIS ONE.
BLUE BLAZES--
--QUASAR?
I THOUGHT YOU WERE IN A BLACK HOLE WITH ALL THE OTHER MOVERS AND SHAKERS--
THE SURFER GOT A LOT OF US OUT-- BUT HE COULDN'T SAVE HIMSELF. HE'S STILL MISSING.*
SORRY, CAN I GET A FRUIT JUICE? KEEP THE CHANGE.
*SEE SILVER SURFER: BLACK #1 NEXT WEEK! --DS
HOW'S GALACTUS TAKING IT?
I'VE SPOKEN TO HIM, BUT...HE'S TOUGH TO READ RIGHT NOW.
THE WHOLE "GOLD GALACTUS" THING, HAVING TO COME BACK FROM THAT-- HE'S KIND OF DOWN LATELY...
SERIOUSLY? THE BIG G GETS DEPRESSED?
WELL...HE'S JUST THIS GUY, YOU KNOW?
LISTEN, RICH...UH, CAN WE TALK FOR A SEC?
WHAT, THIS ISN'T TALKING?
IT'S JUST...YOUR COMMANDER, WHEN I ASKED WHERE YOU WERE...WELL...
HE TOLD ME YOU'RE ON THERAPEUTIC LEAVE.
...YEAH.
YEAH, I GUESS I SHOULD TALK ABOUT THAT.

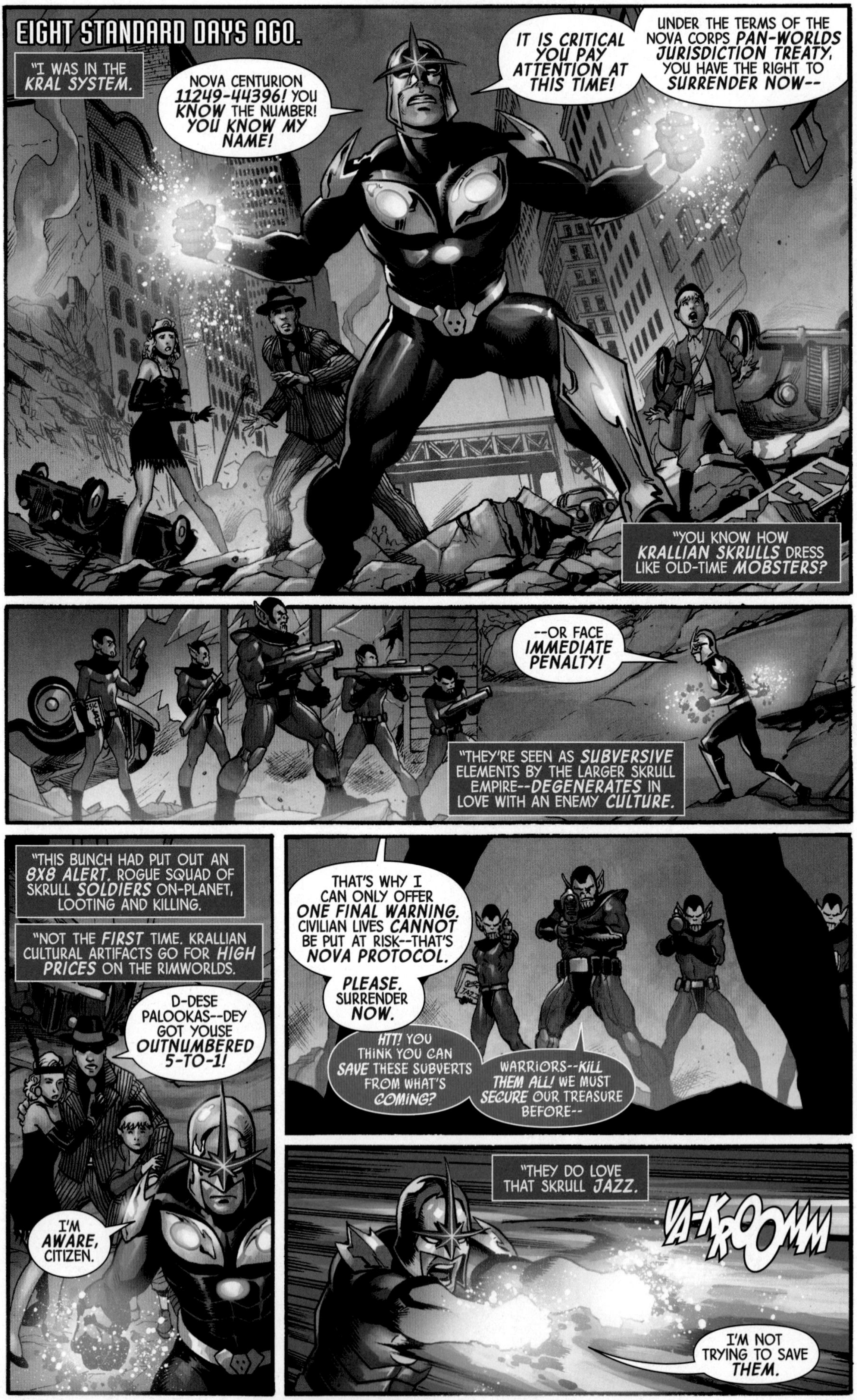
EIGHT STANDARD DAYS AGO.
"I WAS IN THE KRAL SYSTEM.
NOVA CENTURION 11249-44396! YOU KNOW THE NUMBER! YOU KNOW MY NAME!
IT IS CRITICAL YOU PAY ATTENTION AT THIS TIME!
UNDER THE TERMS OF THE NOVA CORPS PAN-WORLDS JURISDICTION TREATY, YOU HAVE THE RIGHT TO SURRENDER NOW--
"YOU KNOW HOW KRALLIAN SKRULLS DRESS LIKE OLD-TIME MOBSTERS?
--OR FACE IMMEDIATE PENALTY!
"THEY'RE SEEN AS SUBVERSIVE ELEMENTS BY THE LARGER SKRULL EMPIRE--DEGENERATES IN LOVE WITH AN ENEMY CULTURE.
"THIS BUNCH HAD PUT OUT AN 8X8 ALERT. ROGUE SQUAD OF SKRULL SOLDIERS ON-PLANET, LOOTING AND KILLING.
"NOT THE FIRST TIME. KRALLIAN CULTURAL ARTIFACTS GO FOR HIGH PRICES ON THE RIMWORLDS.
D-DESE PALOOKAS--DEY GOT YOUSE OUTNUMBERED 5-TO-1!
I'M AWARE, CITIZEN.
THAT'S WHY I CAN ONLY OFFER ONE FINAL WARNING. CIVILIAN LIVES CANNOT BE PUT AT RISK--THAT'S NOVA PROTOCOL.
PLEASE. SURRENDER NOW.
HTT! YOU THINK YOU CAN SAVE THESE SUBVERTS FROM WHAT'S COMING?
WARRIORS--KILL THEM ALL! WE MUST SECURE OUR TREASURE BEFORE--
"THEY DO LOVE THAT SKRULL JAZZ.
VA-KROOMM
I'M NOT TRYING TO SAVE THEM.

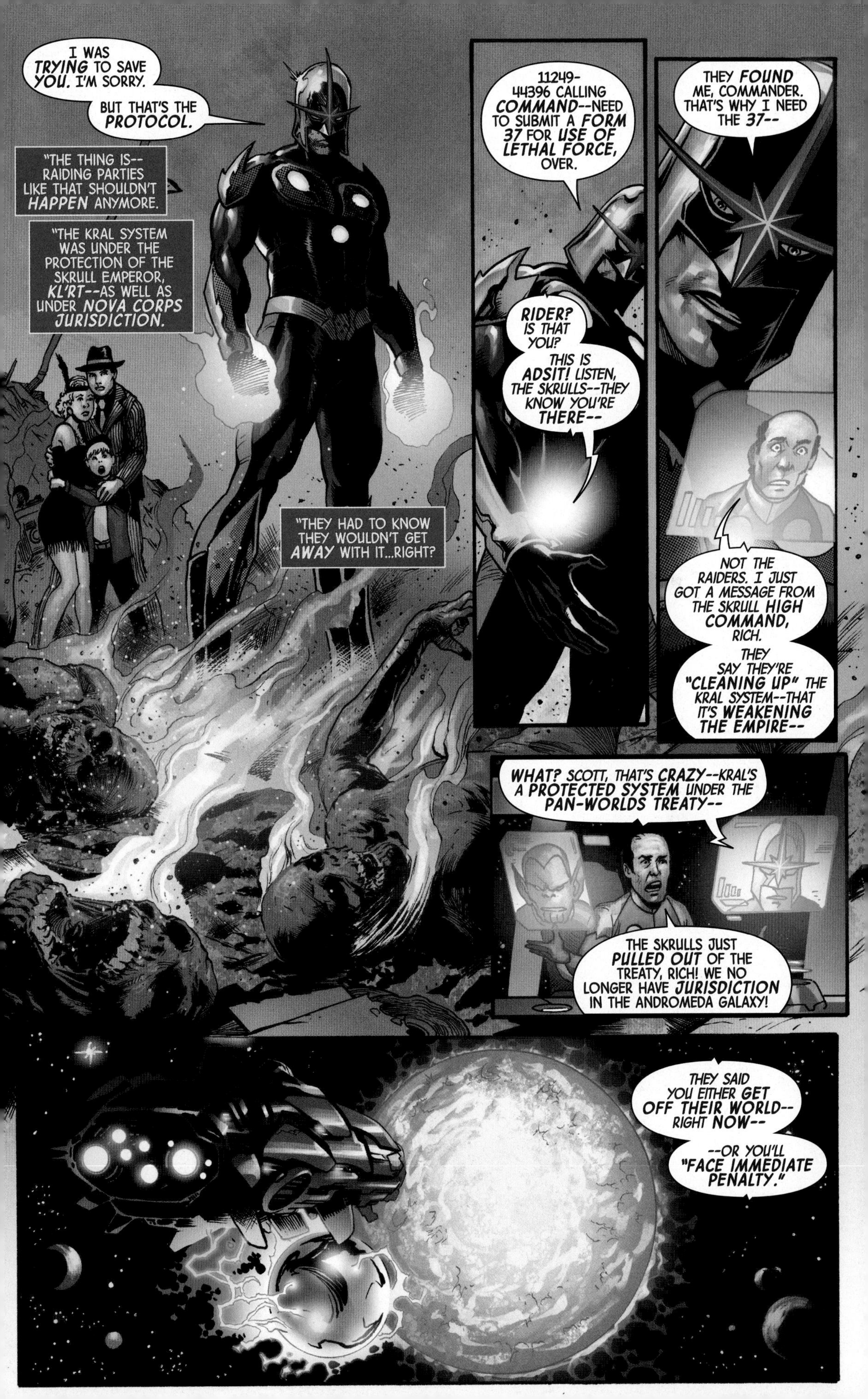
I WAS TRYING TO SAVE YOU. I'M SORRY.
BUT THAT'S THE PROTOCOL.
"THE THING IS-- RAIDING PARTIES LIKE THAT SHOULDN'T HAPPEN ANYMORE.
"THE KRAL SYSTEM WAS UNDER THE PROTECTION OF THE SKRULL EMPEROR, KL'RT--AS WELL AS UNDER NOVA CORPS JURISDICTION.
"THEY HAD TO KNOW THEY WOULDN'T GET AWAY WITH IT...RIGHT?
11249-44396 CALLING COMMAND--NEED TO SUBMIT A FORM 37 FOR USE OF LETHAL FORCE, OVER.
RIDER? IS THAT YOU?
THIS IS ADSIT! LISTEN, THE SKRULLS--THEY KNOW YOU'RE THERE--
THEY FOUND ME, COMMANDER. THAT'S WHY I NEED THE 37--
NOT THE RAIDERS. I JUST GOT A MESSAGE FROM THE SKRULL HIGH COMMAND, RICH.
THEY SAY THEY'RE "CLEANING UP" THE KRAL SYSTEM--THAT IT'S WEAKENING THE EMPIRE--
WHAT? SCOTT, THAT'S CRAZY--KRAL'S A PROTECTED SYSTEM UNDER THE PAN-WORLDS TREATY--
THE SKRULLS JUST PULLED OUT OF THE TREATY, RICH! WE NO LONGER HAVE JURISDICTION IN THE ANDROMEDA GALAXY!
THEY SAID YOU EITHER GET OFF THEIR WORLD-- RIGHT NOW--
--OR YOU'LL "FACE IMMEDIATE PENALTY."

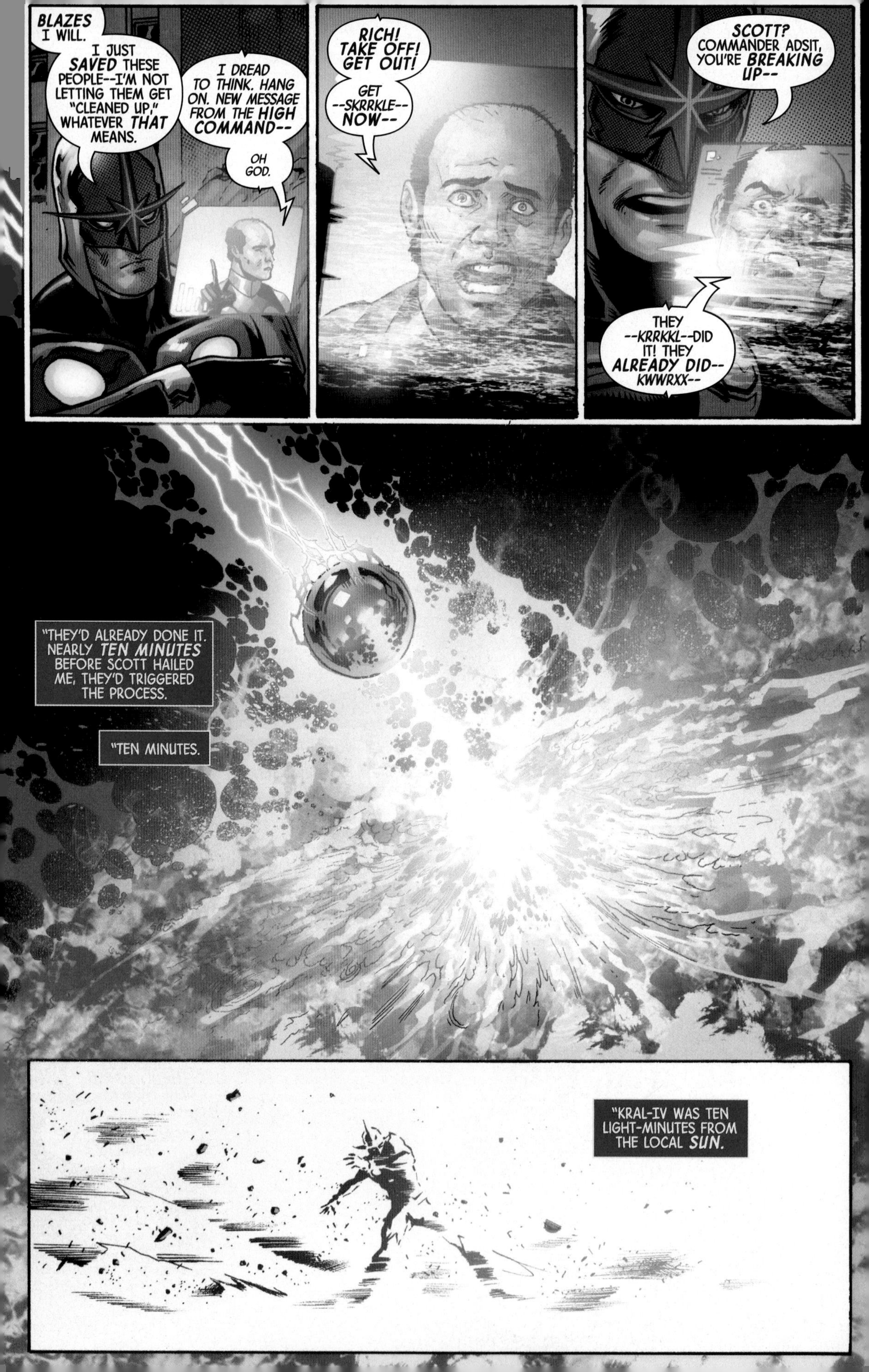

BLAZES I WILL.
I JUST SAVED THESE PEOPLE--I'M NOT LETTING THEM GET "CLEANED UP," WHATEVER THAT MEANS.
I DREAD TO THINK. HANG ON. NEW MESSAGE FROM THE HIGH COMMAND--
OH GOD.
RICH! TAKE OFF! GET OUT!
GET --SKRRKLE-- NOW--
SCOTT? COMMANDER ADSIT, YOU'RE BREAKING UP--
THEY --KRRKKL--DID IT! THEY ALREADY DID-- KWWRXX--
"THEY'D ALREADY DONE IT. NEARLY TEN MINUTES BEFORE SCOTT HAILED ME, THEY'D TRIGGERED THE PROCESS.
"TEN MINUTES.
"KRAL-IV WAS TEN LIGHT-MINUTES FROM THE LOCAL SUN.

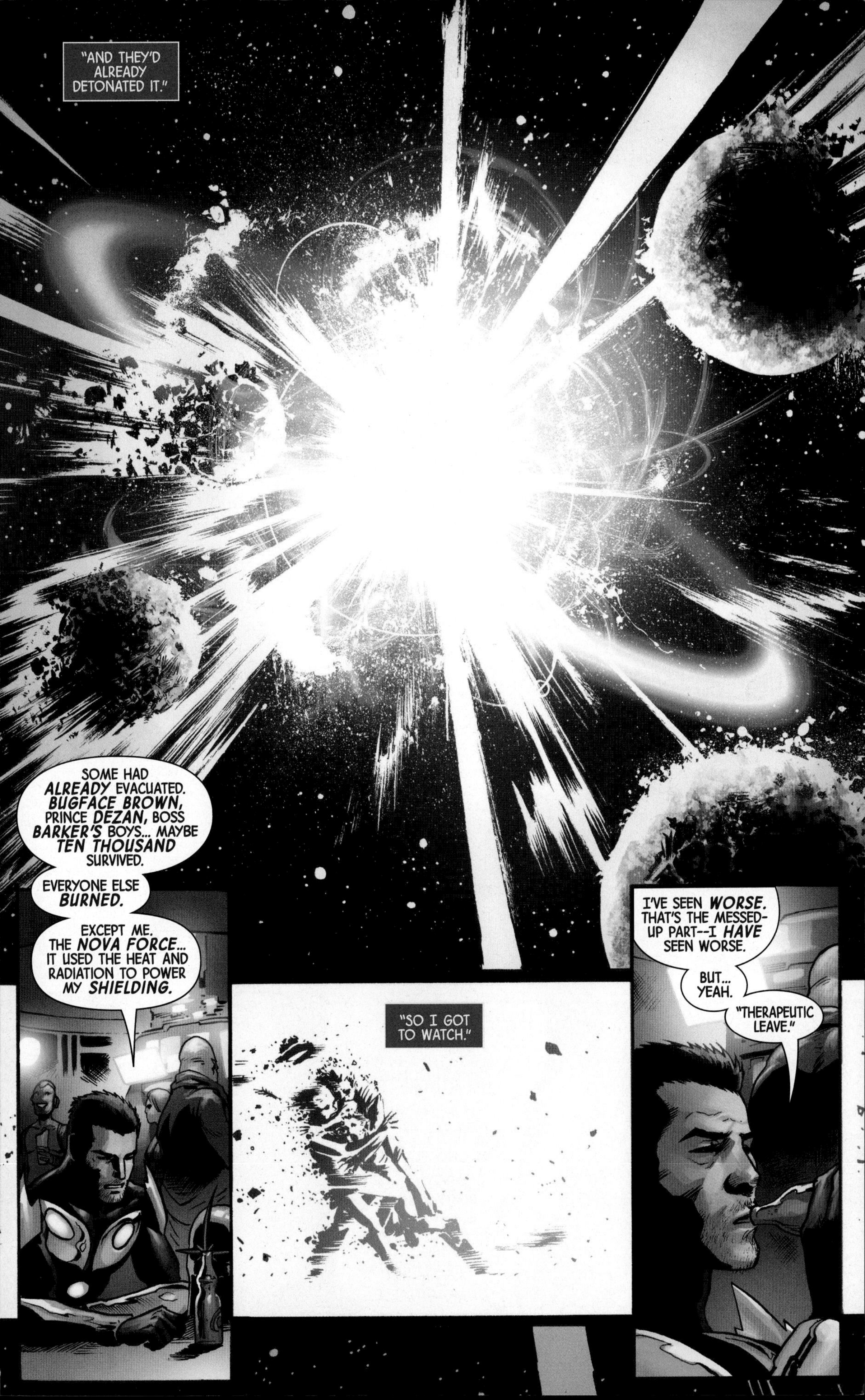
"AND THEY'D ALREADY DETONATED IT."
SOME HAD ALREADY EVACUATED. BUGFACE BROWN, PRINCE DEZAN, BOSS BARKER'S BOYS... MAYBE TEN THOUSAND SURVIVED.
EVERYONE ELSE BURNED.
EXCEPT ME. THE NOVA FORCE... IT USED THE HEAT AND RADIATION TO POWER MY SHIELDING.
"SO I GOT TO WATCH."
I'VE SEEN WORSE. THAT'S THE MESSED-UP PART--I HAVE SEEN WORSE.
BUT... YEAH.
"THERAPEUTIC LEAVE."

I'M SO SORRY.

EMPEROR KL'RT—THE *SUPER SKRULL*—HE *APPROVED* THAT?

OR SOMEONE WENT BEHIND HIS *BACK*. THAT MIGHT BE *WORSE*... IF HE COULDN'T *STOP* IT...

BUT EITHER WAY, THE *HARD-LINE* SKRULLS ARE ON THE RISE.

AND IT'S THE SAME STORY WITH THE *KREE*.

I DON'T KNOW IF YOU *HEARD*—THEY GREW A NEW *SUPREMOR* FROM AN OTHER-DIMENSIONAL *"PLEX INTELLIGENCE."*

BIG SWING TOWARD *UTOPIANISM*.

"ONLY THERE WAS A FACTION OF KREE *EXPLORERS*— WARRIOR TYPES—THAT DIDN'T *LIKE* THAT. THEY STAGED A COUP.

"NOW IT'S A *CIVIL WAR*. THE *UTOPIAN* KREE—THEY'RE GETTING *STOMPED*.

"RONAN THE ACCUSER... HE'S ALREADY *DEAD*."*

*SEE *DEATH OF THE INHUMANS!* --DS

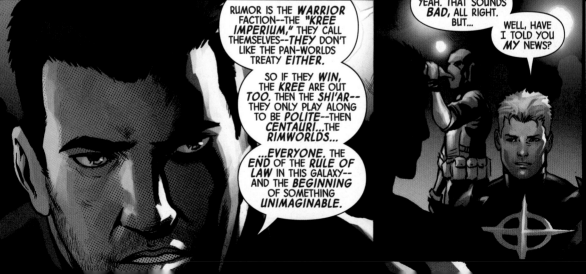

RUMOR IS THE *WARRIOR* FACTION—THE *"KREE IMPERIUM,"* THEY CALL THEMSELVES—*THEY* DON'T LIKE THE PAN-WORLDS TREATY *EITHER*.

SO IF THEY *WIN*, THE *KREE* ARE OUT *TOO*. THEN THE *SHI'AR*— THEY ONLY PLAY ALONG TO BE *POLITE*—THEN *CENTAURI*...THE *RIMWORLDS*...

...*EVERYONE*. THE *END* OF THE *RULE OF LAW* IN THIS GALAXY— AND THE *BEGINNING* OF SOMETHING *UNIMAGINABLE*.

YEAH. THAT SOUNDS *BAD*, ALL RIGHT. BUT...

WELL, HAVE I TOLD YOU *MY* NEWS?

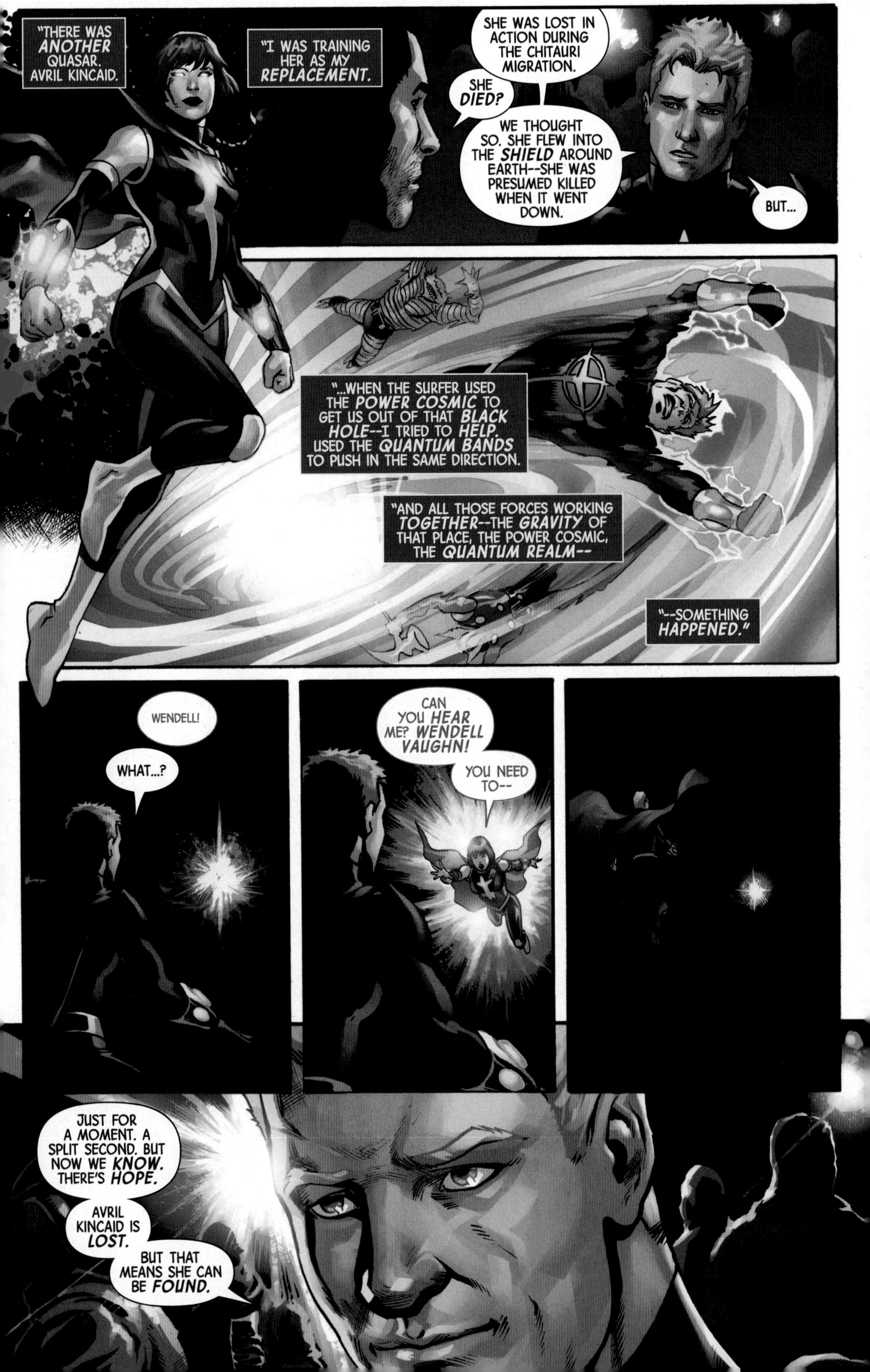

"THERE WAS ANOTHER QUASAR. AVRIL KINCAID.
"I WAS TRAINING HER AS MY REPLACEMENT.
SHE DIED?
SHE WAS LOST IN ACTION DURING THE CHITAURI MIGRATION.
WE THOUGHT SO. SHE FLEW INTO THE SHIELD AROUND EARTH--SHE WAS PRESUMED KILLED WHEN IT WENT DOWN.
BUT...
"...WHEN THE SURFER USED THE POWER COSMIC TO GET US OUT OF THAT BLACK HOLE--I TRIED TO HELP. USED THE QUANTUM BANDS TO PUSH IN THE SAME DIRECTION.
"AND ALL THOSE FORCES WORKING TOGETHER--THE GRAVITY OF THAT PLACE, THE POWER COSMIC, THE QUANTUM REALM--
"--SOMETHING HAPPENED."
WENDELL!
WHAT...?
CAN YOU HEAR ME? WENDELL VAUGHN!
YOU NEED TO--
JUST FOR A MOMENT. A SPLIT SECOND. BUT NOW WE KNOW. THERE'S HOPE.
AVRIL KINCAID IS LOST.
BUT THAT MEANS SHE CAN BE FOUND.

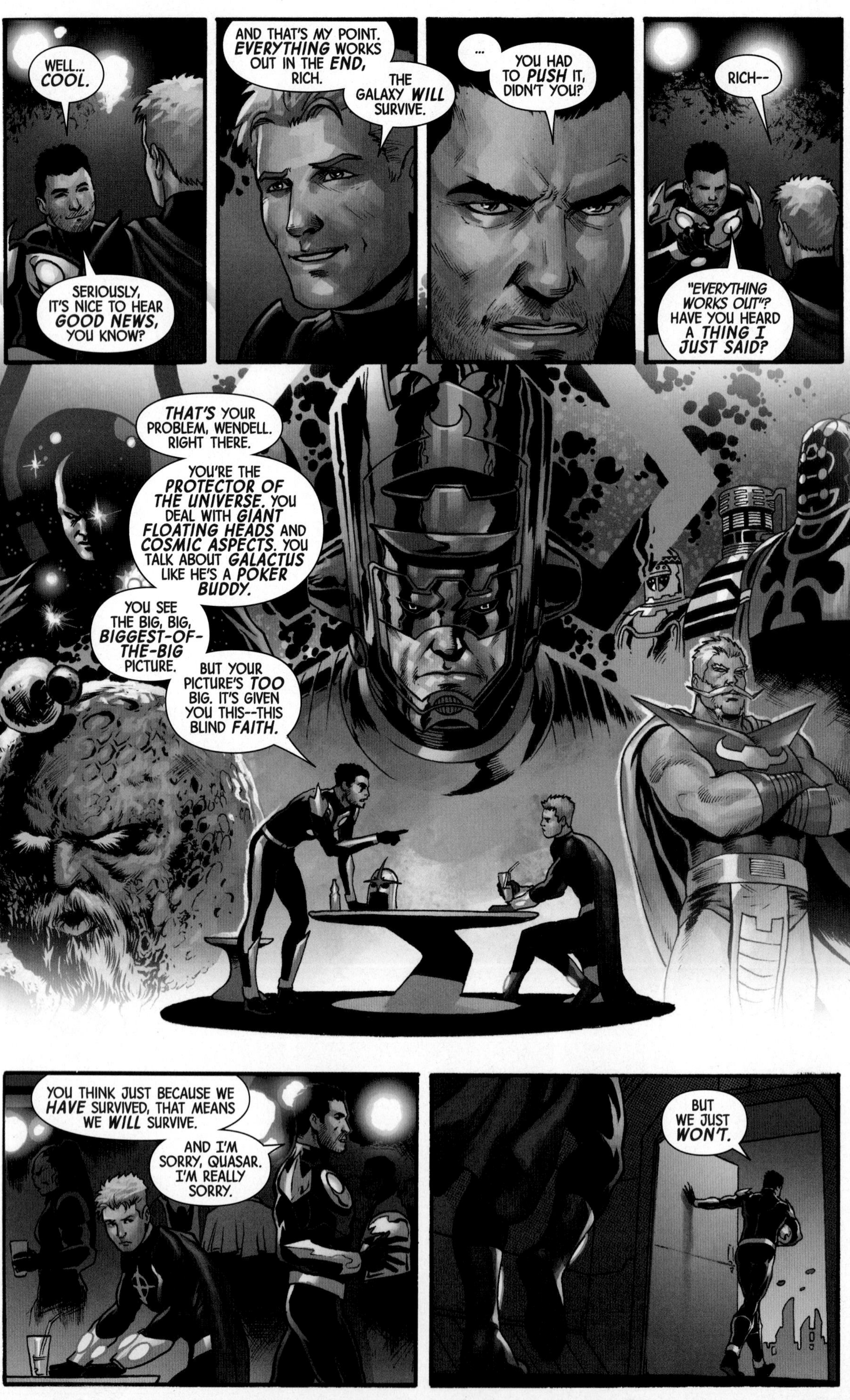
WELL... COOL.
SERIOUSLY, IT'S NICE TO HEAR GOOD NEWS, YOU KNOW?
AND THAT'S MY POINT. EVERYTHING WORKS OUT IN THE END, RICH.
THE GALAXY WILL SURVIVE.
...
YOU HAD TO PUSH IT, DIDN'T YOU?
RICH--
"EVERYTHING WORKS OUT"? HAVE YOU HEARD A THING I JUST SAID?
THAT'S YOUR PROBLEM, WENDELL. RIGHT THERE.
YOU'RE THE PROTECTOR OF THE UNIVERSE. YOU DEAL WITH GIANT FLOATING HEADS AND COSMIC ASPECTS. YOU TALK ABOUT GALACTUS LIKE HE'S A POKER BUDDY.
YOU SEE THE BIG, BIG, BIGGEST-OF-THE-BIG PICTURE.
BUT YOUR PICTURE'S TOO BIG. IT'S GIVEN YOU THIS--THIS BLIND FAITH.
YOU THINK JUST BECAUSE WE HAVE SURVIVED, THAT MEANS WE WILL SURVIVE.
AND I'M SORRY, QUASAR. I'M REALLY SORRY.
BUT WE JUST WON'T.

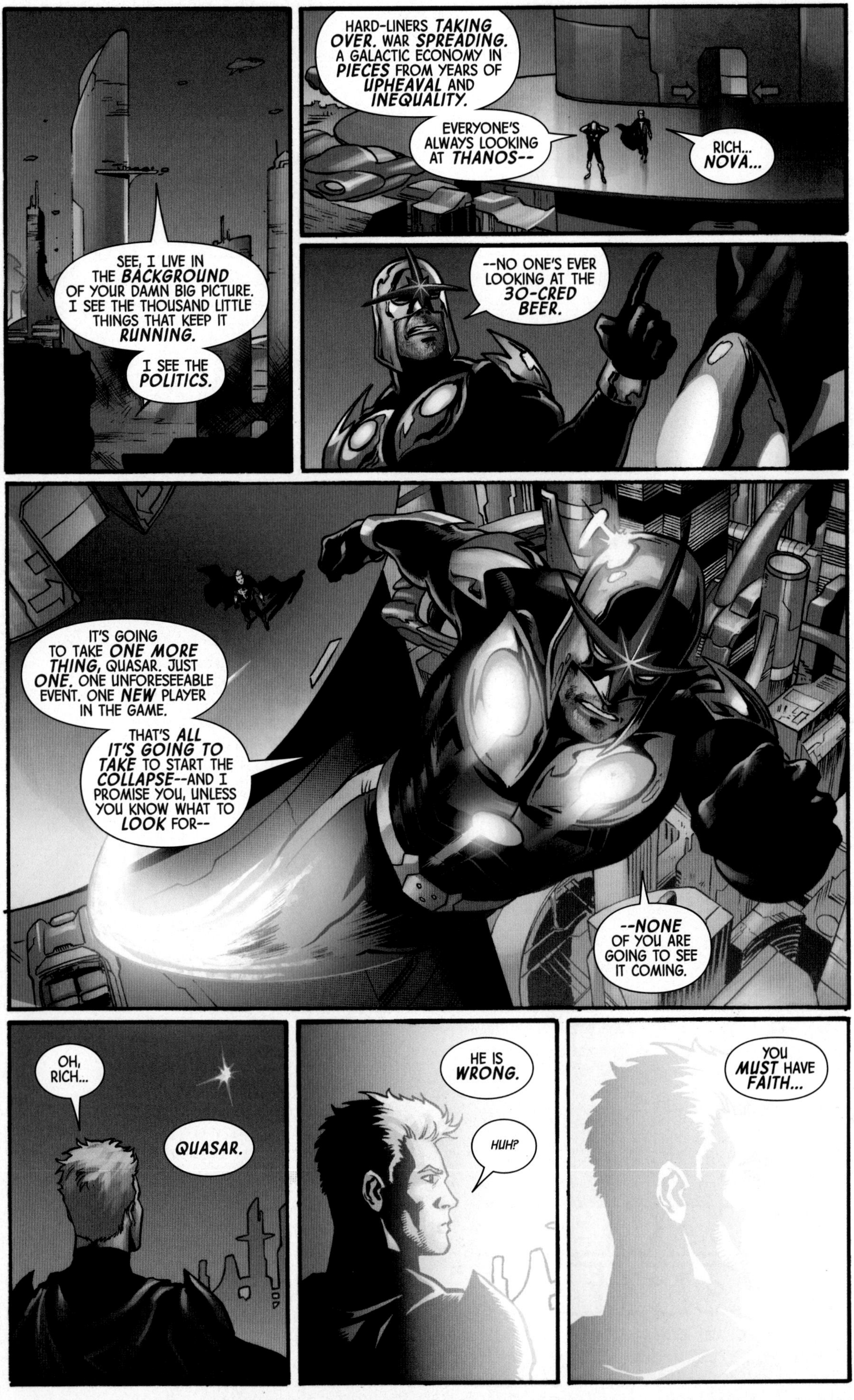
SEE, I LIVE IN THE BACKGROUND OF YOUR DAMN BIG PICTURE. I SEE THE THOUSAND LITTLE THINGS THAT KEEP IT RUNNING.
I SEE THE POLITICS.
HARD-LINERS TAKING OVER. WAR SPREADING. A GALACTIC ECONOMY IN PIECES FROM YEARS OF UPHEAVAL AND INEQUALITY.
EVERYONE'S ALWAYS LOOKING AT THANOS--
RICH... NOVA...
--NO ONE'S EVER LOOKING AT THE 30-CRED BEER.
IT'S GOING TO TAKE ONE MORE THING, QUASAR. JUST ONE. ONE UNFORESEEABLE EVENT. ONE NEW PLAYER IN THE GAME.
THAT'S ALL IT'S GOING TO TAKE TO START THE COLLAPSE--AND I PROMISE YOU, UNLESS YOU KNOW WHAT TO LOOK FOR--
--NONE OF YOU ARE GOING TO SEE IT COMING.
OH, RICH...
QUASAR.
HE IS WRONG.
HUH?
YOU MUST HAVE FAITH...

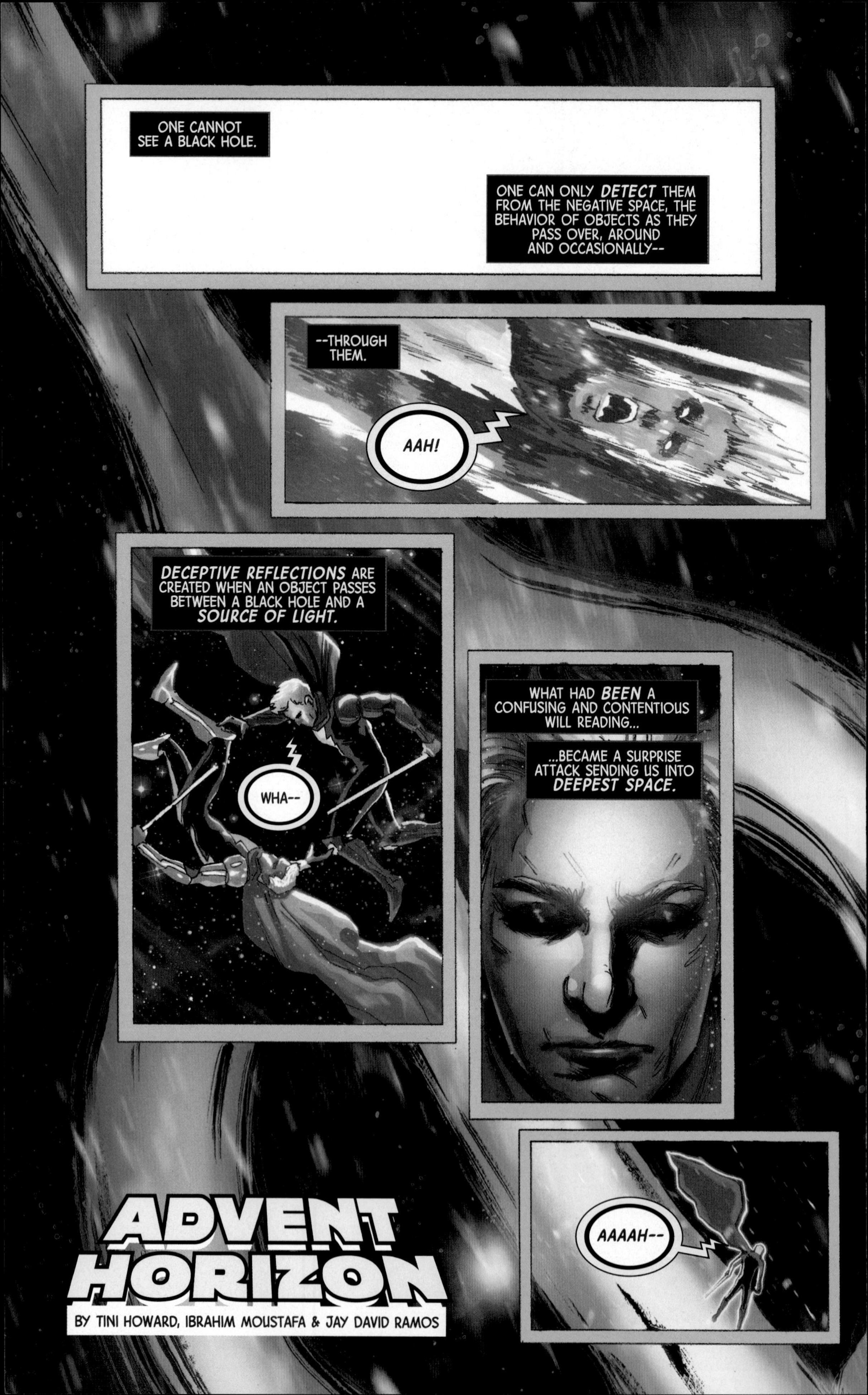
ONE CANNOT SEE A BLACK HOLE.
ONE CAN ONLY DETECT THEM FROM THE NEGATIVE SPACE, THE BEHAVIOR OF OBJECTS AS THEY PASS OVER, AROUND AND OCCASIONALLY--
--THROUGH THEM.
AAH!
DECEPTIVE REFLECTIONS ARE CREATED WHEN AN OBJECT PASSES BETWEEN A BLACK HOLE AND A SOURCE OF LIGHT.
WHA--
WHAT HAD BEEN A CONFUSING AND CONTENTIOUS WILL READING...
...BECAME A SURPRISE ATTACK SENDING US INTO DEEPEST SPACE.
ADVENT HORIZON
BY TINI HOWARD, IBRAHIM MOUSTAFA & JAY DAVID RAMOS
AAAAH--

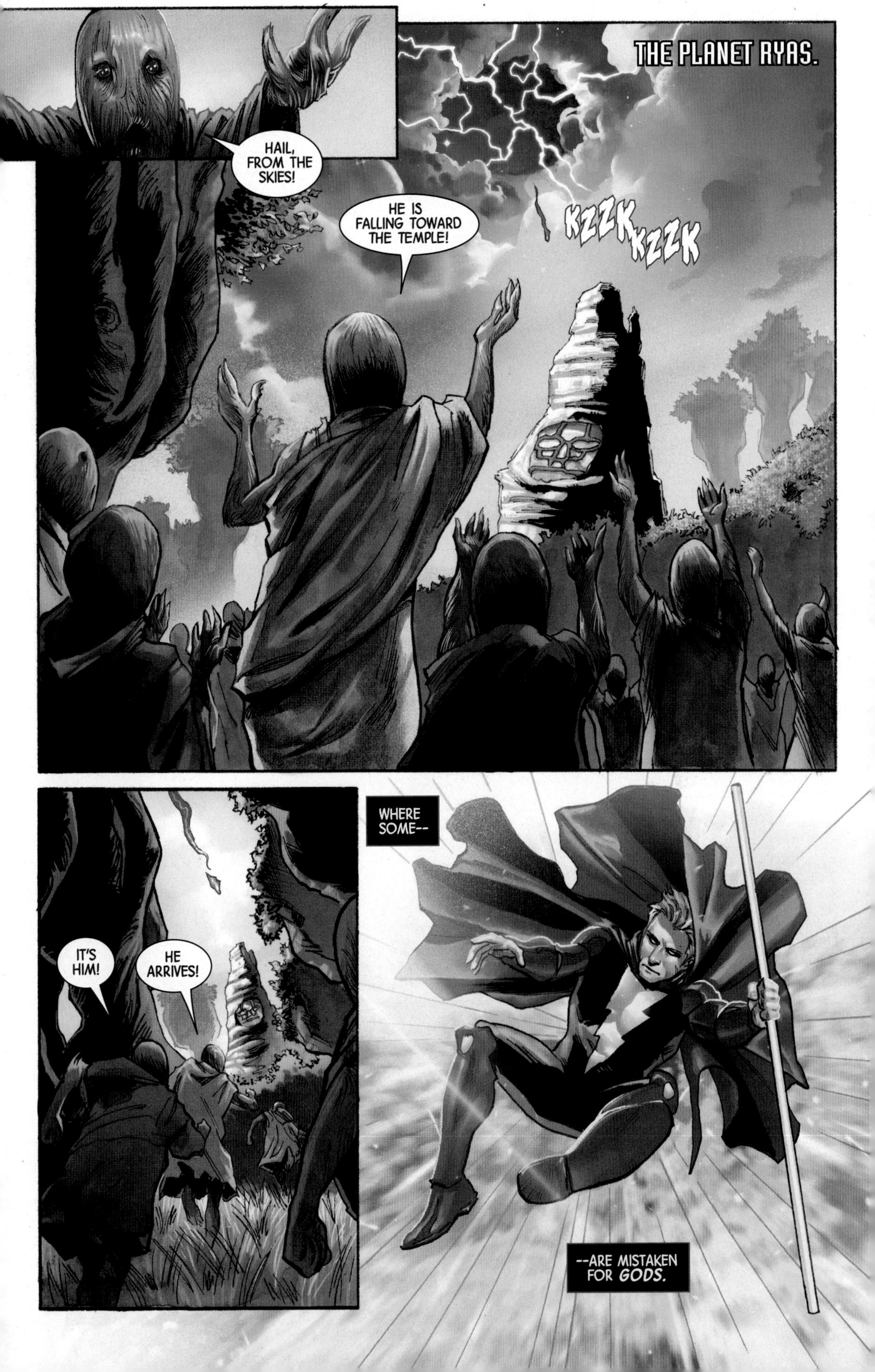
THE PLANET RYAS.
HAIL, FROM THE SKIES!
HE IS FALLING TOWARD THE TEMPLE!
KZZK KZZK
IT'S HIM!
HE ARRIVES!
WHERE SOME--
--ARE MISTAKEN FOR GODS.

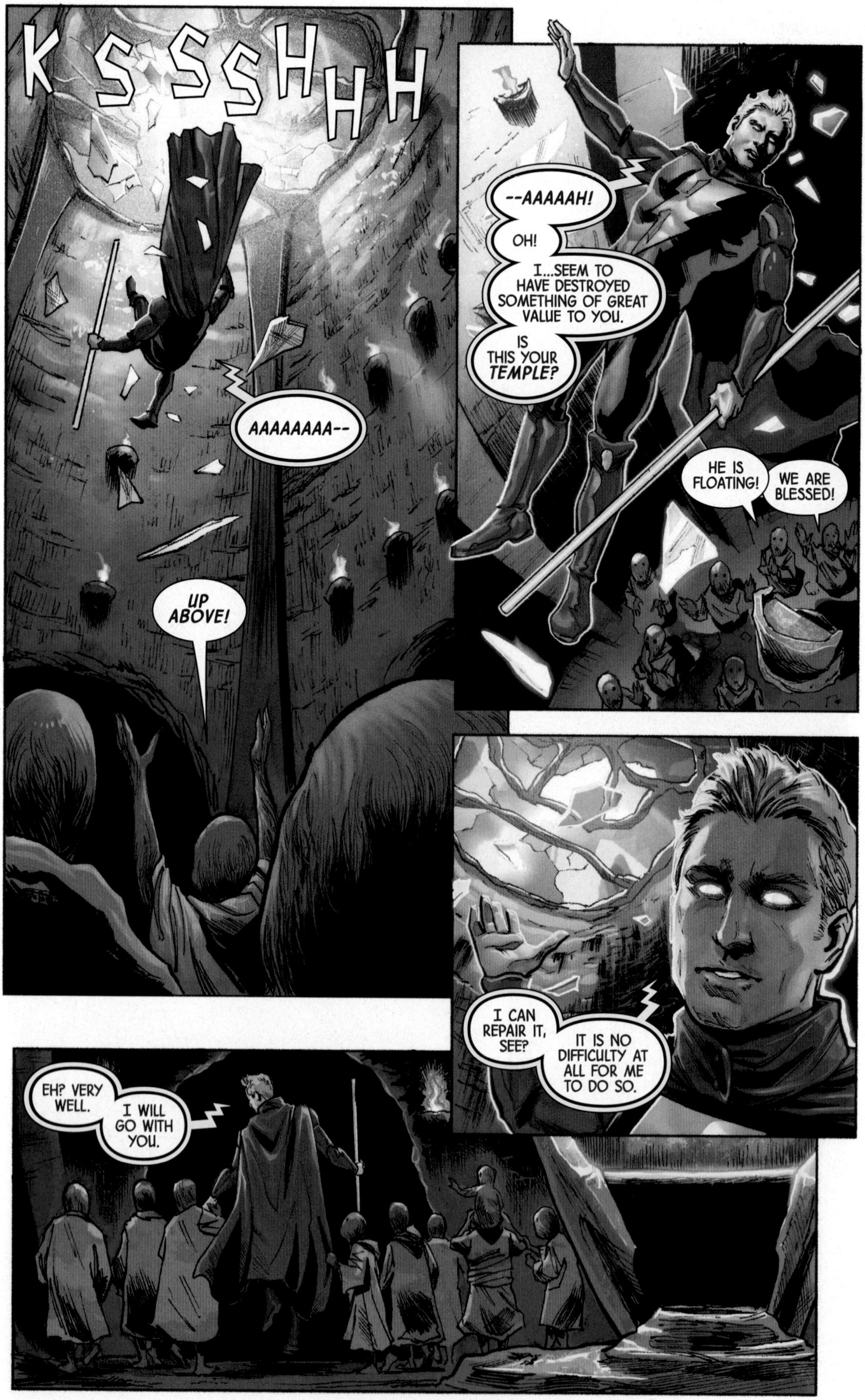
KSSSHHH
AAAAAAAA--
UP ABOVE!
--AAAAAH!
OH!
I...SEEM TO HAVE DESTROYED SOMETHING OF GREAT VALUE TO YOU.
IS THIS YOUR *TEMPLE?*
HE IS FLOATING!
WE ARE BLESSED!
I CAN REPAIR IT, SEE?
IT IS NO DIFFICULTY AT ALL FOR ME TO DO SO.
EH? VERY WELL.
I WILL GO WITH YOU.

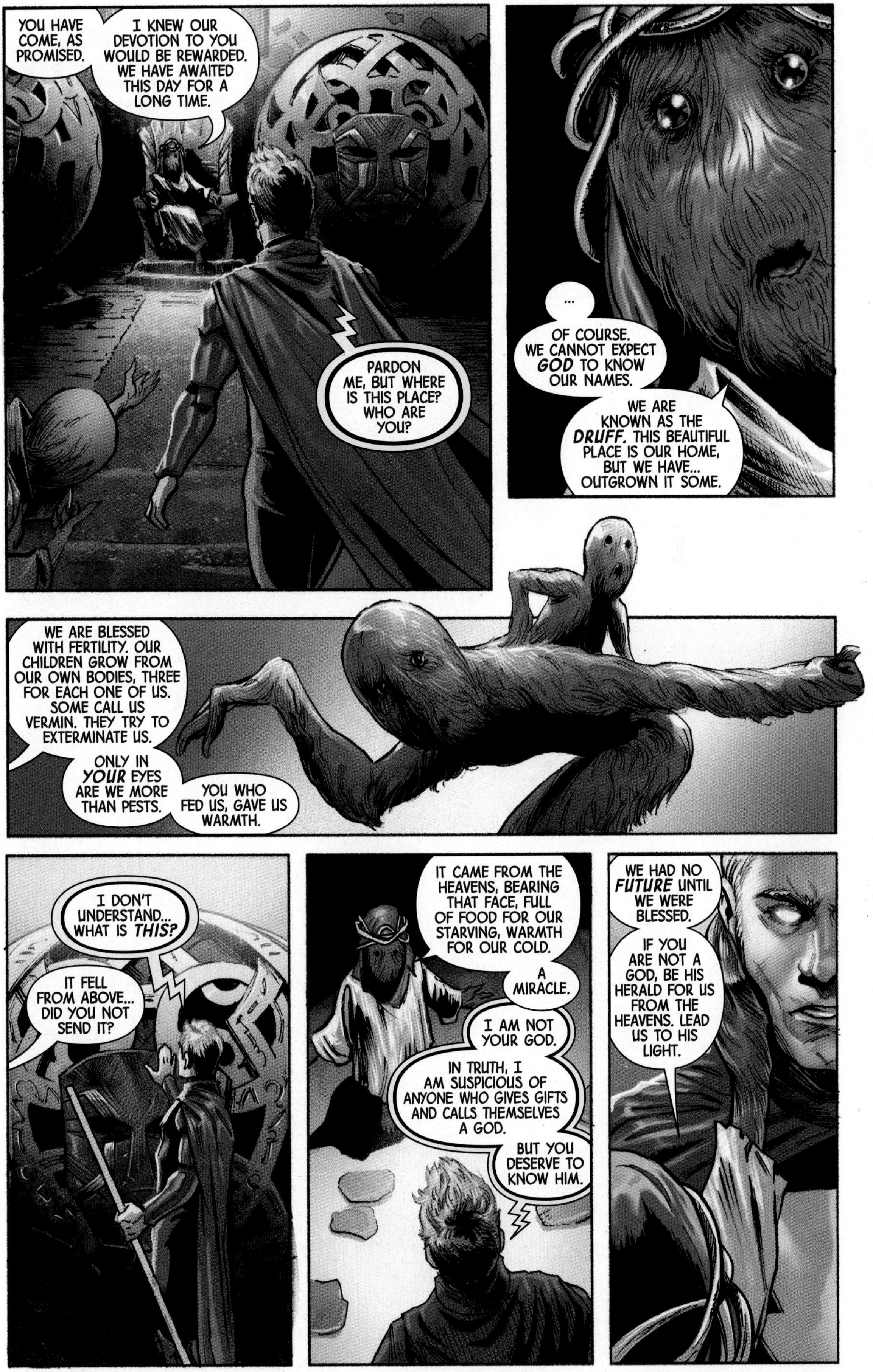

YOU HAVE COME, AS PROMISED.
I KNEW OUR DEVOTION TO YOU WOULD BE REWARDED. WE HAVE AWAITED THIS DAY FOR A LONG TIME.
PARDON ME, BUT WHERE IS THIS PLACE? WHO ARE YOU?
...
OF COURSE. WE CANNOT EXPECT GOD TO KNOW OUR NAMES.
WE ARE KNOWN AS THE DRUFF. THIS BEAUTIFUL PLACE IS OUR HOME, BUT WE HAVE... OUTGROWN IT SOME.
WE ARE BLESSED WITH FERTILITY. OUR CHILDREN GROW FROM OUR OWN BODIES, THREE FOR EACH ONE OF US. SOME CALL US VERMIN. THEY TRY TO EXTERMINATE US.
ONLY IN YOUR EYES ARE WE MORE THAN PESTS.
YOU WHO FED US, GAVE US WARMTH.
I DON'T UNDERSTAND... WHAT IS THIS?
IT FELL FROM ABOVE... DID YOU NOT SEND IT?
IT CAME FROM THE HEAVENS, BEARING THAT FACE, FULL OF FOOD FOR OUR STARVING, WARMTH FOR OUR COLD.
A MIRACLE.
I AM NOT YOUR GOD.
IN TRUTH, I AM SUSPICIOUS OF ANYONE WHO GIVES GIFTS AND CALLS THEMSELVES A GOD.
BUT YOU DESERVE TO KNOW HIM.
WE HAD NO FUTURE UNTIL WE WERE BLESSED.
IF YOU ARE NOT A GOD, BE HIS HERALD FOR US FROM THE HEAVENS. LEAD US TO HIS LIGHT.

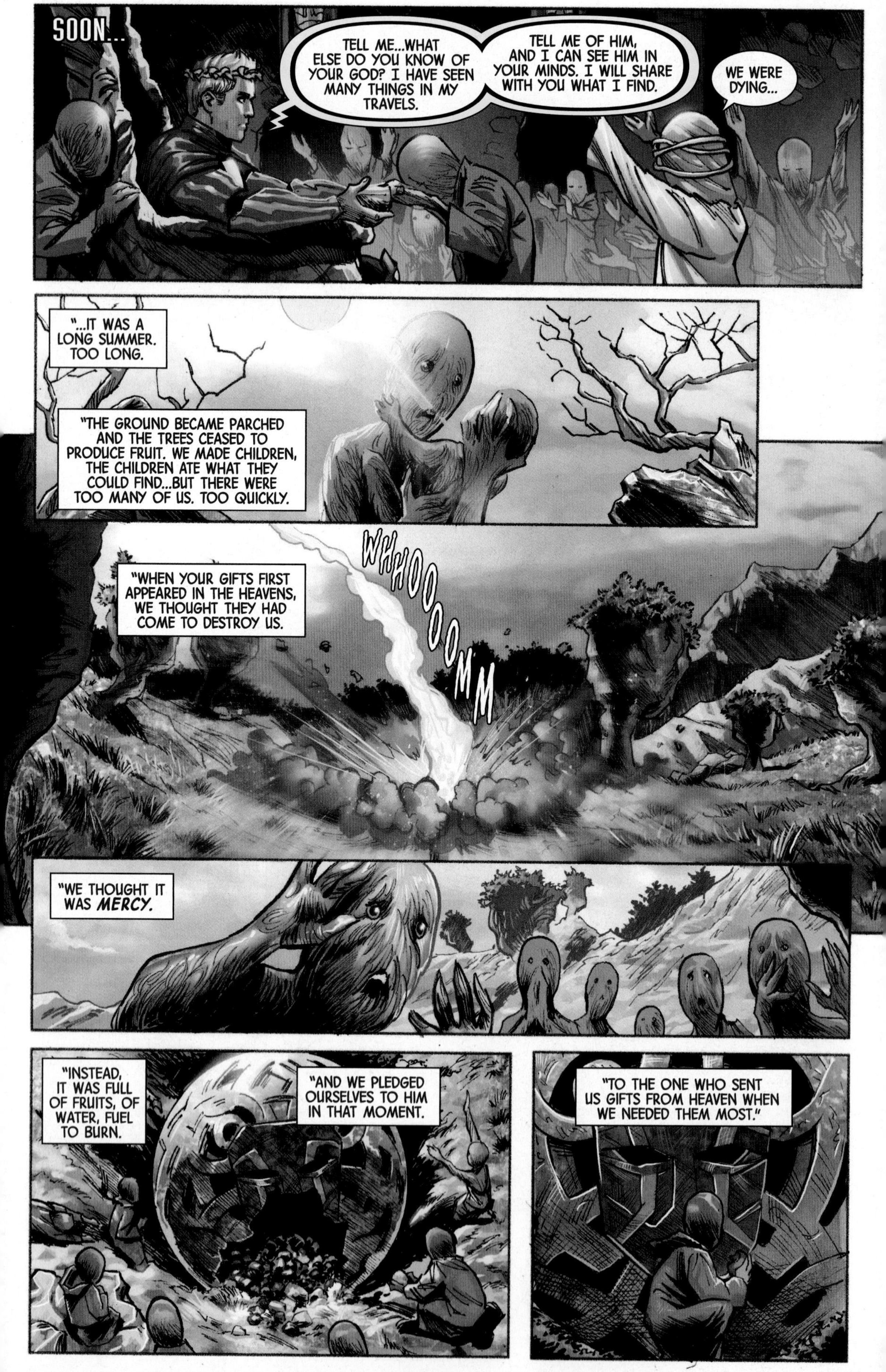
SOON...
TELL ME...WHAT ELSE DO YOU KNOW OF YOUR GOD? I HAVE SEEN MANY THINGS IN MY TRAVELS.
TELL ME OF HIM, AND I CAN SEE HIM IN YOUR MINDS. I WILL SHARE WITH YOU WHAT I FIND.
WE WERE DYING...
"...IT WAS A LONG SUMMER. TOO LONG.
"THE GROUND BECAME PARCHED AND THE TREES CEASED TO PRODUCE FRUIT. WE MADE CHILDREN, THE CHILDREN ATE WHAT THEY COULD FIND...BUT THERE WERE TOO MANY OF US. TOO QUICKLY.
"WHEN YOUR GIFTS FIRST APPEARED IN THE HEAVENS, WE THOUGHT THEY HAD COME TO DESTROY US.
WHHOOOOOMM
"WE THOUGHT IT WAS *MERCY.*
"INSTEAD, IT WAS FULL OF FRUITS, OF WATER, FUEL TO BURN.
"AND WE PLEDGED OURSELVES TO HIM IN THAT MOMENT.
"TO THE ONE WHO SENT US GIFTS FROM HEAVEN WHEN WE NEEDED THEM MOST."

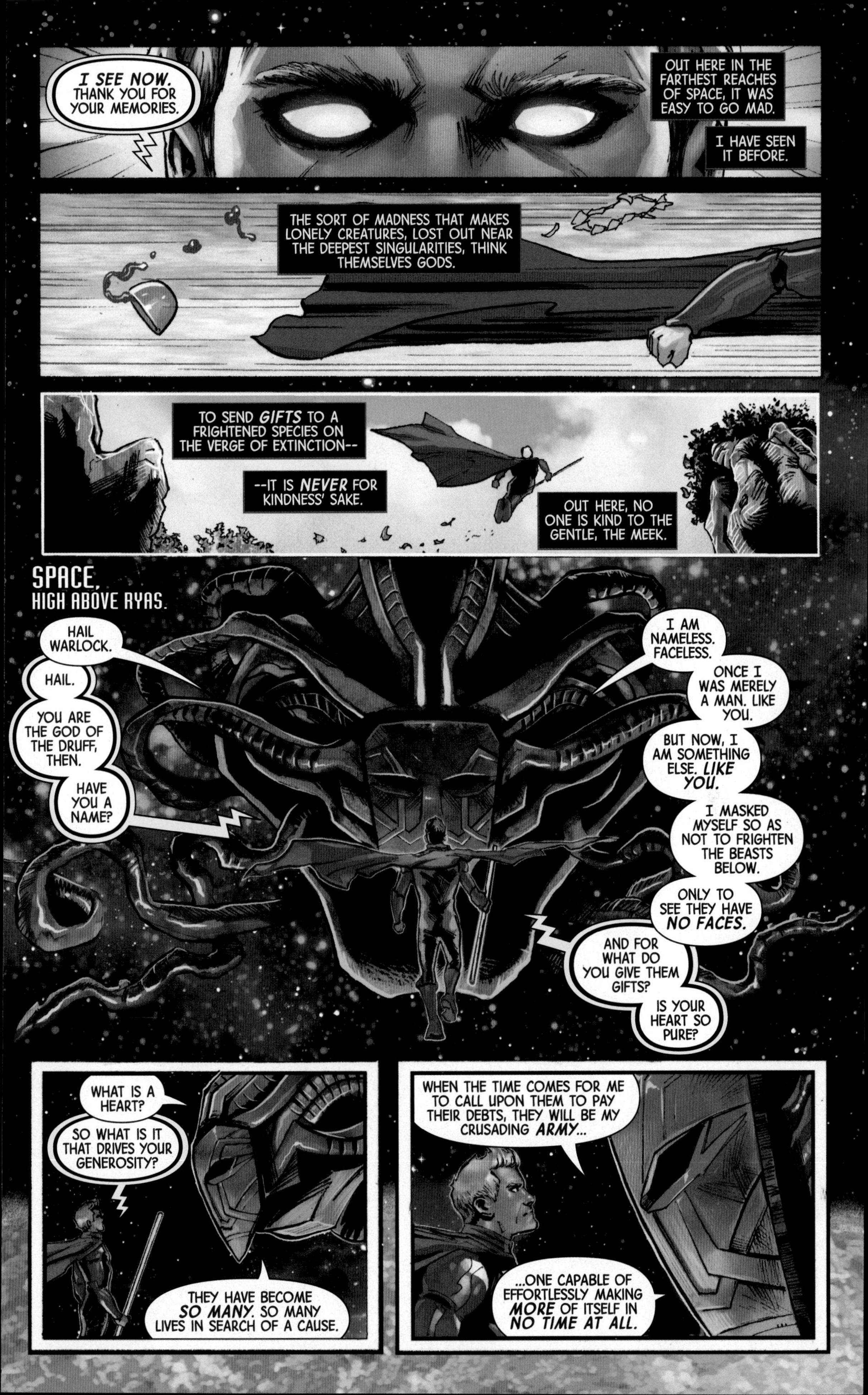
I SEE NOW. THANK YOU FOR YOUR MEMORIES.
OUT HERE IN THE FARTHEST REACHES OF SPACE, IT WAS EASY TO GO MAD.
I HAVE SEEN IT BEFORE.
THE SORT OF MADNESS THAT MAKES LONELY CREATURES, LOST OUT NEAR THE DEEPEST SINGULARITIES, THINK THEMSELVES GODS.
TO SEND GIFTS TO A FRIGHTENED SPECIES ON THE VERGE OF EXTINCTION--
--IT IS NEVER FOR KINDNESS' SAKE.
OUT HERE, NO ONE IS KIND TO THE GENTLE, THE MEEK.
SPACE, HIGH ABOVE RYAS.
HAIL WARLOCK.
HAIL.
YOU ARE THE GOD OF THE DRUFF, THEN.
HAVE YOU A NAME?
I AM NAMELESS. FACELESS.
ONCE I WAS MERELY A MAN. LIKE YOU.
BUT NOW, I AM SOMETHING ELSE. LIKE YOU.
I MASKED MYSELF SO AS NOT TO FRIGHTEN THE BEASTS BELOW.
ONLY TO SEE THEY HAVE NO FACES.
AND FOR WHAT DO YOU GIVE THEM GIFTS?
IS YOUR HEART SO PURE?
WHAT IS A HEART?
SO WHAT IS IT THAT DRIVES YOUR GENEROSITY?
THEY HAVE BECOME SO MANY. SO MANY LIVES IN SEARCH OF A CAUSE.
WHEN THE TIME COMES FOR ME TO CALL UPON THEM TO PAY THEIR DEBTS, THEY WILL BE MY CRUSADING ARMY...
...ONE CAPABLE OF EFFORTLESSLY MAKING MORE OF ITSELF IN NO TIME AT ALL.

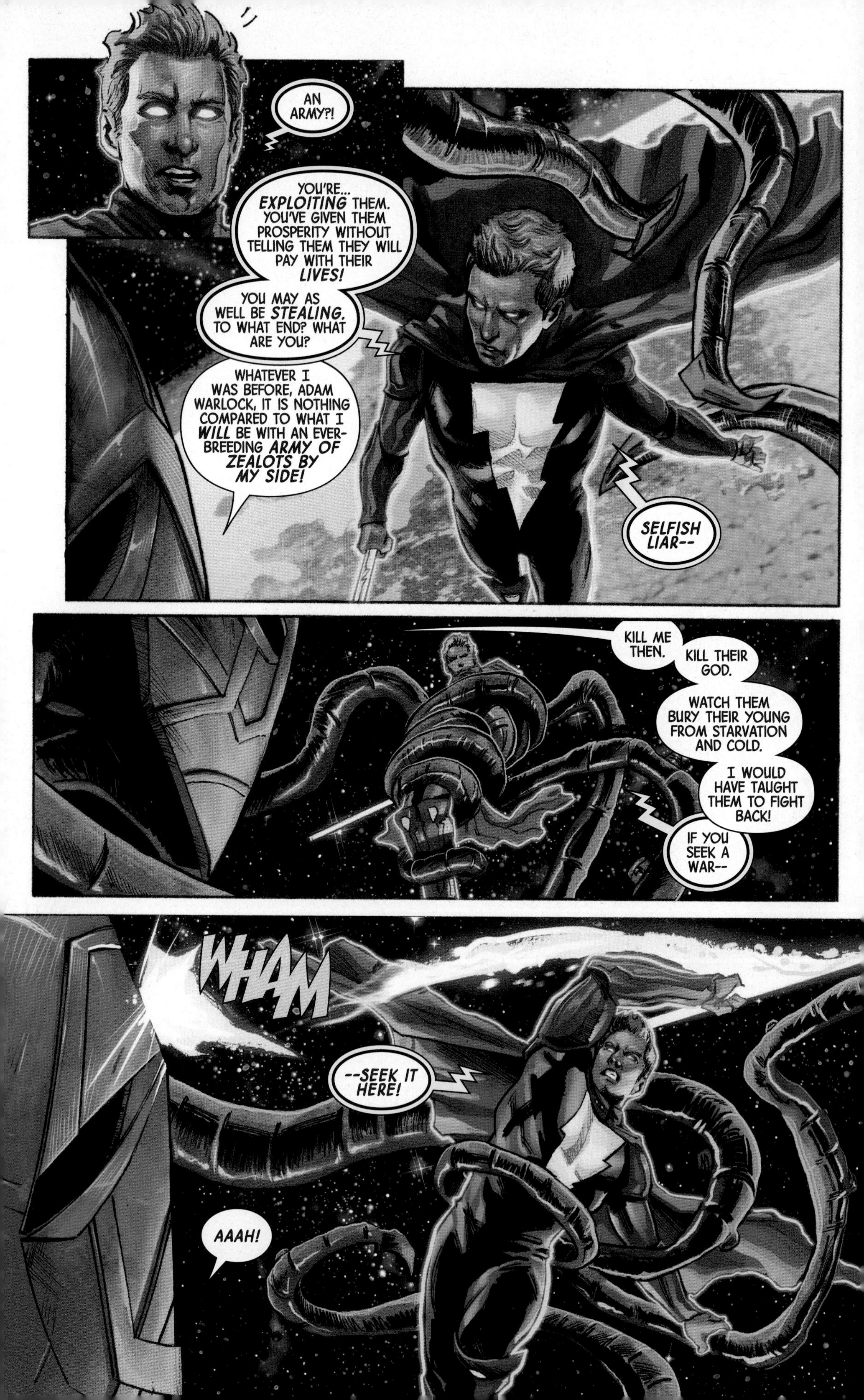
AN ARMY?!
YOU'RE... EXPLOITING THEM. YOU'VE GIVEN THEM PROSPERITY WITHOUT TELLING THEM THEY WILL PAY WITH THEIR LIVES!
YOU MAY AS WELL BE STEALING. TO WHAT END? WHAT ARE YOU?
WHATEVER I WAS BEFORE, ADAM WARLOCK, IT IS NOTHING COMPARED TO WHAT I WILL BE WITH AN EVER-BREEDING ARMY OF ZEALOTS BY MY SIDE!
SELFISH LIAR--
KILL ME THEN.
KILL THEIR GOD.
WATCH THEM BURY THEIR YOUNG FROM STARVATION AND COLD.
I WOULD HAVE TAUGHT THEM TO FIGHT BACK!
IF YOU SEEK A WAR--
WHAM
--SEEK IT HERE!
AAAH!

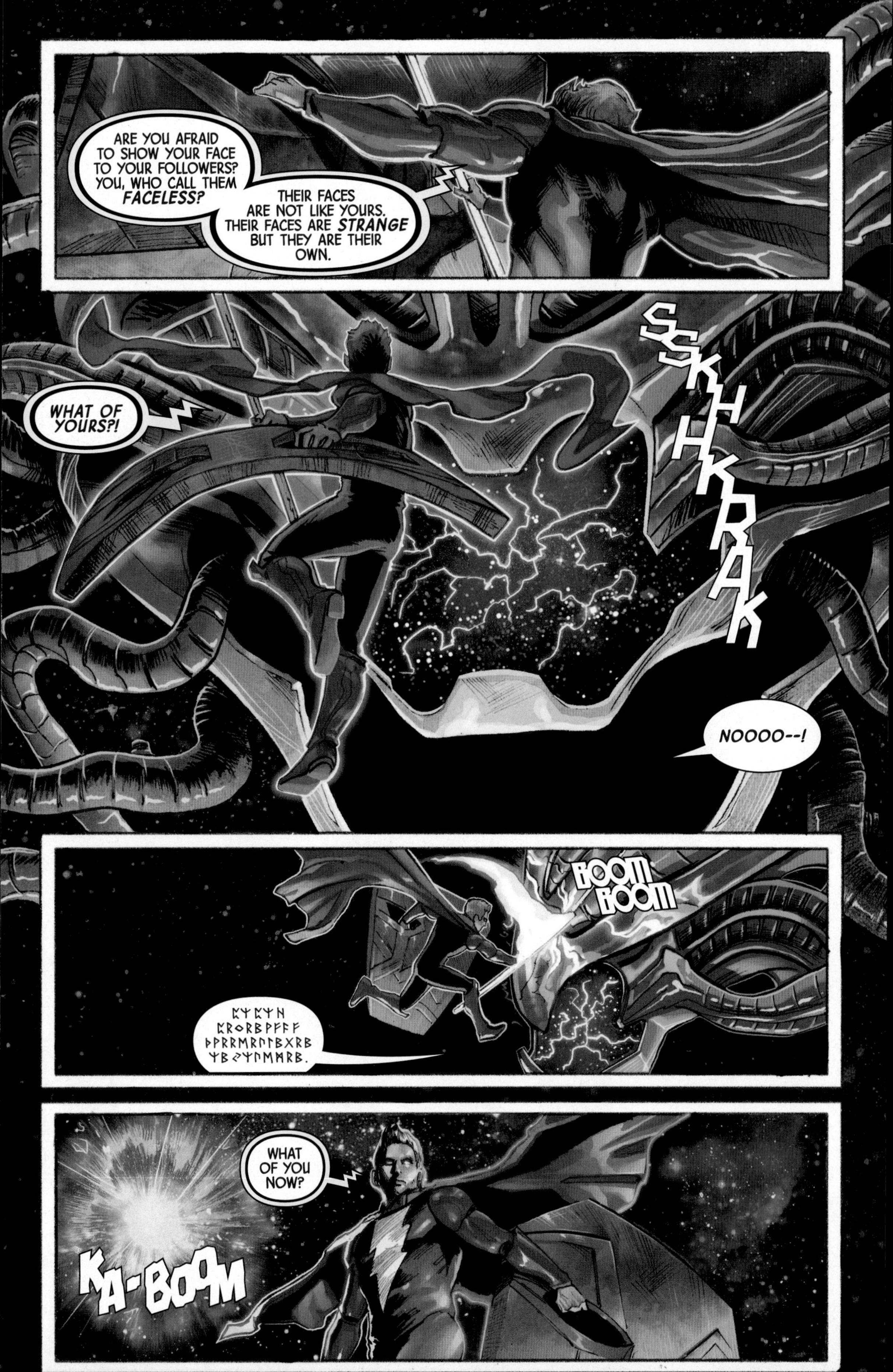
ARE YOU AFRAID TO SHOW YOUR FACE TO YOUR FOLLOWERS? YOU, WHO CALL THEM *FACELESS?*
THEIR FACES ARE NOT LIKE YOURS. THEIR FACES ARE *STRANGE* BUT THEY ARE THEIR OWN.
SSKHHKRAK
WHAT OF YOURS?!
NOOOO--!
BOOM BOOM
WHAT OF YOU NOW?
KA-BOOM

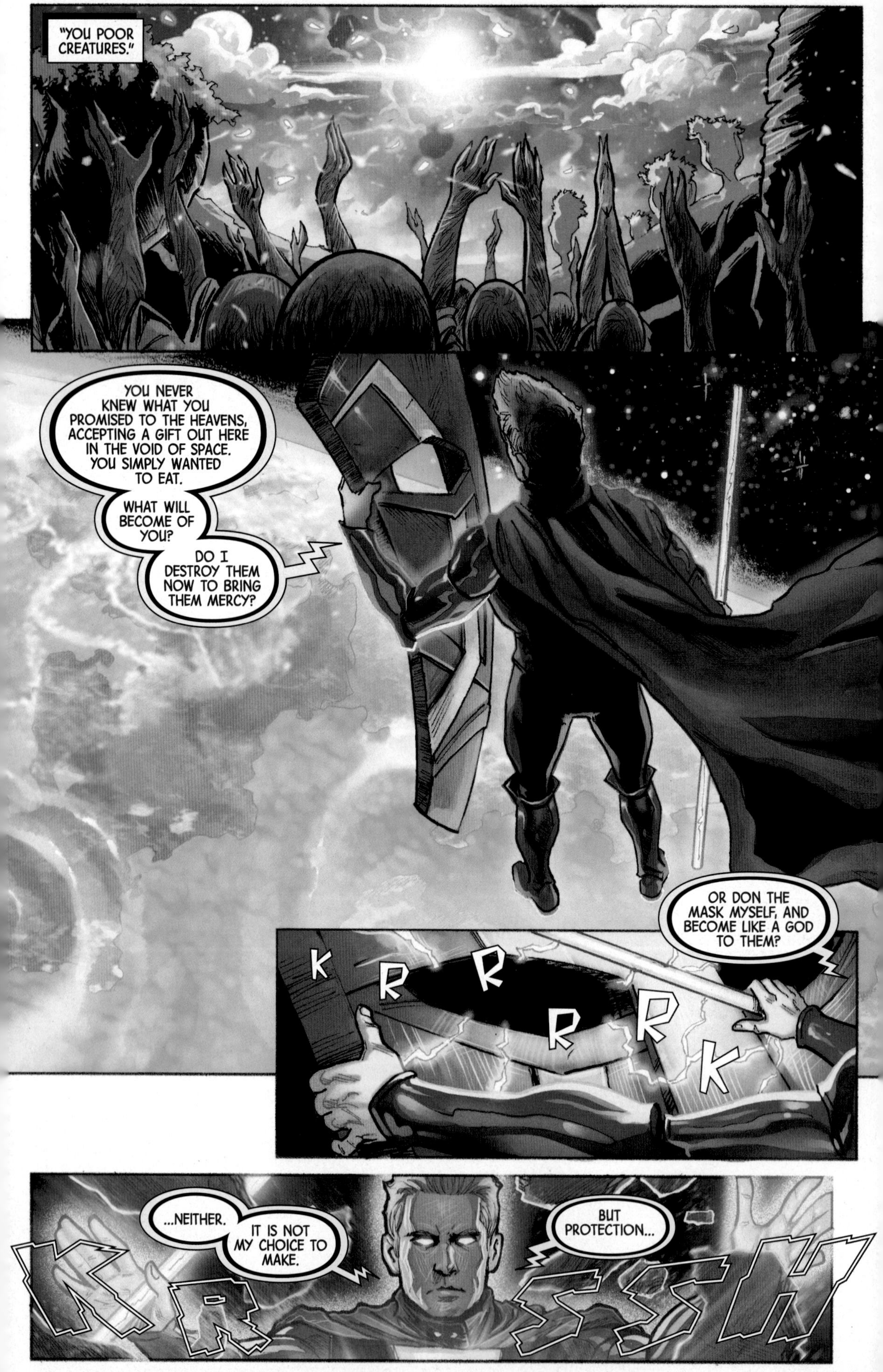
"YOU POOR CREATURES."
YOU NEVER KNEW WHAT YOU PROMISED TO THE HEAVENS, ACCEPTING A GIFT OUT HERE IN THE VOID OF SPACE. YOU SIMPLY WANTED TO EAT.
WHAT WILL BECOME OF YOU?
DO I DESTROY THEM NOW TO BRING THEM MERCY?
OR DON THE MASK MYSELF, AND BECOME LIKE A GOD TO THEM?
KRRRRK
...NEITHER.
IT IS NOT MY CHOICE TO MAKE.
BUT PROTECTION...
KRASSH

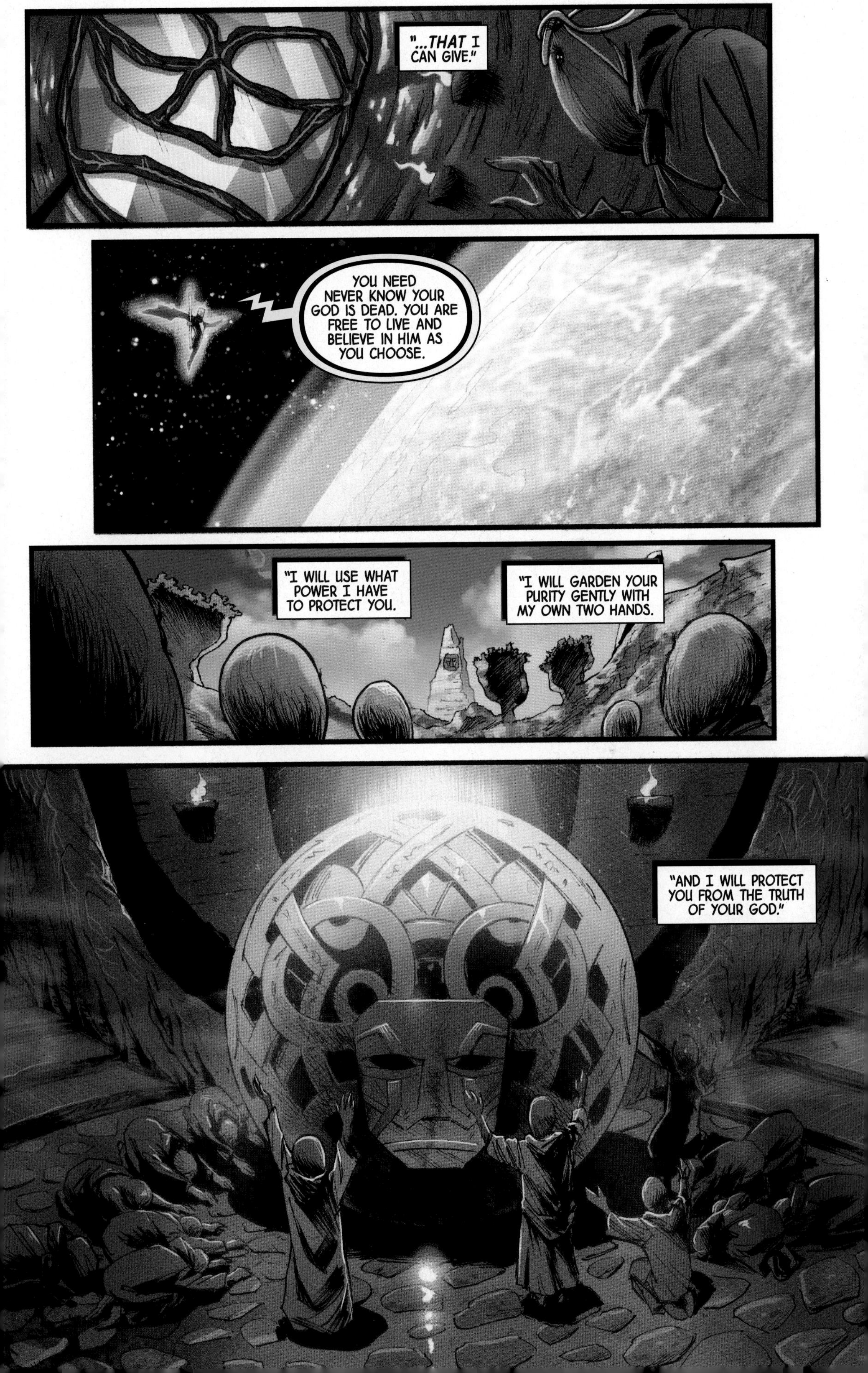
"...THAT I CAN GIVE."
YOU NEED NEVER KNOW YOUR GOD IS DEAD. YOU ARE FREE TO LIVE AND BELIEVE IN HIM AS YOU CHOOSE.
"I WILL USE WHAT POWER I HAVE TO PROTECT YOU.
"I WILL GARDEN YOUR PURITY GENTLY WITH MY OWN TWO HANDS.
"AND I WILL PROTECT YOU FROM THE TRUTH OF YOUR GOD."

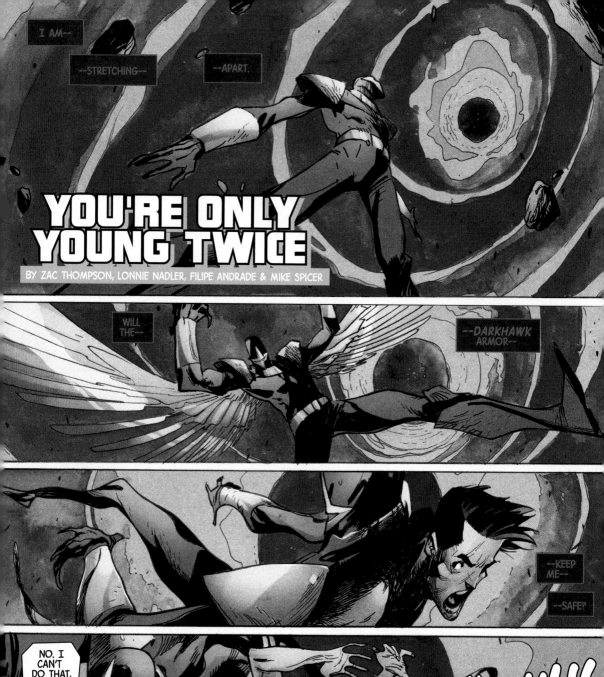

I AM--

--STRETCHING--

--APART.

YOU'RE ONLY YOUNG TWICE

BY ZAC THOMPSON, LONNIE NADLER, FILIPE ANDRADE & MIKE SPICER

WILL THE--

--DARKHAWK ARMOR--

--KEEP ME--

--SAFE?

NO. I CAN'T DO THAT, CHRIS.

AHHHHHHH!

HOW IS...

MY BODY HERE?

LOOKING AT YOU.

WE ARE...

I CAN'T BE...

NO LONGER LINKED.

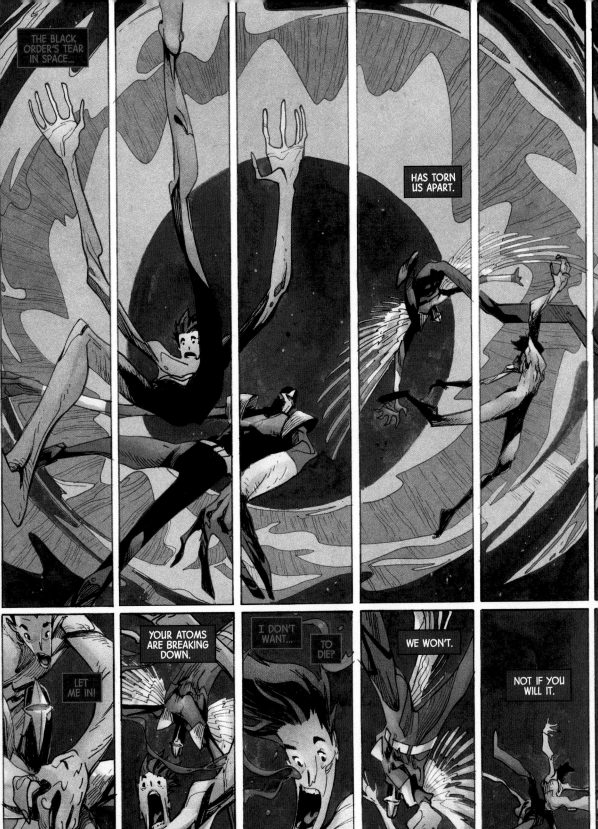

THE BLACK ORDER'S TEAR IN SPACE...

HAS TORN US APART.

LET ME IN!

YOUR ATOMS ARE BREAKING DOWN.

I DON'T WANT...

TO DIE?

WE WON'T.

NOT IF YOU WILL IT.

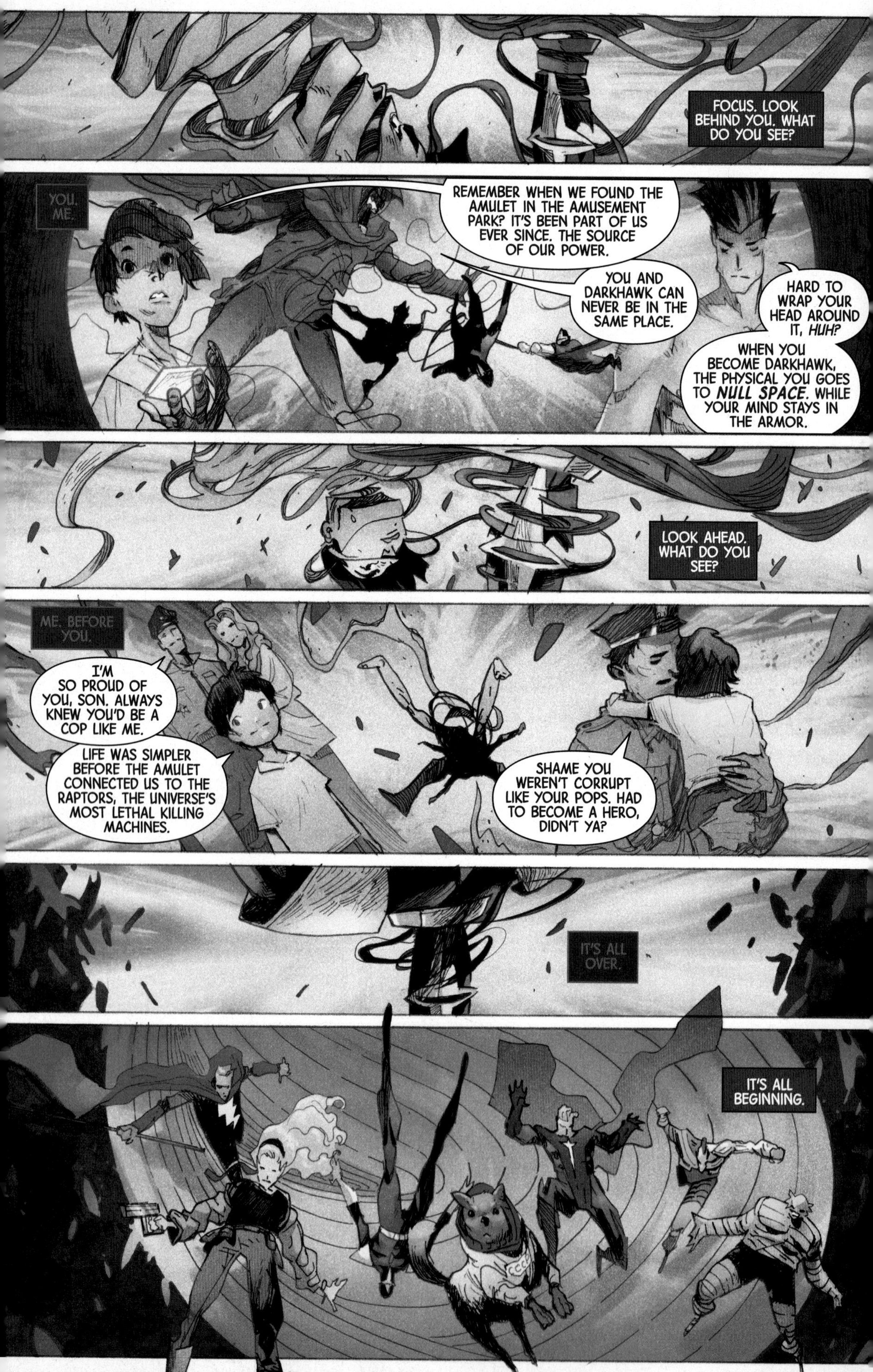
FOCUS. LOOK BEHIND YOU. WHAT DO YOU SEE?
YOU. ME.
REMEMBER WHEN WE FOUND THE AMULET IN THE AMUSEMENT PARK? IT'S BEEN PART OF US EVER SINCE. THE SOURCE OF OUR POWER.
YOU AND DARKHAWK CAN NEVER BE IN THE SAME PLACE.
HARD TO WRAP YOUR HEAD AROUND IT, *HUH?*
WHEN YOU BECOME DARKHAWK, THE PHYSICAL YOU GOES TO ***NULL SPACE***. WHILE YOUR MIND STAYS IN THE ARMOR.
LOOK AHEAD. WHAT DO YOU SEE?
ME, BEFORE YOU.
I'M SO PROUD OF YOU, SON. ALWAYS KNEW YOU'D BE A COP LIKE ME.
LIFE WAS SIMPLER BEFORE THE AMULET CONNECTED US TO THE RAPTORS, THE UNIVERSE'S MOST LETHAL KILLING MACHINES.
SHAME YOU WEREN'T CORRUPT LIKE YOUR POPS. HAD TO BECOME A HERO, DIDN'T YA?
IT'S ALL OVER.
IT'S ALL BEGINNING.

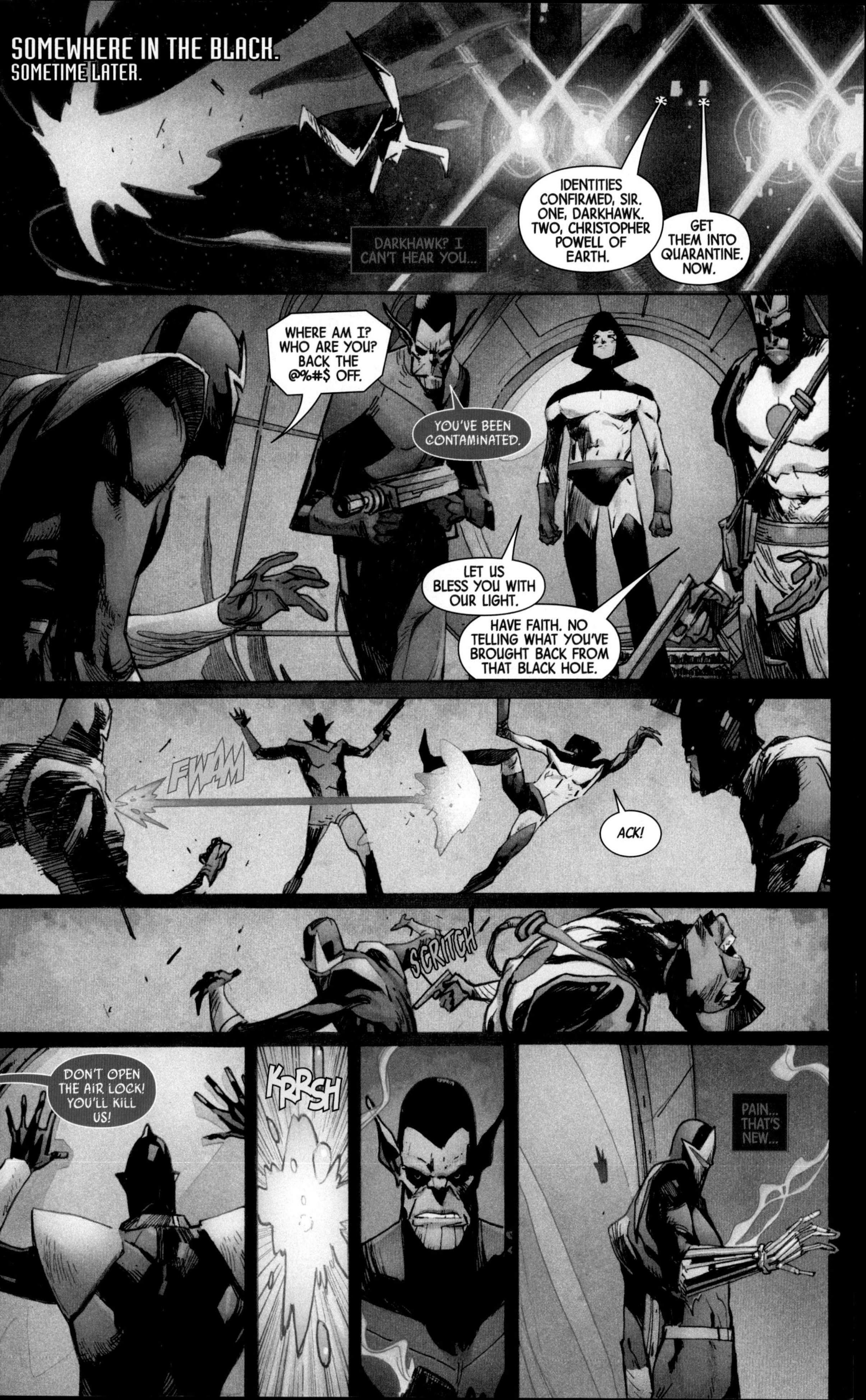
SOMEWHERE IN THE BLACK.
SOMETIME LATER.
DARKHAWK? I CAN'T HEAR YOU...
IDENTITIES CONFIRMED, SIR. ONE, DARKHAWK. TWO, CHRISTOPHER POWELL OF EARTH.
GET THEM INTO QUARANTINE. NOW.
WHERE AM I? WHO ARE YOU? BACK THE @%#$ OFF.
YOU'VE BEEN CONTAMINATED.
LET US BLESS YOU WITH OUR LIGHT.
HAVE FAITH. NO TELLING WHAT YOU'VE BROUGHT BACK FROM THAT BLACK HOLE.
FWAM
ACK!
SCRITCH
DON'T OPEN THE AIR LOCK! YOU'LL KILL US!
KRRSH
PAIN... THAT'S NEW...

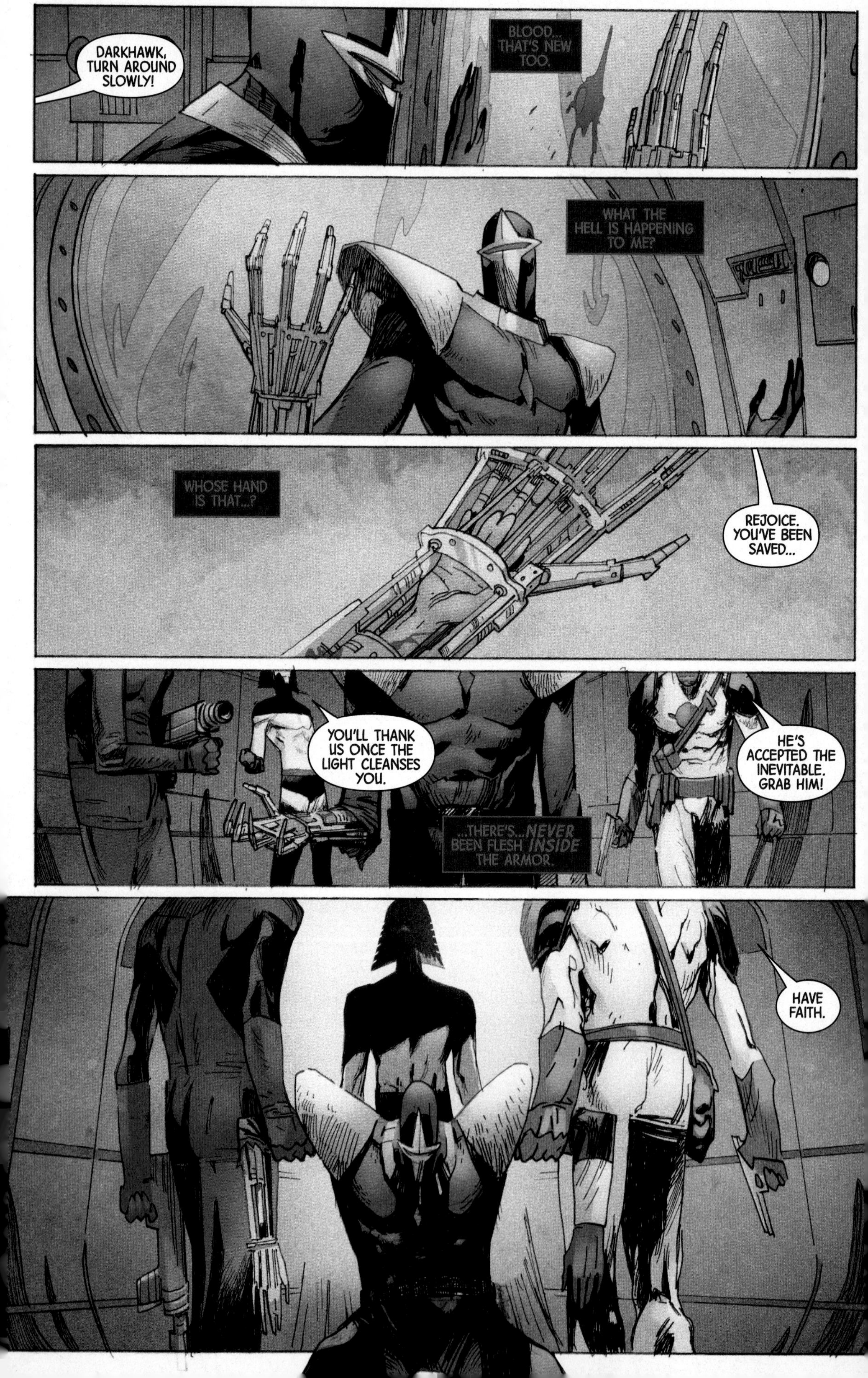

DARKHAWK, TURN AROUND SLOWLY!
BLOOD... THAT'S NEW TOO.
WHAT THE HELL IS HAPPENING TO ME?
WHOSE HAND IS THAT...?
REJOICE. YOU'VE BEEN SAVED...
YOU'LL THANK US ONCE THE LIGHT CLEANSES YOU.
HE'S ACCEPTED THE INEVITABLE. GRAB HIM!
...THERE'S...NEVER BEEN FLESH INSIDE THE ARMOR.
HAVE FAITH.

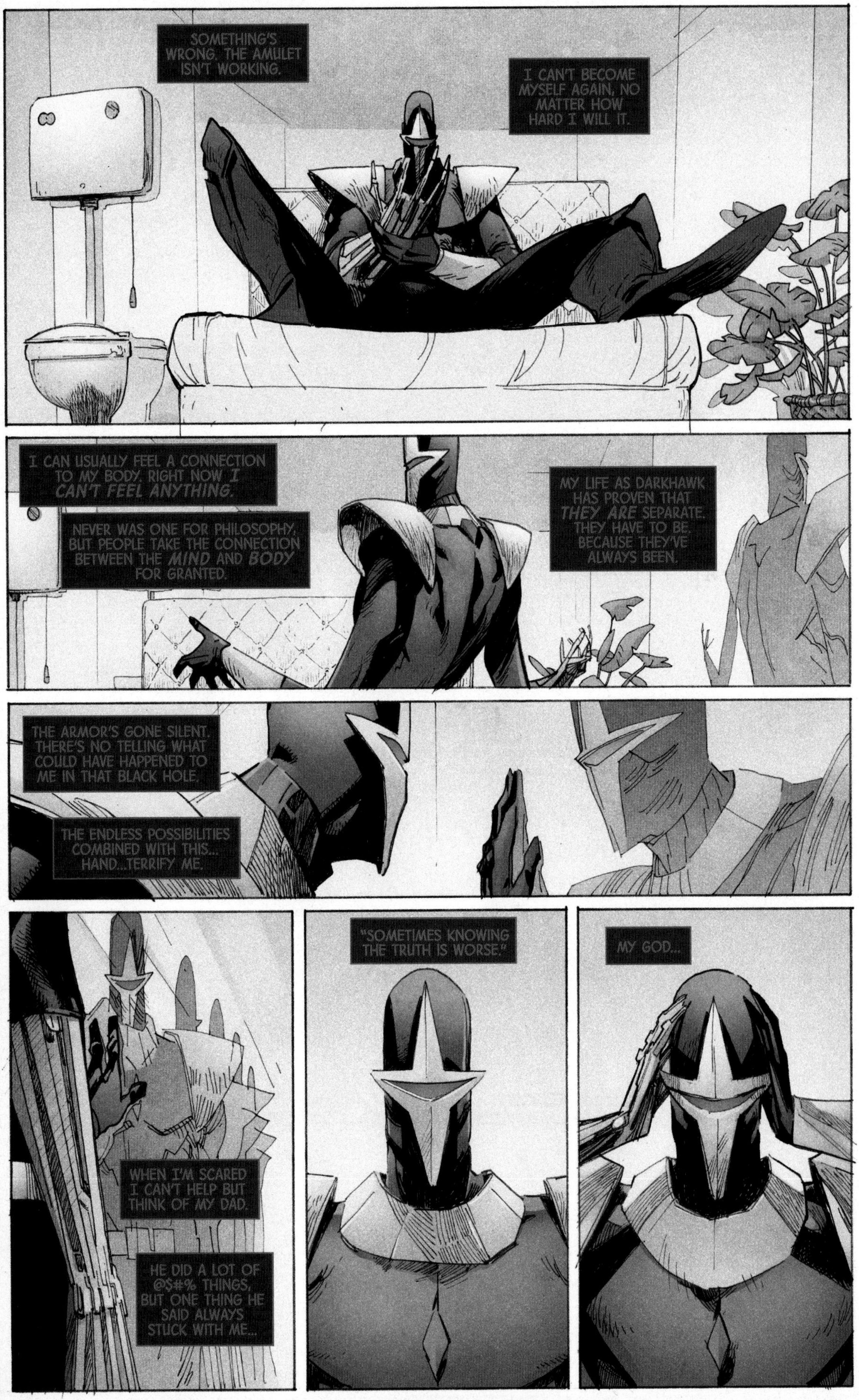
SOMETHING'S WRONG. THE AMULET ISN'T WORKING.
I CAN'T BECOME MYSELF AGAIN, NO MATTER HOW HARD I WILL IT.
I CAN USUALLY FEEL A CONNECTION TO *MY* BODY. RIGHT NOW *I CAN'T FEEL ANYTHING.*
NEVER WAS ONE FOR PHILOSOPHY, BUT PEOPLE TAKE THE CONNECTION BETWEEN THE *MIND* AND *BODY* FOR GRANTED.
MY LIFE AS DARKHAWK HAS PROVEN THAT *THEY ARE* SEPARATE. THEY HAVE TO BE, BECAUSE THEY'VE ALWAYS BEEN.
THE ARMOR'S GONE SILENT. THERE'S NO TELLING WHAT COULD HAVE HAPPENED TO ME IN THAT BLACK HOLE.
THE ENDLESS POSSIBILITIES COMBINED WITH THIS... HAND...TERRIFY ME.
WHEN I'M SCARED I CAN'T HELP BUT THINK OF *MY* DAD.
HE DID A LOT OF @$#% THINGS, BUT ONE THING HE SAID ALWAYS STUCK WITH ME...
"SOMETIMES KNOWING THE TRUTH IS WORSE."
MY GOD...

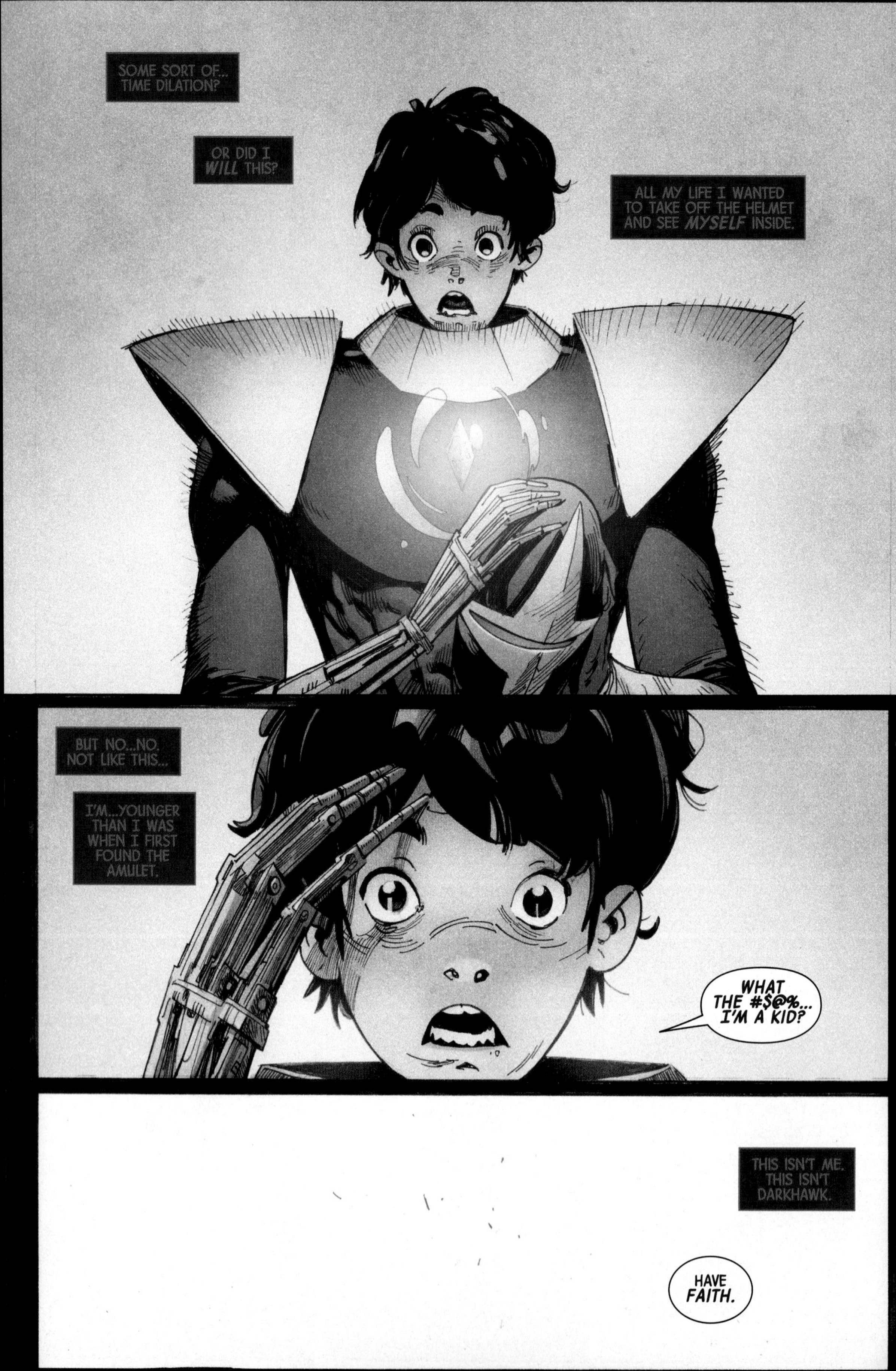
SOME SORT OF... TIME DILATION?
OR DID I *WILL* THIS?
ALL MY LIFE I WANTED TO TAKE OFF THE HELMET AND SEE *MYSELF* INSIDE.
BUT NO...NO. NOT LIKE THIS...
I'M...YOUNGER THAN I WAS WHEN I FIRST FOUND THE AMULET.
WHAT THE #$@%... I'M A KID?
THIS ISN'T ME. THIS ISN'T DARKHAWK.
HAVE *FAITH.*

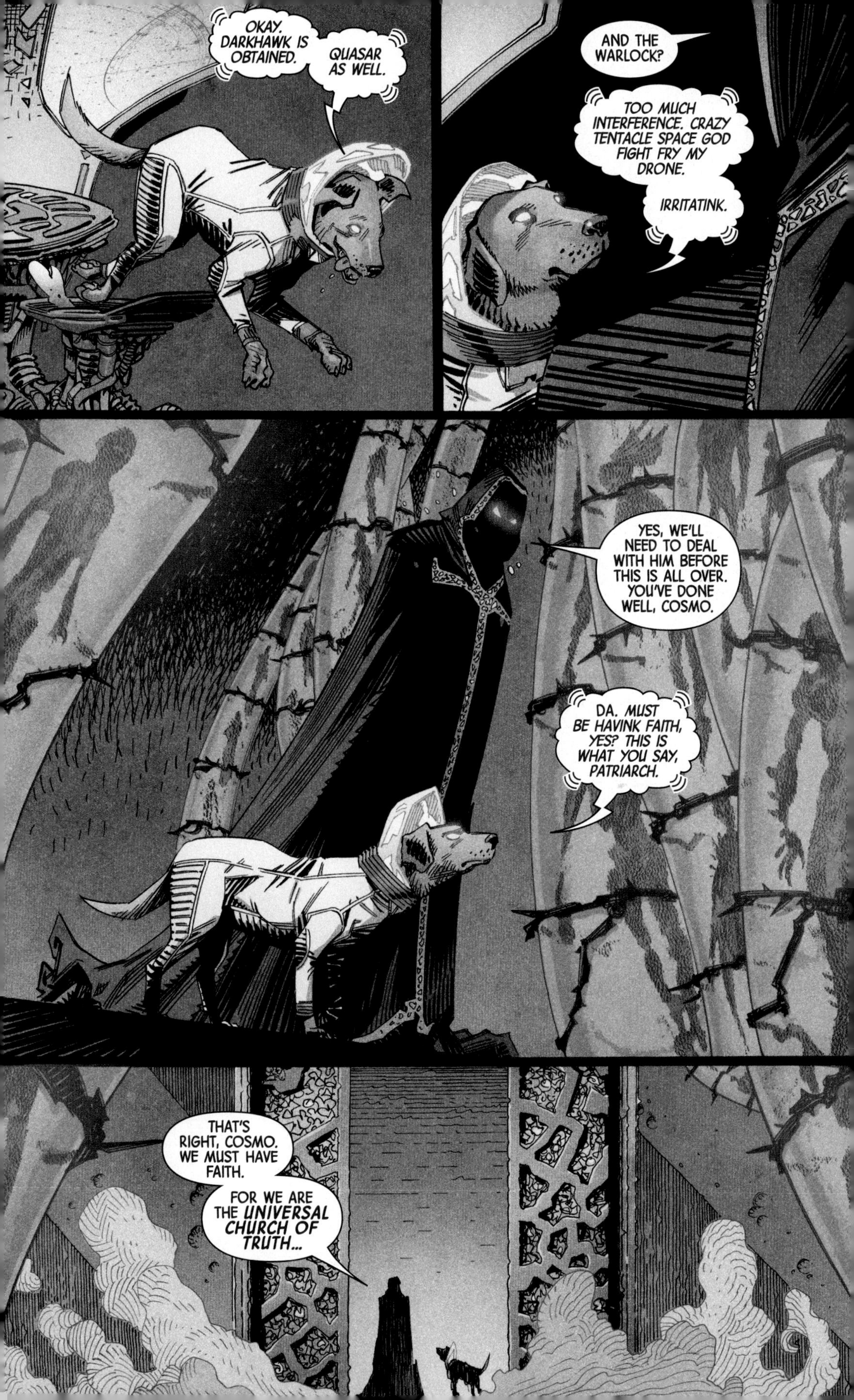
OKAY. DARKHAWK IS OBTAINED.
QUASAR AS WELL.
AND THE WARLOCK?
TOO MUCH INTERFERENCE. CRAZY TENTACLE SPACE GOD FIGHT FRY MY DRONE.
IRRITATINK.
YES, WE'LL NEED TO DEAL WITH HIM BEFORE THIS IS ALL OVER. YOU'VE DONE WELL, COSMO.
DA. MUST BE HAVINK FAITH, YES? THIS IS WHAT YOU SAY, PATRIARCH.
THAT'S RIGHT, COSMO. WE MUST HAVE FAITH.
FOR WE ARE THE UNIVERSAL CHURCH OF TRUTH...

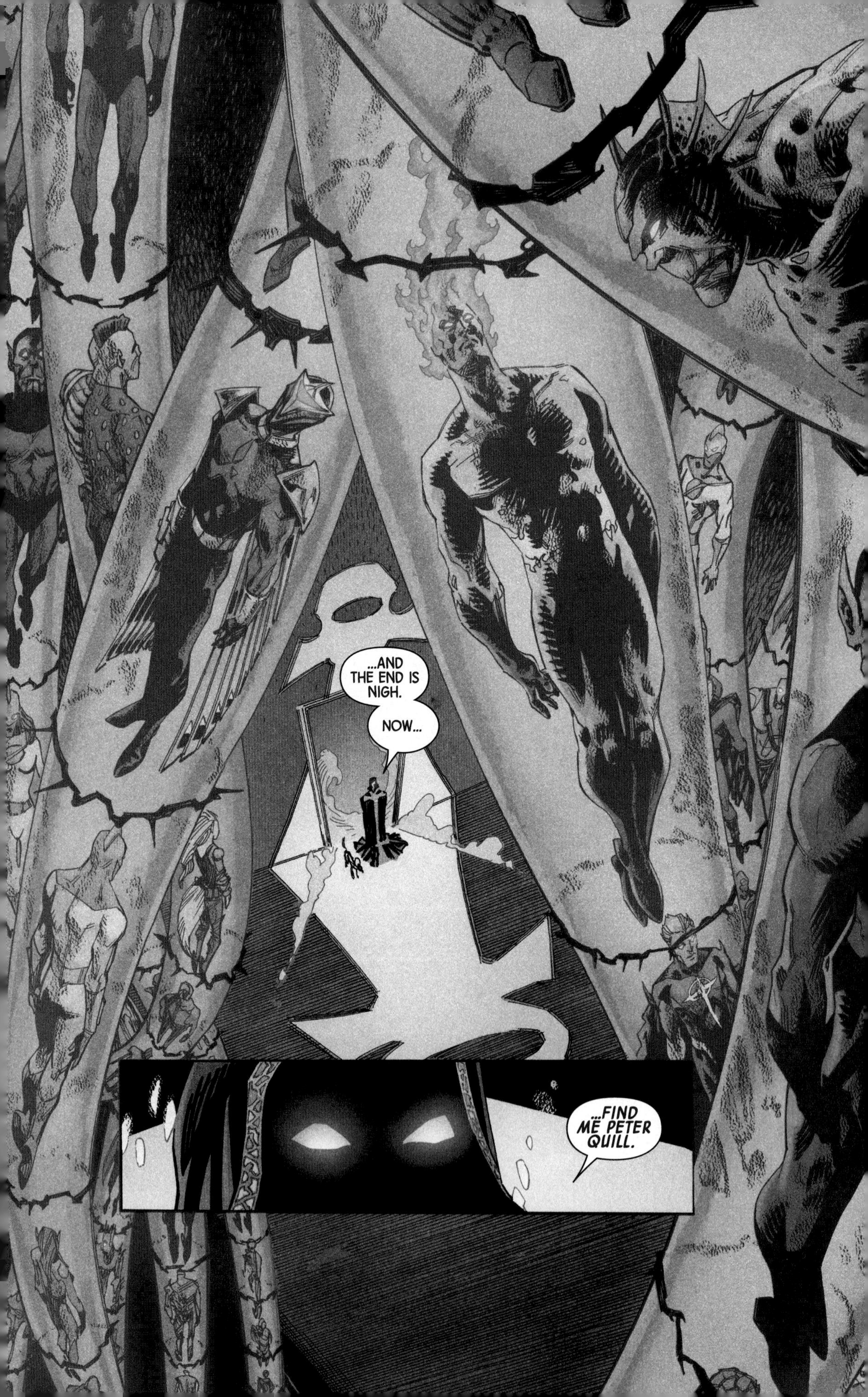
...AND THE END IS NIGH.
NOW...
...FIND ME PETER QUILL.

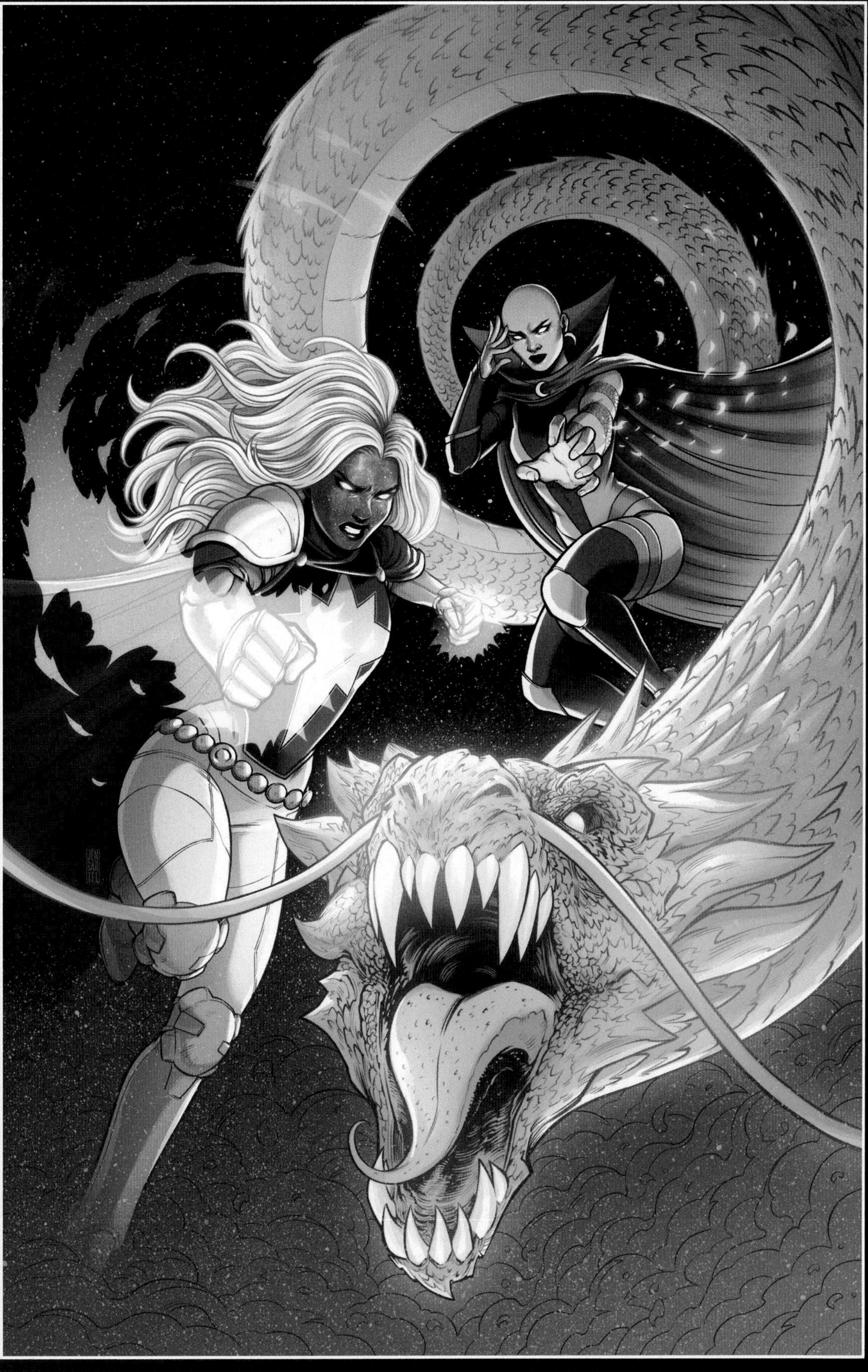

JEN BARTEL
ANNUAL #1 Variant

SEVEN

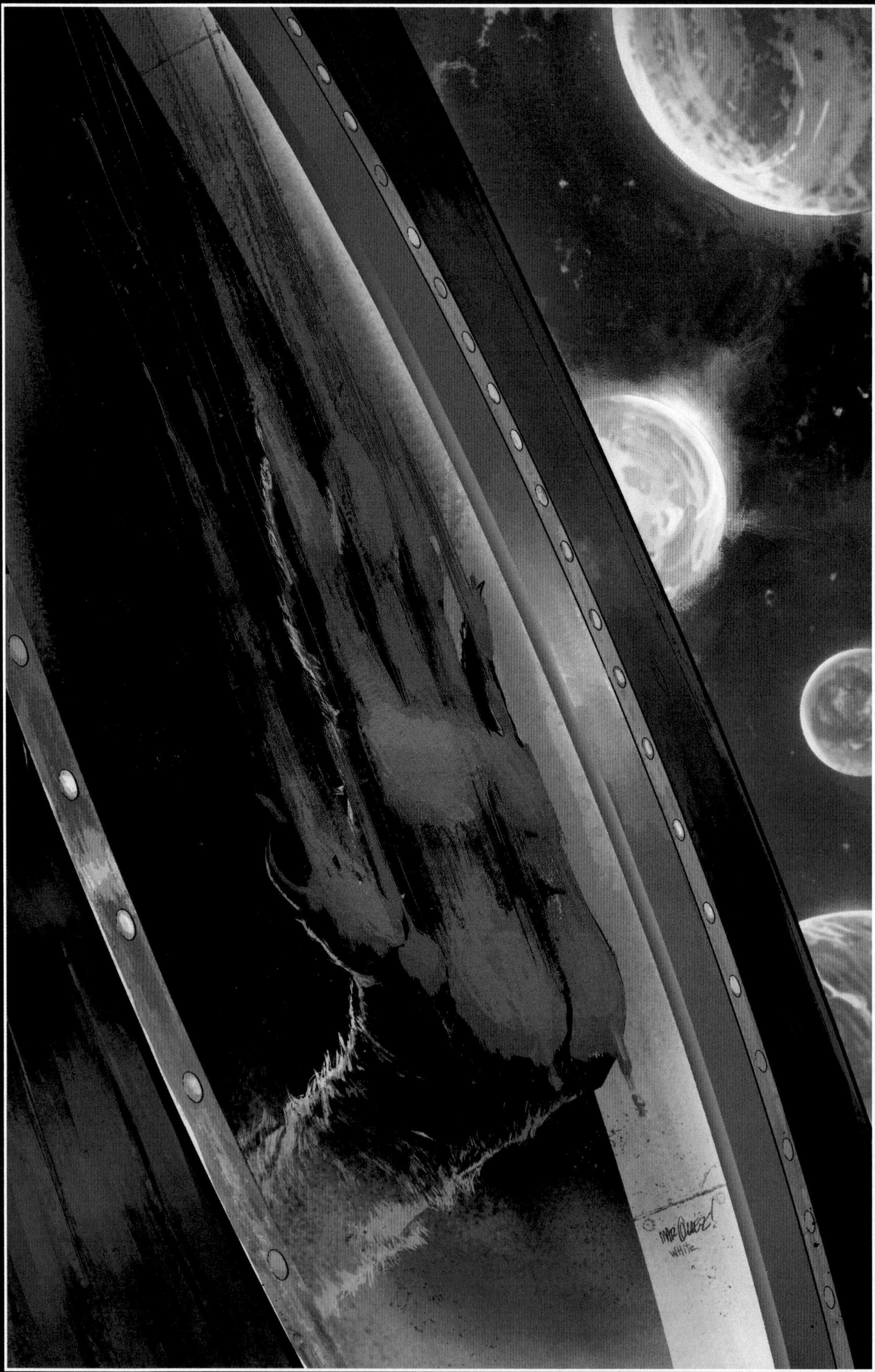

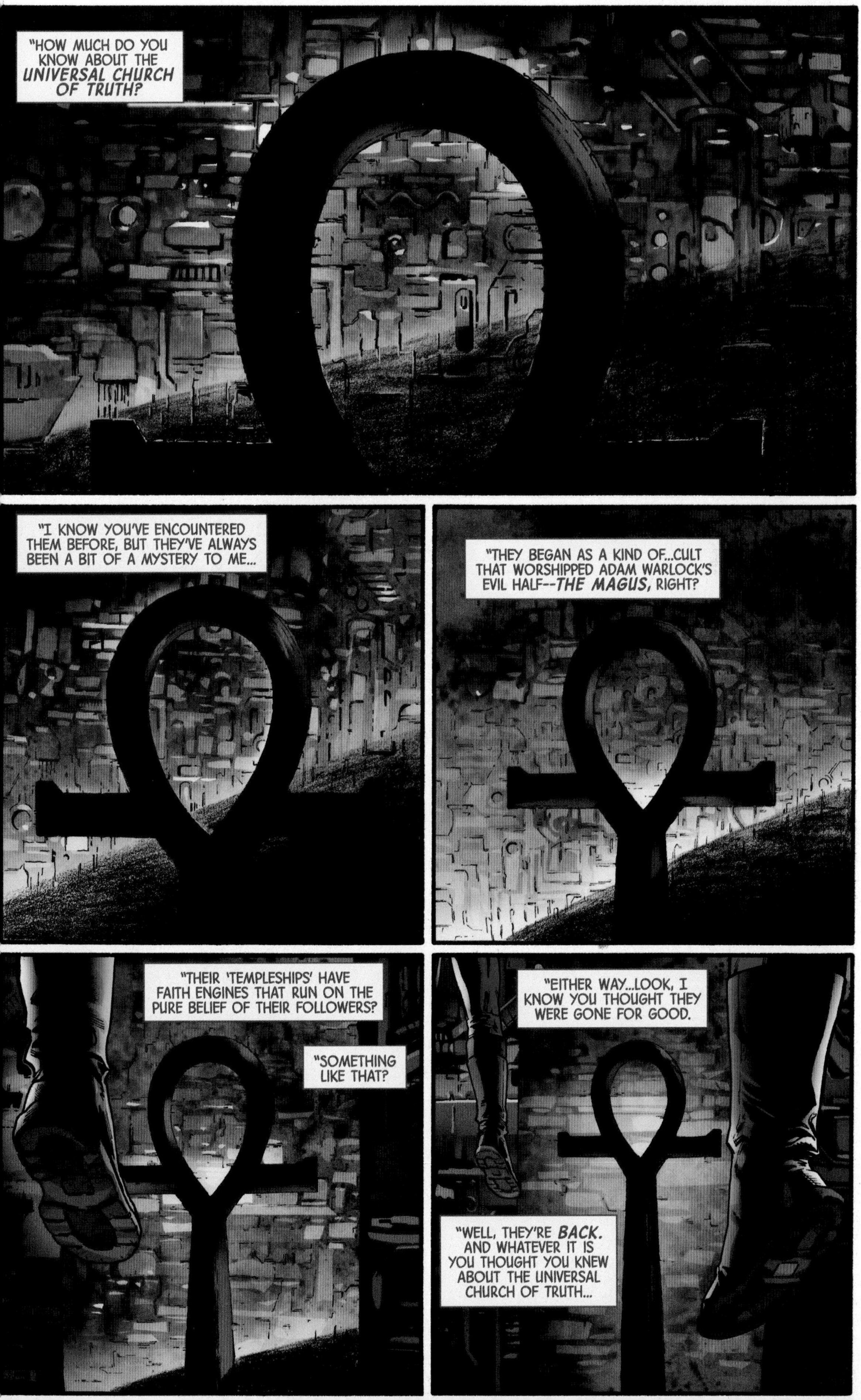
"HOW MUCH DO YOU KNOW ABOUT THE *UNIVERSAL CHURCH OF TRUTH?*
"I KNOW YOU'VE ENCOUNTERED THEM BEFORE, BUT THEY'VE ALWAYS BEEN A BIT OF A MYSTERY TO ME...
"THEY BEGAN AS A KIND OF...CULT THAT WORSHIPPED ADAM WARLOCK'S EVIL HALF--*THE MAGUS,* RIGHT?
"THEIR 'TEMPLESHIPS' HAVE FAITH ENGINES THAT RUN ON THE PURE BELIEF OF THEIR FOLLOWERS?
"SOMETHING LIKE THAT?
"EITHER WAY...LOOK, I KNOW YOU THOUGHT THEY WERE GONE FOR GOOD.
"WELL, THEY'RE *BACK.* AND WHATEVER IT IS YOU THOUGHT YOU KNEW ABOUT THE UNIVERSAL CHURCH OF TRUTH...

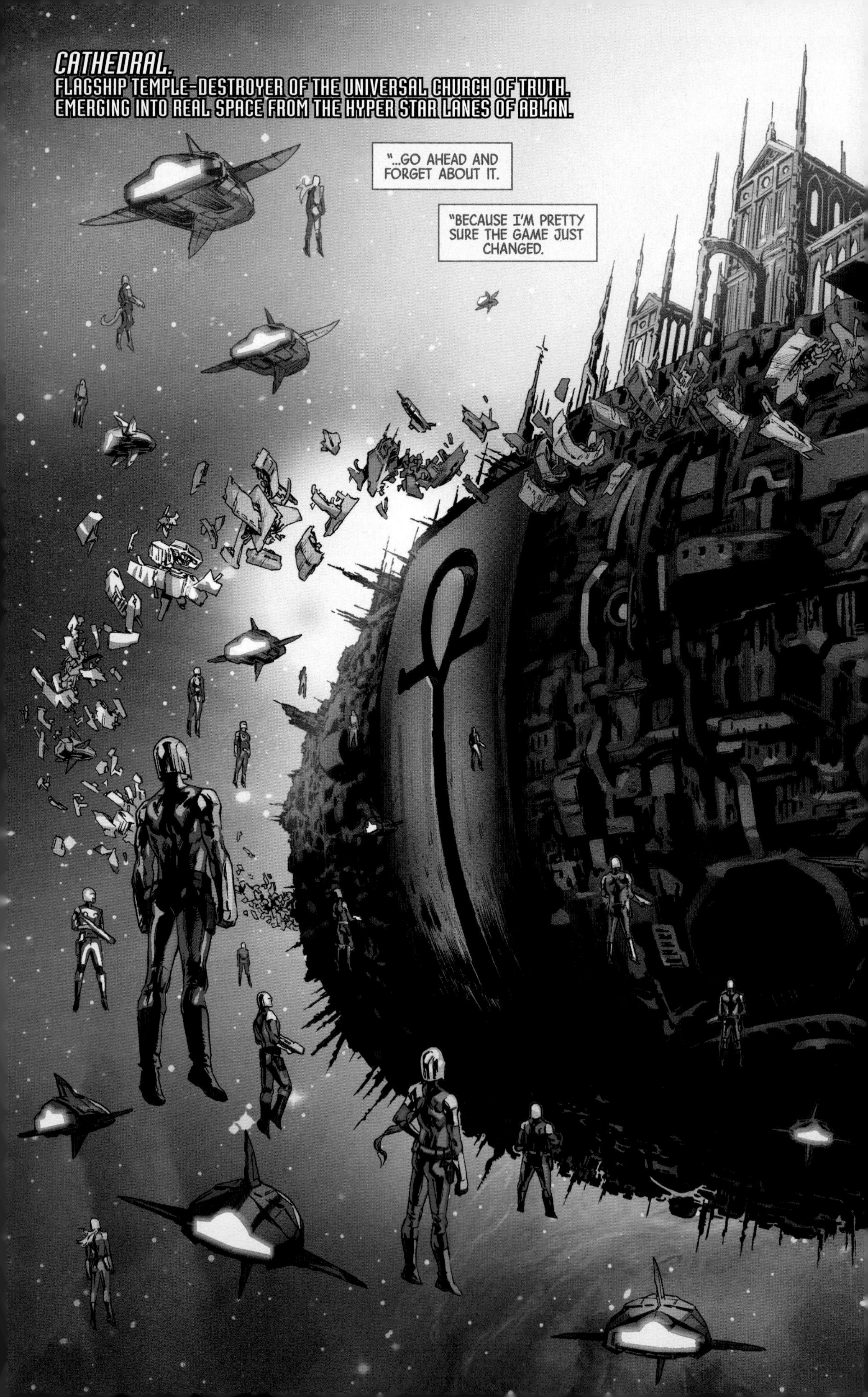
CATHEDRAL.
FLAGSHIP TEMPLE-DESTROYER OF THE UNIVERSAL CHURCH OF TRUTH.
EMERGING INTO REAL SPACE FROM THE HYPER STAR LANES OF ABLAN.
"...GO AHEAD AND FORGET ABOUT IT.
"BECAUSE I'M PRETTY SURE THE GAME JUST CHANGED.

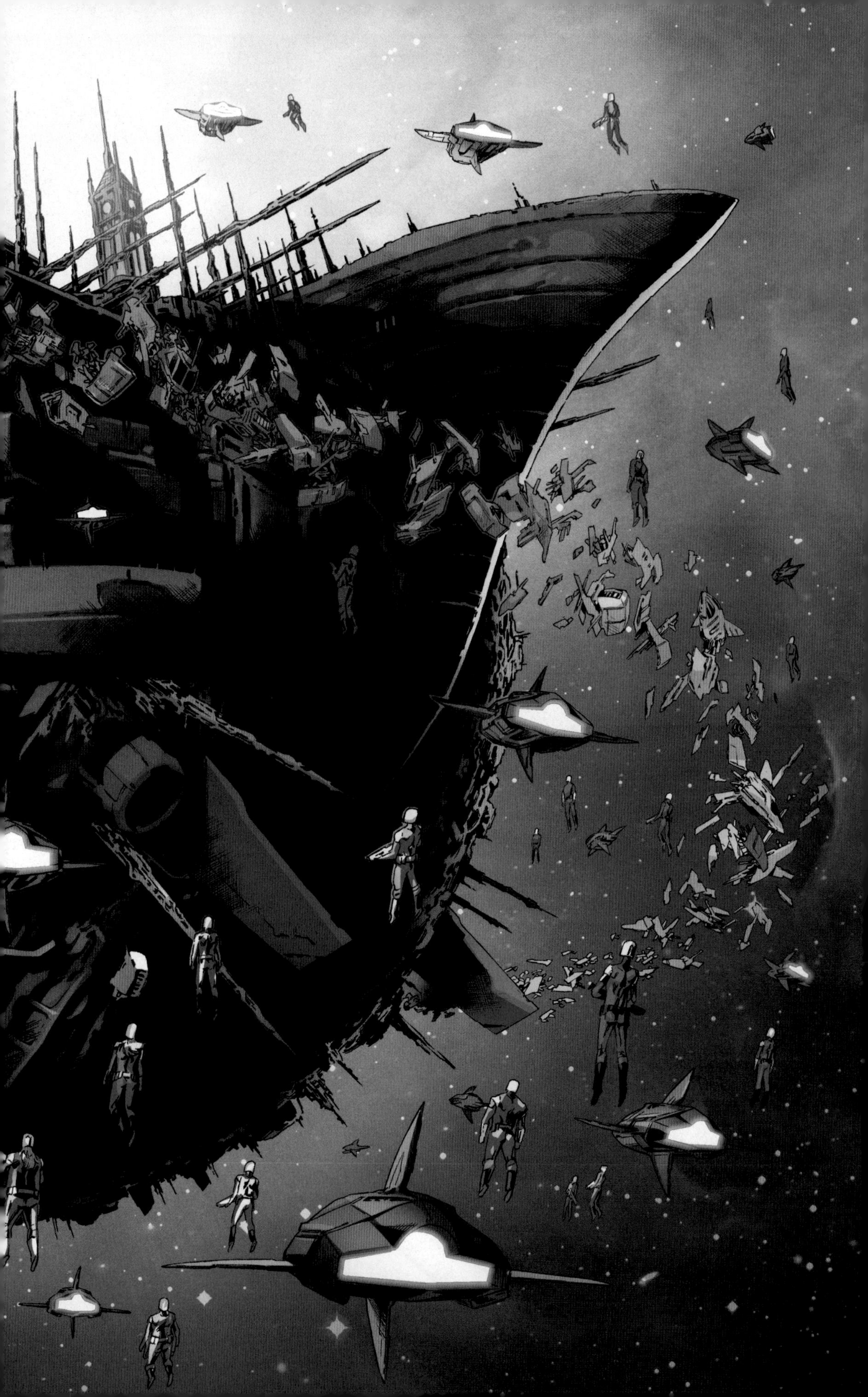

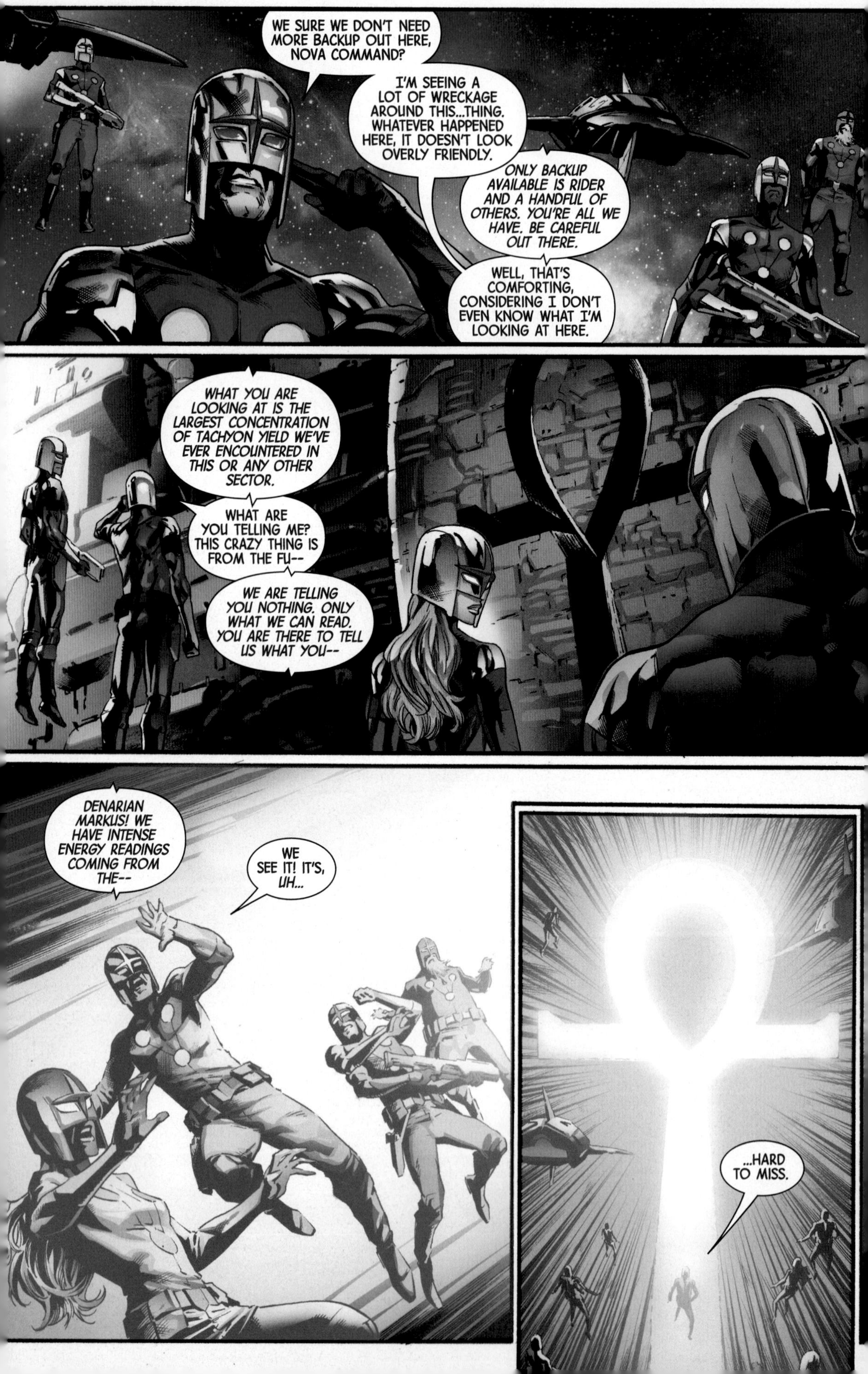
WE SURE WE DON'T NEED MORE BACKUP OUT HERE, NOVA COMMAND?
I'M SEEING A LOT OF WRECKAGE AROUND THIS...THING. WHATEVER HAPPENED HERE, IT DOESN'T LOOK OVERLY FRIENDLY.
ONLY BACKUP AVAILABLE IS RIDER AND A HANDFUL OF OTHERS. YOU'RE ALL WE HAVE. BE CAREFUL OUT THERE.
WELL, THAT'S COMFORTING, CONSIDERING I DON'T EVEN KNOW WHAT I'M LOOKING AT HERE.
WHAT YOU ARE LOOKING AT IS THE LARGEST CONCENTRATION OF TACHYON YIELD WE'VE EVER ENCOUNTERED IN THIS OR ANY OTHER SECTOR.
WHAT ARE YOU TELLING ME? THIS CRAZY THING IS FROM THE FU--
WE ARE TELLING YOU NOTHING. ONLY WHAT WE CAN READ. YOU ARE THERE TO TELL US WHAT YOU--
DENARIAN MARKUS! WE HAVE INTENSE ENERGY READINGS COMING FROM THE--
WE SEE IT! IT'S, UH...
...HARD TO MISS.

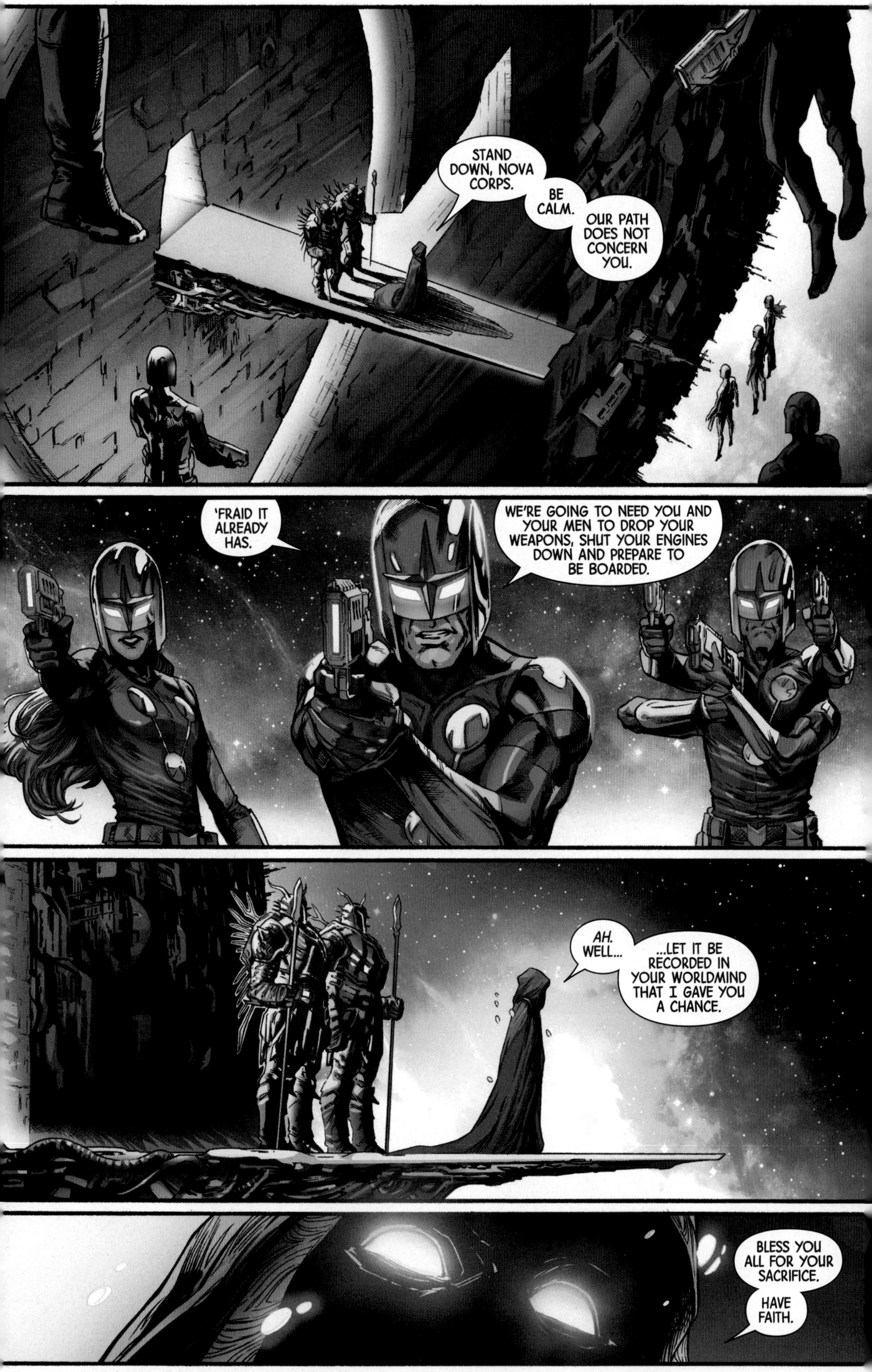
STAND DOWN, NOVA CORPS.
BE CALM.
OUR PATH DOES NOT CONCERN YOU.
'FRAID IT ALREADY HAS.
WE'RE GOING TO NEED YOU AND YOUR MEN TO DROP YOUR WEAPONS, SHUT YOUR ENGINES DOWN AND PREPARE TO BE BOARDED.
AH. WELL...
...LET IT BE RECORDED IN YOUR WORLDMIND THAT I GAVE YOU A CHANCE.
BLESS YOU ALL FOR YOUR SACRIFICE.
HAVE FAITH.

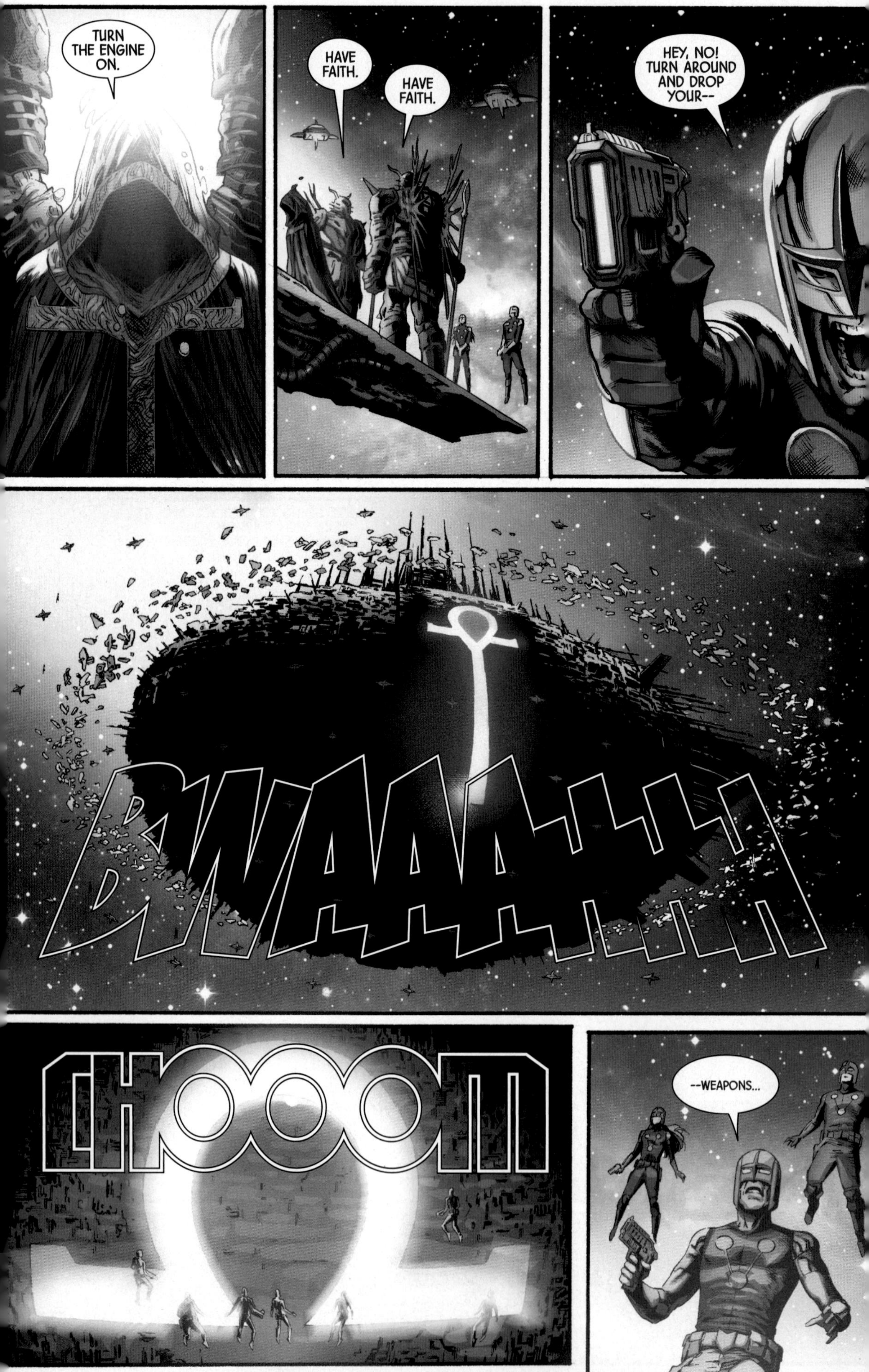
TURN THE ENGINE ON.
HAVE FAITH.
HAVE FAITH.
HEY, NO! TURN AROUND AND DROP YOUR--
BWAAAHHHH
CHOOOM
--WEAPONS...

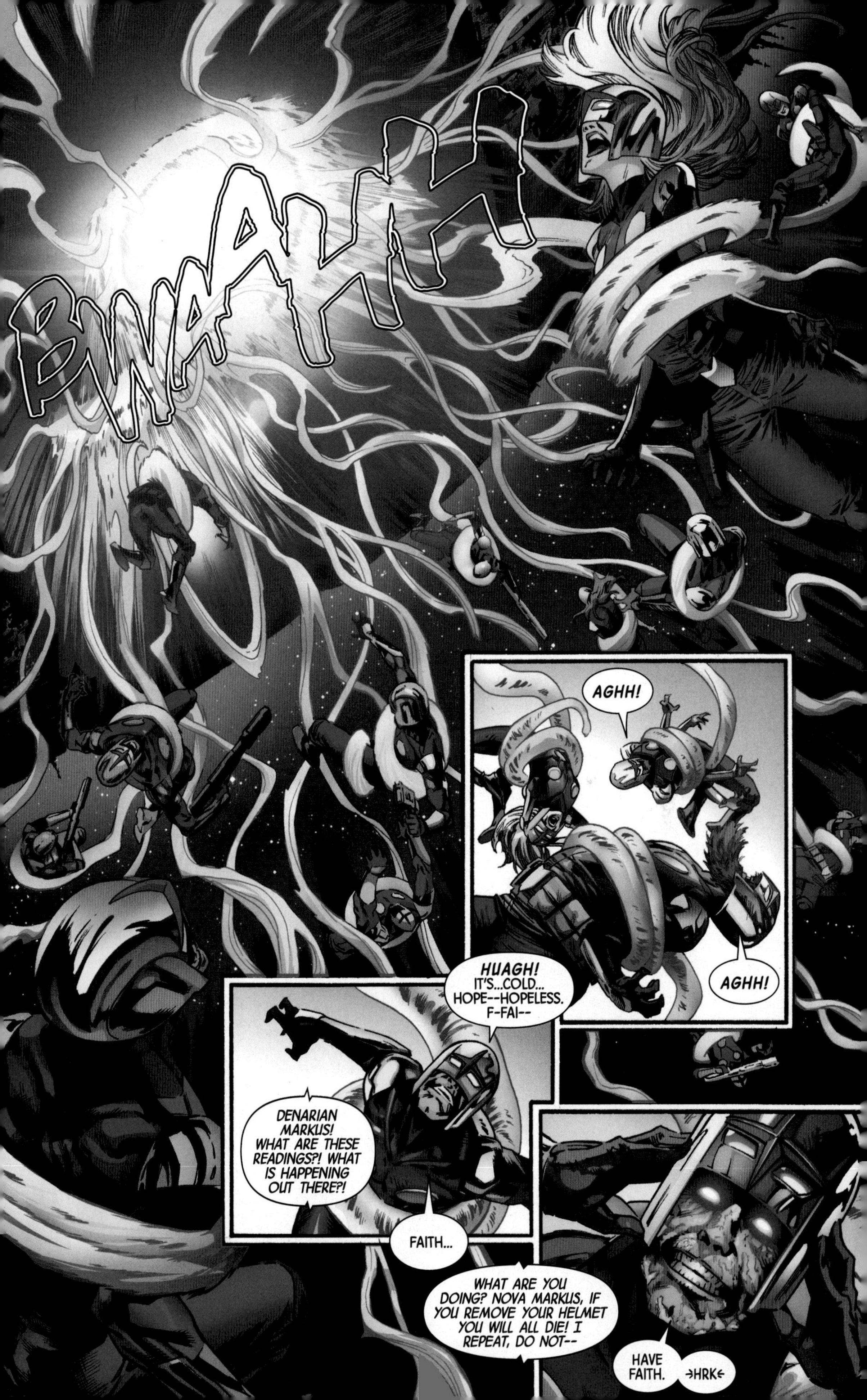
BWAAAH
AGHH!
AGHH!
HUAGH! IT'S...COLD... HOPE--HOPELESS. F-FAI--
DENARIAN MARKUS! WHAT ARE THESE READINGS?! WHAT IS HAPPENING OUT THERE?!
FAITH...
WHAT ARE YOU DOING? NOVA MARKUS, IF YOU REMOVE YOUR HELMET YOU WILL ALL DIE! I REPEAT, DO NOT--
HAVE FAITH.
HRK

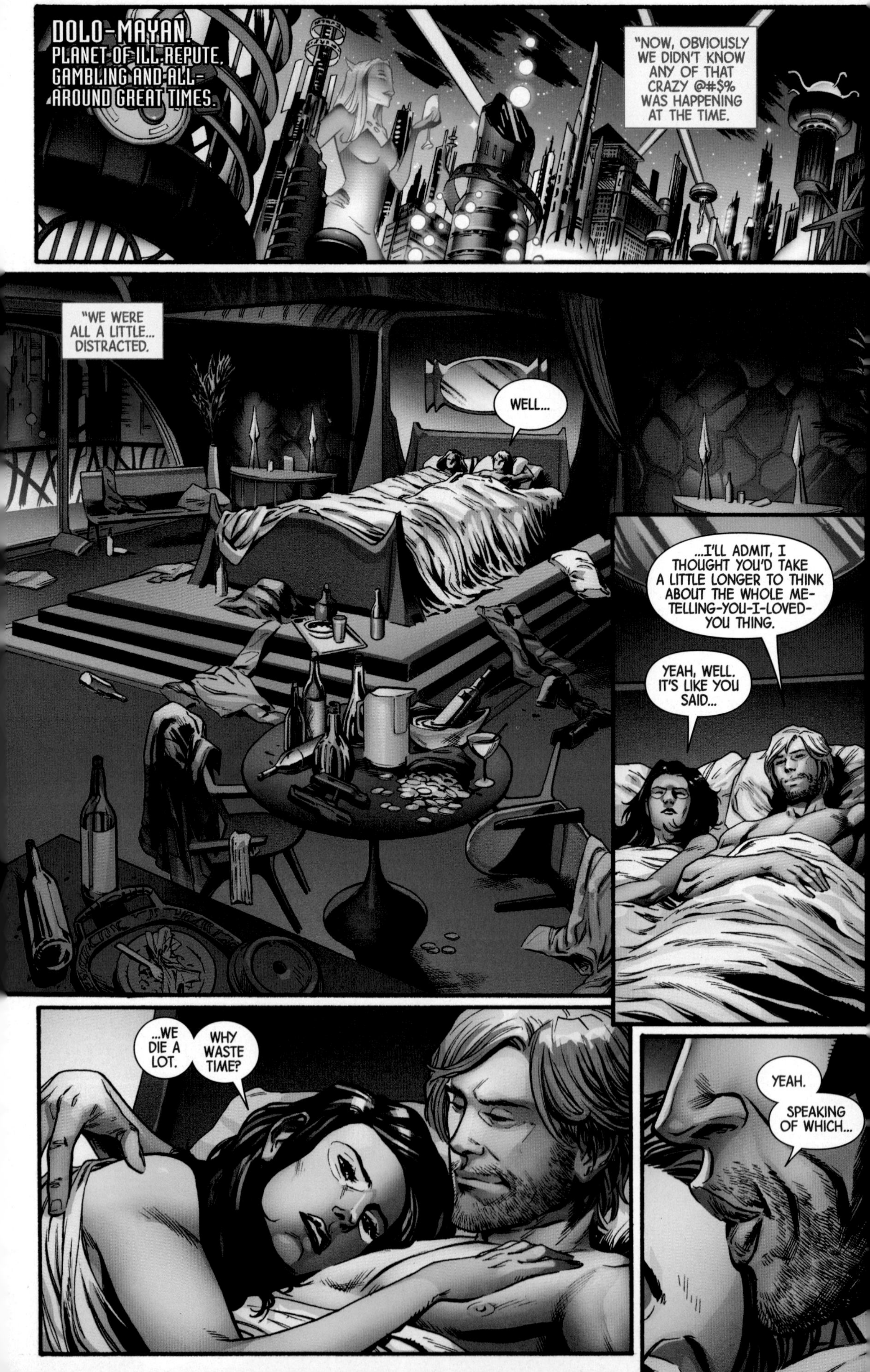
DOLO-MAYAN.
PLANET OF ILL REPUTE, GAMBLING AND ALL-AROUND GREAT TIMES.
"NOW, OBVIOUSLY WE DIDN'T KNOW ANY OF THAT CRAZY @#$% WAS HAPPENING AT THE TIME.
"WE WERE ALL A LITTLE... DISTRACTED.
WELL...
...I'LL ADMIT, I THOUGHT YOU'D TAKE A LITTLE LONGER TO THINK ABOUT THE WHOLE ME-TELLING-YOU-I-LOVED-YOU THING.
YEAH, WELL. IT'S LIKE YOU SAID...
...WE DIE A LOT.
WHY WASTE TIME?
YEAH.
SPEAKING OF WHICH...

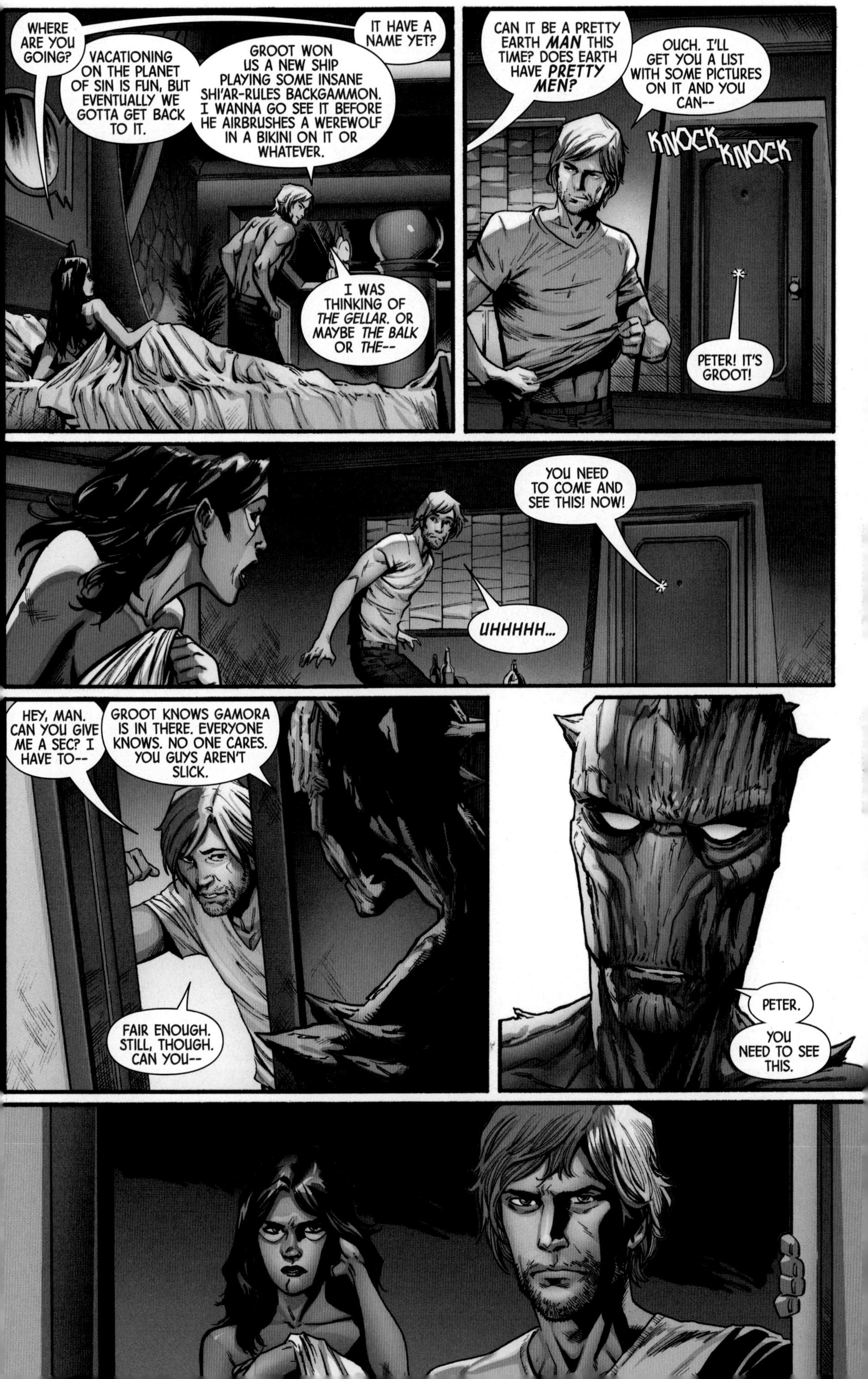
WHERE ARE YOU GOING?
VACATIONING ON THE PLANET OF SIN IS FUN, BUT EVENTUALLY WE GOTTA GET BACK TO IT.
GROOT WON US A NEW SHIP PLAYING SOME INSANE SHI'AR-RULES BACKGAMMON. I WANNA GO SEE IT BEFORE HE AIRBRUSHES A WEREWOLF IN A BIKINI ON IT OR WHATEVER.
IT HAVE A NAME YET?
I WAS THINKING OF THE GELLAR. OR MAYBE THE BALK OR THE--
CAN IT BE A PRETTY EARTH MAN THIS TIME? DOES EARTH HAVE PRETTY MEN?
OUCH. I'LL GET YOU A LIST WITH SOME PICTURES ON IT AND YOU CAN--
KNOCK KNOCK
PETER! IT'S GROOT!
YOU NEED TO COME AND SEE THIS! NOW!
UHHHHH...
HEY, MAN. CAN YOU GIVE ME A SEC? I HAVE TO--
GROOT KNOWS GAMORA IS IN THERE. EVERYONE KNOWS. NO ONE CARES. YOU GUYS AREN'T SLICK.
FAIR ENOUGH. STILL, THOUGH. CAN YOU--
PETER.
YOU NEED TO SEE THIS.

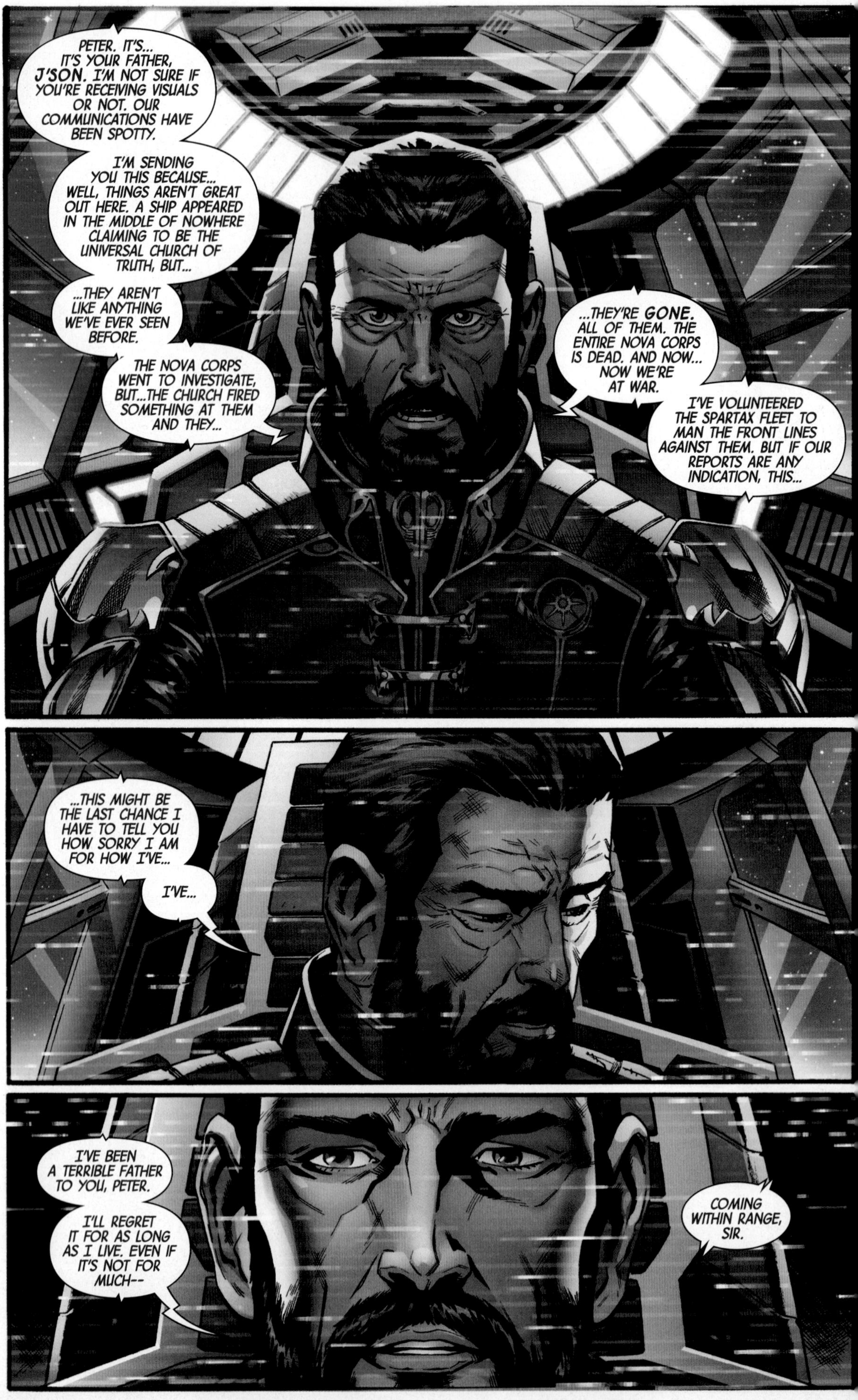
PETER. IT'S... IT'S YOUR FATHER, J'SON. I'M NOT SURE IF YOU'RE RECEIVING VISUALS OR NOT. OUR COMMUNICATIONS HAVE BEEN SPOTTY.
I'M SENDING YOU THIS BECAUSE... WELL, THINGS AREN'T GREAT OUT HERE. A SHIP APPEARED IN THE MIDDLE OF NOWHERE CLAIMING TO BE THE UNIVERSAL CHURCH OF TRUTH, BUT...
...THEY AREN'T LIKE ANYTHING WE'VE EVER SEEN BEFORE.
THE NOVA CORPS WENT TO INVESTIGATE, BUT...THE CHURCH FIRED SOMETHING AT THEM AND THEY...
...THEY'RE GONE. ALL OF THEM. THE ENTIRE NOVA CORPS IS DEAD. AND NOW... NOW WE'RE AT WAR.
I'VE VOLUNTEERED THE SPARTAX FLEET TO MAN THE FRONT LINES AGAINST THEM. BUT IF OUR REPORTS ARE ANY INDICATION, THIS...
...THIS MIGHT BE THE LAST CHANCE I HAVE TO TELL YOU HOW SORRY I AM FOR HOW I'VE...
I'VE...
I'VE BEEN A TERRIBLE FATHER TO YOU, PETER.
I'LL REGRET IT FOR AS LONG AS I LIVE. EVEN IF IT'S NOT FOR MUCH--
COMING WITHIN RANGE, SIR.

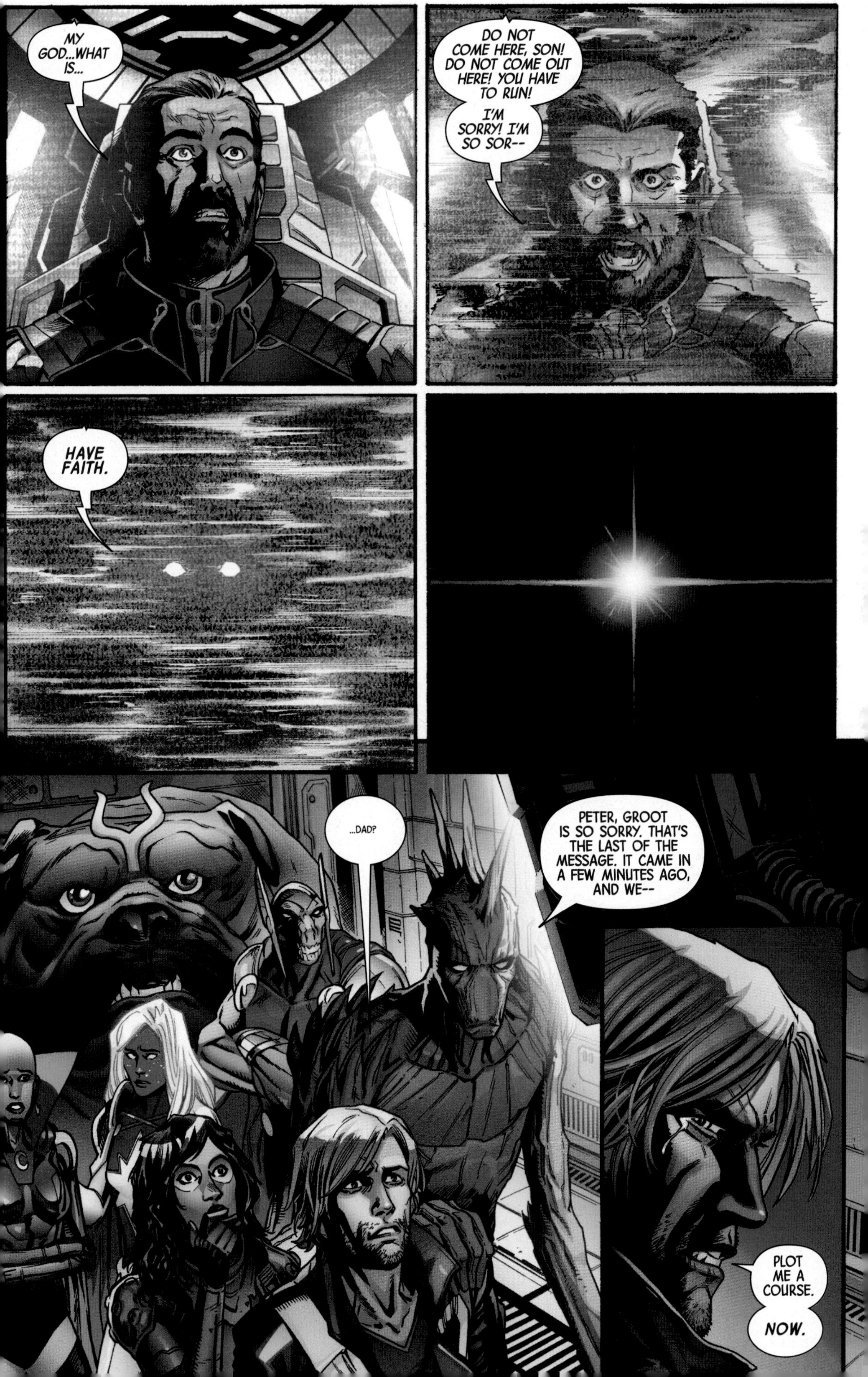

MY GOD...WHAT IS...
DO NOT COME HERE, SON! DO NOT COME OUT HERE! YOU HAVE TO RUN!
I'M SORRY! I'M SO SOR--
HAVE FAITH.
...DAD?
PETER, GROOT IS SO SORRY. THAT'S THE LAST OF THE MESSAGE. IT CAME IN A FEW MINUTES AGO, AND WE--
PLOT ME A COURSE.
NOW.

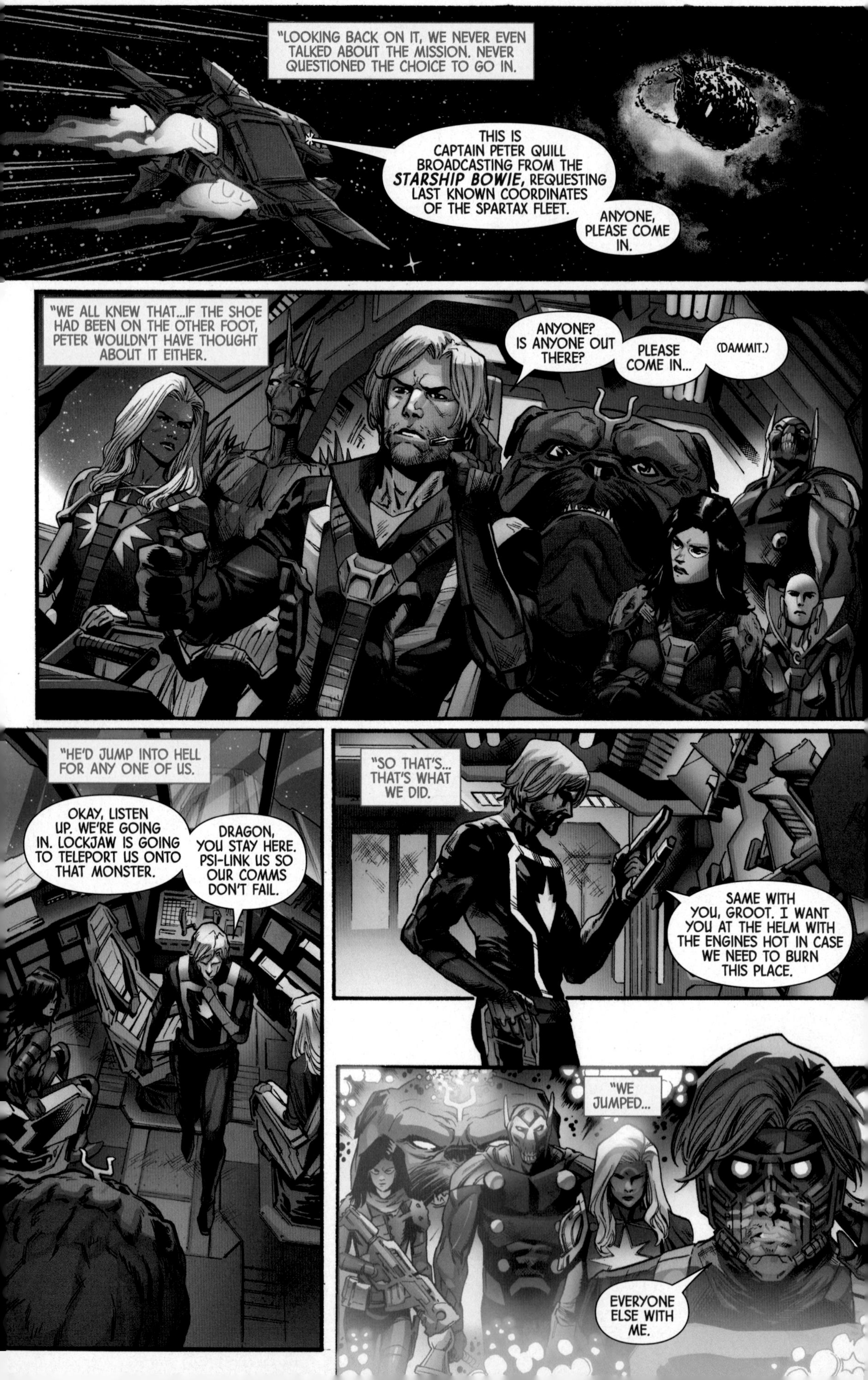
"LOOKING BACK ON IT, WE NEVER EVEN TALKED ABOUT THE MISSION. NEVER QUESTIONED THE CHOICE TO GO IN.
THIS IS CAPTAIN PETER QUILL BROADCASTING FROM THE STARSHIP BOWIE, REQUESTING LAST KNOWN COORDINATES OF THE SPARTAX FLEET.
ANYONE, PLEASE COME IN.
"WE ALL KNEW THAT...IF THE SHOE HAD BEEN ON THE OTHER FOOT, PETER WOULDN'T HAVE THOUGHT ABOUT IT EITHER.
ANYONE? IS ANYONE OUT THERE?
PLEASE COME IN...
(DAMMIT.)
"HE'D JUMP INTO HELL FOR ANY ONE OF US.
OKAY, LISTEN UP. WE'RE GOING IN. LOCKJAW IS GOING TO TELEPORT US ONTO THAT MONSTER.
DRAGON, YOU STAY HERE. PSI-LINK US SO OUR COMMS DON'T FAIL.
"SO THAT'S... THAT'S WHAT WE DID.
SAME WITH YOU, GROOT. I WANT YOU AT THE HELM WITH THE ENGINES HOT IN CASE WE NEED TO BURN THIS PLACE.
"WE JUMPED...
EVERYONE ELSE WITH ME.

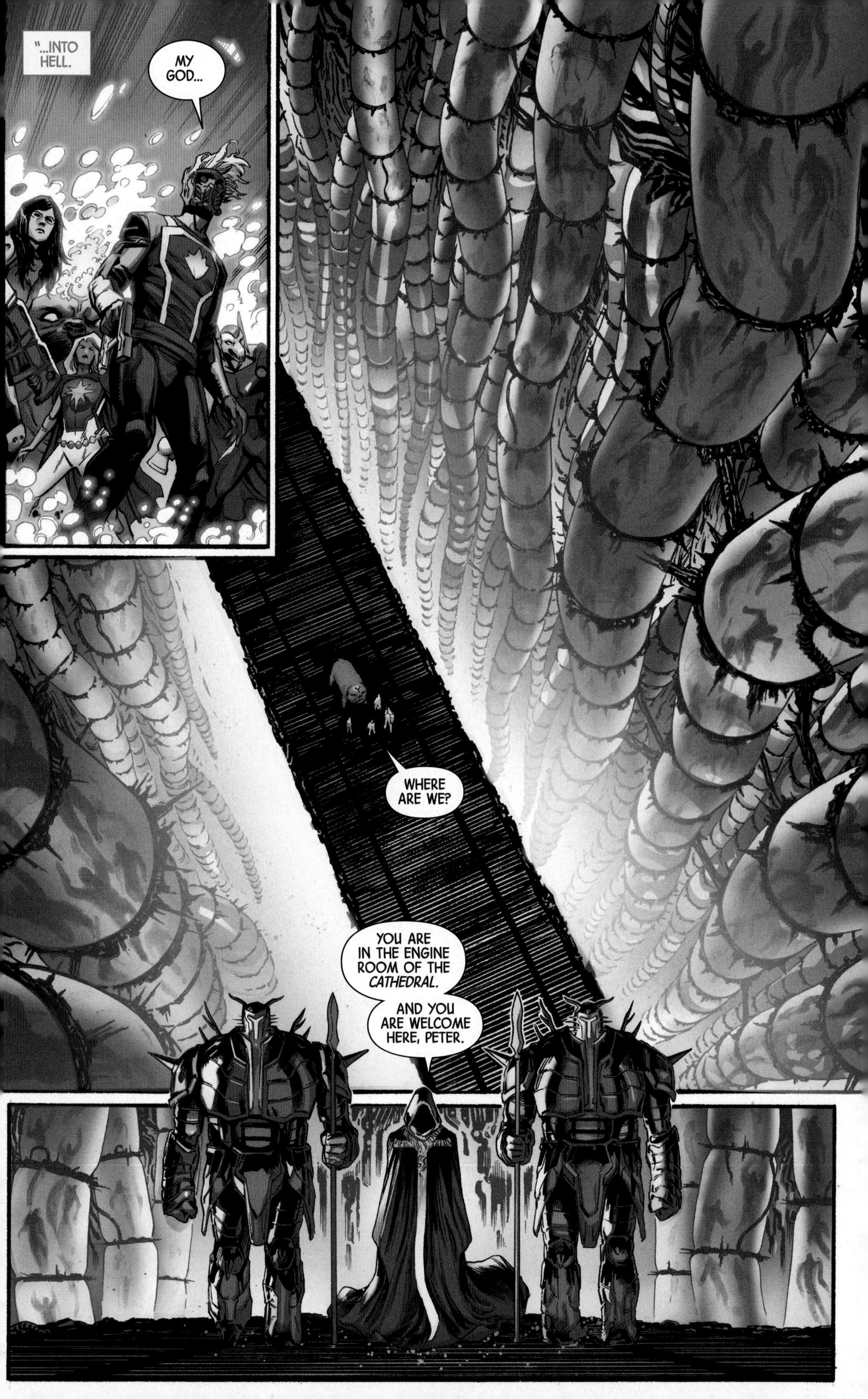
"...INTO HELL.
MY GOD...
WHERE ARE WE?
YOU ARE IN THE ENGINE ROOM OF THE *CATHEDRAL.*
AND YOU ARE WELCOME HERE, PETER.

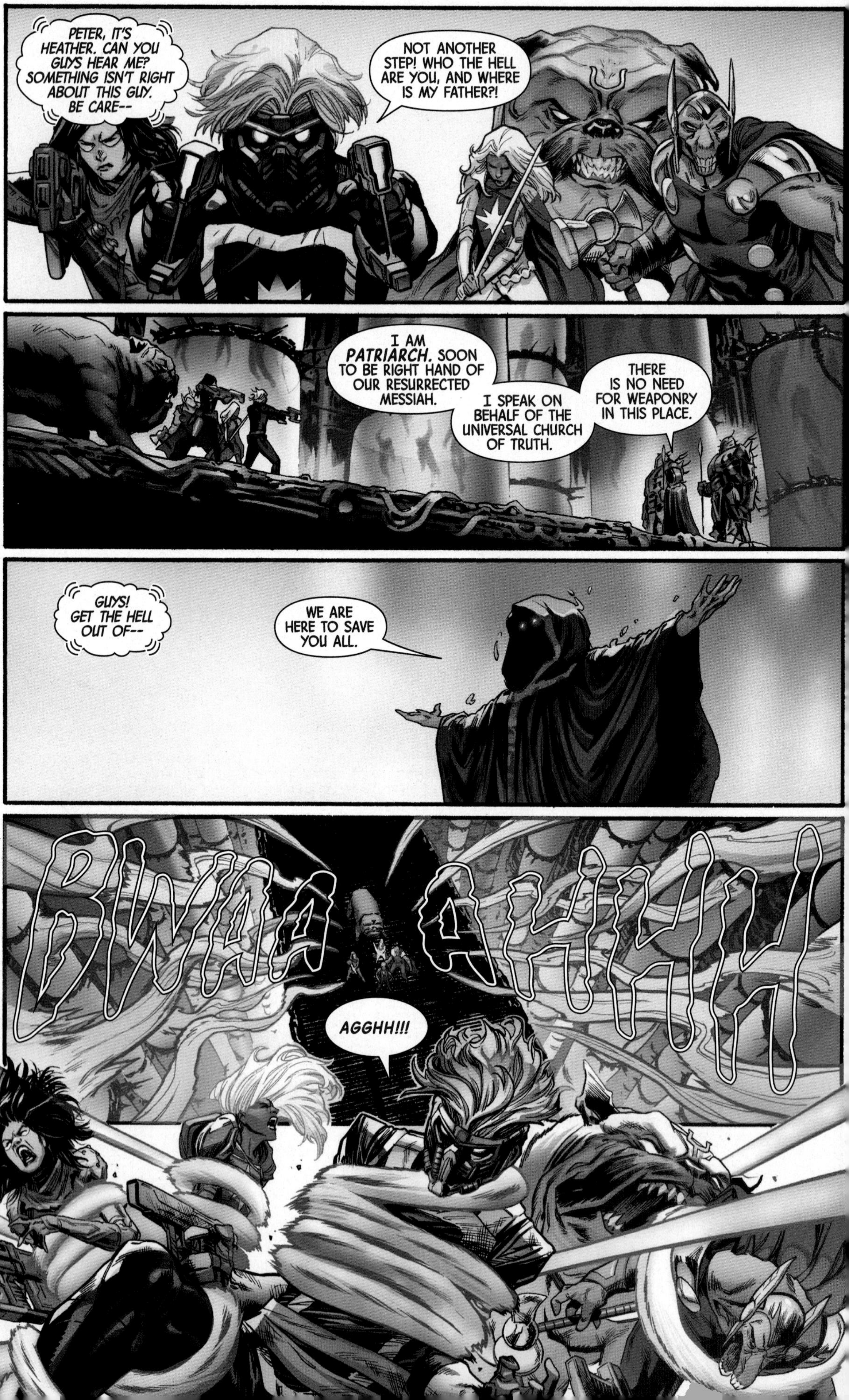

PETER, IT'S HEATHER. CAN YOU GUYS HEAR ME? SOMETHING ISN'T RIGHT ABOUT THIS GUY. BE CARE--
NOT ANOTHER STEP! WHO THE HELL ARE YOU, AND WHERE IS MY FATHER?!
I AM PATRIARCH. SOON TO BE RIGHT HAND OF OUR RESURRECTED MESSIAH.
I SPEAK ON BEHALF OF THE UNIVERSAL CHURCH OF TRUTH.
THERE IS NO NEED FOR WEAPONRY IN THIS PLACE.
GUYS! GET THE HELL OUT OF--
WE ARE HERE TO SAVE YOU ALL.
BWAA AHHHH
AGGHH!!!

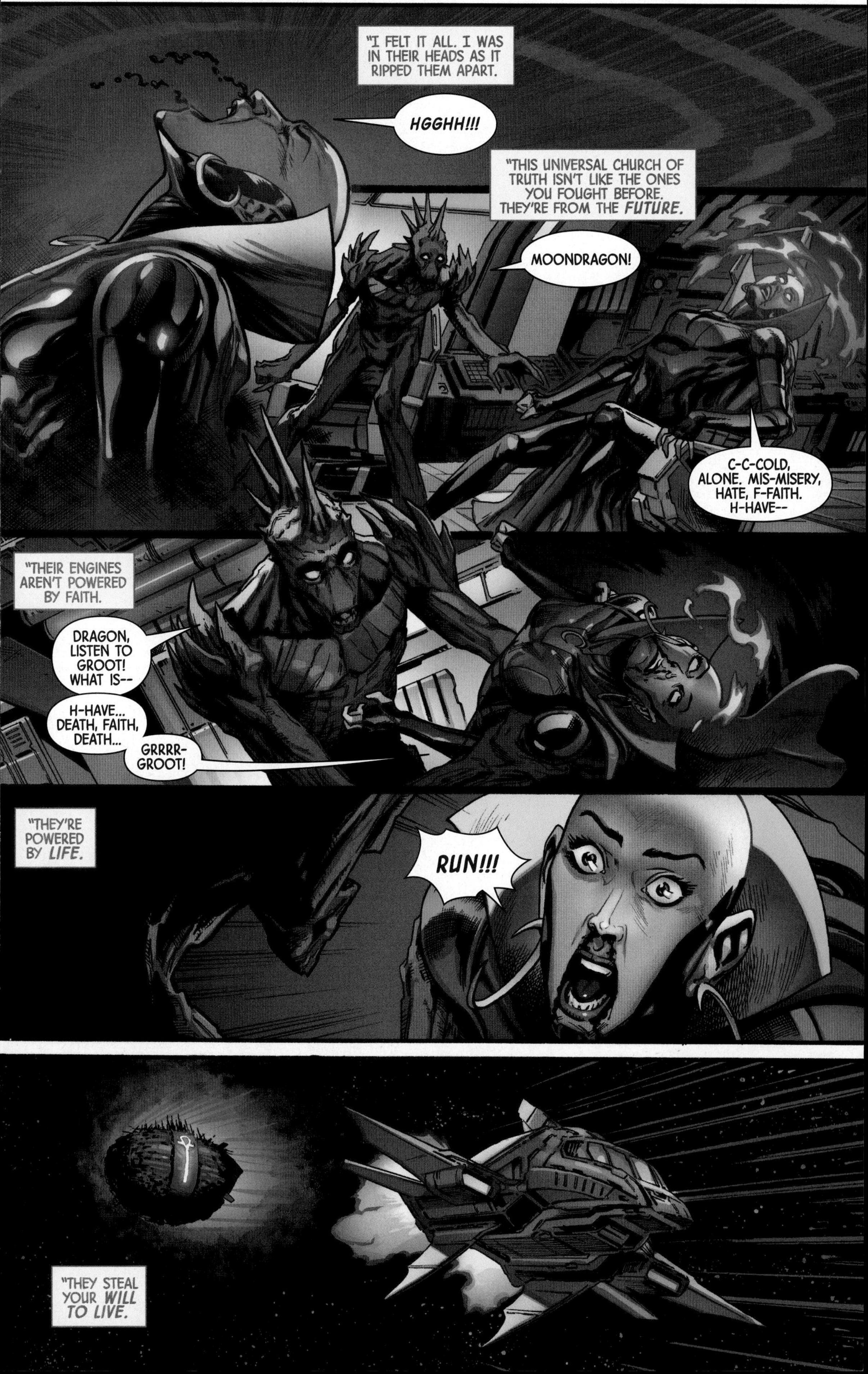
"I FELT IT ALL. I WAS IN THEIR HEADS AS IT RIPPED THEM APART.
HGGHH!!!
"THIS UNIVERSAL CHURCH OF TRUTH ISN'T LIKE THE ONES YOU FOUGHT BEFORE. THEY'RE FROM THE FUTURE.
MOONDRAGON!
C-C-COLD, ALONE. MIS-MISERY, HATE, F-FAITH. H-HAVE--
"THEIR ENGINES AREN'T POWERED BY FAITH.
DRAGON, LISTEN TO GROOT! WHAT IS--
H-HAVE... DEATH, FAITH, DEATH...
GRRRR-GROOT!
"THEY'RE POWERED BY LIFE.
RUN!!!
"THEY STEAL YOUR WILL TO LIVE.

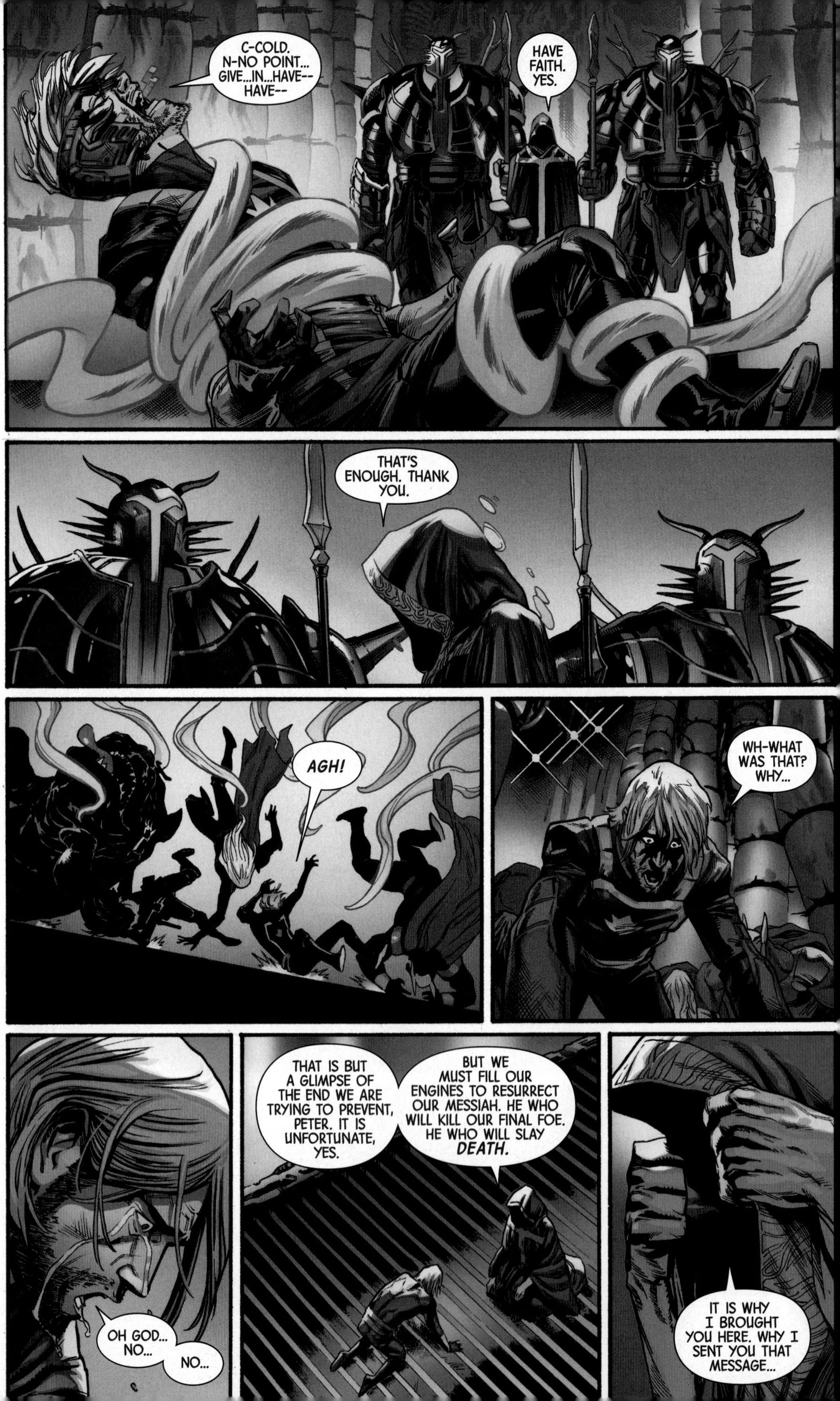
C-COLD. N-NO POINT... GIVE...IN...HAVE-- HAVE--
HAVE FAITH. YES.
THAT'S ENOUGH. THANK YOU.
AGH!
WH-WHAT WAS THAT? WHY...
OH GOD... NO...
NO...
THAT IS BUT A GLIMPSE OF THE END WE ARE TRYING TO PREVENT, PETER. IT IS UNFORTUNATE, YES.
BUT WE MUST FILL OUR ENGINES TO RESURRECT OUR MESSIAH. HE WHO WILL KILL OUR FINAL FOE. HE WHO WILL SLAY DEATH.
IT IS WHY I BROUGHT YOU HERE. WHY I SENT YOU THAT MESSAGE...

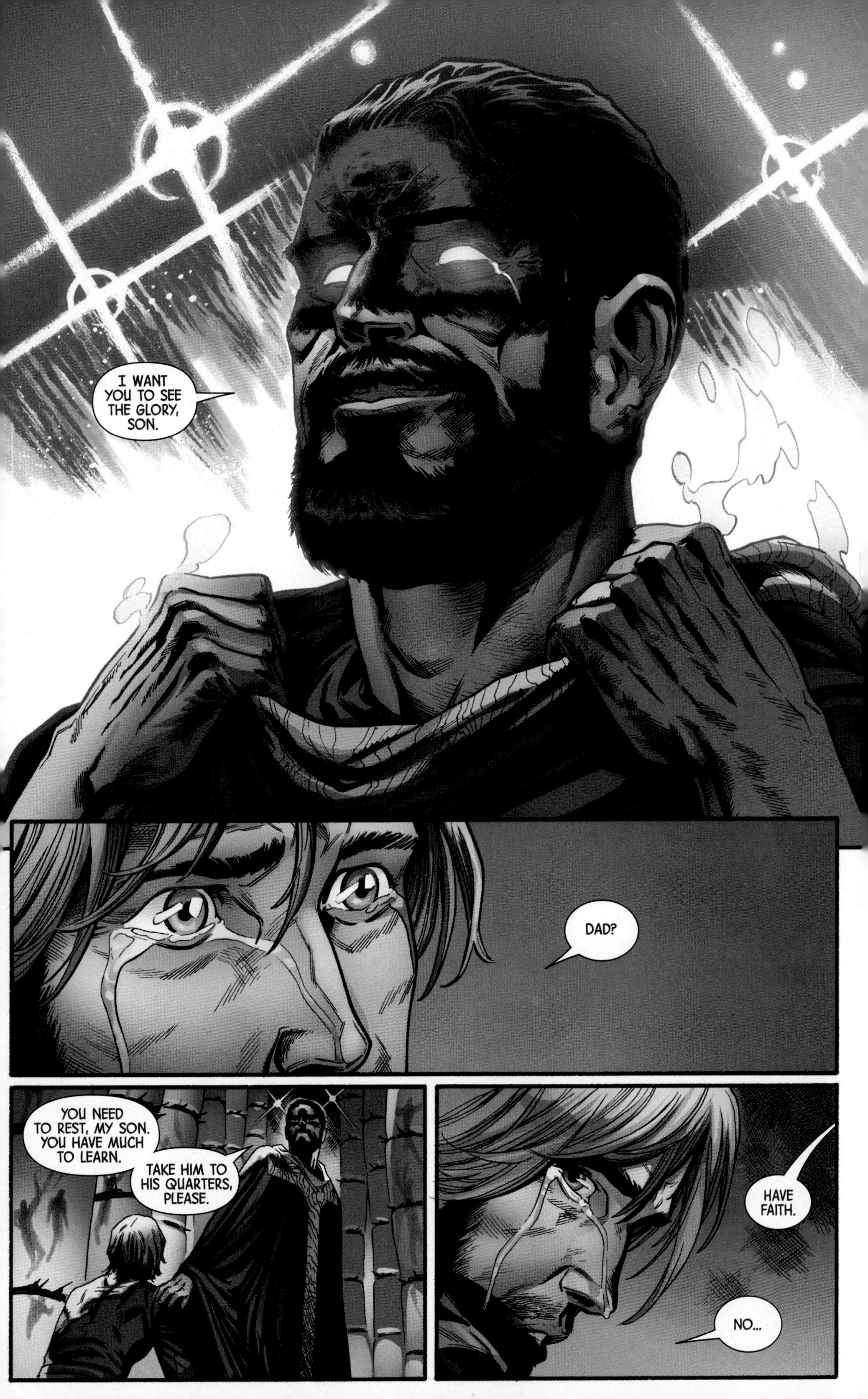
I WANT YOU TO SEE THE GLORY, SON.
DAD?
YOU NEED TO REST, MY SON. YOU HAVE MUCH TO LEARN.
TAKE HIM TO HIS QUARTERS, PLEASE.
HAVE FAITH.
NO...

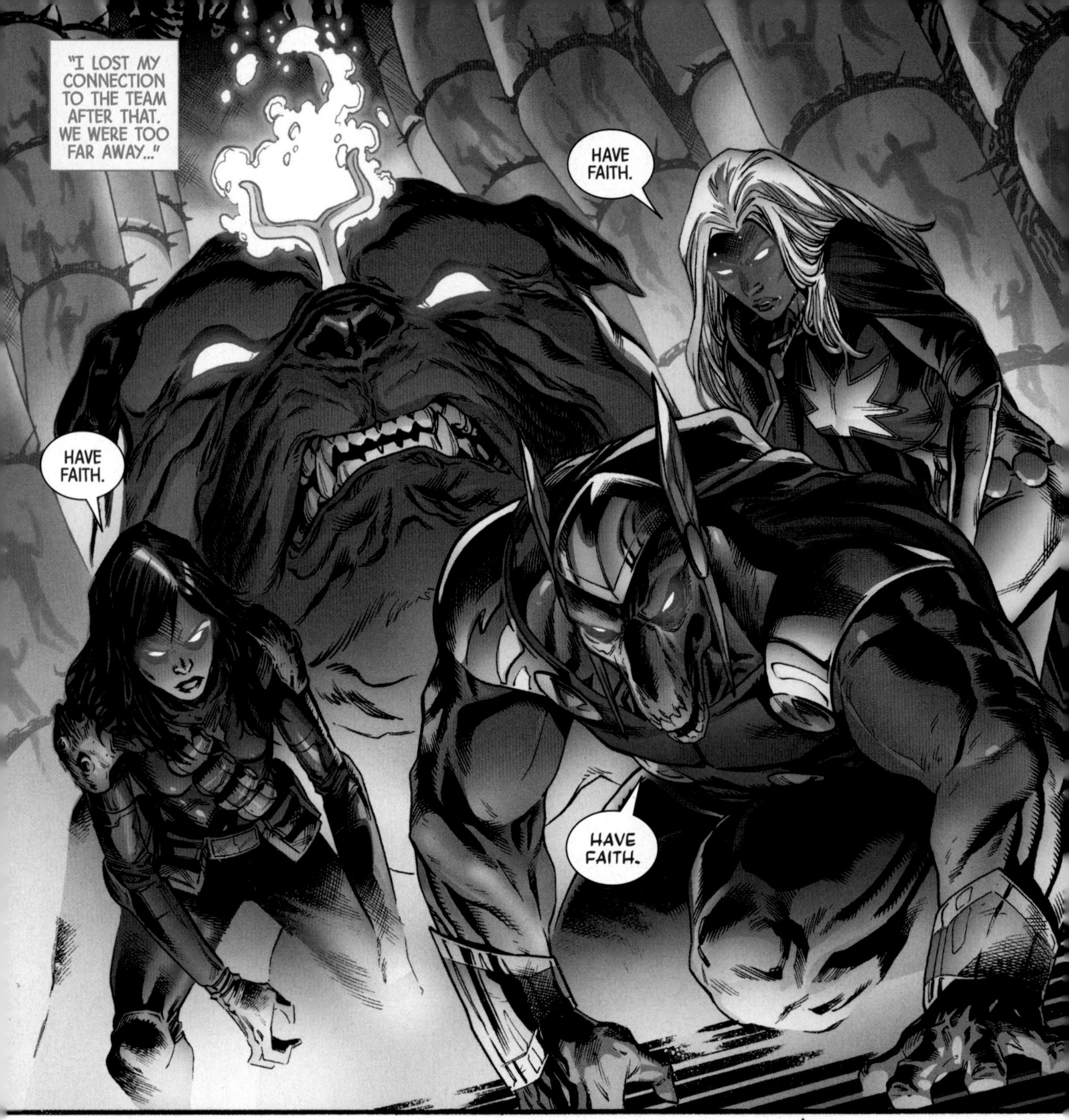
"I LOST MY CONNECTION TO THE TEAM AFTER THAT. WE WERE TOO FAR AWAY..."
HAVE FAITH.
HAVE FAITH.
HAVE FAITH.

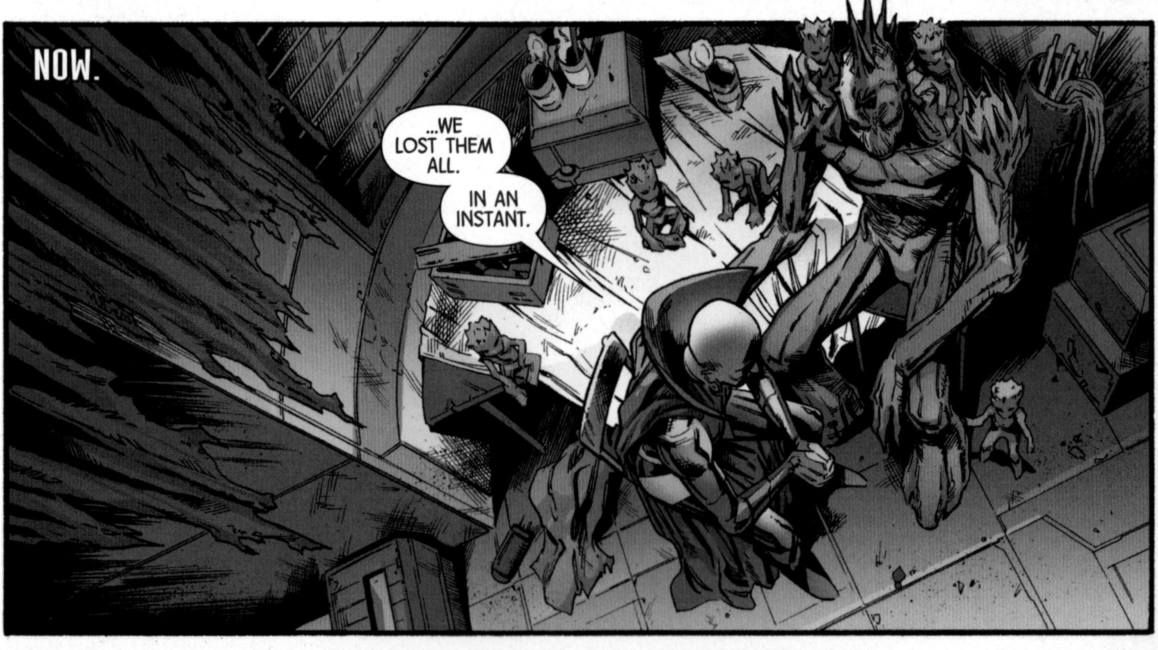
NOW.
...WE LOST THEM ALL.
IN AN INSTANT.

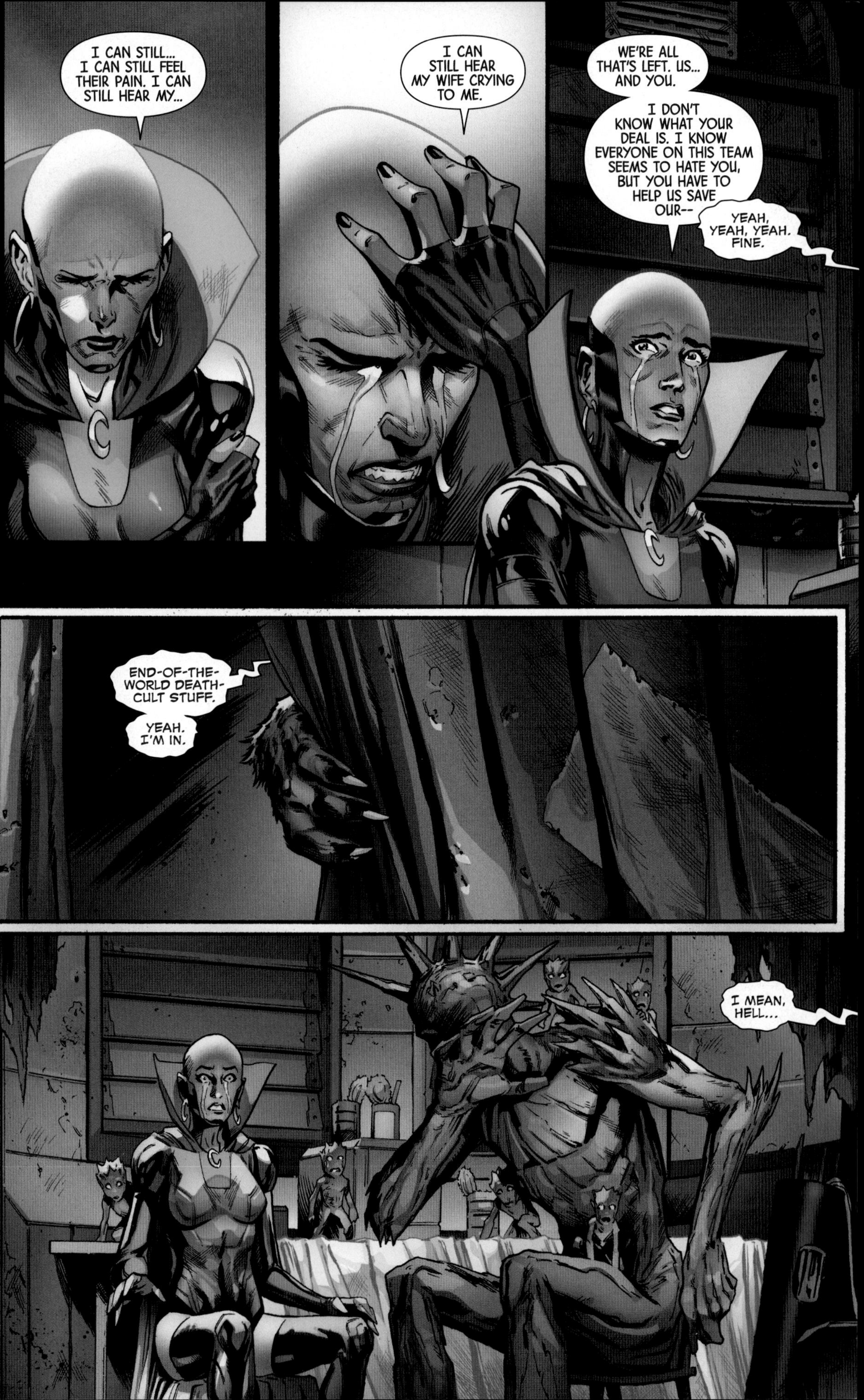
I CAN STILL... I CAN STILL FEEL THEIR PAIN. I CAN STILL HEAR MY...
I CAN STILL HEAR MY WIFE CRYING TO ME.
WE'RE ALL THAT'S LEFT. US... AND YOU.
I DON'T KNOW WHAT YOUR DEAL IS. I KNOW EVERYONE ON THIS TEAM SEEMS TO HATE YOU, BUT YOU HAVE TO HELP US SAVE OUR--
YEAH, YEAH, YEAH. FINE.
END-OF-THE-WORLD DEATH-CULT STUFF.
YEAH. I'M IN.
I MEAN, HELL...

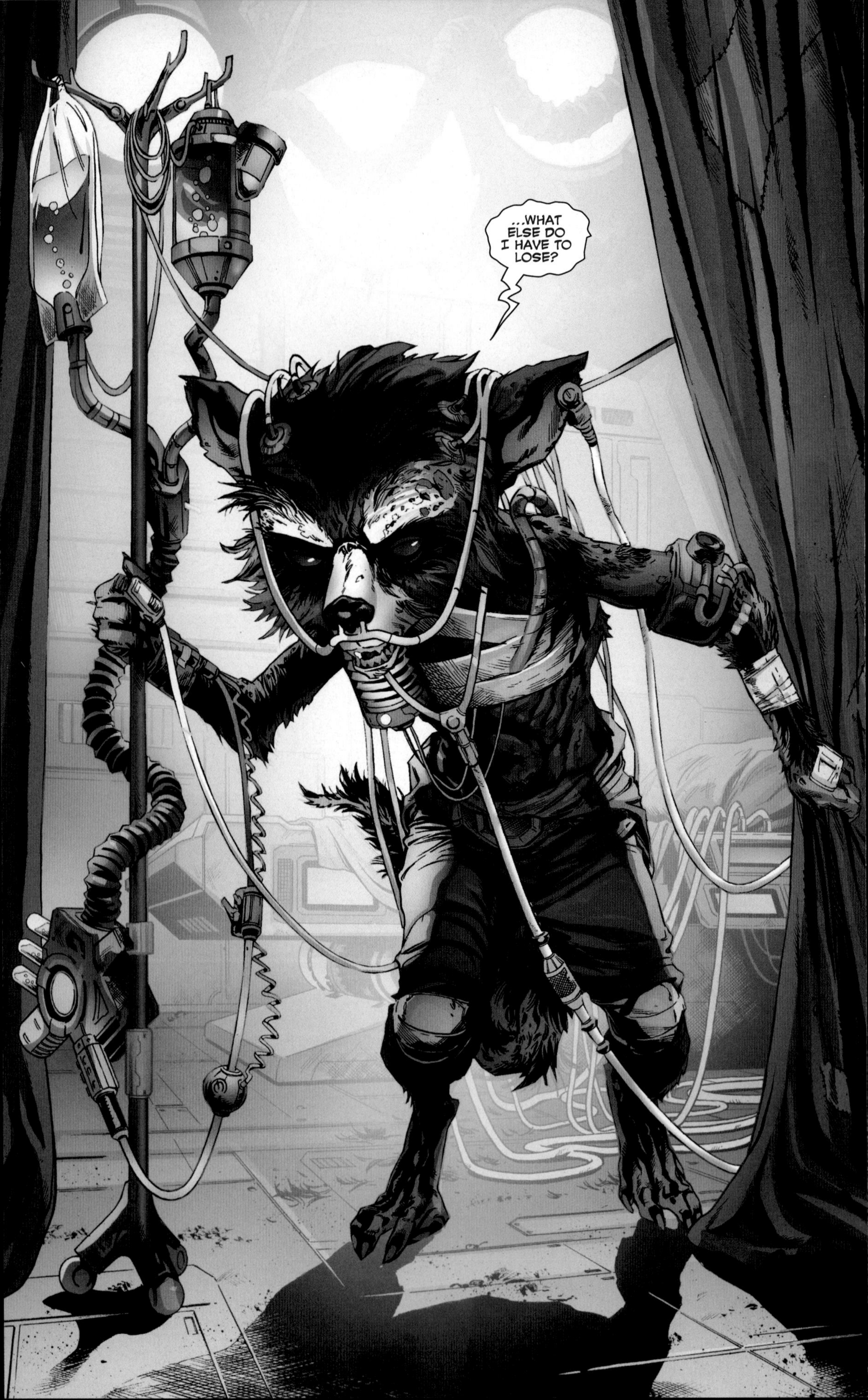
...WHAT ELSE DO I HAVE TO LOSE?

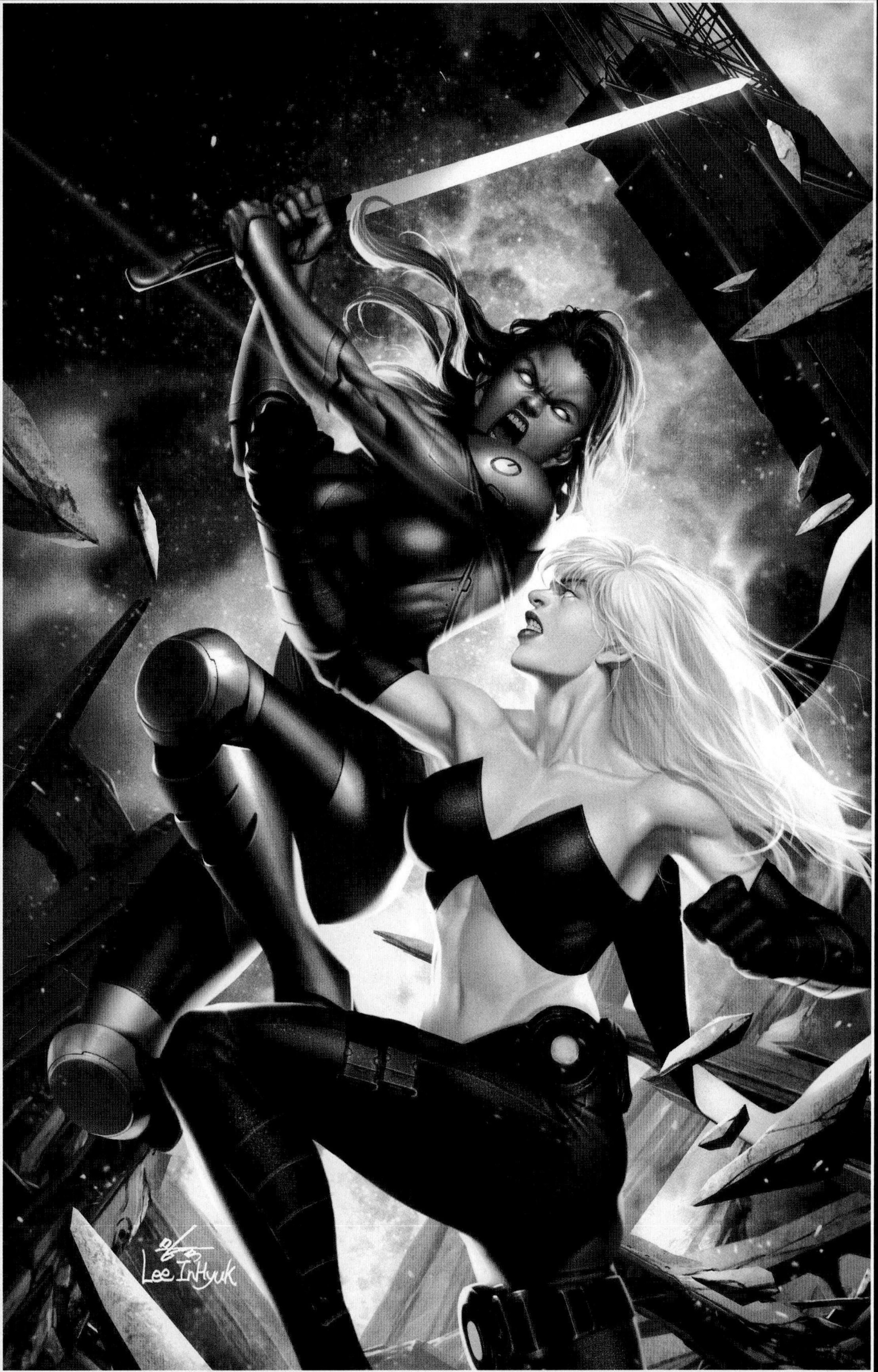
Lee InHyuk

INHYUK LEE
ANNUAL #1 Bring on the Bad Guys variant

EIGHT

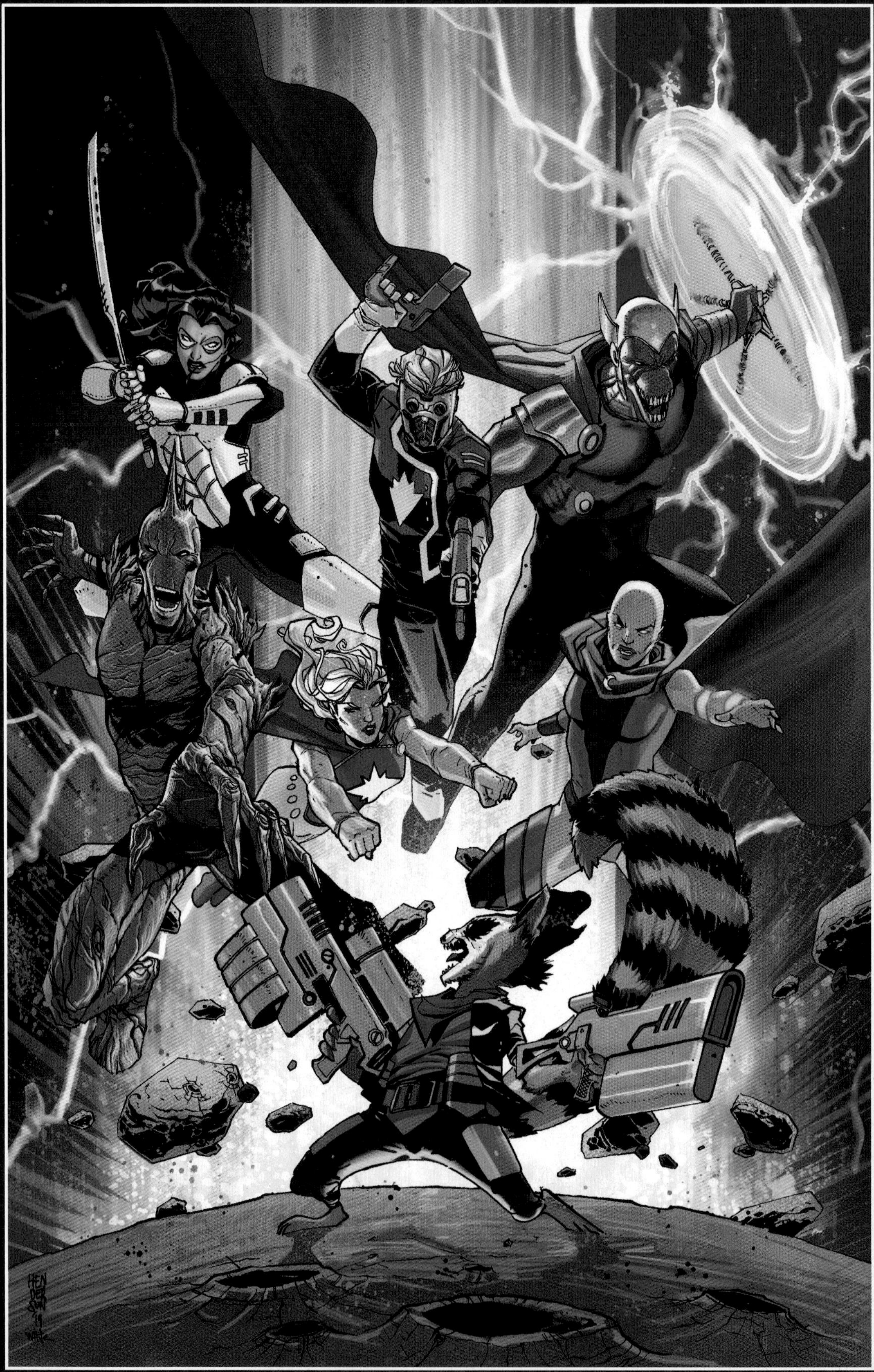

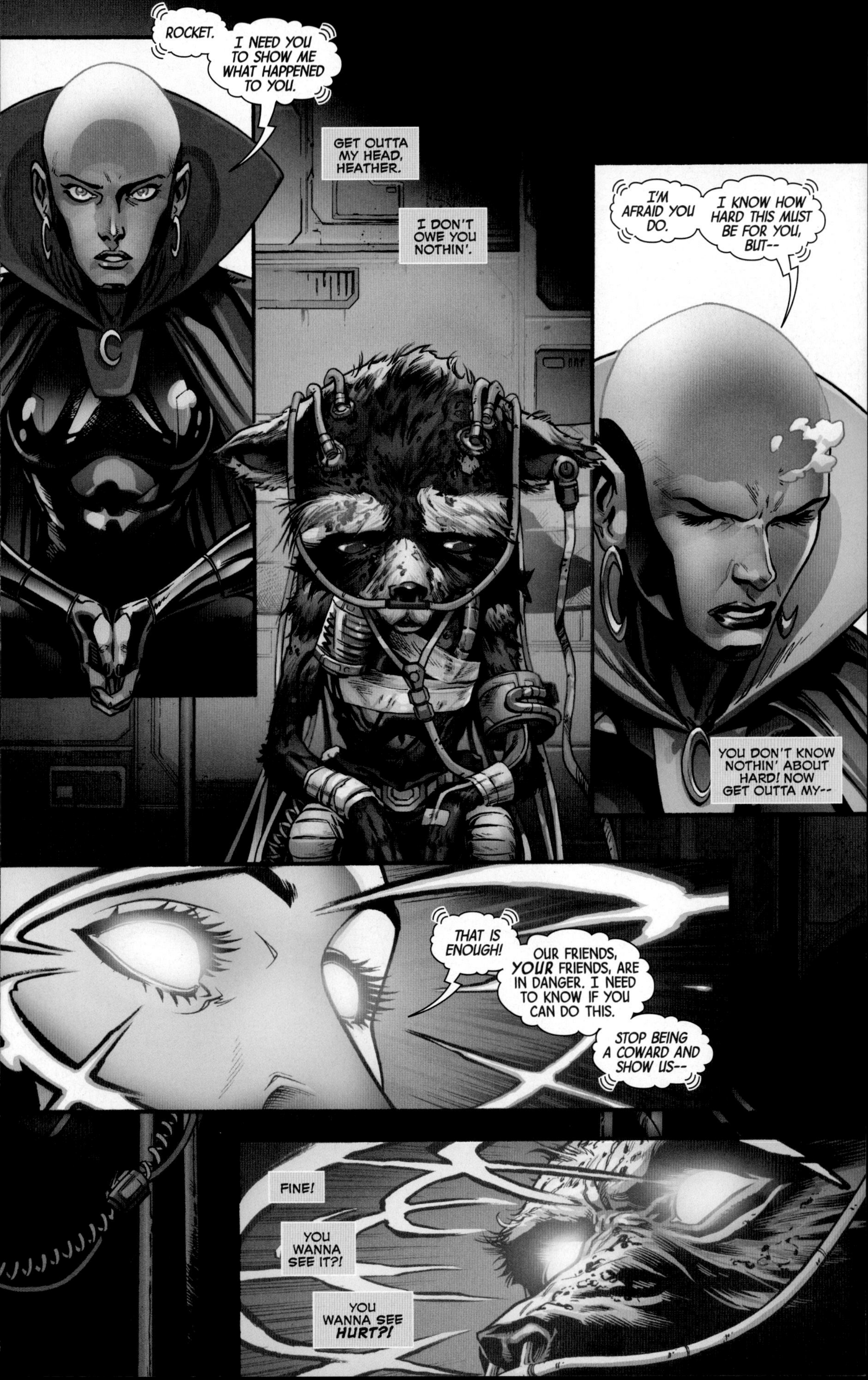
ROCKET.
I NEED YOU TO SHOW ME WHAT HAPPENED TO YOU.
GET OUTTA MY HEAD, HEATHER.
I DON'T OWE YOU NOTHIN'.
I'M AFRAID YOU DO.
I KNOW HOW HARD THIS MUST BE FOR YOU, BUT--
YOU DON'T KNOW NOTHIN' ABOUT HARD! NOW GET OUTTA MY--
THAT IS ENOUGH!
OUR FRIENDS, YOUR FRIENDS, ARE IN DANGER. I NEED TO KNOW IF YOU CAN DO THIS.
STOP BEING A COWARD AND SHOW US--
FINE!
YOU WANNA SEE IT?!
YOU WANNA SEE HURT?!

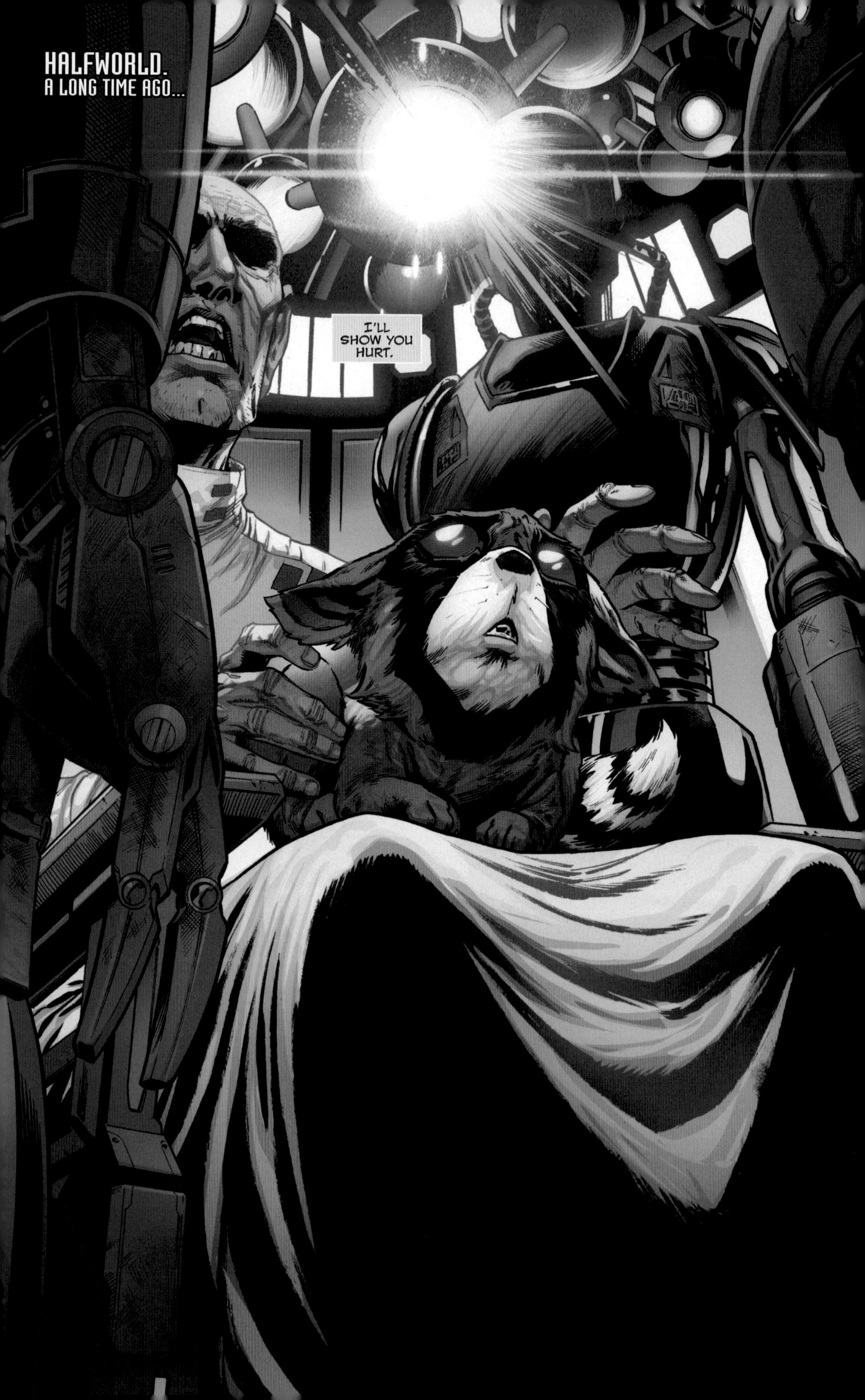
HALFWORLD.
A LONG TIME AGO...
I'LL SHOW YOU HURT.

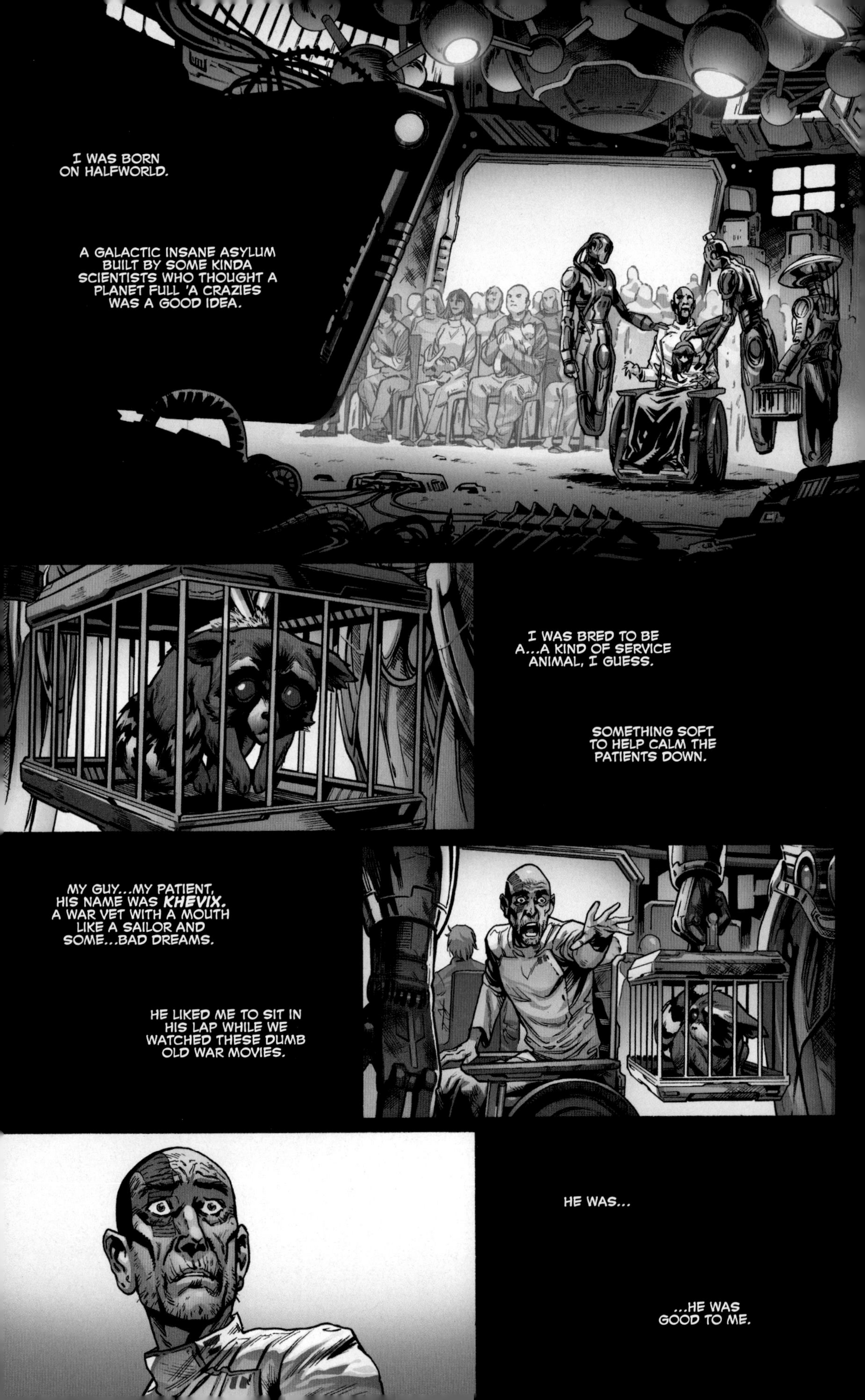
I WAS BORN ON HALFWORLD.
A GALACTIC INSANE ASYLUM BUILT BY SOME KINDA SCIENTISTS WHO THOUGHT A PLANET FULL 'A CRAZIES WAS A GOOD IDEA.
I WAS BRED TO BE A...A KIND OF SERVICE ANIMAL, I GUESS.
SOMETHING SOFT TO HELP CALM THE PATIENTS DOWN.
MY GUY...MY PATIENT, HIS NAME WAS ***KHEVIX.*** A WAR VET WITH A MOUTH LIKE A SAILOR AND SOME...BAD DREAMS.
HE LIKED ME TO SIT IN HIS LAP WHILE WE WATCHED THESE DUMB OLD WAR MOVIES.
HE WAS...
...HE WAS GOOD TO ME.

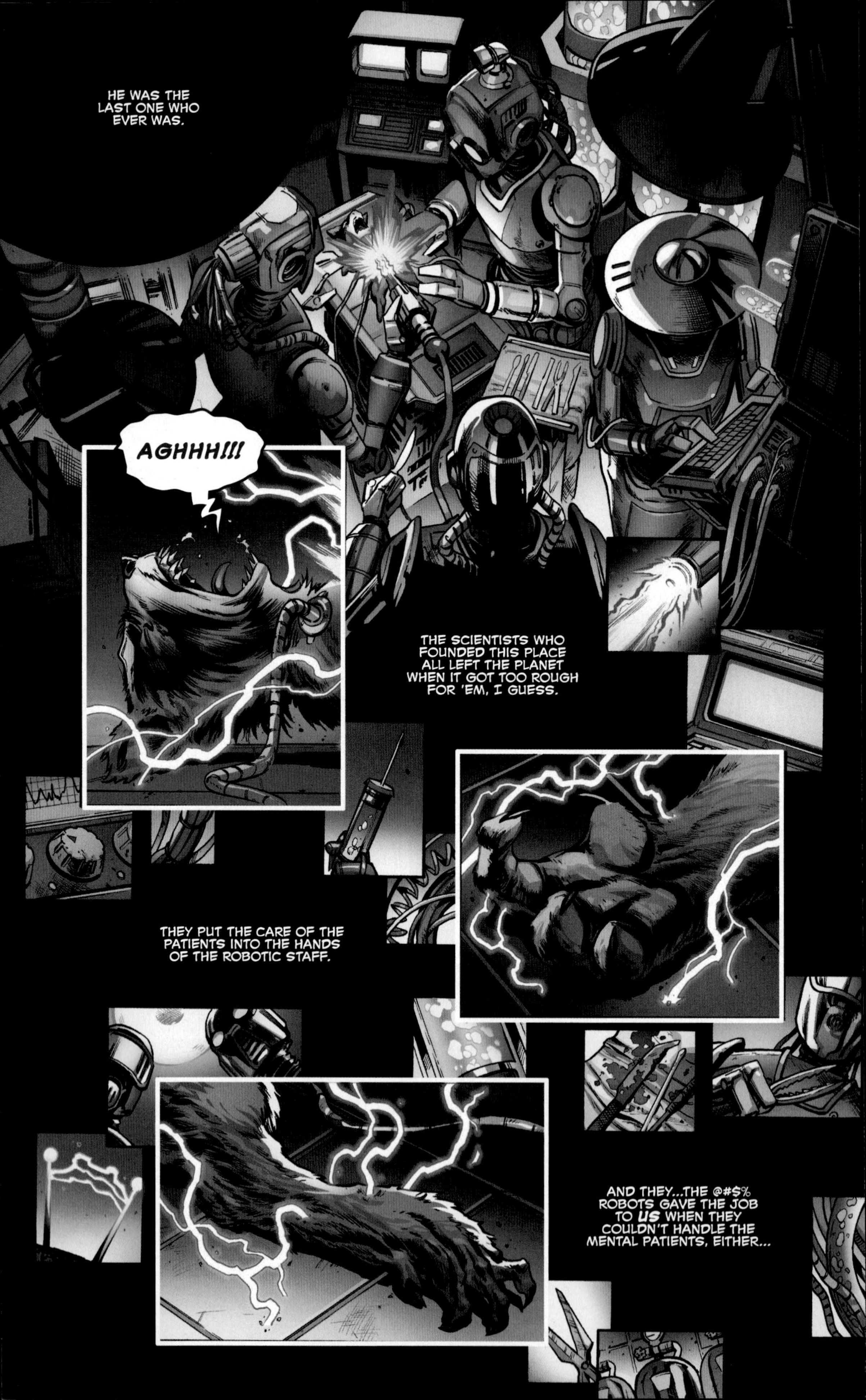
HE WAS THE LAST ONE WHO EVER WAS.
AGHHH!!!
THE SCIENTISTS WHO FOUNDED THIS PLACE ALL LEFT THE PLANET WHEN IT GOT TOO ROUGH FOR 'EM, I GUESS.
THEY PUT THE CARE OF THE PATIENTS INTO THE HANDS OF THE ROBOTIC STAFF.
AND THEY...THE @#$% ROBOTS GAVE THE JOB TO US WHEN THEY COULDN'T HANDLE THE MENTAL PATIENTS, EITHER...

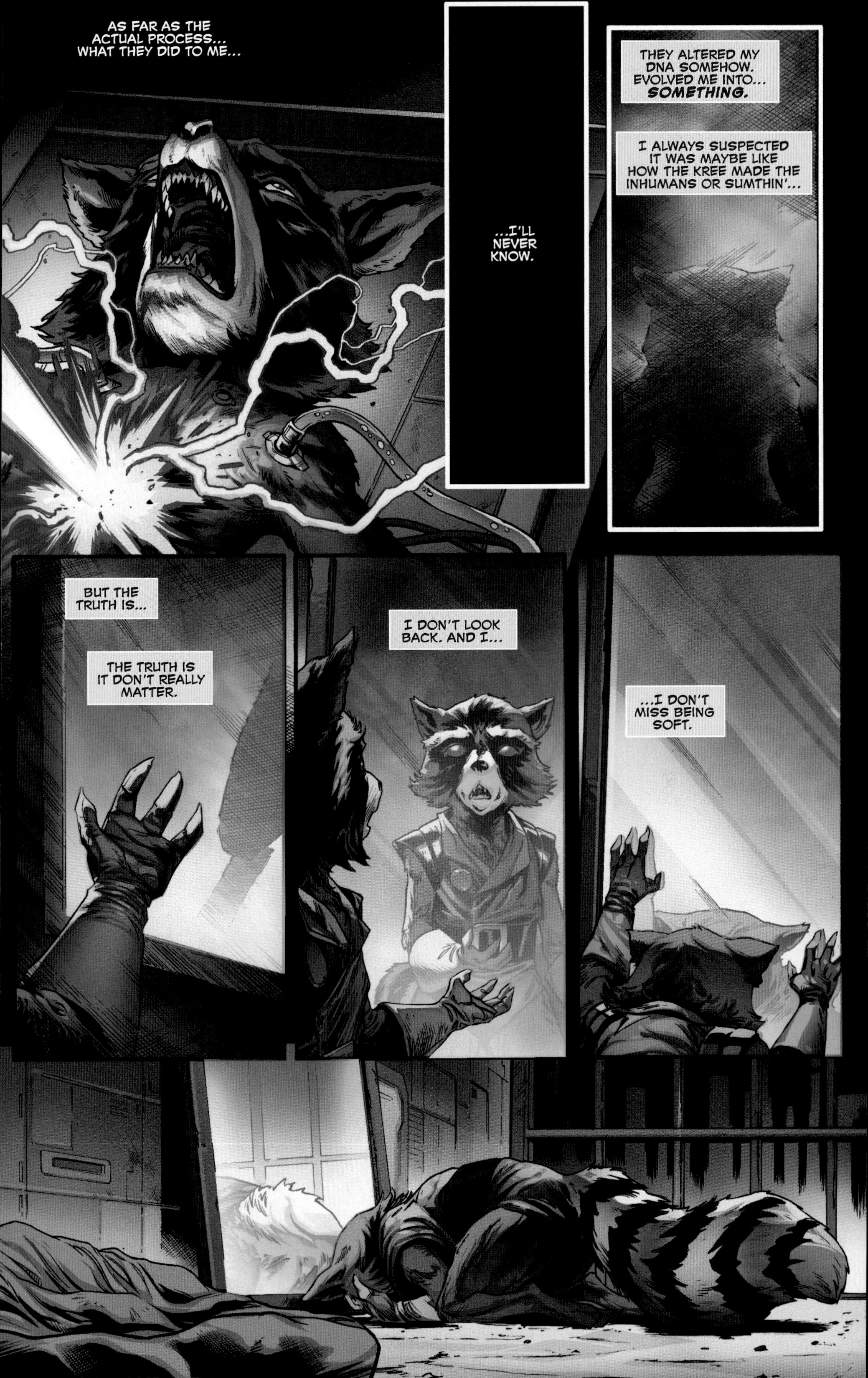
AS FAR AS THE ACTUAL PROCESS... WHAT THEY DID TO ME...
...I'LL NEVER KNOW.
THEY ALTERED MY DNA SOMEHOW. EVOLVED ME INTO... SOMETHING.
I ALWAYS SUSPECTED IT WAS MAYBE LIKE HOW THE KREE MADE THE INHUMANS OR SUMTHIN'...
BUT THE TRUTH IS...
THE TRUTH IS IT DON'T REALLY MATTER.
I DON'T LOOK BACK. AND I...
...I DON'T MISS BEING SOFT.

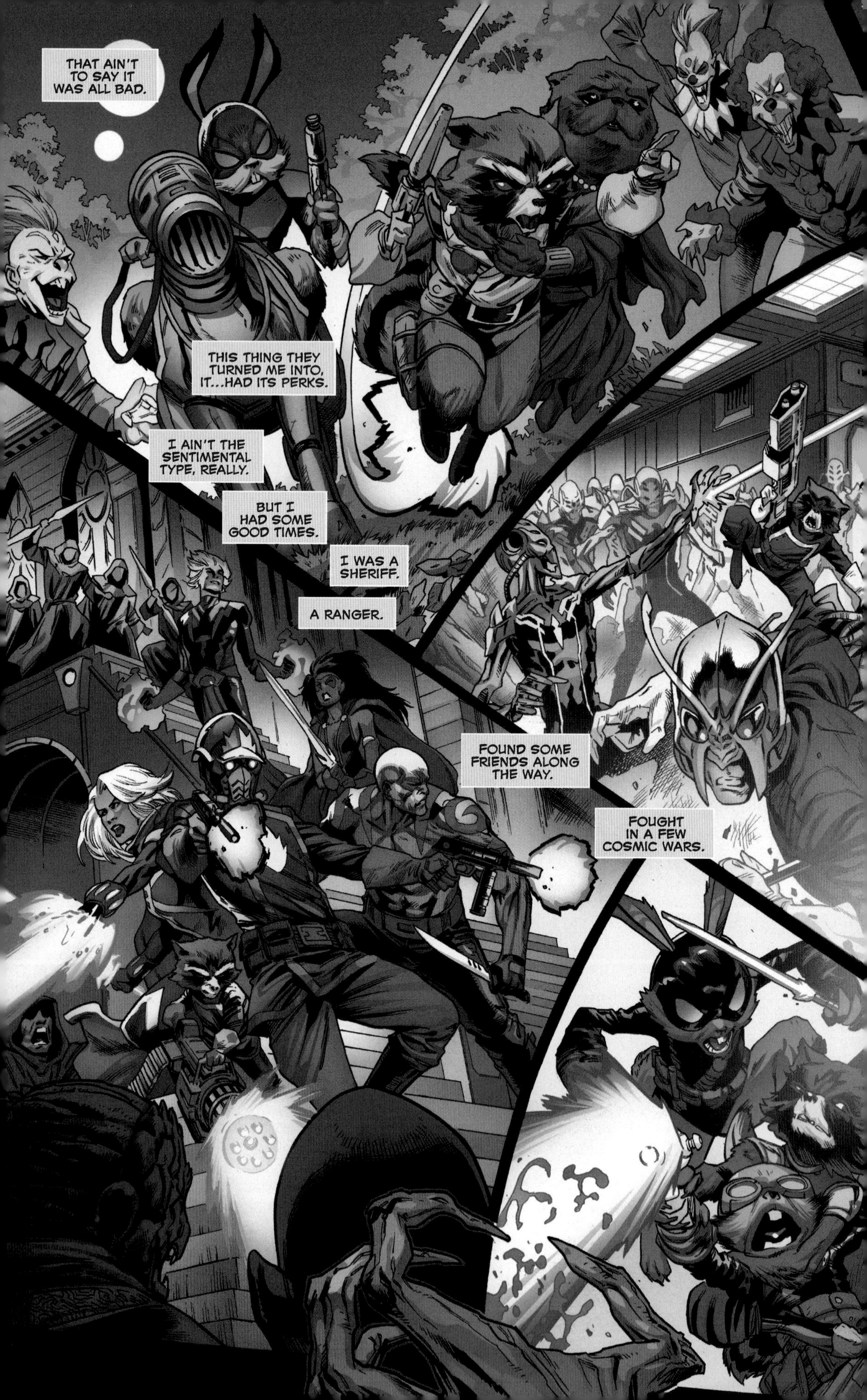
THAT AIN'T TO SAY IT WAS ALL BAD.
THIS THING THEY TURNED ME INTO, IT...HAD ITS PERKS.
I AIN'T THE SENTIMENTAL TYPE, REALLY.
BUT I HAD SOME GOOD TIMES.
I WAS A SHERIFF.
A RANGER.
FOUND SOME FRIENDS ALONG THE WAY.
FOUGHT IN A FEW COSMIC WARS.

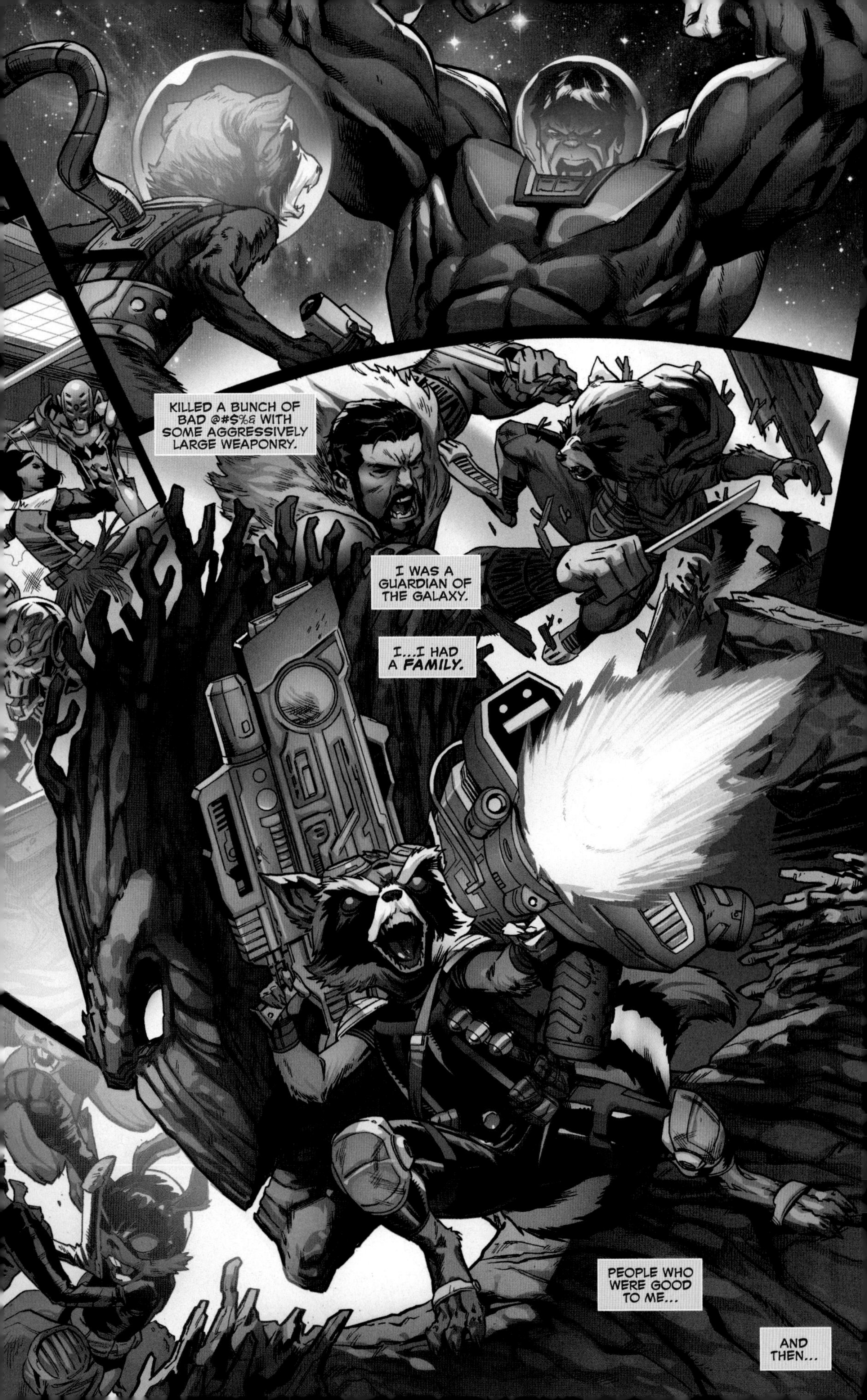
KILLED A BUNCH OF BAD @#$%& WITH SOME AGGRESSIVELY LARGE WEAPONRY.
I WAS A GUARDIAN OF THE GALAXY.
I...I HAD A FAMILY.
PEOPLE WHO WERE GOOD TO ME...
AND THEN...

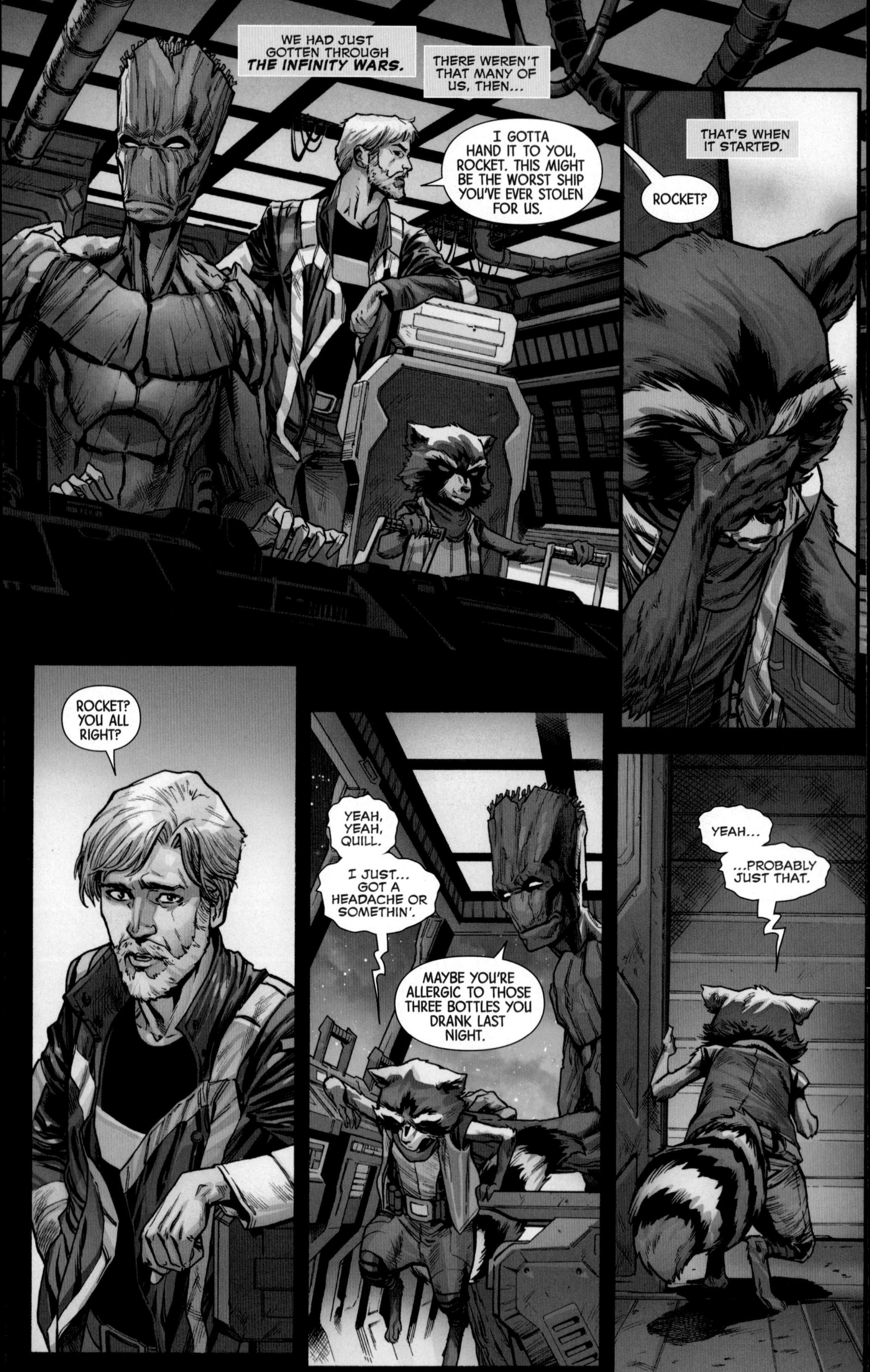
WE HAD JUST GOTTEN THROUGH THE INFINITY WARS.
THERE WEREN'T THAT MANY OF US, THEN...
I GOTTA HAND IT TO YOU, ROCKET. THIS MIGHT BE THE WORST SHIP YOU'VE EVER STOLEN FOR US.
THAT'S WHEN IT STARTED.
ROCKET?
ROCKET? YOU ALL RIGHT?
YEAH, YEAH, QUILL.
I JUST... GOT A HEADACHE OR SOMETHIN'.
MAYBE YOU'RE ALLERGIC TO THOSE THREE BOTTLES YOU DRANK LAST NIGHT.
YEAH...
...PROBABLY JUST THAT.

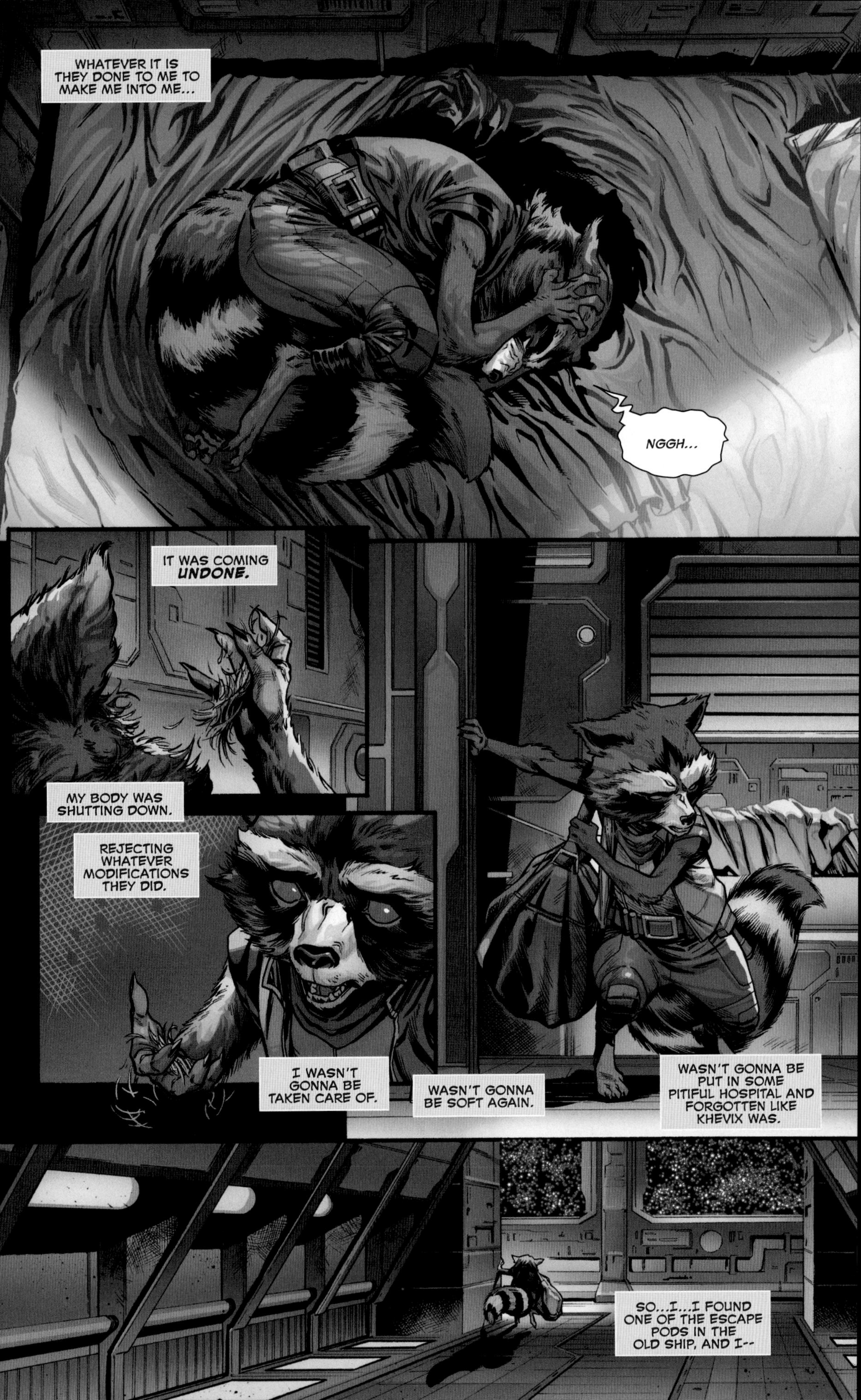
WHATEVER IT IS THEY DONE TO ME TO MAKE ME INTO ME...
NGGH...
IT WAS COMING UNDONE.
MY BODY WAS SHUTTING DOWN.
REJECTING WHATEVER MODIFICATIONS THEY DID.
I WASN'T GONNA BE TAKEN CARE OF.
WASN'T GONNA BE SOFT AGAIN.
WASN'T GONNA BE PUT IN SOME PITIFUL HOSPITAL AND FORGOTTEN LIKE KHEVIX WAS.
SO...I...I FOUND ONE OF THE ESCAPE PODS IN THE OLD SHIP, AND I--

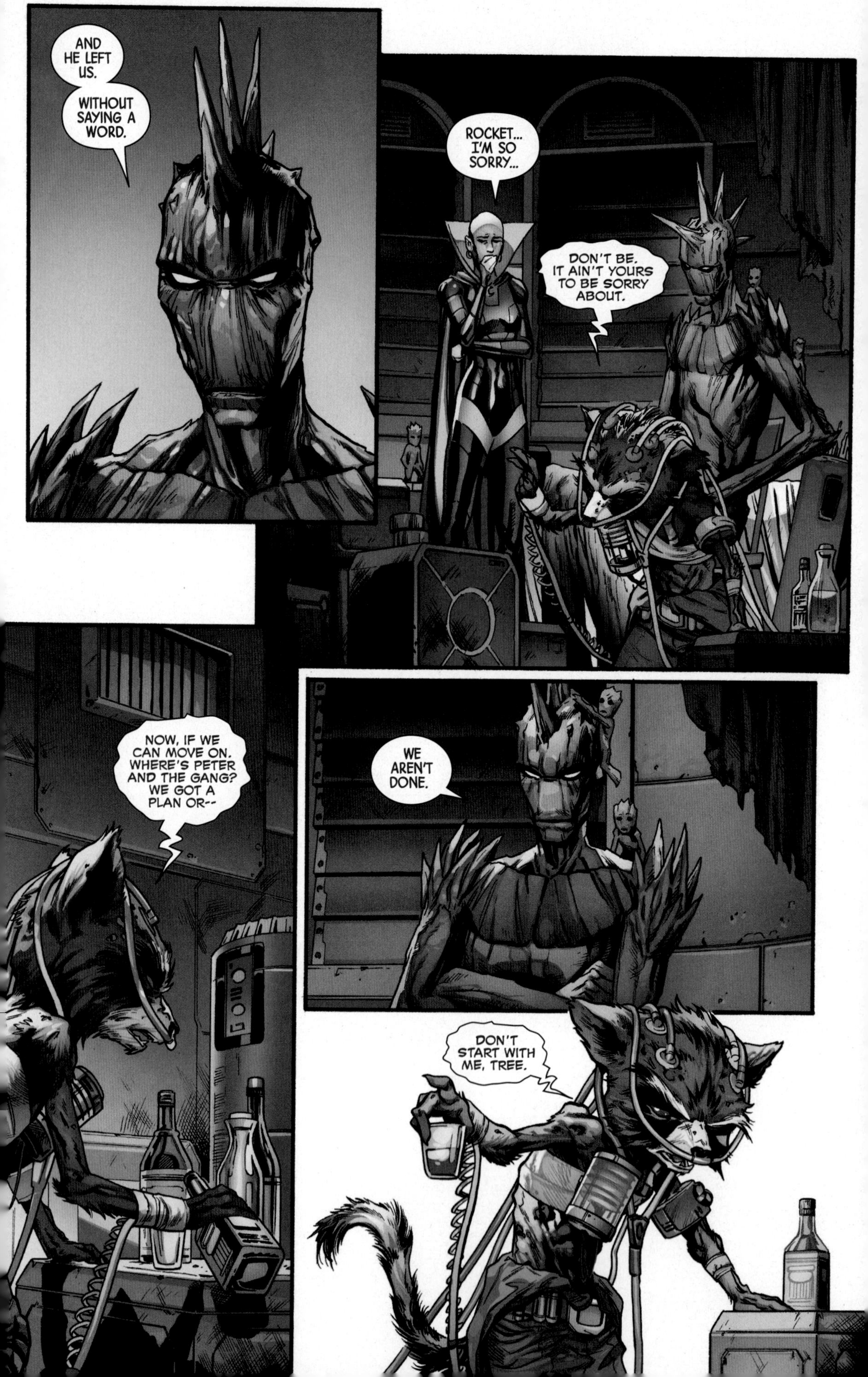
AND HE LEFT US.
WITHOUT SAYING A WORD.
ROCKET... I'M SO SORRY...
DON'T BE. IT AIN'T YOURS TO BE SORRY ABOUT.
NOW, IF WE CAN MOVE ON. WHERE'S PETER AND THE GANG? WE GOT A PLAN OR--
WE AREN'T DONE.
DON'T START WITH ME, TREE.

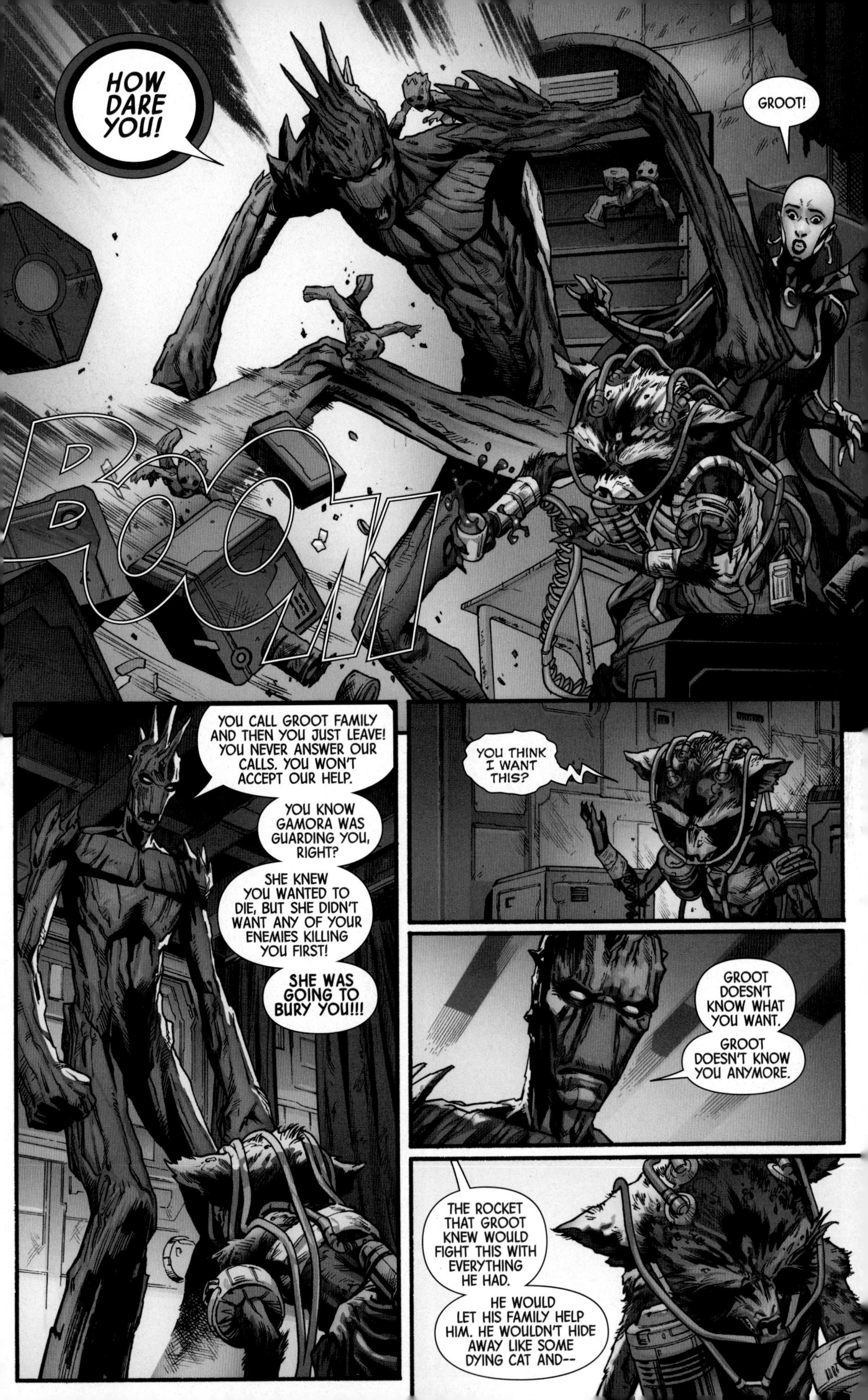
HOW DARE YOU!
GROOT!
BOOM
YOU CALL GROOT FAMILY AND THEN YOU JUST LEAVE! YOU NEVER ANSWER OUR CALLS. YOU WON'T ACCEPT OUR HELP.
YOU KNOW GAMORA WAS GUARDING YOU, RIGHT?
SHE KNEW YOU WANTED TO DIE, BUT SHE DIDN'T WANT ANY OF YOUR ENEMIES KILLING YOU FIRST!
SHE WAS GOING TO BURY YOU!!!
YOU THINK I WANT THIS?
GROOT DOESN'T KNOW WHAT YOU WANT.
GROOT DOESN'T KNOW YOU ANYMORE.
THE ROCKET THAT GROOT KNEW WOULD FIGHT THIS WITH EVERYTHING HE HAD.
HE WOULD LET HIS FAMILY HELP HIM. HE WOULDN'T HIDE AWAY LIKE SOME DYING CAT AND--

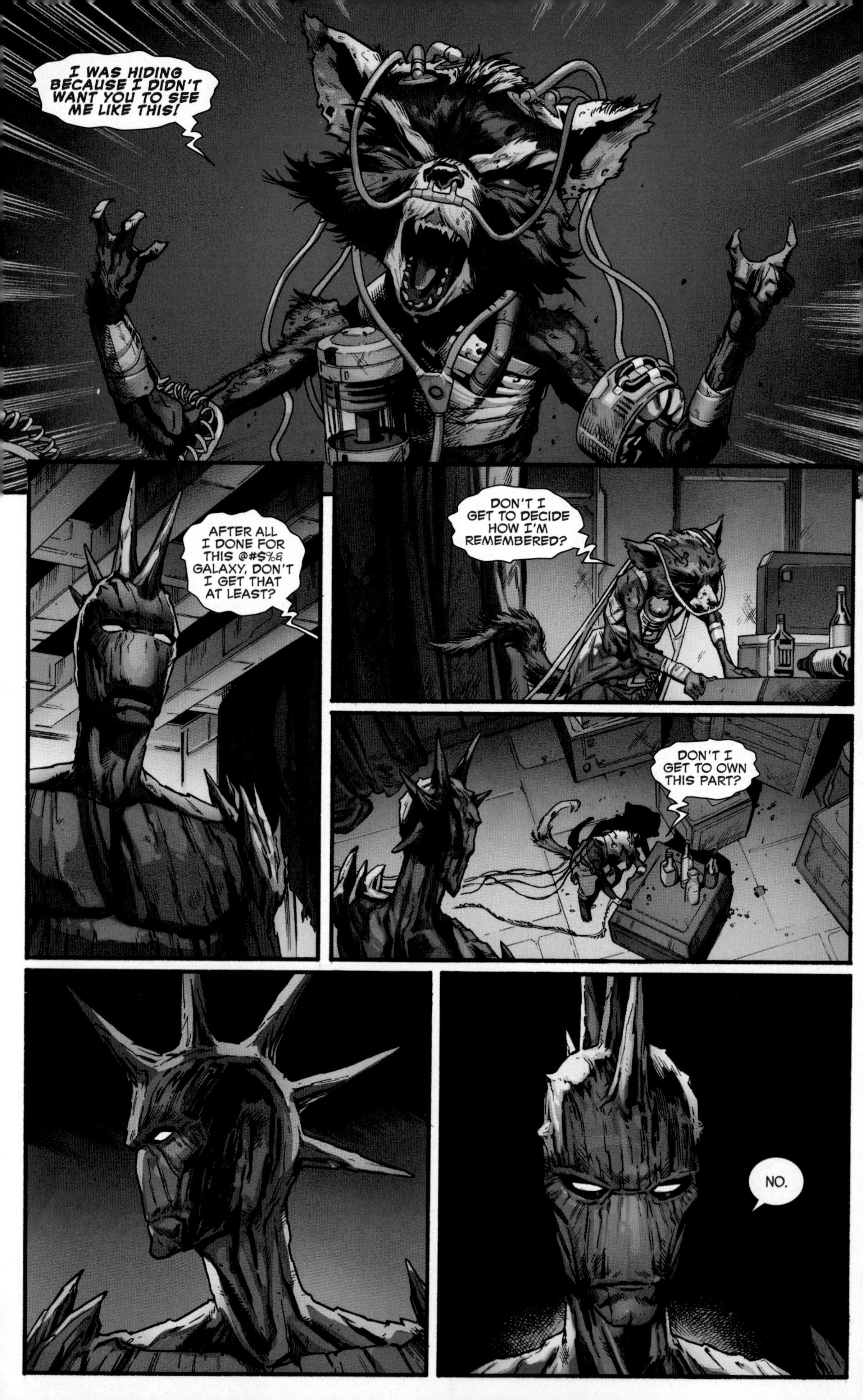
I WAS HIDING BECAUSE I DIDN'T WANT YOU TO SEE ME LIKE THIS!
DON'T I GET TO DECIDE HOW I'M REMEMBERED?
AFTER ALL I DONE FOR THIS @#$%& GALAXY, DON'T I GET THAT AT LEAST?
DON'T I GET TO OWN THIS PART?
NO.

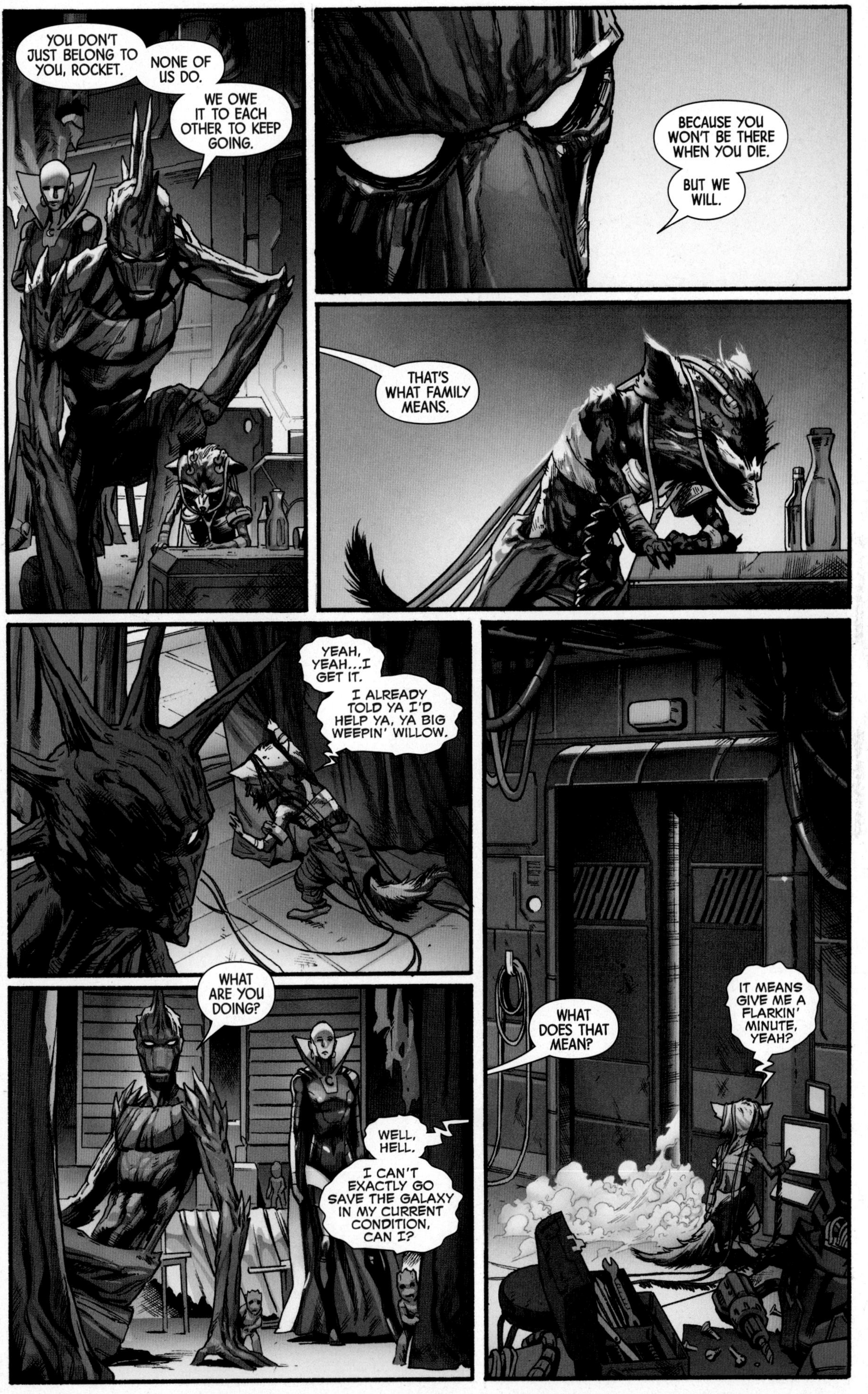
YOU DON'T JUST BELONG TO YOU, ROCKET.
NONE OF US DO.
WE OWE IT TO EACH OTHER TO KEEP GOING.
BECAUSE YOU WON'T BE THERE WHEN YOU DIE.
BUT WE WILL.
THAT'S WHAT FAMILY MEANS.
YEAH, YEAH...I GET IT.
I ALREADY TOLD YA I'D HELP YA, YA BIG WEEPIN' WILLOW.
WHAT ARE YOU DOING?
WELL, HELL.
I CAN'T EXACTLY GO SAVE THE GALAXY IN MY CURRENT CONDITION, CAN I?
WHAT DOES THAT MEAN?
IT MEANS GIVE ME A FLARKIN' MINUTE, YEAH?

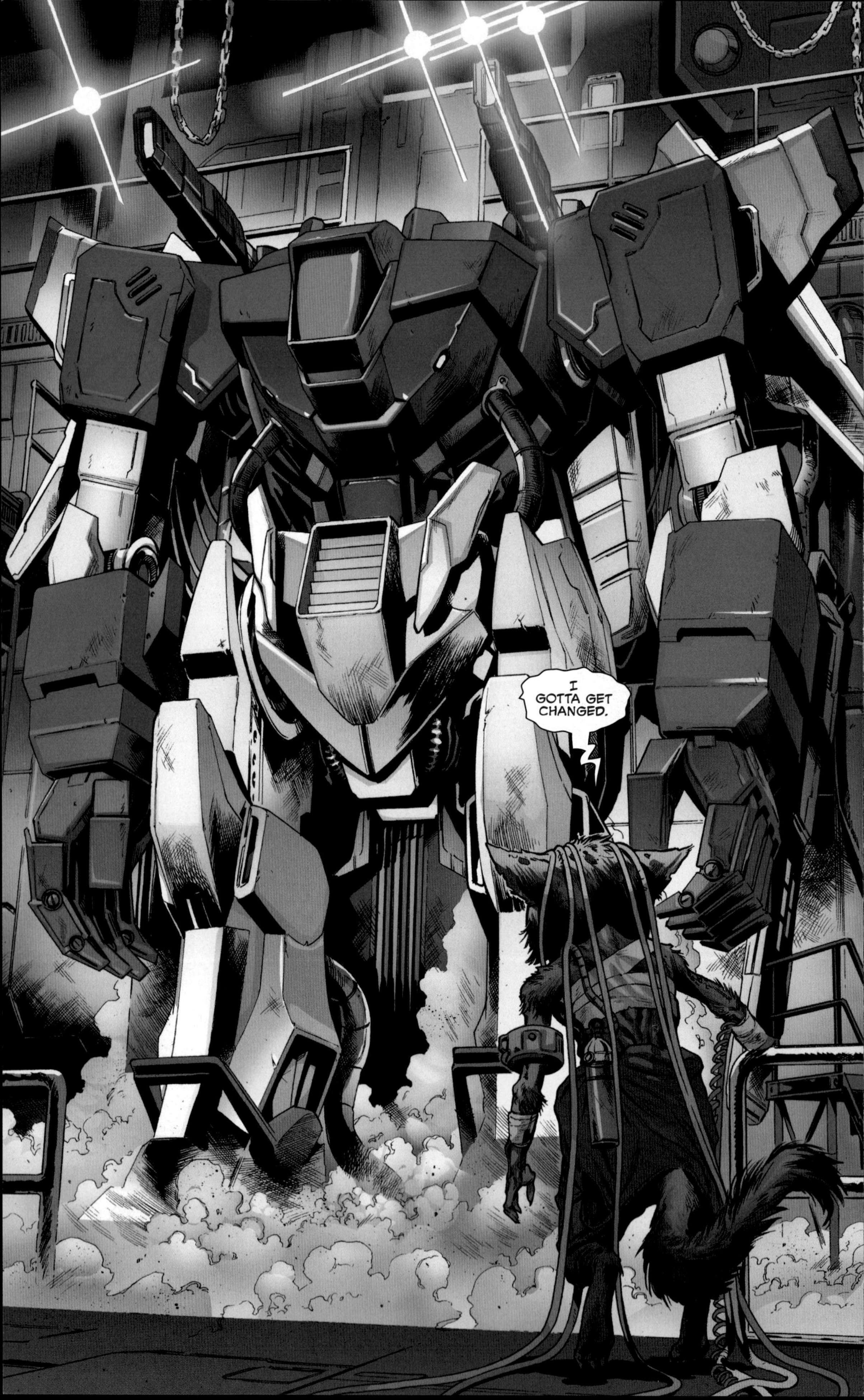
I GOTTA GET CHANGED.

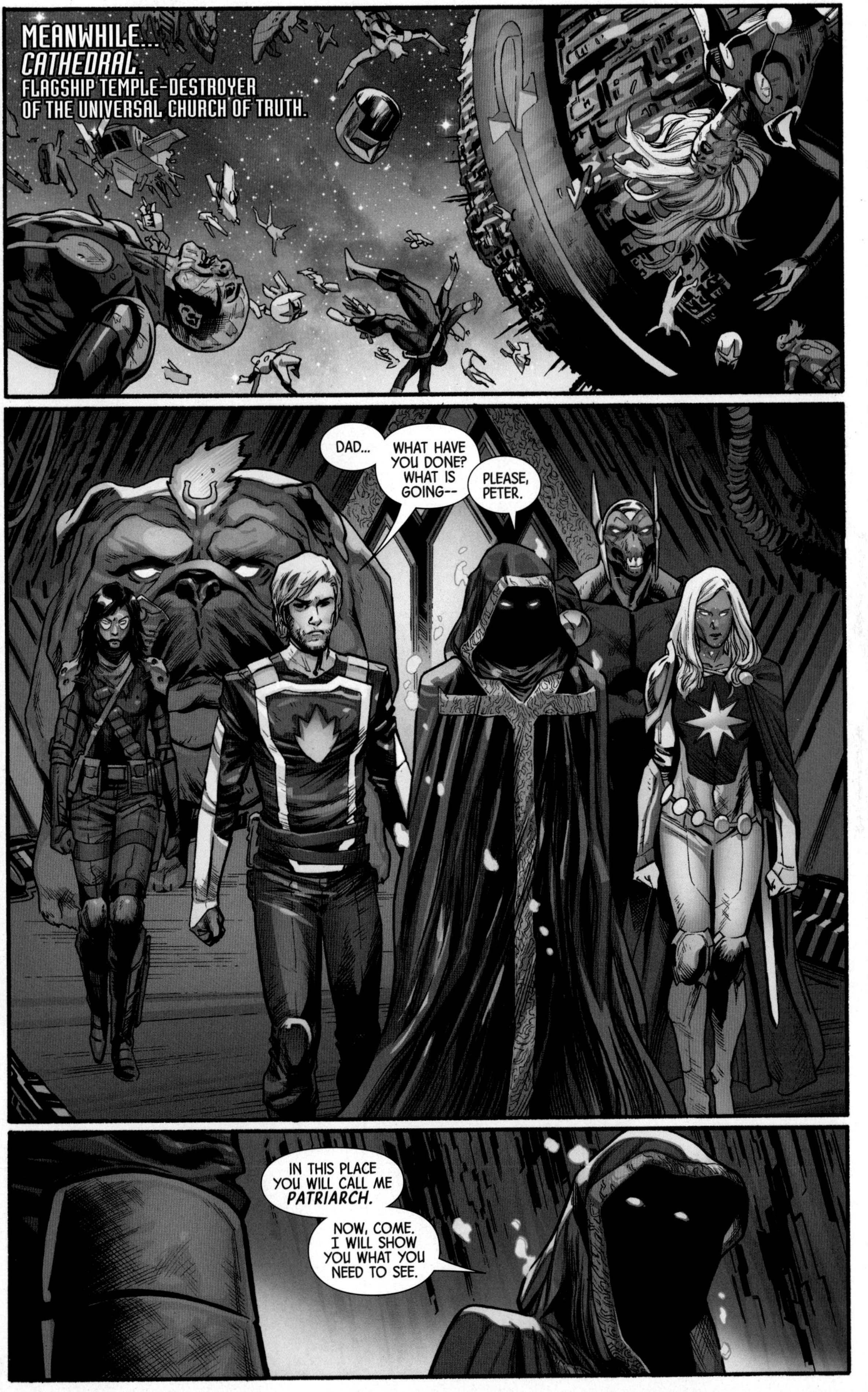
MEANWHILE...
CATHEDRAL.
FLAGSHIP TEMPLE-DESTROYER OF THE UNIVERSAL CHURCH OF TRUTH.
DAD...
WHAT HAVE YOU DONE? WHAT IS GOING--
PLEASE, PETER.
IN THIS PLACE YOU WILL CALL ME PATRIARCH.
NOW, COME. I WILL SHOW YOU WHAT YOU NEED TO SEE.

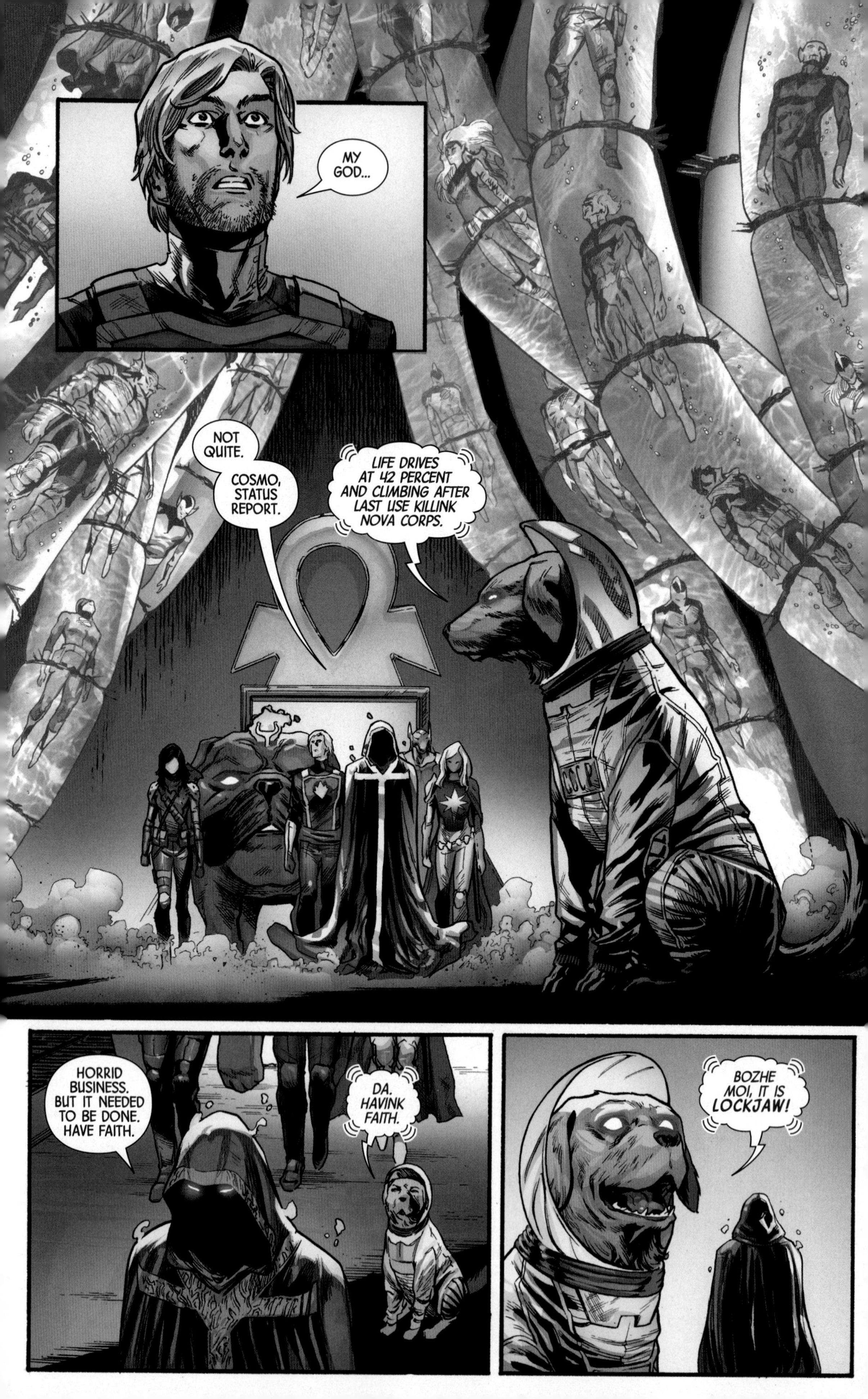
MY GOD...
NOT QUITE.
COSMO, STATUS REPORT.
LIFE DRIVES AT 42 PERCENT AND CLIMBING AFTER LAST USE KILLINK NOVA CORPS.
HORRID BUSINESS. BUT IT NEEDED TO BE DONE. HAVE FAITH.
DA. HAVINK FAITH.
BOZHE MOI, IT IS LOCKJAW!

‹IT IS HONOR TO MEET YOU AGAIN, GREAT HOUND GOD.›

‹RISE AND WELL MET, HONORED SPACE KNIGHT. YOU SHOW YOUR BELLY TO NO ONE.›

SPACE DOGS, MAN...

ARF! ROOF, ROOF! WOOF!

WOOF, WOOF! RRRR ARF!

COME ALONG, PETER.

IS THAT QUASAR? DARKHAWK? WHAT...WHAT HAVE YOU DONE TO THEM, DAD? ARE THEY--

THEY YET LIVE, SON.

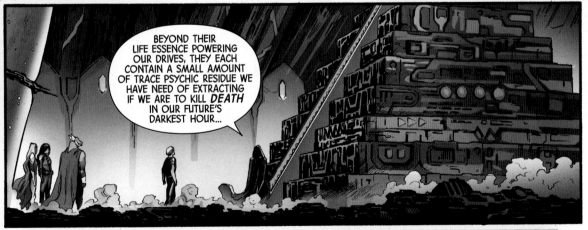

BEYOND THEIR LIFE ESSENCE POWERING OUR DRIVES, THEY EACH CONTAIN A SMALL AMOUNT OF TRACE PSYCHIC RESIDUE WE HAVE NEED OF EXTRACTING IF WE ARE TO KILL *DEATH* IN OUR FUTURE'S DARKEST HOUR...

PSYCHIC... EXTRACTING?

WHAT...WHAT THE HELL DOES THIS ALL MEAN?

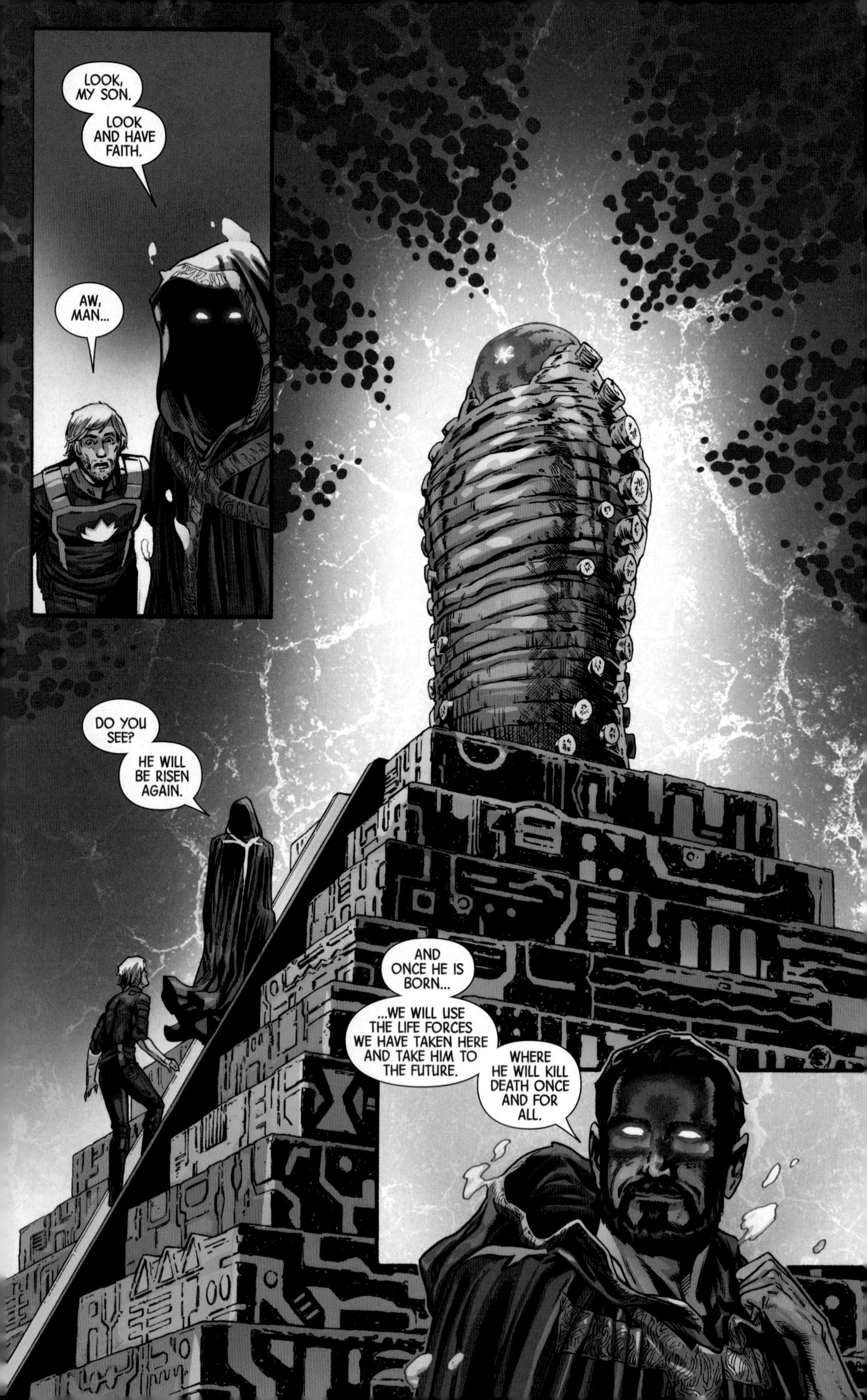
LOOK, MY SON.
LOOK AND HAVE FAITH.
AW, MAN...
DO YOU SEE?
HE WILL BE RISEN AGAIN.
AND ONCE HE IS BORN...
...WE WILL USE THE LIFE FORCES WE HAVE TAKEN HERE AND TAKE HIM TO THE FUTURE.
WHERE HE WILL KILL DEATH ONCE AND FOR ALL.

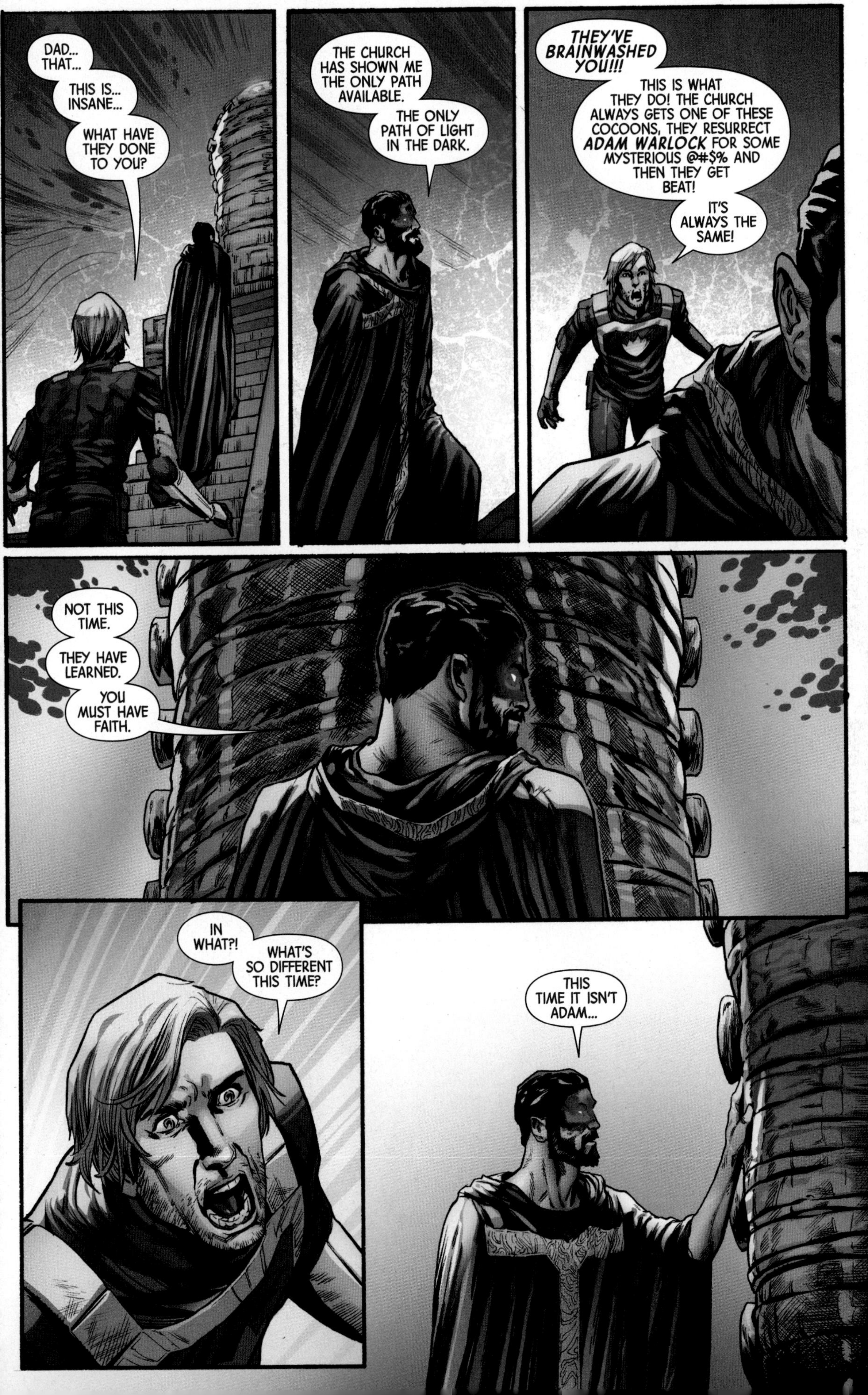

DAD... THAT...
THIS IS... INSANE...
WHAT HAVE THEY DONE TO YOU?
THE CHURCH HAS SHOWN ME THE ONLY PATH AVAILABLE.
THE ONLY PATH OF LIGHT IN THE DARK.
THEY'VE BRAINWASHED YOU!!!
THIS IS WHAT THEY DO! THE CHURCH ALWAYS GETS ONE OF THESE COCOONS, THEY RESURRECT ADAM WARLOCK FOR SOME MYSTERIOUS @#$% AND THEN THEY GET BEAT!
IT'S ALWAYS THE SAME!
NOT THIS TIME.
THEY HAVE LEARNED.
YOU MUST HAVE FAITH.
IN WHAT?!
WHAT'S SO DIFFERENT THIS TIME?
THIS TIME IT ISN'T ADAM...

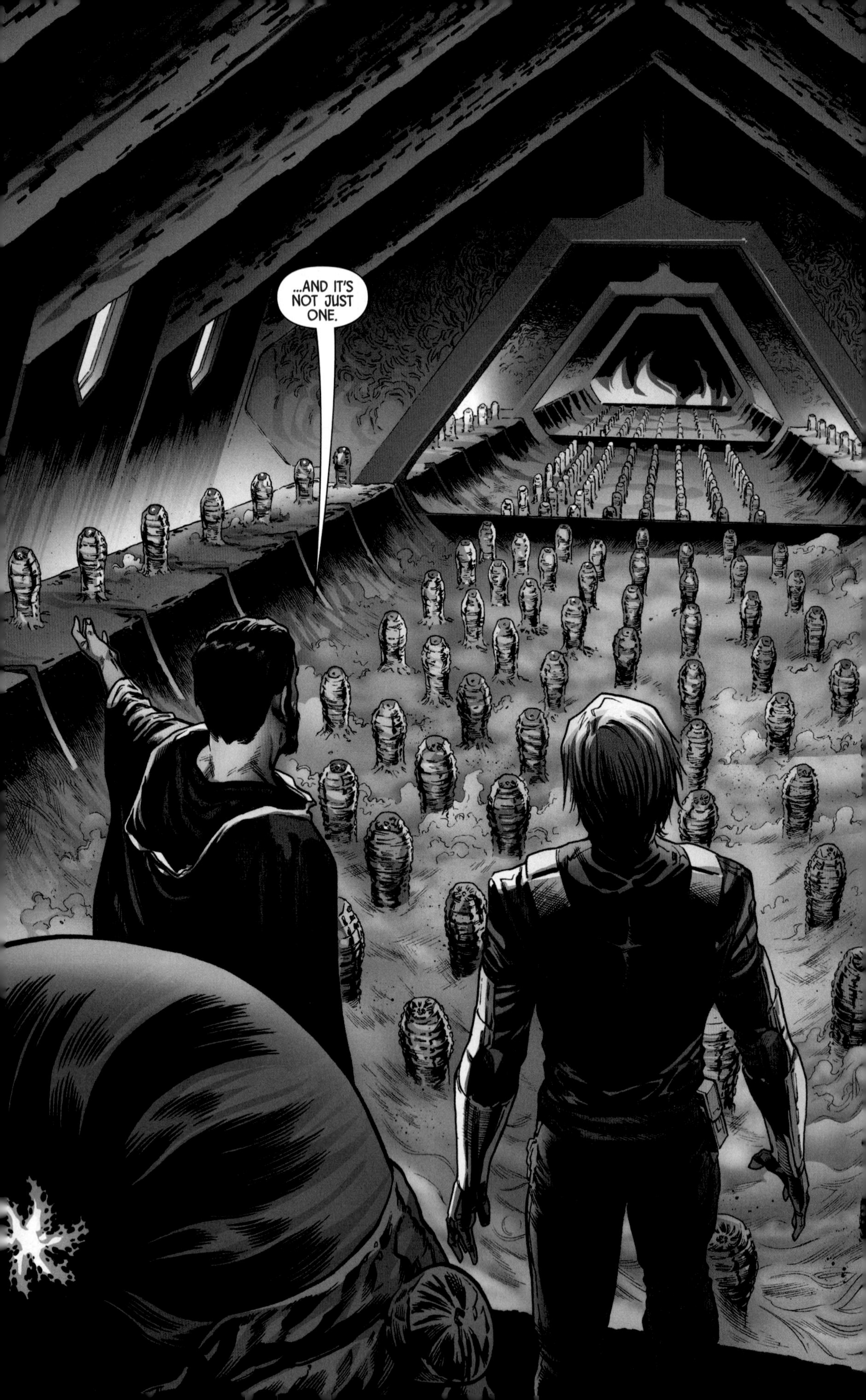
...AND IT'S NOT JUST ONE.

NINE

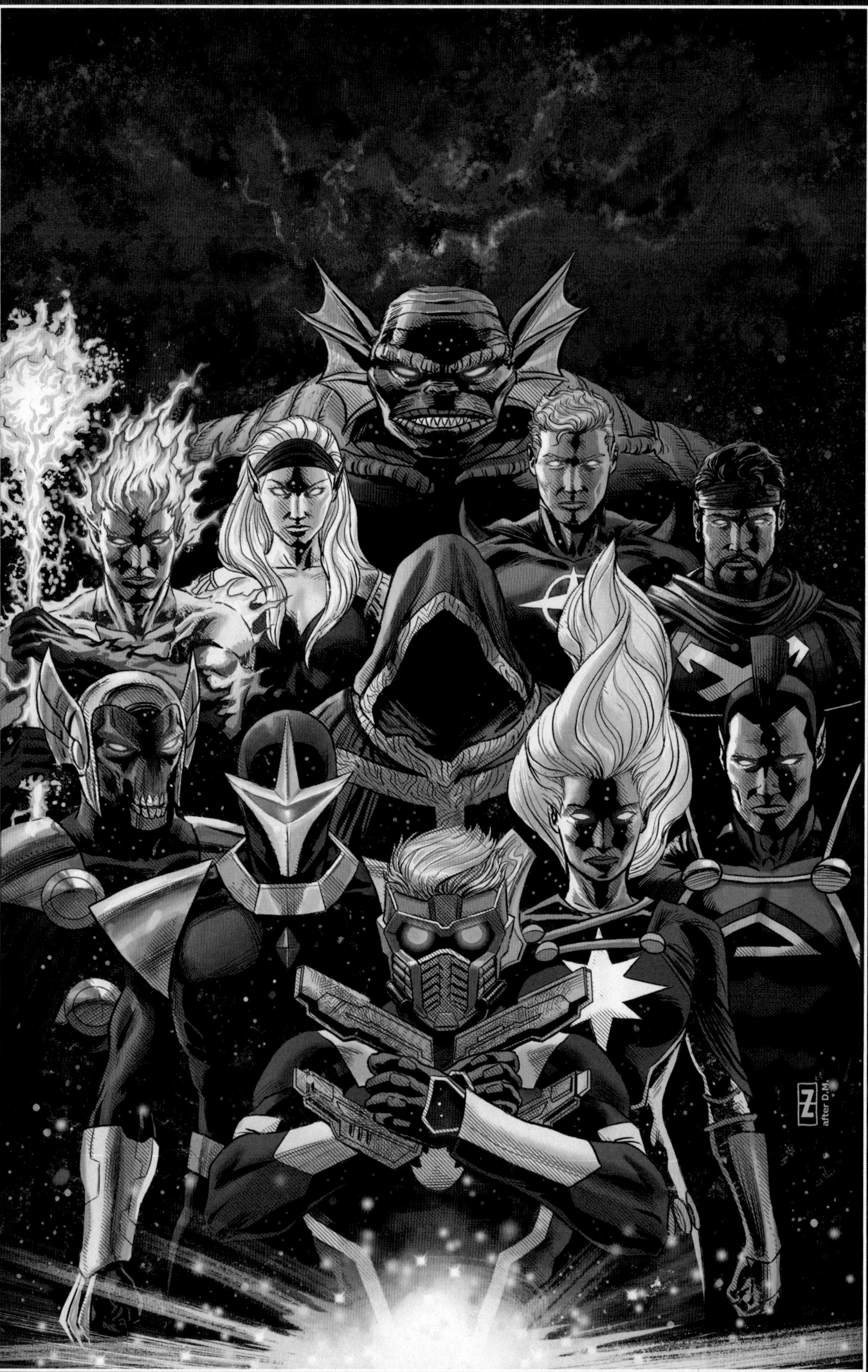
after D.M.

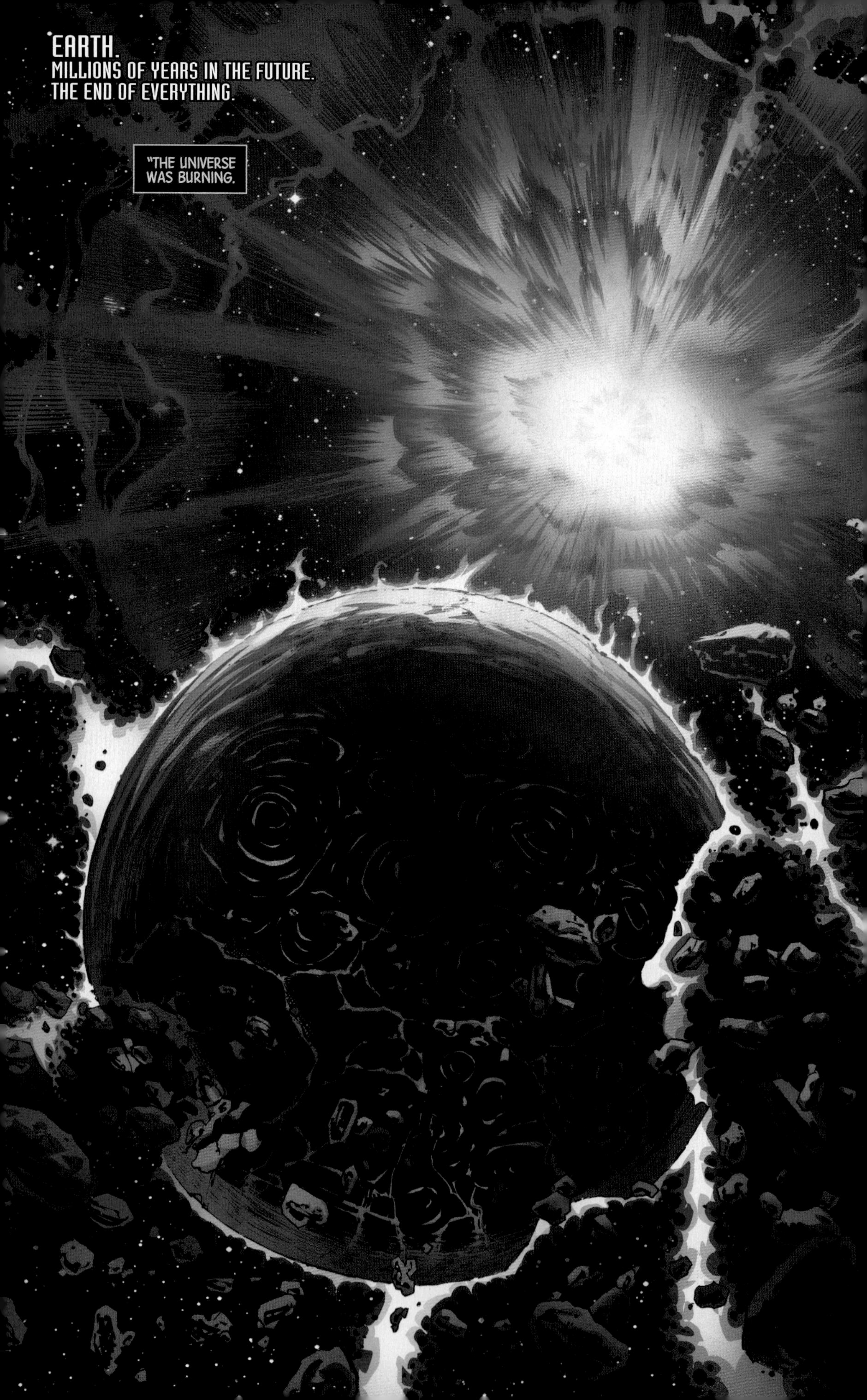
EARTH.
MILLIONS OF YEARS IN THE FUTURE.
THE END OF EVERYTHING.
"THE UNIVERSE WAS BURNING.

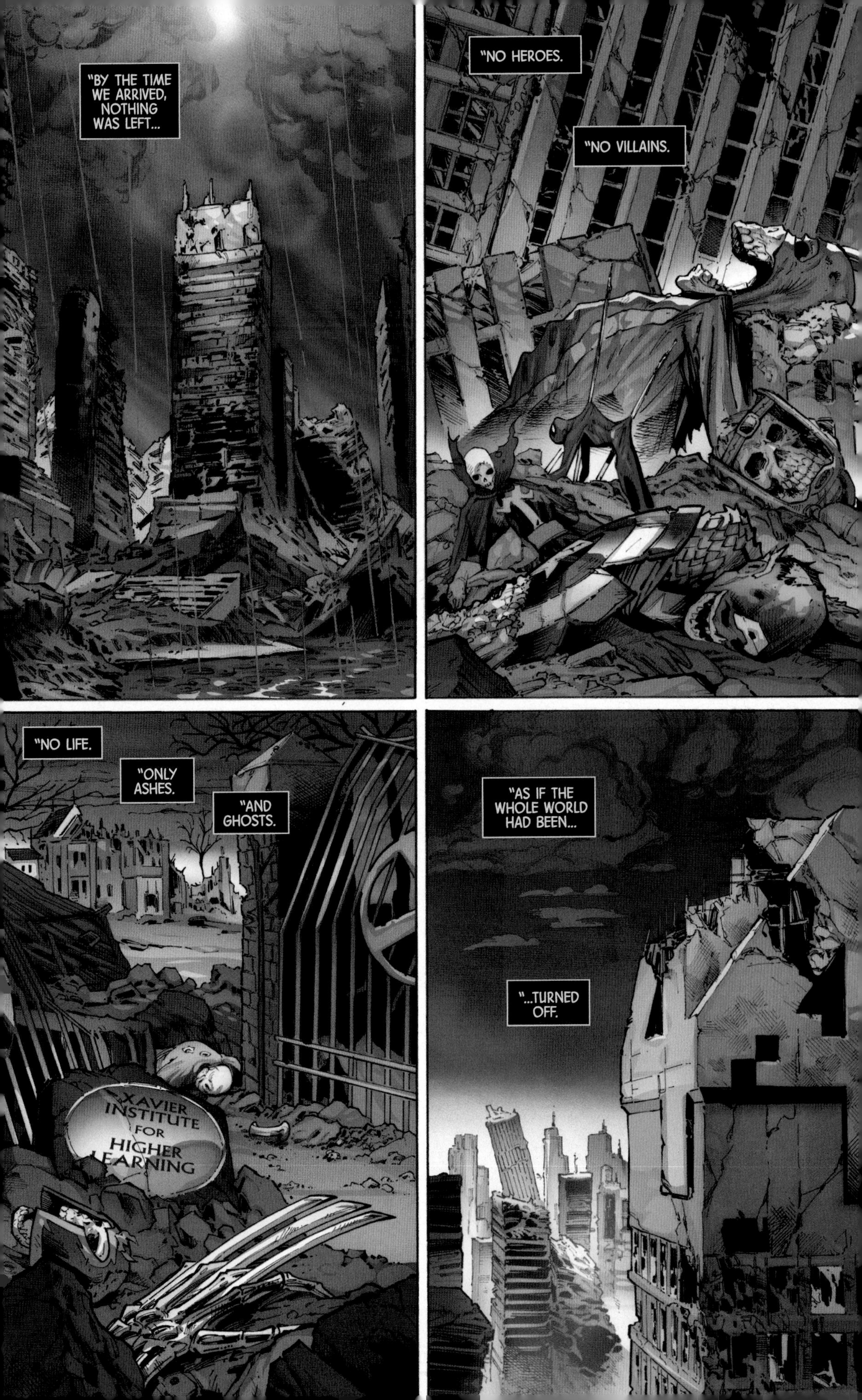
"BY THE TIME WE ARRIVED, NOTHING WAS LEFT...
"NO HEROES.
"NO VILLAINS.
"NO LIFE.
"ONLY ASHES.
"AND GHOSTS.
XAVIER INSTITUTE FOR HIGHER LEARNING
"AS IF THE WHOLE WORLD HAD BEEN...
"...TURNED OFF.

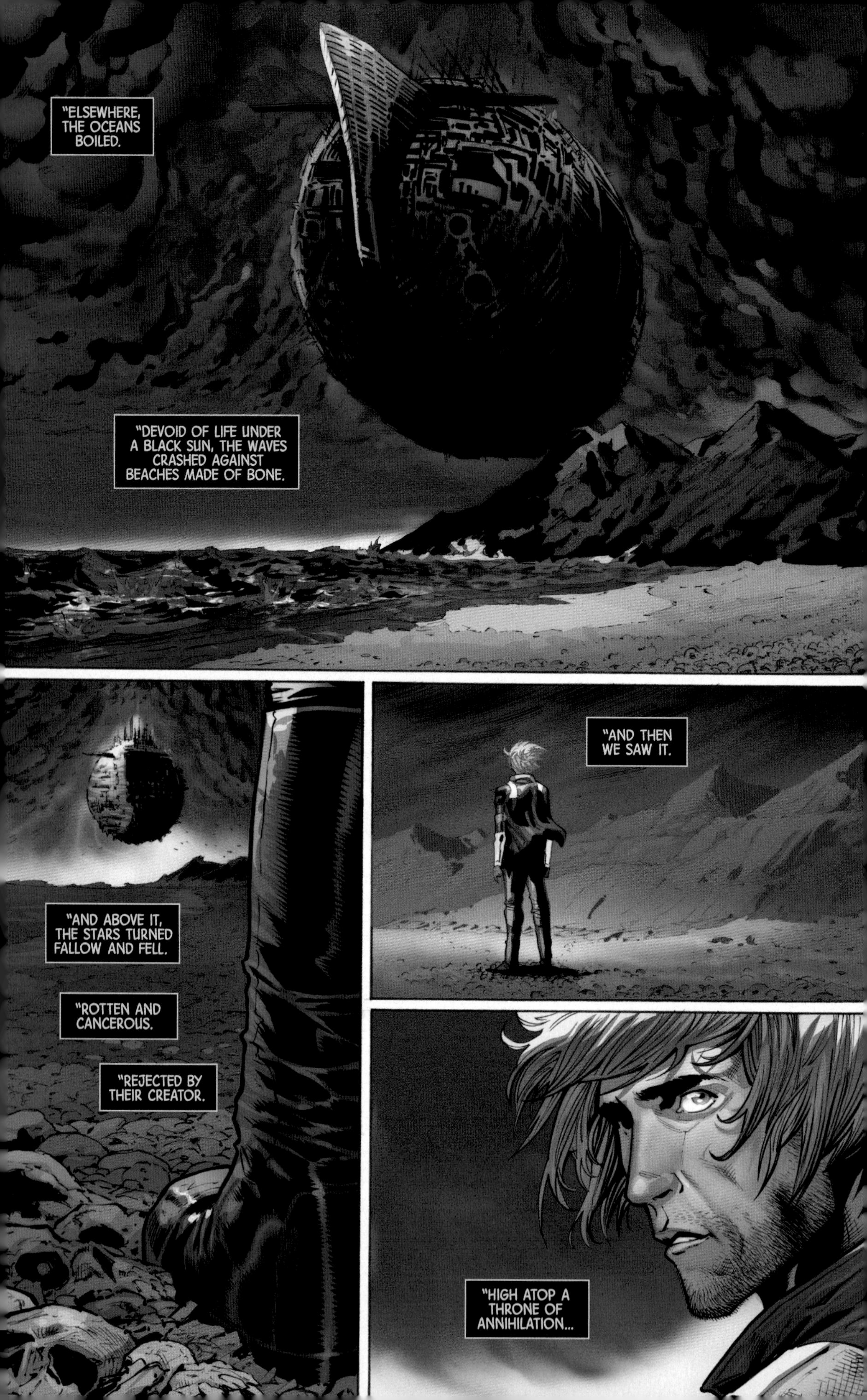
"ELSEWHERE, THE OCEANS BOILED.
"DEVOID OF LIFE UNDER A BLACK SUN, THE WAVES CRASHED AGAINST BEACHES MADE OF BONE.
"AND ABOVE IT, THE STARS TURNED FALLOW AND FELL.
"ROTTEN AND CANCEROUS.
"REJECTED BY THEIR CREATOR.
"AND THEN WE SAW IT.
"HIGH ATOP A THRONE OF ANNIHILATION...

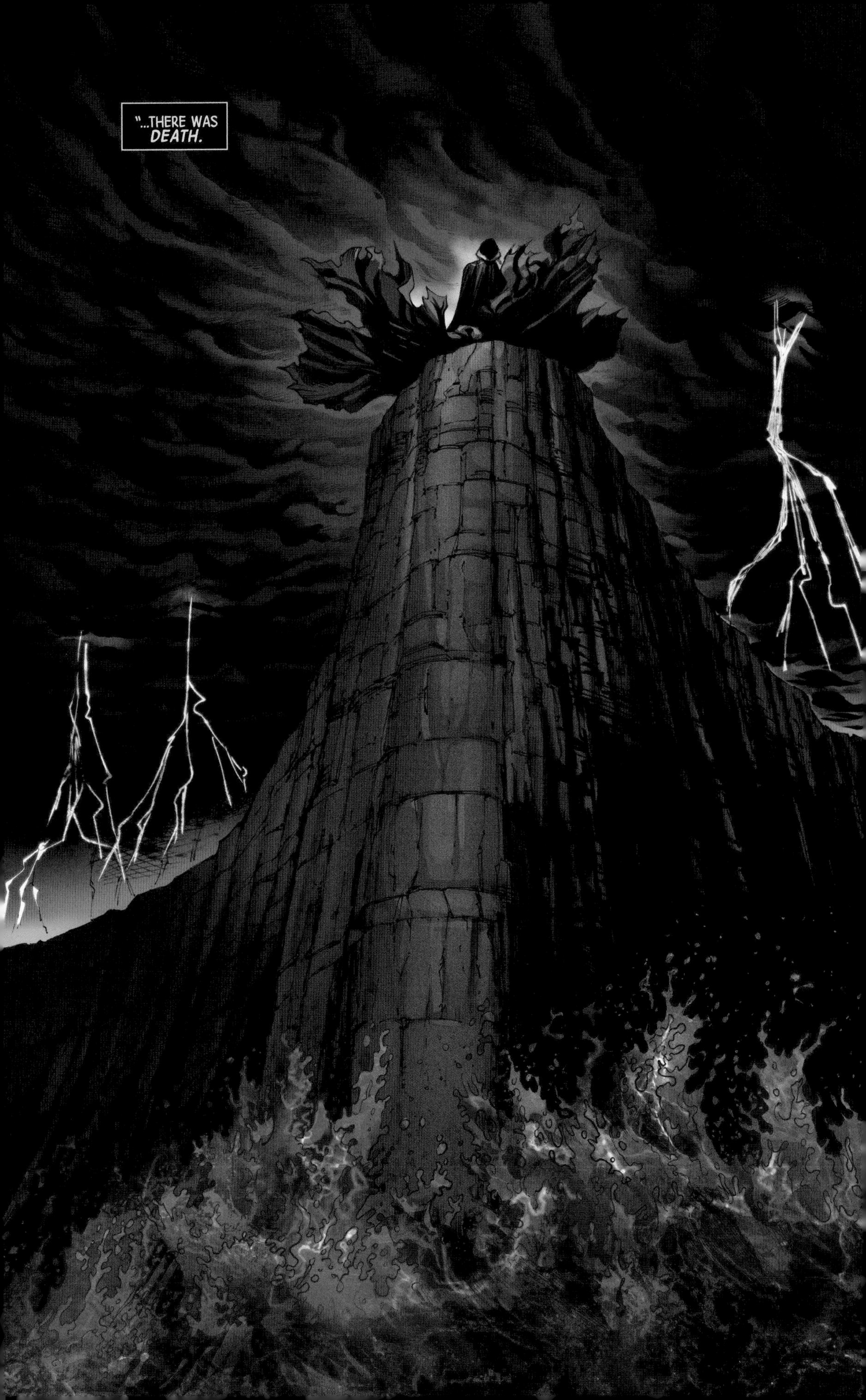
"...THERE WAS DEATH.

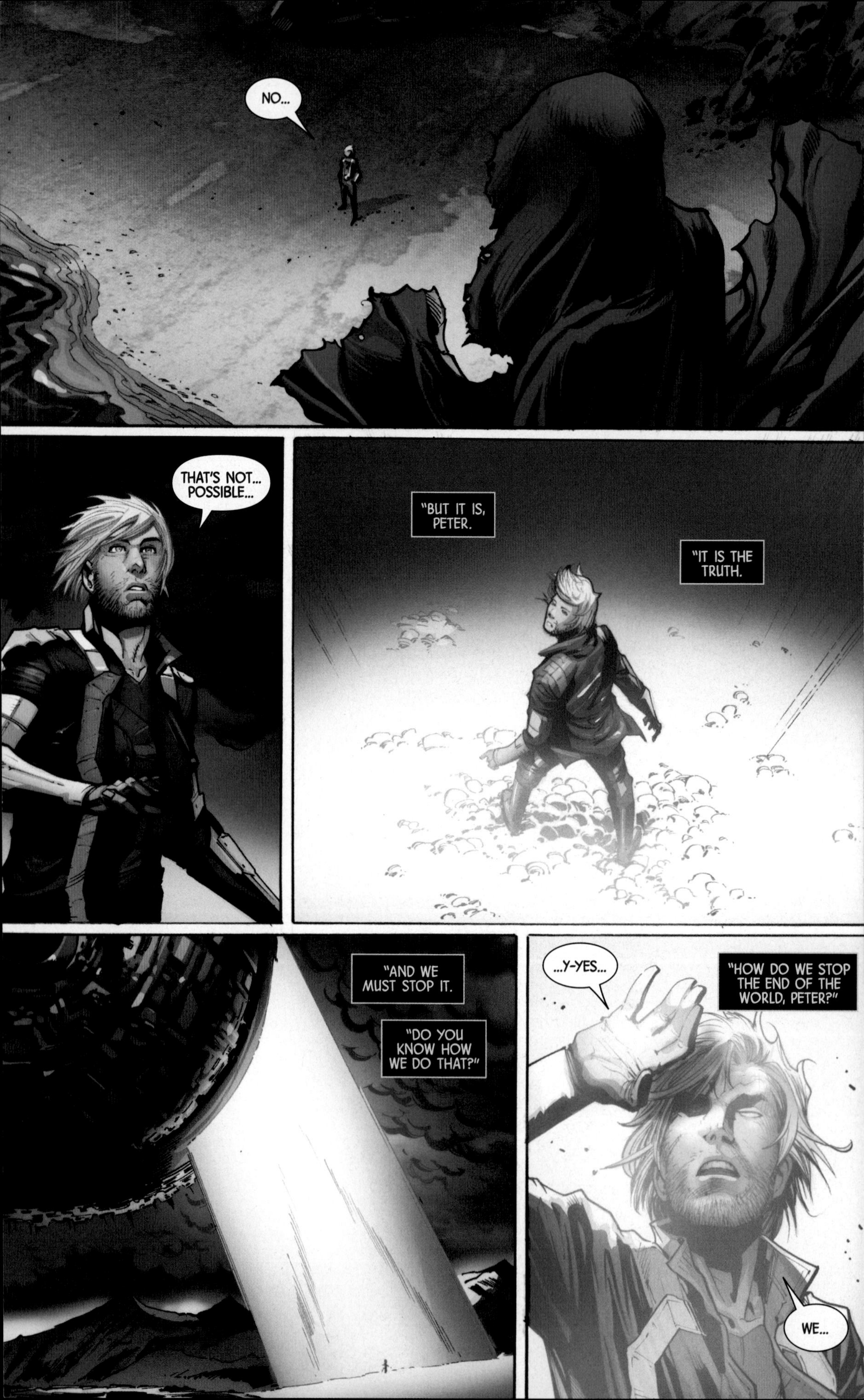
NO...
THAT'S NOT... POSSIBLE...
"BUT IT IS, PETER.
"IT IS THE TRUTH.
"AND WE MUST STOP IT.
"DO YOU KNOW HOW WE DO THAT?"
...Y-YES...
"HOW DO WE STOP THE END OF THE WORLD, PETER?"
WE...

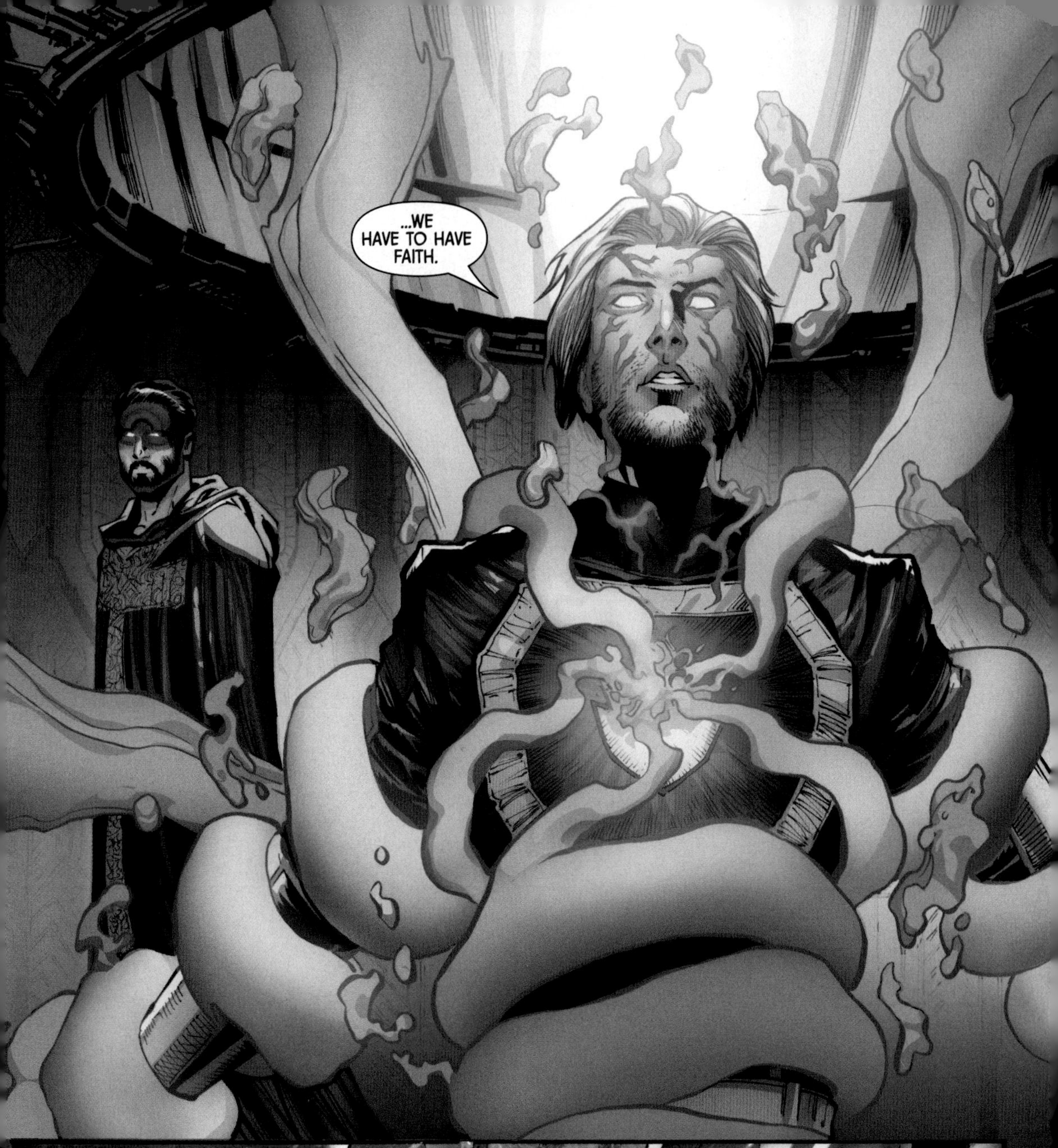
...WE HAVE TO HAVE FAITH.

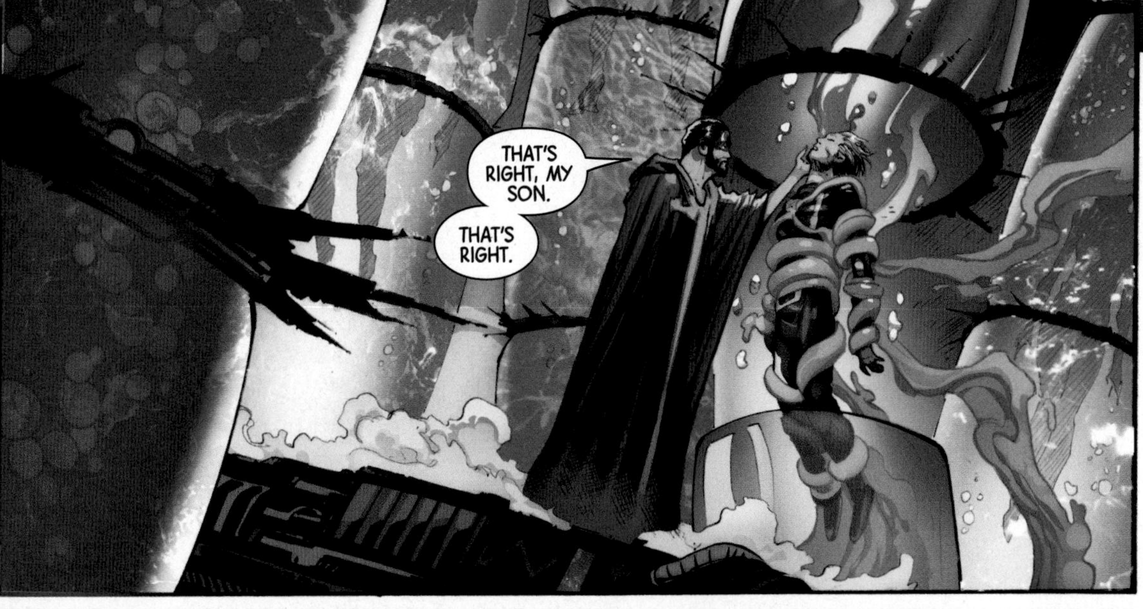
THAT'S RIGHT, MY SON.
THAT'S RIGHT.

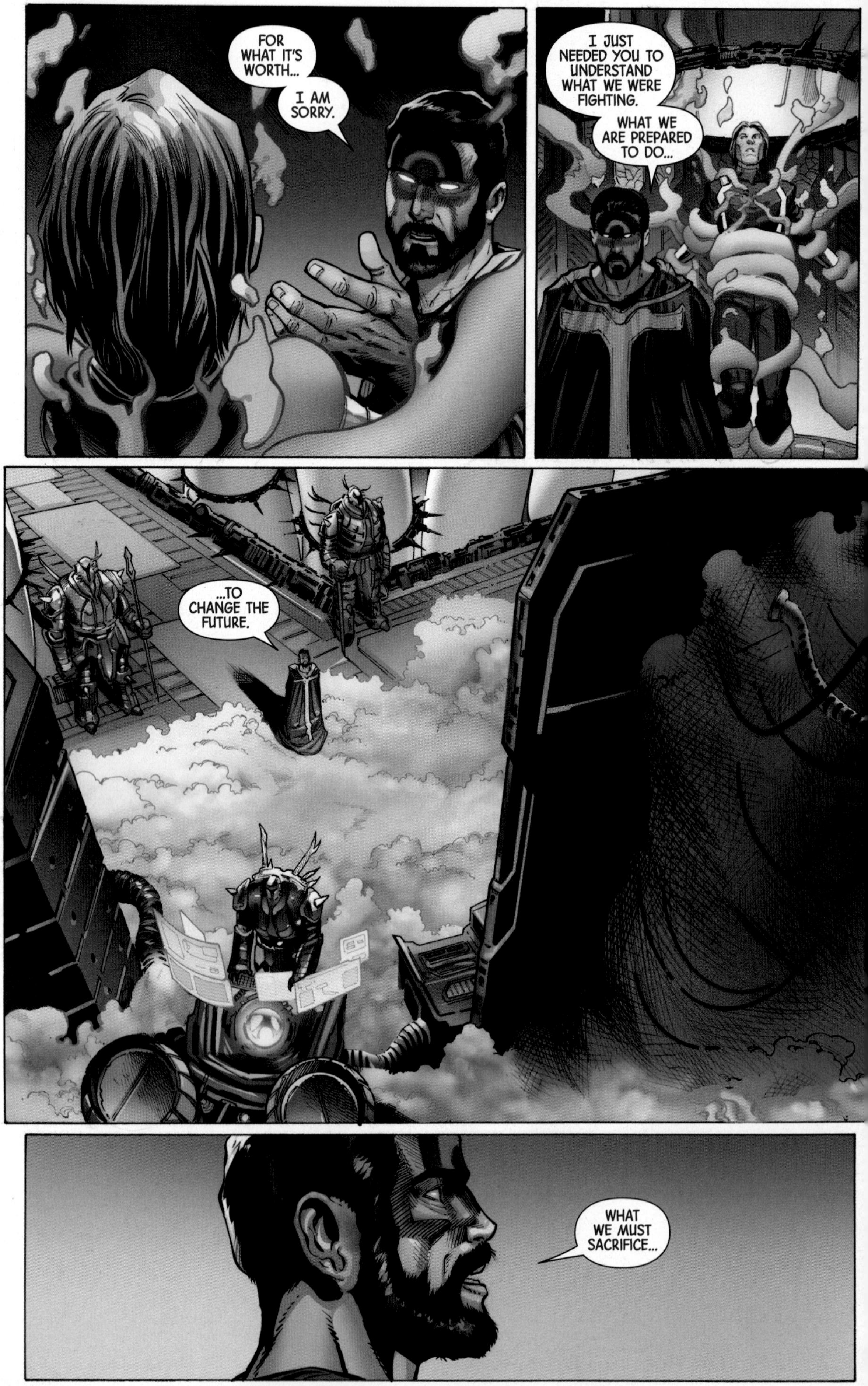
FOR WHAT IT'S WORTH...
I AM SORRY.
I JUST NEEDED YOU TO UNDERSTAND WHAT WE WERE FIGHTING.
WHAT WE ARE PREPARED TO DO...
...TO CHANGE THE FUTURE.
WHAT WE MUST SACRIFICE...

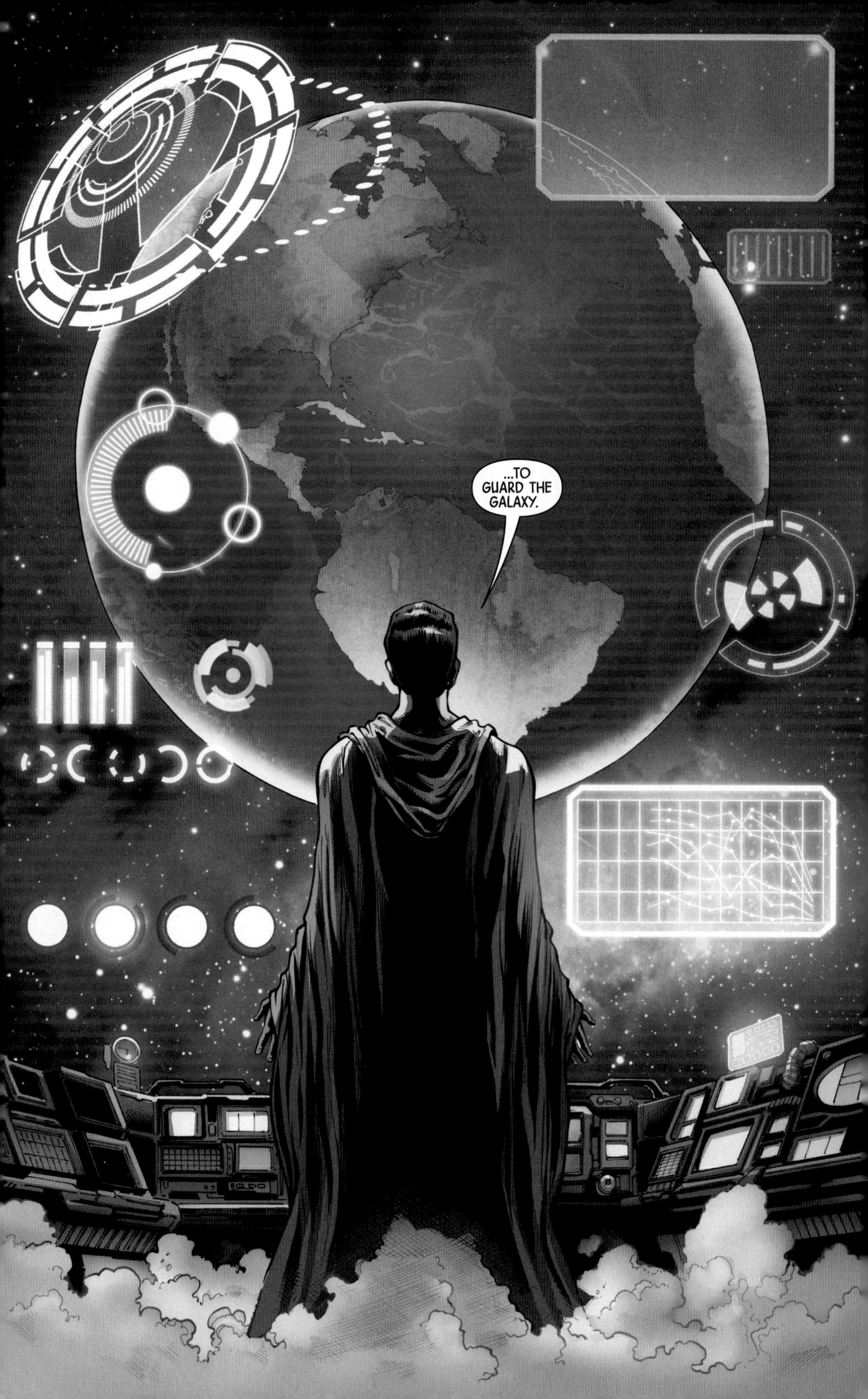
...TO GUARD THE GALAXY.

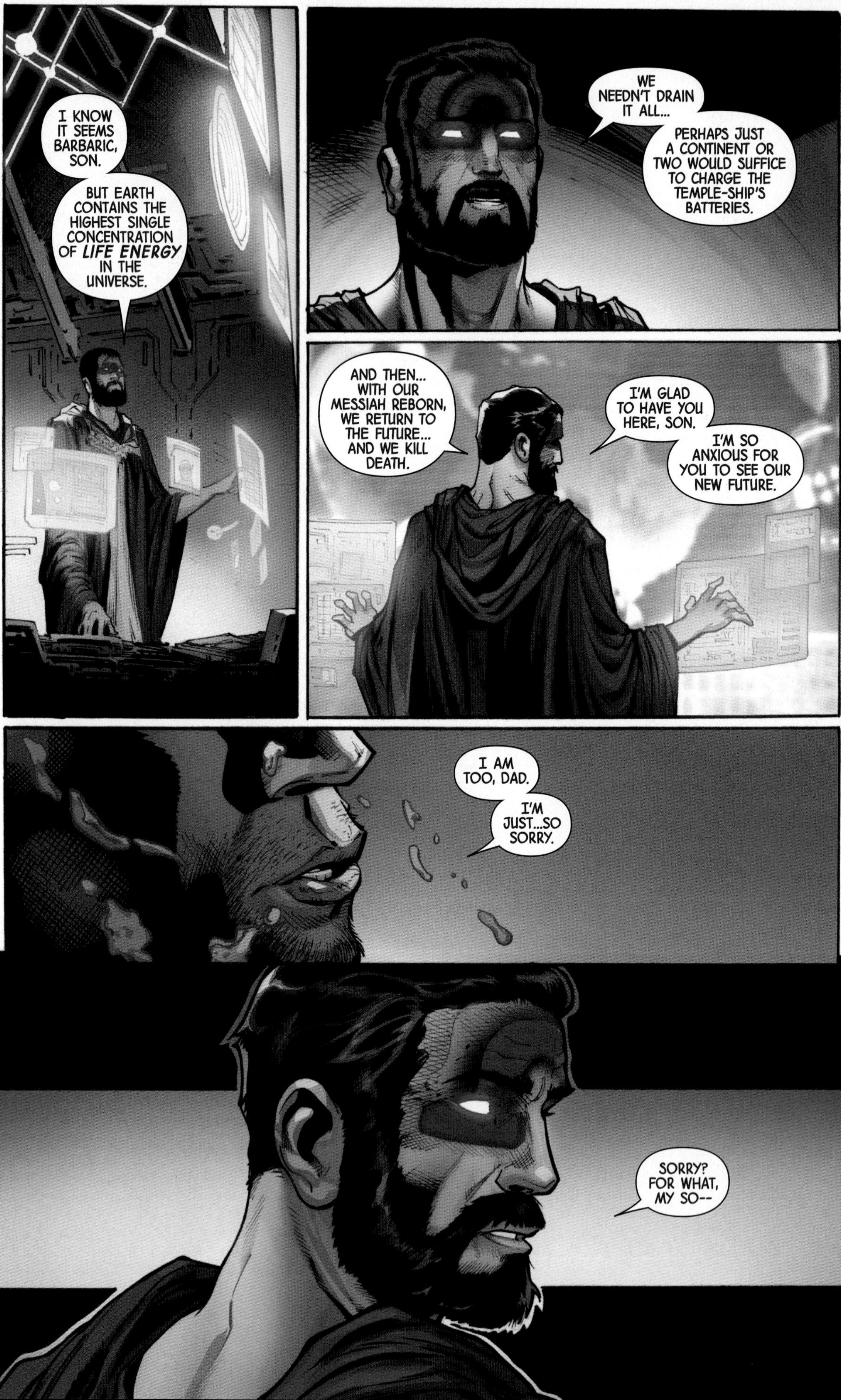
I KNOW IT SEEMS BARBARIC, SON.
BUT EARTH CONTAINS THE HIGHEST SINGLE CONCENTRATION OF LIFE ENERGY IN THE UNIVERSE.
WE NEEDN'T DRAIN IT ALL...
PERHAPS JUST A CONTINENT OR TWO WOULD SUFFICE TO CHARGE THE TEMPLE-SHIP'S BATTERIES.
AND THEN... WITH OUR MESSIAH REBORN, WE RETURN TO THE FUTURE... AND WE KILL DEATH.
I'M GLAD TO HAVE YOU HERE, SON.
I'M SO ANXIOUS FOR YOU TO SEE OUR NEW FUTURE.
I AM TOO, DAD.
I'M JUST...SO SORRY.
SORRY? FOR WHAT, MY SO--

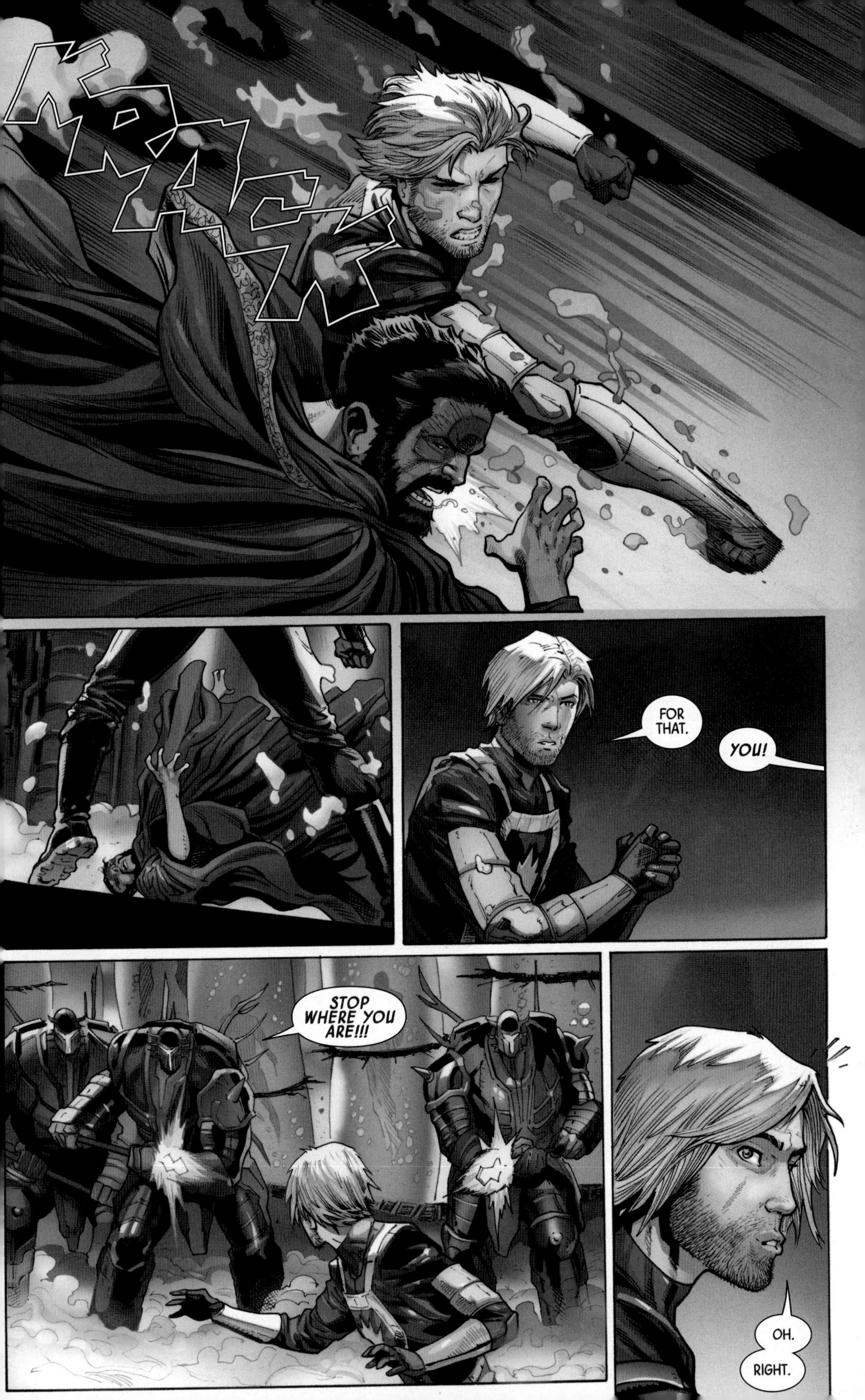
KRACK
FOR THAT.
YOU!
STOP WHERE YOU ARE!!!
OH.
RIGHT.

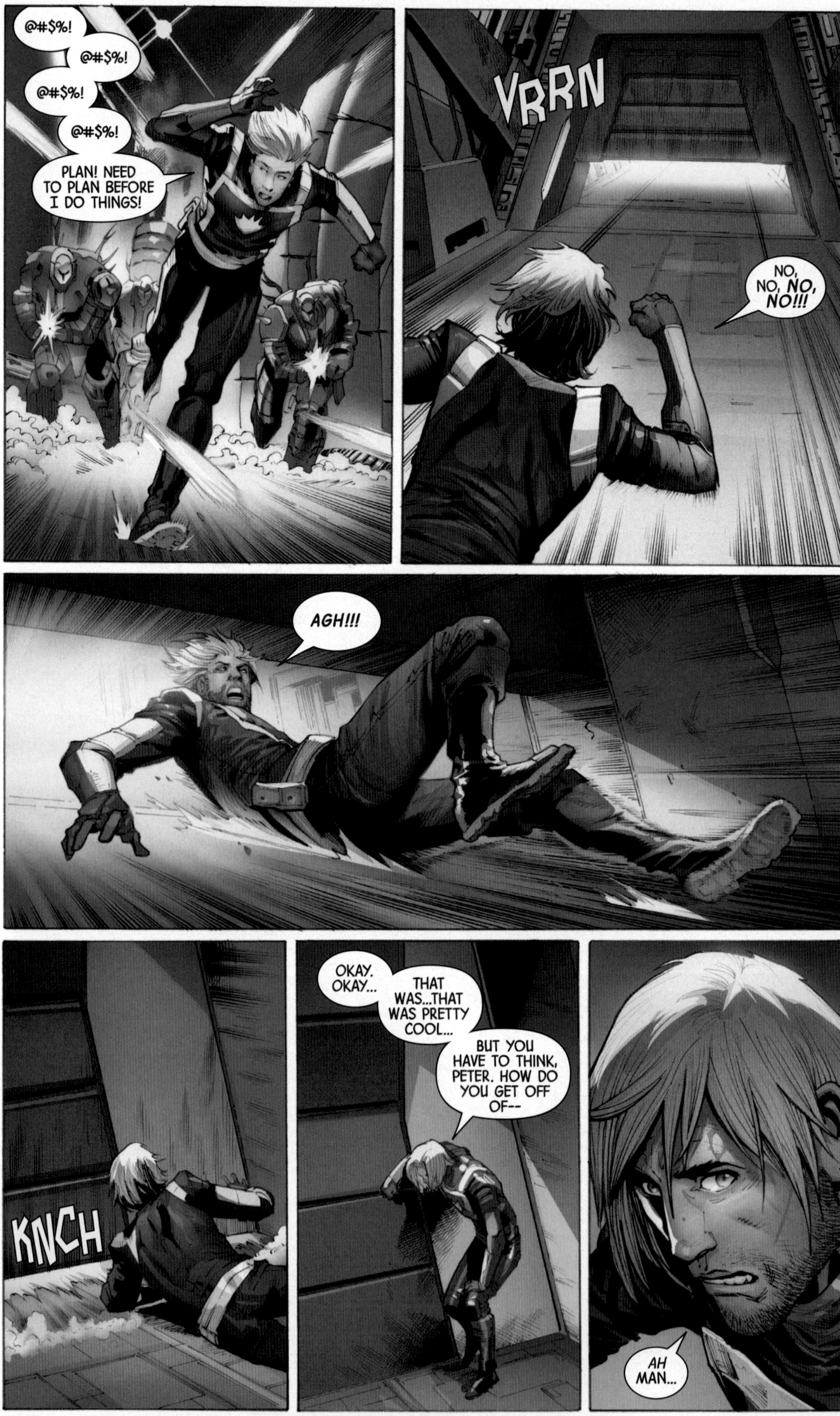
@#$%!
@#$%!
@#$%!
@#$%!
PLAN! NEED TO PLAN BEFORE I DO THINGS!
VRRN
NO, NO, NO, NO!!!
AGH!!!
KNCH
OKAY. OKAY...
THAT WAS...THAT WAS PRETTY COOL...
BUT YOU HAVE TO THINK, PETER. HOW DO YOU GET OFF OF--
AH MAN...

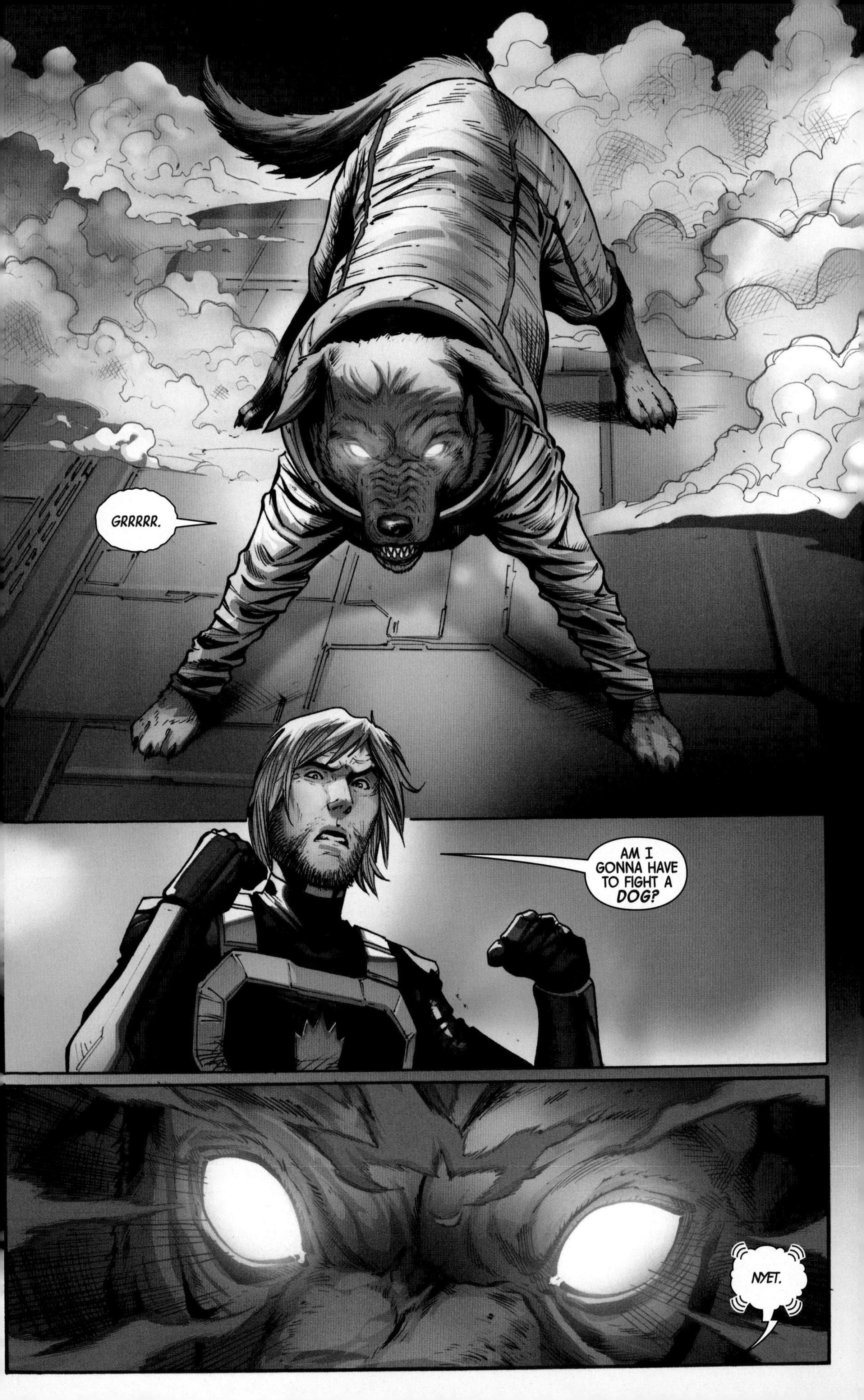
GRRRRR.
AM I GONNA HAVE TO FIGHT A *DOG?*
NYET.

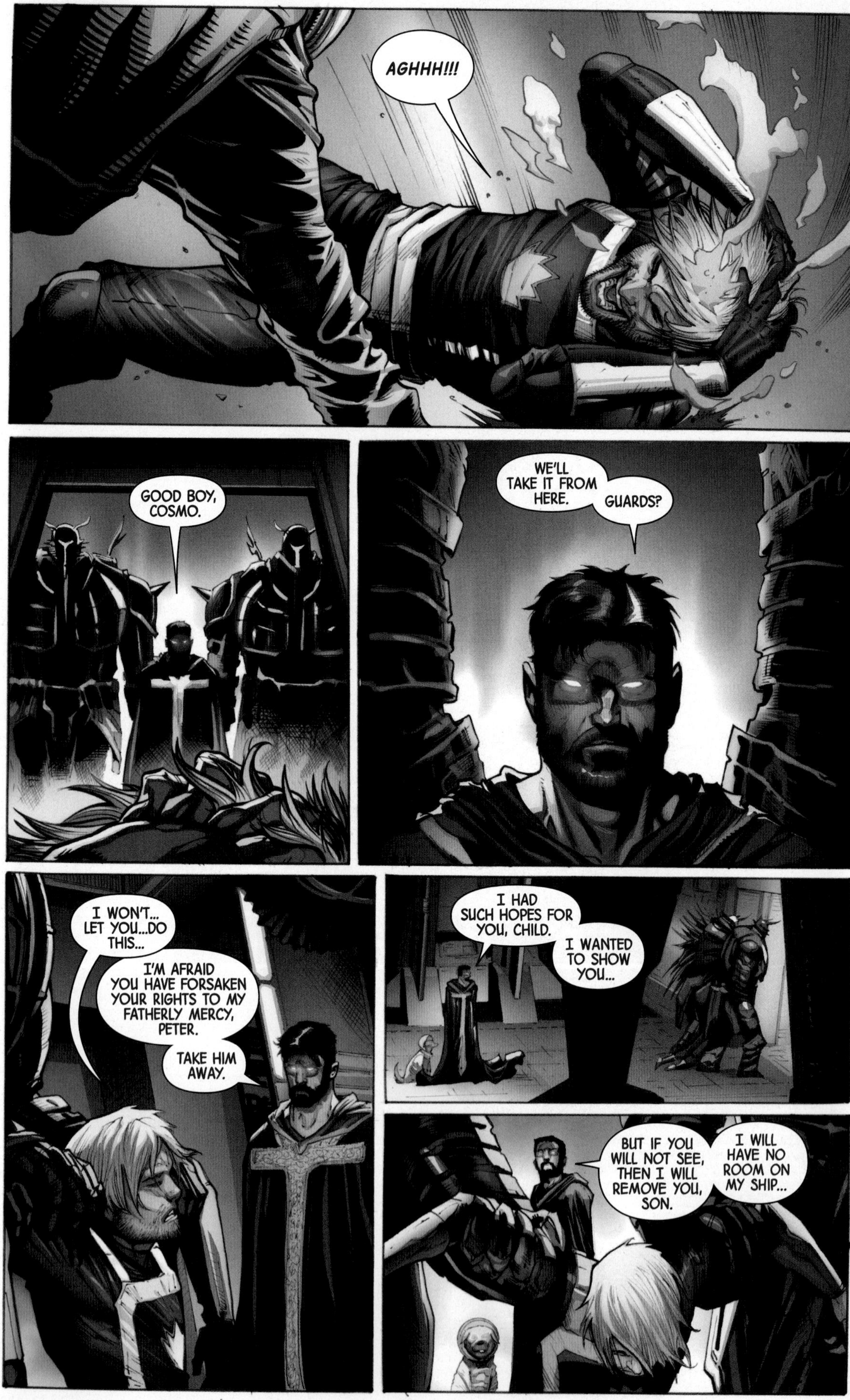
AGHHH!!!
GOOD BOY, COSMO.
WE'LL TAKE IT FROM HERE.
GUARDS?
I WON'T... LET YOU...DO THIS...
I'M AFRAID YOU HAVE FORSAKEN YOUR RIGHTS TO MY FATHERLY MERCY, PETER.
TAKE HIM AWAY.
I HAD SUCH HOPES FOR YOU, CHILD.
I WANTED TO SHOW YOU...
BUT IF YOU WILL NOT SEE, THEN I WILL REMOVE YOU, SON.
I WILL HAVE NO ROOM ON MY SHIP...

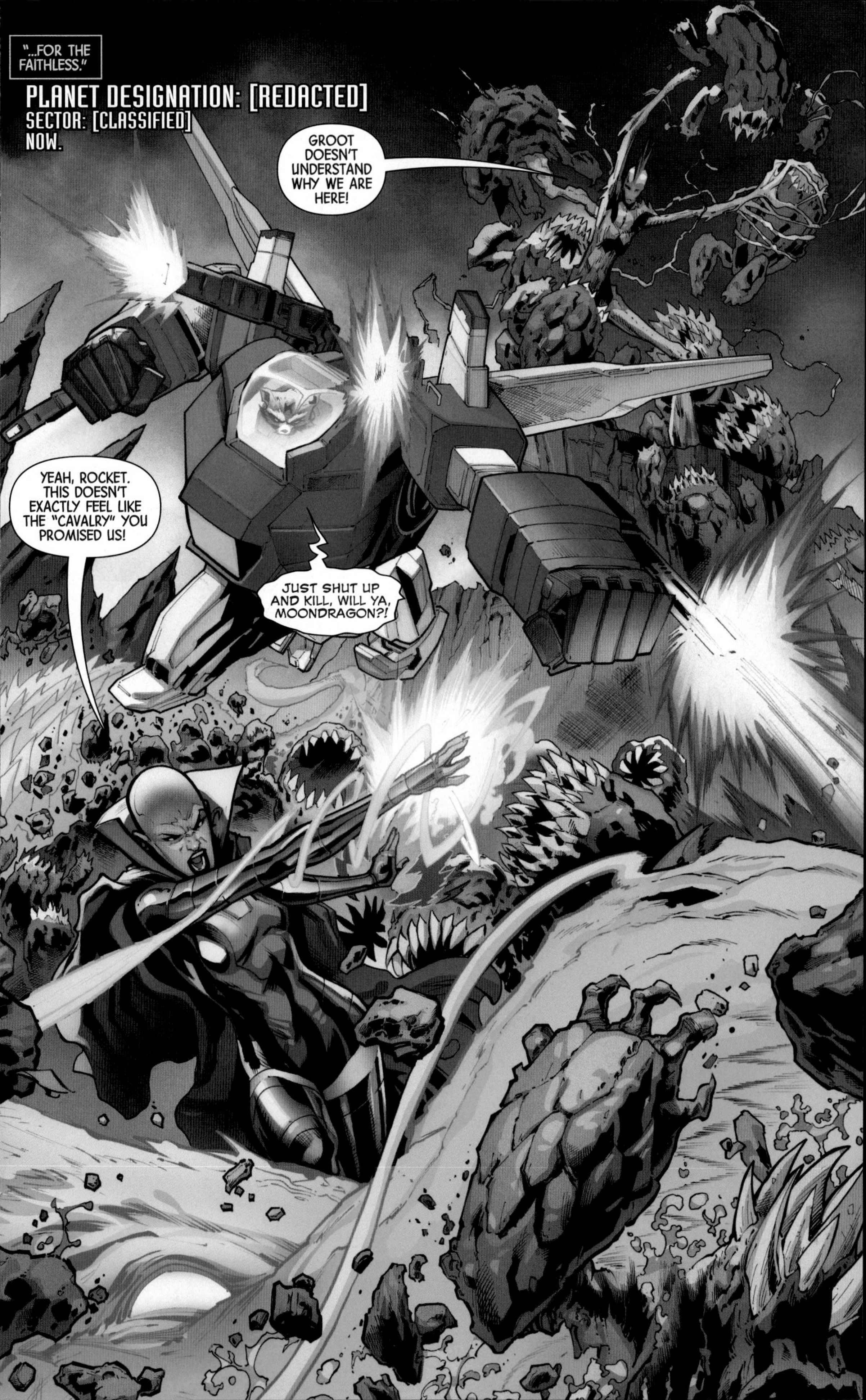
"...FOR THE FAITHLESS."
PLANET DESIGNATION: [REDACTED]
SECTOR: [CLASSIFIED]
NOW.
GROOT DOESN'T UNDERSTAND WHY WE ARE HERE!
YEAH, ROCKET. THIS DOESN'T EXACTLY FEEL LIKE THE "CAVALRY" YOU PROMISED US!
JUST SHUT UP AND KILL, WILL YA, MOONDRAGON?!

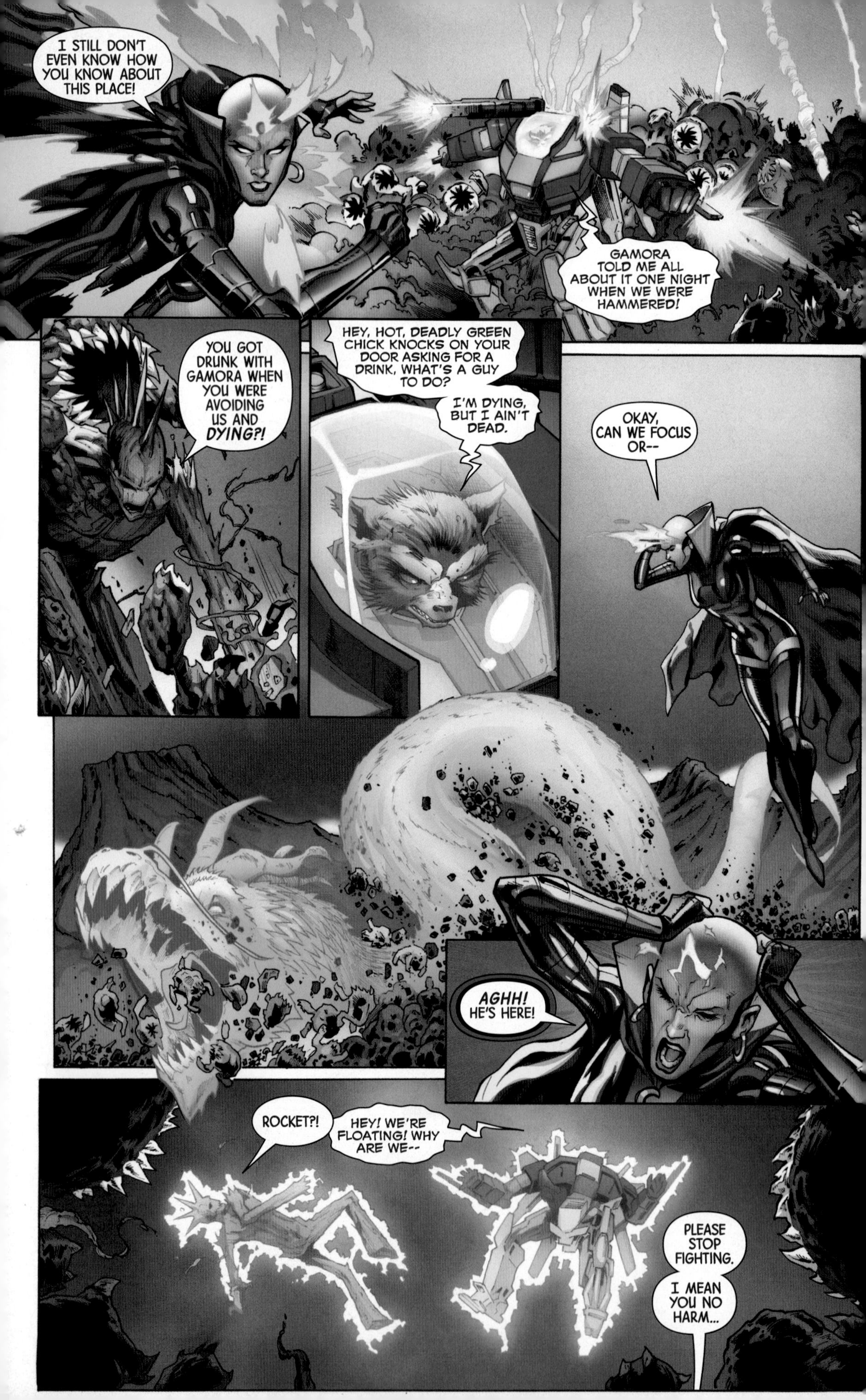
I STILL DON'T EVEN KNOW HOW YOU KNOW ABOUT THIS PLACE!
GAMORA TOLD ME ALL ABOUT IT ONE NIGHT WHEN WE WERE HAMMERED!
YOU GOT DRUNK WITH GAMORA WHEN YOU WERE AVOIDING US AND DYING?!
HEY, HOT, DEADLY GREEN CHICK KNOCKS ON YOUR DOOR ASKING FOR A DRINK, WHAT'S A GUY TO DO?
I'M DYING, BUT I AIN'T DEAD.
OKAY, CAN WE FOCUS OR--
AGHH! HE'S HERE!
ROCKET?!
HEY! WE'RE FLOATING! WHY ARE WE--
PLEASE STOP FIGHTING.
I MEAN YOU NO HARM...

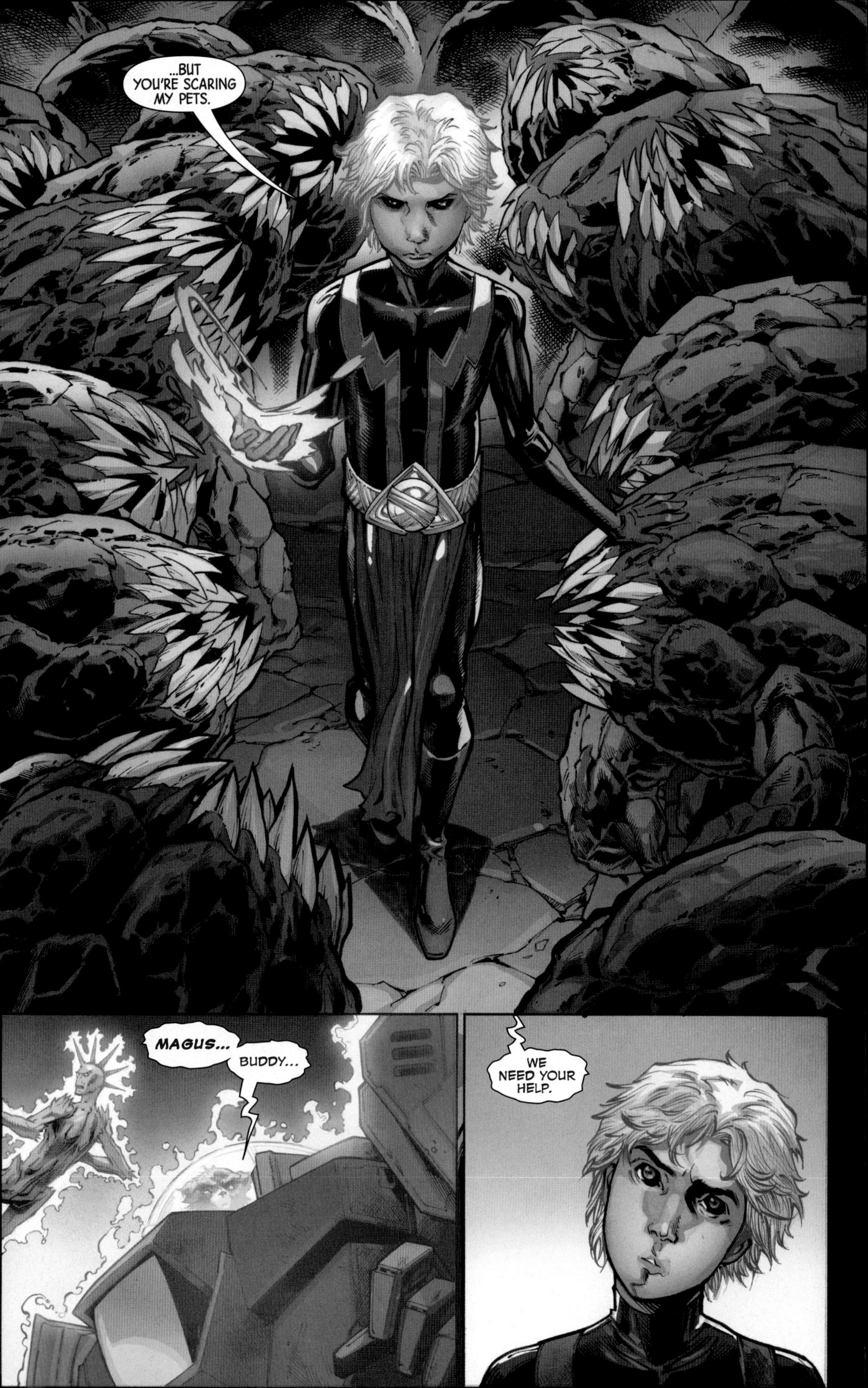
...BUT YOU'RE SCARING MY PETS.
MAGUS...
BUDDY...
WE NEED YOUR HELP.

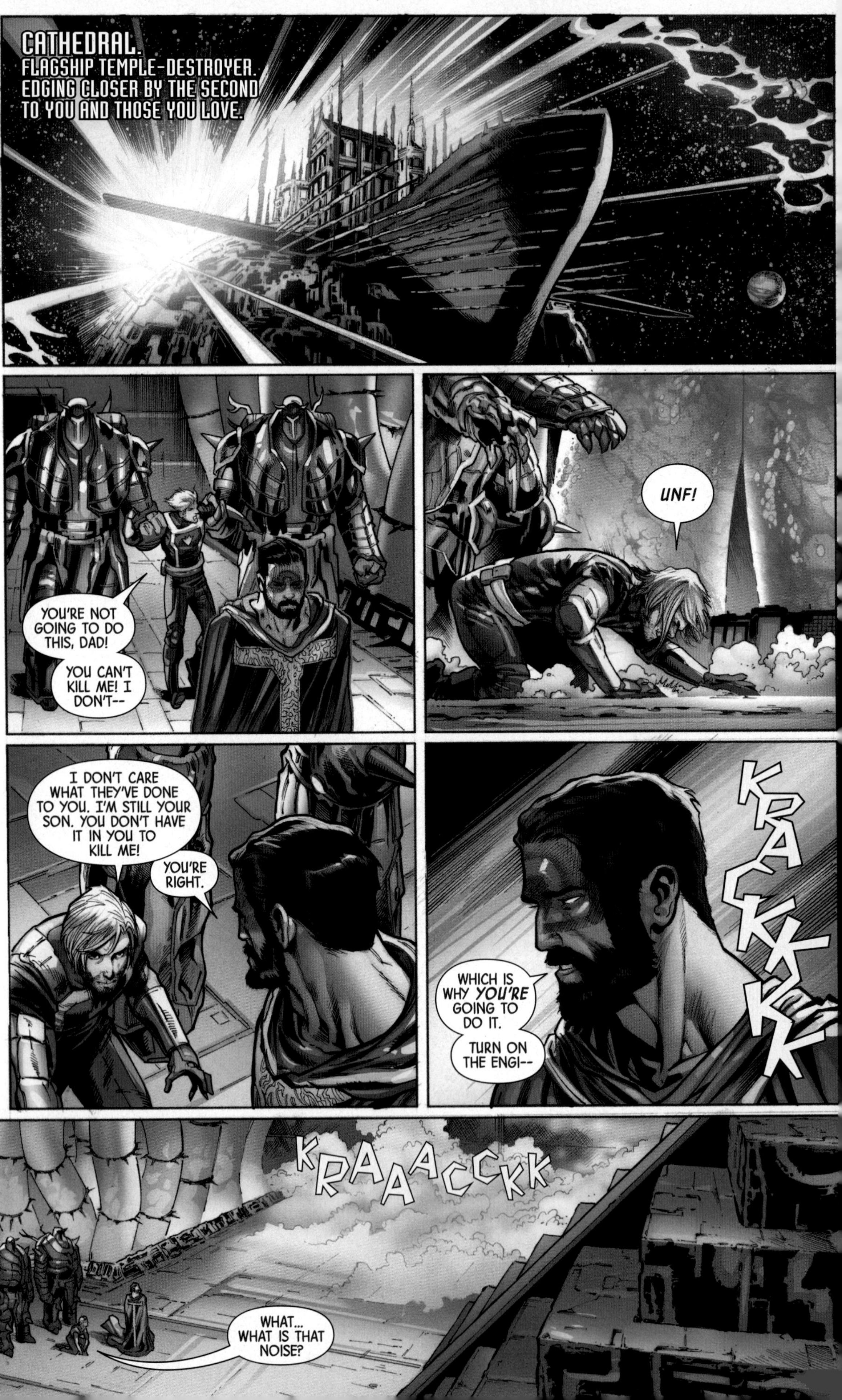
CATHEDRAL.
FLAGSHIP TEMPLE-DESTROYER. EDGING CLOSER BY THE SECOND TO YOU AND THOSE YOU LOVE.
YOU'RE NOT GOING TO DO THIS, DAD!
YOU CAN'T KILL ME! I DON'T--
UNF!
I DON'T CARE WHAT THEY'VE DONE TO YOU. I'M STILL YOUR SON. YOU DON'T HAVE IT IN YOU TO KILL ME!
YOU'RE RIGHT.
KRACKKKK
WHICH IS WHY YOU'RE GOING TO DO IT.
TURN ON THE ENGI--
KRAAACCKK
WHAT... WHAT IS THAT NOISE?

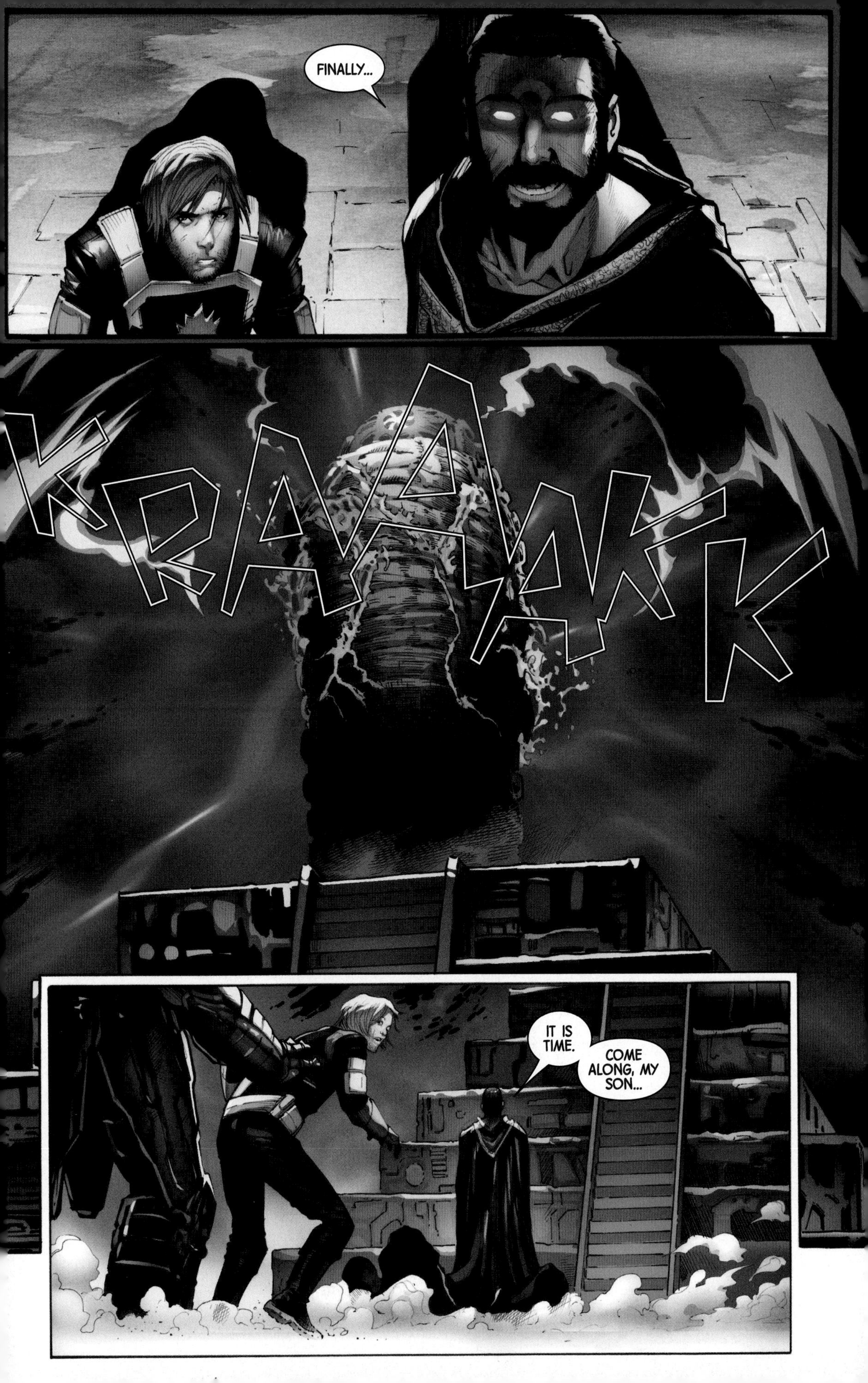
FINALLY...
KRAAAKK
IT IS TIME.
COME ALONG, MY SON...

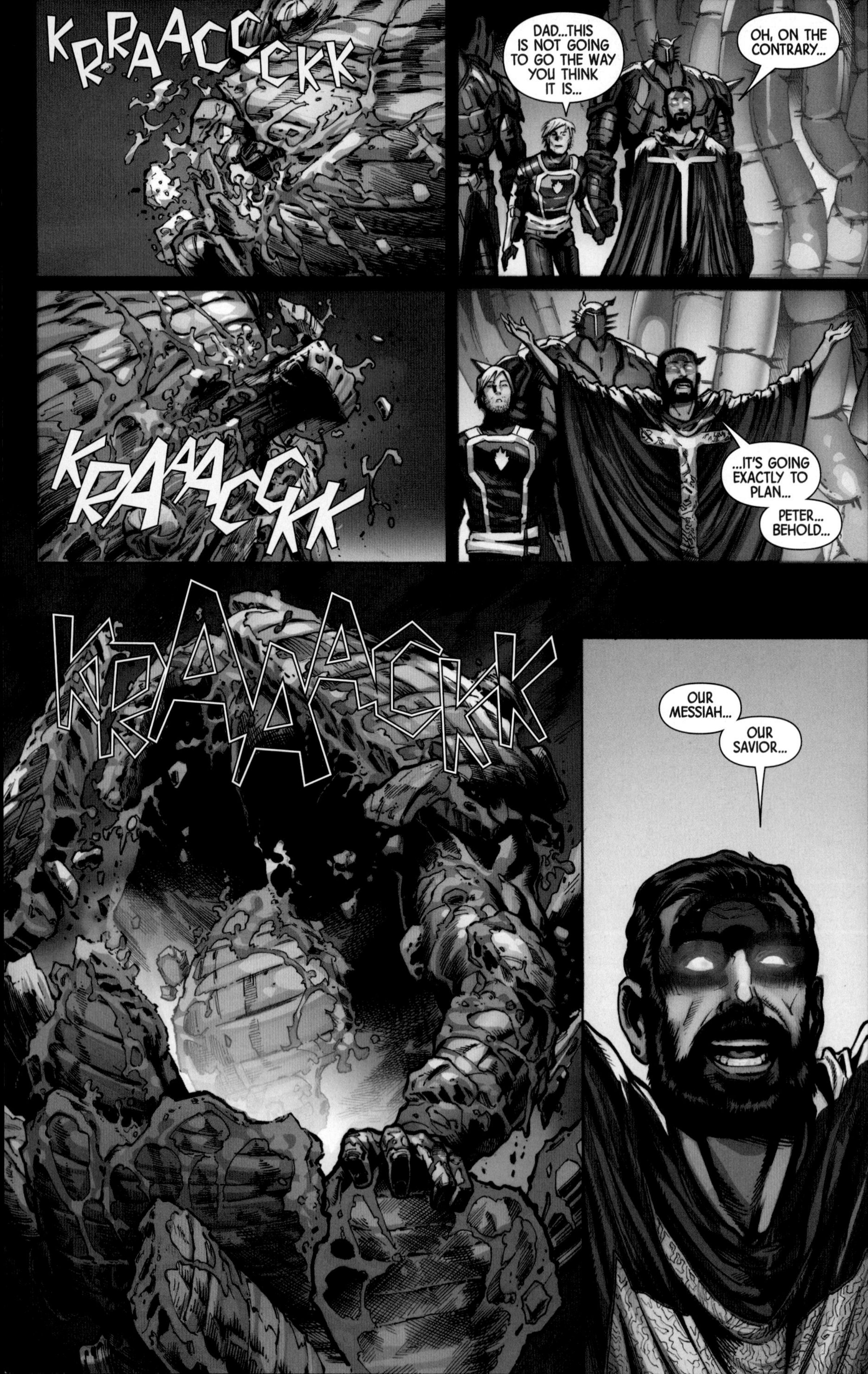
KRRAACCCKK
DAD...THIS IS NOT GOING TO GO THE WAY YOU THINK IT IS...
OH, ON THE CONTRARY...
KRAAAACCKK
...IT'S GOING EXACTLY TO PLAN...
PETER... BEHOLD...
KRAAAACKK
OUR MESSIAH...
OUR SAVIOR...

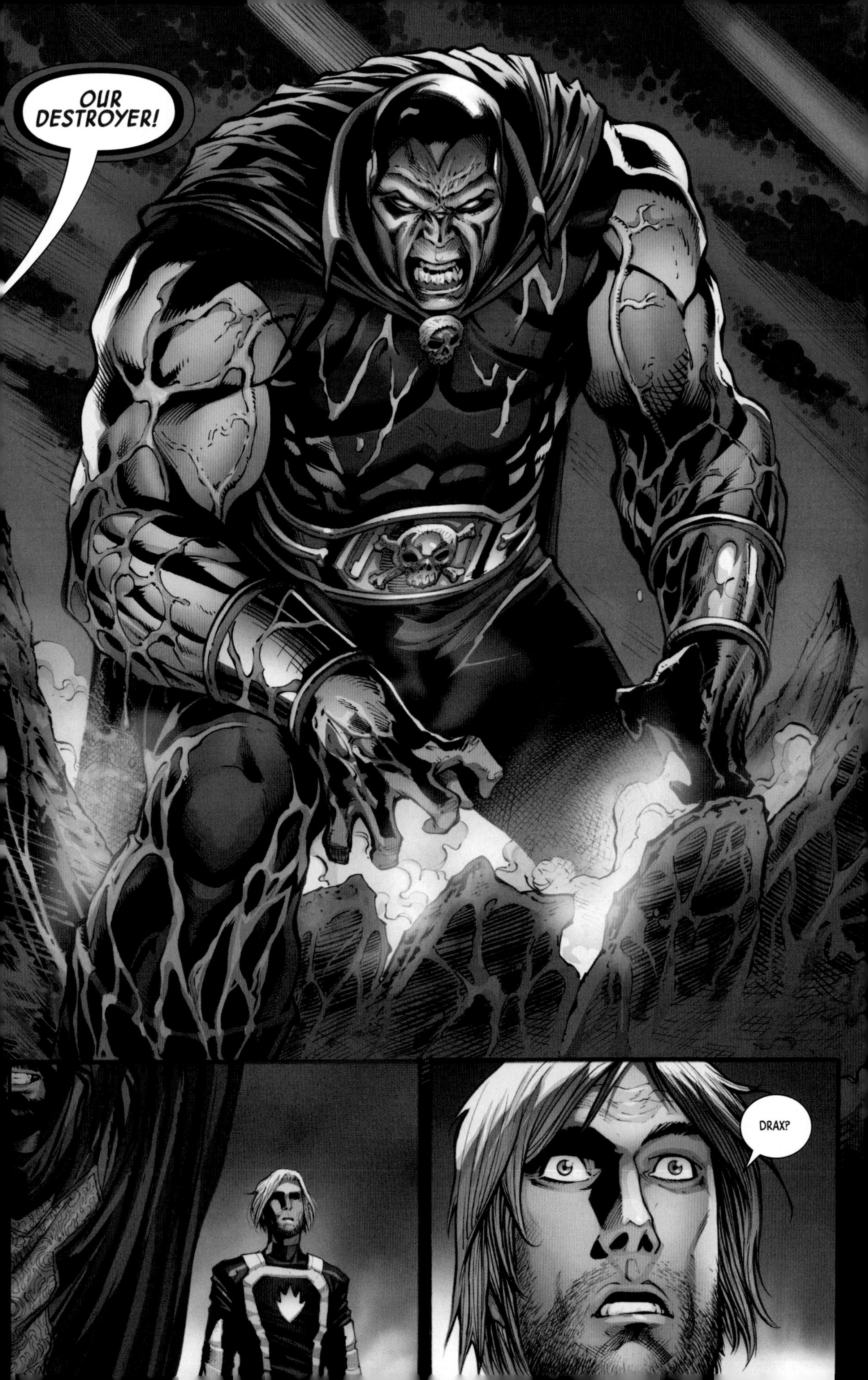
OUR DESTROYER!
DRAX?

TEN

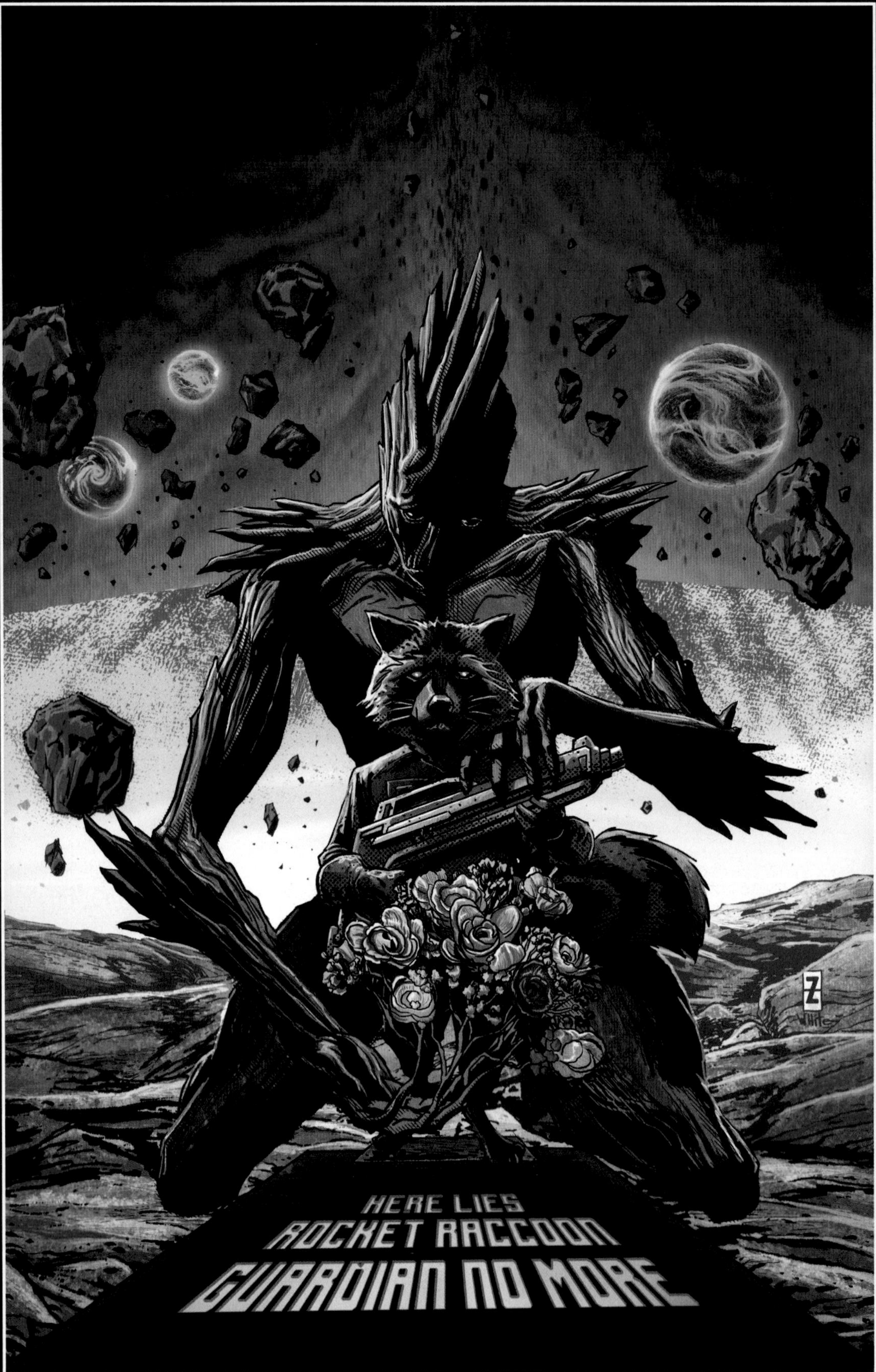
HERE LIES
ROCKET RACCOON
GUARDIAN NO MORE

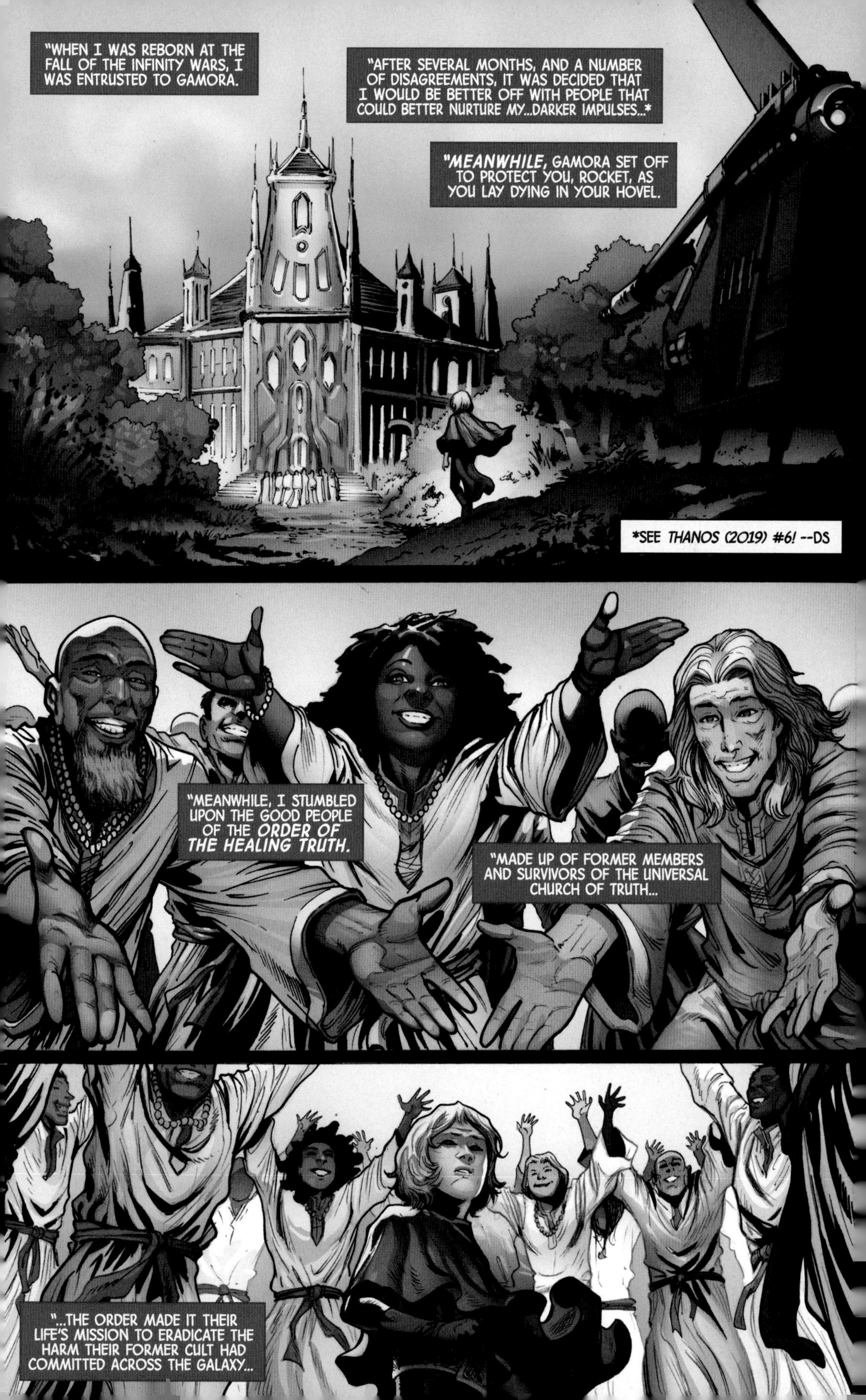
"WHEN I WAS REBORN AT THE FALL OF THE INFINITY WARS, I WAS ENTRUSTED TO GAMORA.
"AFTER SEVERAL MONTHS, AND A NUMBER OF DISAGREEMENTS, IT WAS DECIDED THAT I WOULD BE BETTER OFF WITH PEOPLE THAT COULD BETTER NURTURE MY...DARKER IMPULSES...*
"MEANWHILE, GAMORA SET OFF TO PROTECT YOU, ROCKET, AS YOU LAY DYING IN YOUR HOVEL.
*SEE THANOS (2019) #6! --DS
"MEANWHILE, I STUMBLED UPON THE GOOD PEOPLE OF THE ORDER OF THE HEALING TRUTH.
"MADE UP OF FORMER MEMBERS AND SURVIVORS OF THE UNIVERSAL CHURCH OF TRUTH...
"...THE ORDER MADE IT THEIR LIFE'S MISSION TO ERADICATE THE HARM THEIR FORMER CULT HAD COMMITTED ACROSS THE GALAXY...

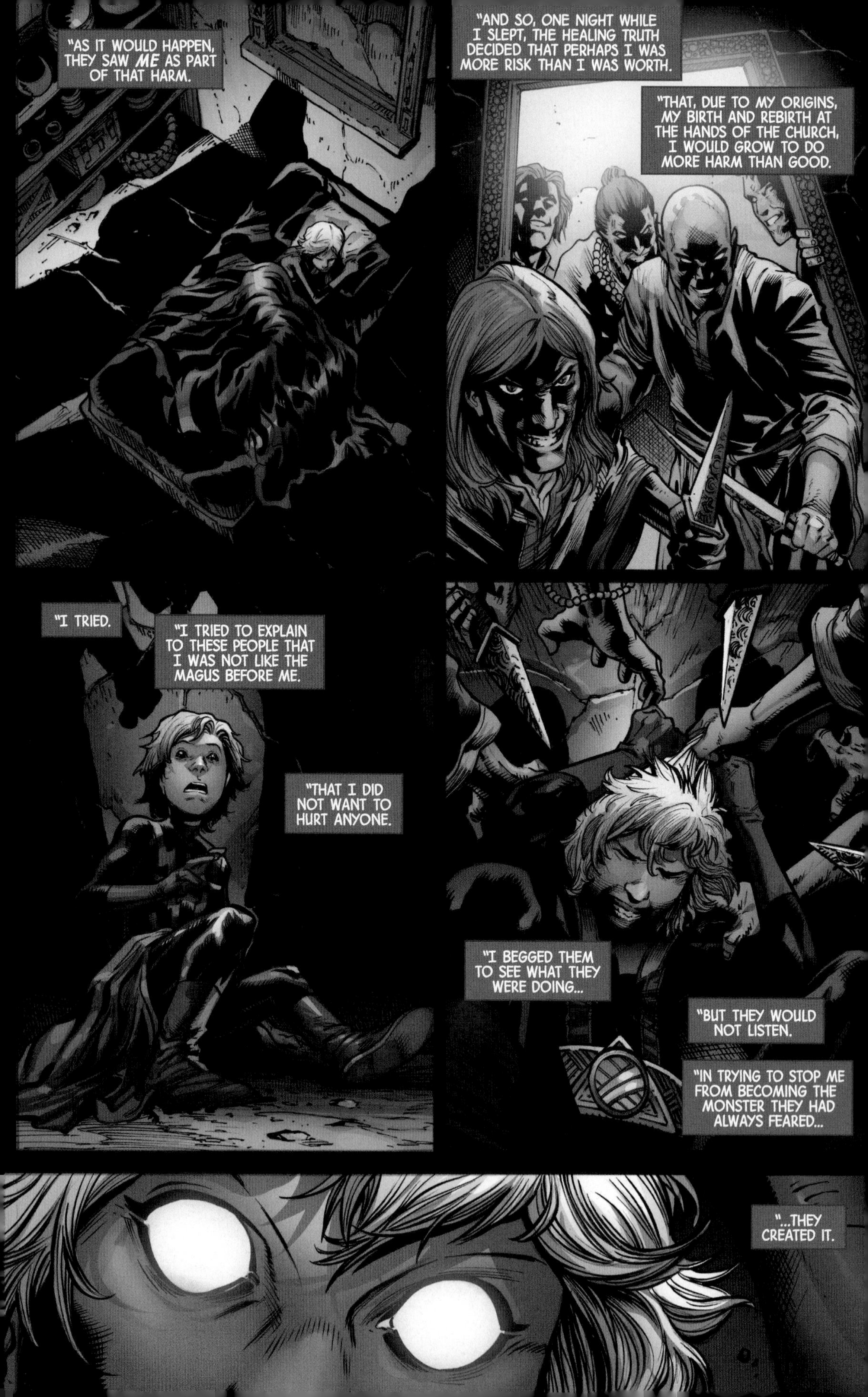
"AS IT WOULD HAPPEN, THEY SAW *ME* AS PART OF THAT HARM.
"AND SO, ONE NIGHT WHILE I SLEPT, THE HEALING TRUTH DECIDED THAT PERHAPS I WAS MORE RISK THAN I WAS WORTH.
"THAT, DUE TO MY ORIGINS, MY BIRTH AND REBIRTH AT THE HANDS OF THE CHURCH, I WOULD GROW TO DO MORE HARM THAN GOOD.
"I TRIED.
"I TRIED TO EXPLAIN TO THESE PEOPLE THAT I WAS NOT LIKE THE MAGUS BEFORE ME.
"THAT I DID NOT WANT TO HURT ANYONE.
"I BEGGED THEM TO SEE WHAT THEY WERE DOING...
"BUT THEY WOULD NOT LISTEN.
"IN TRYING TO STOP ME FROM BECOMING THE MONSTER THEY HAD ALWAYS FEARED...
"...THEY CREATED IT.

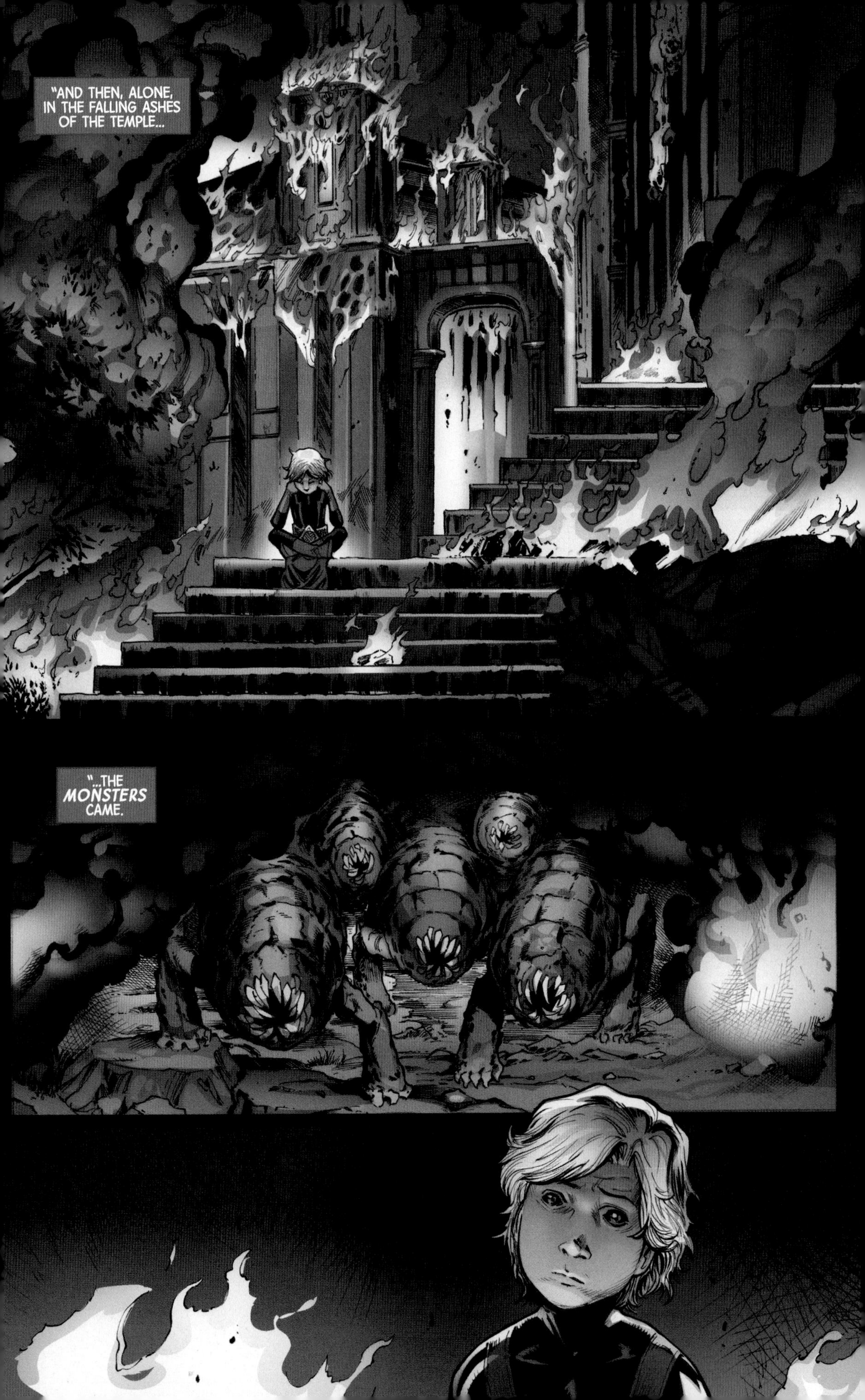
"AND THEN, ALONE, IN THE FALLING ASHES OF THE TEMPLE...
"...THE *MONSTERS* CAME.

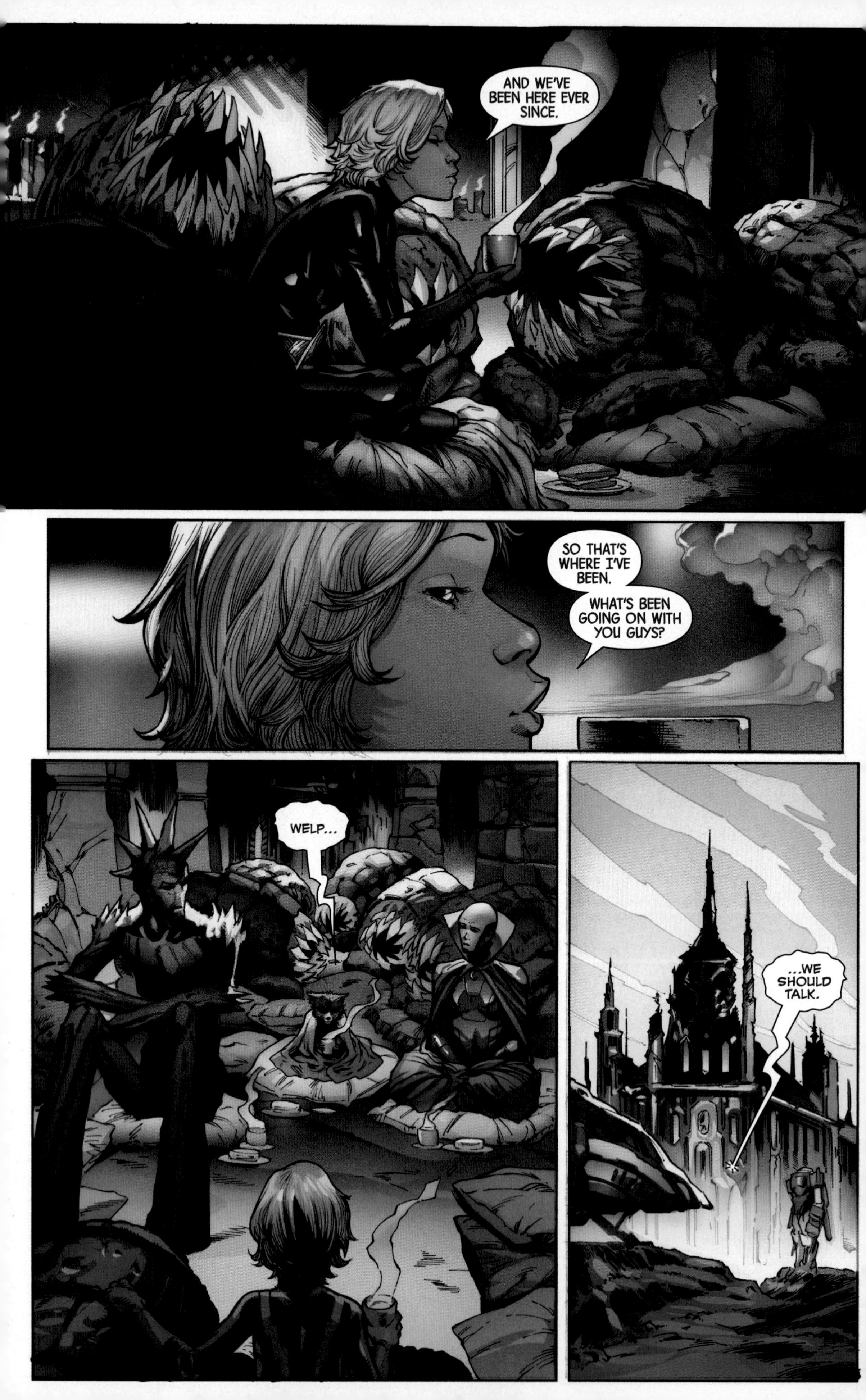
AND WE'VE BEEN HERE EVER SINCE.
SO THAT'S WHERE I'VE BEEN.
WHAT'S BEEN GOING ON WITH YOU GUYS?
WELP...
...WE SHOULD TALK.

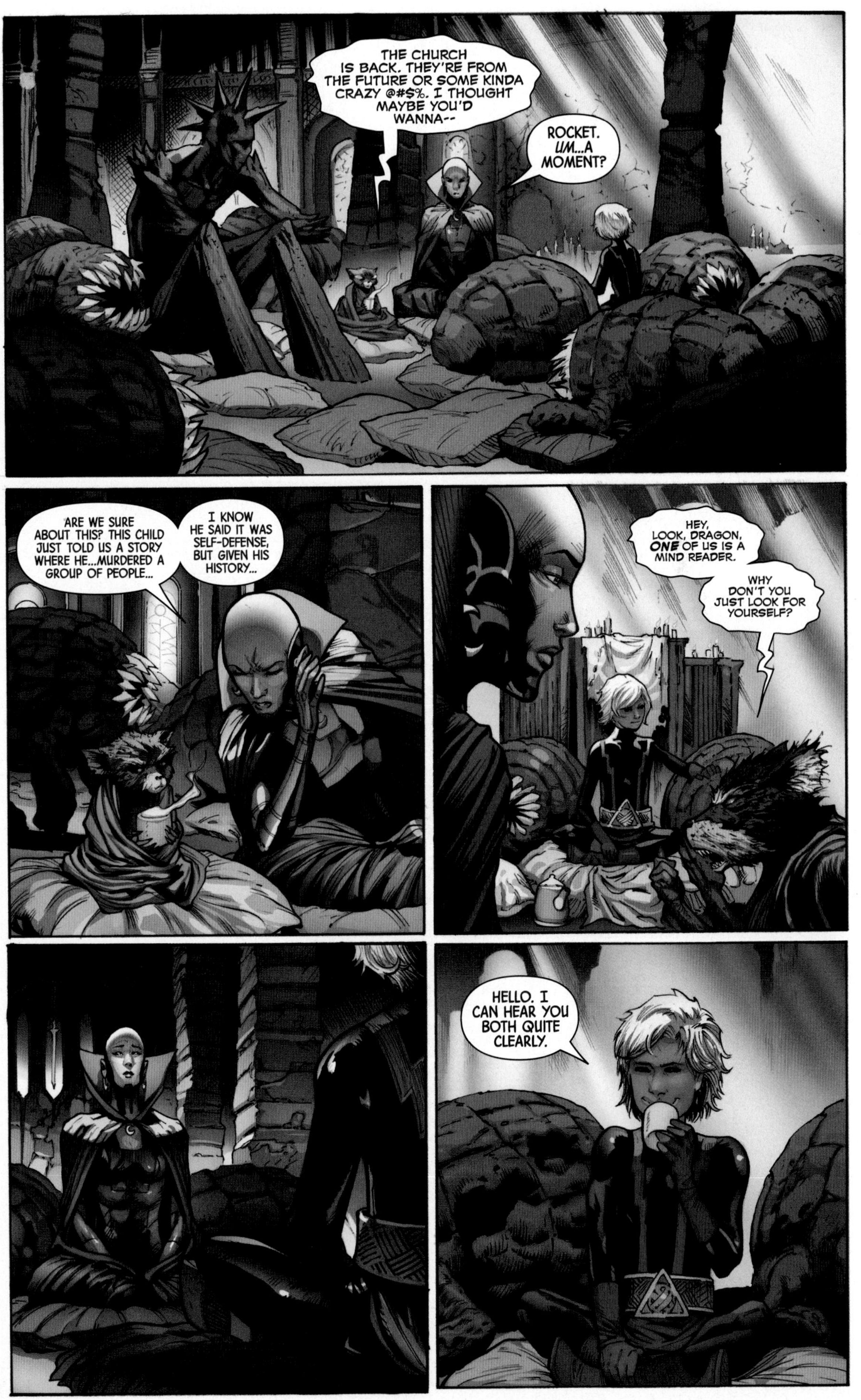
THE CHURCH IS BACK. THEY'RE FROM THE FUTURE OR SOME KINDA CRAZY @#$%. I THOUGHT MAYBE YOU'D WANNA--
ROCKET. UM...A MOMENT?
ARE WE SURE ABOUT THIS? THIS CHILD JUST TOLD US A STORY WHERE HE...MURDERED A GROUP OF PEOPLE...
I KNOW HE SAID IT WAS SELF-DEFENSE, BUT GIVEN HIS HISTORY...
HEY, LOOK, DRAGON, ONE OF US IS A MIND READER.
WHY DON'T YOU JUST LOOK FOR YOURSELF?
HELLO. I CAN HEAR YOU BOTH QUITE CLEARLY.

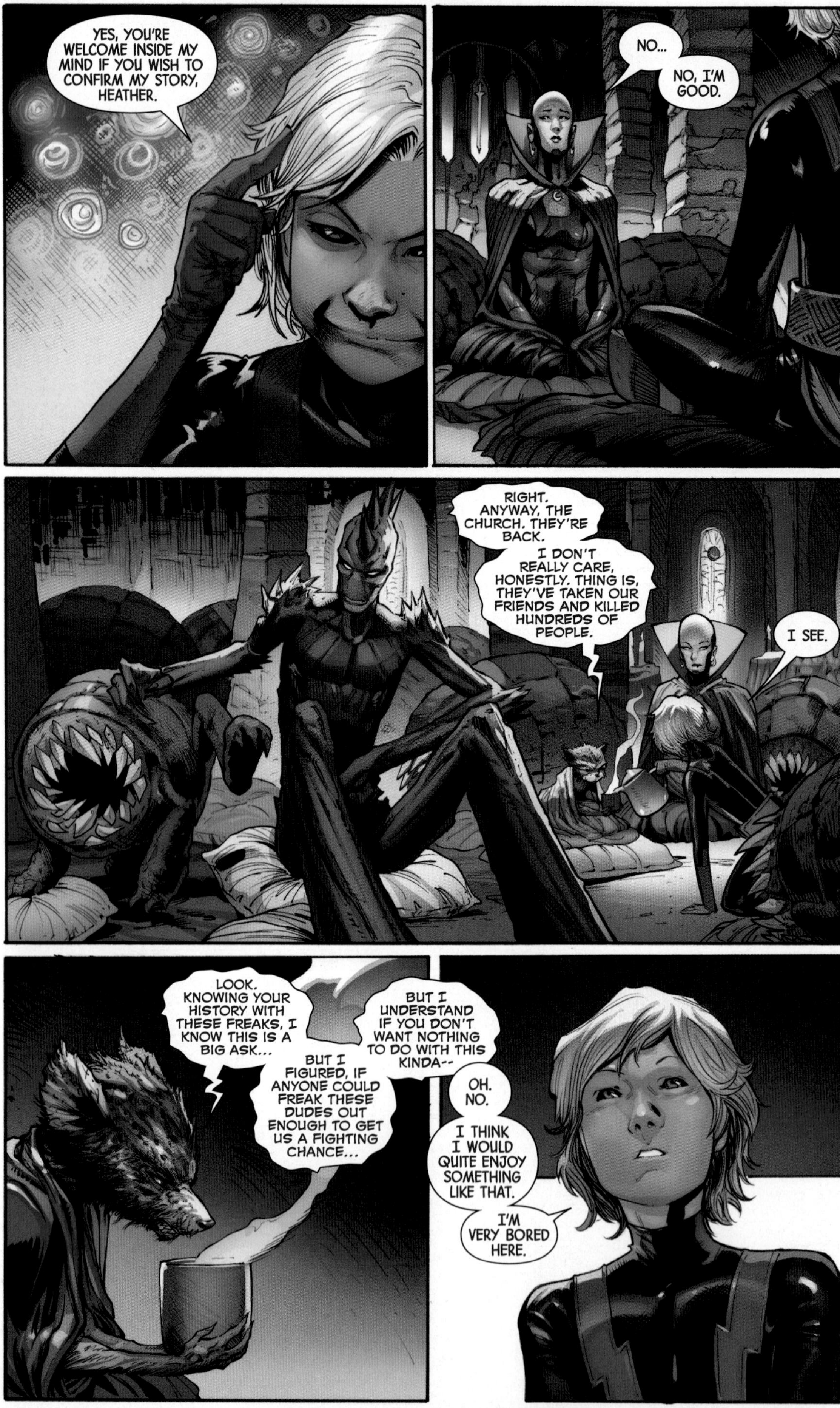
YES, YOU'RE WELCOME INSIDE MY MIND IF YOU WISH TO CONFIRM MY STORY, HEATHER.
NO...
NO, I'M GOOD.
RIGHT. ANYWAY, THE CHURCH. THEY'RE BACK.
I DON'T REALLY CARE, HONESTLY. THING IS, THEY'VE TAKEN OUR FRIENDS AND KILLED HUNDREDS OF PEOPLE.
I SEE.
LOOK. KNOWING YOUR HISTORY WITH THESE FREAKS, I KNOW THIS IS A BIG ASK...
BUT I FIGURED, IF ANYONE COULD FREAK THESE DUDES OUT ENOUGH TO GET US A FIGHTING CHANCE...
BUT I UNDERSTAND IF YOU DON'T WANT NOTHING TO DO WITH THIS KINDA--
OH. NO.
I THINK I WOULD QUITE ENJOY SOMETHING LIKE THAT.
I'M VERY BORED HERE.

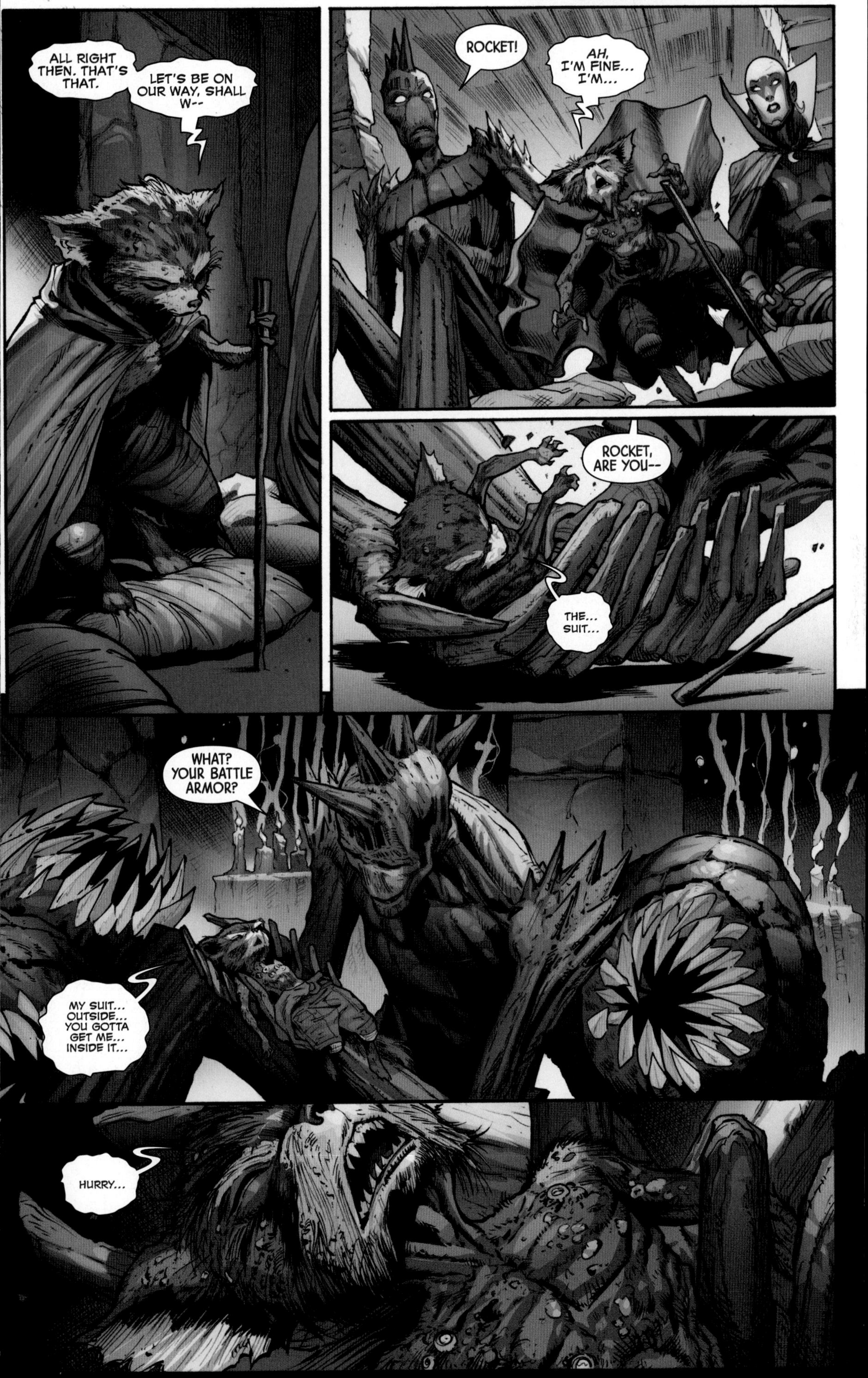
ALL RIGHT THEN. THAT'S THAT.
LET'S BE ON OUR WAY, SHALL W--
ROCKET!
AH, I'M FINE... I'M...
ROCKET, ARE YOU--
THE... SUIT...
WHAT? YOUR BATTLE ARMOR?
MY SUIT... OUTSIDE... YOU GOTTA GET ME... INSIDE IT...
HURRY...

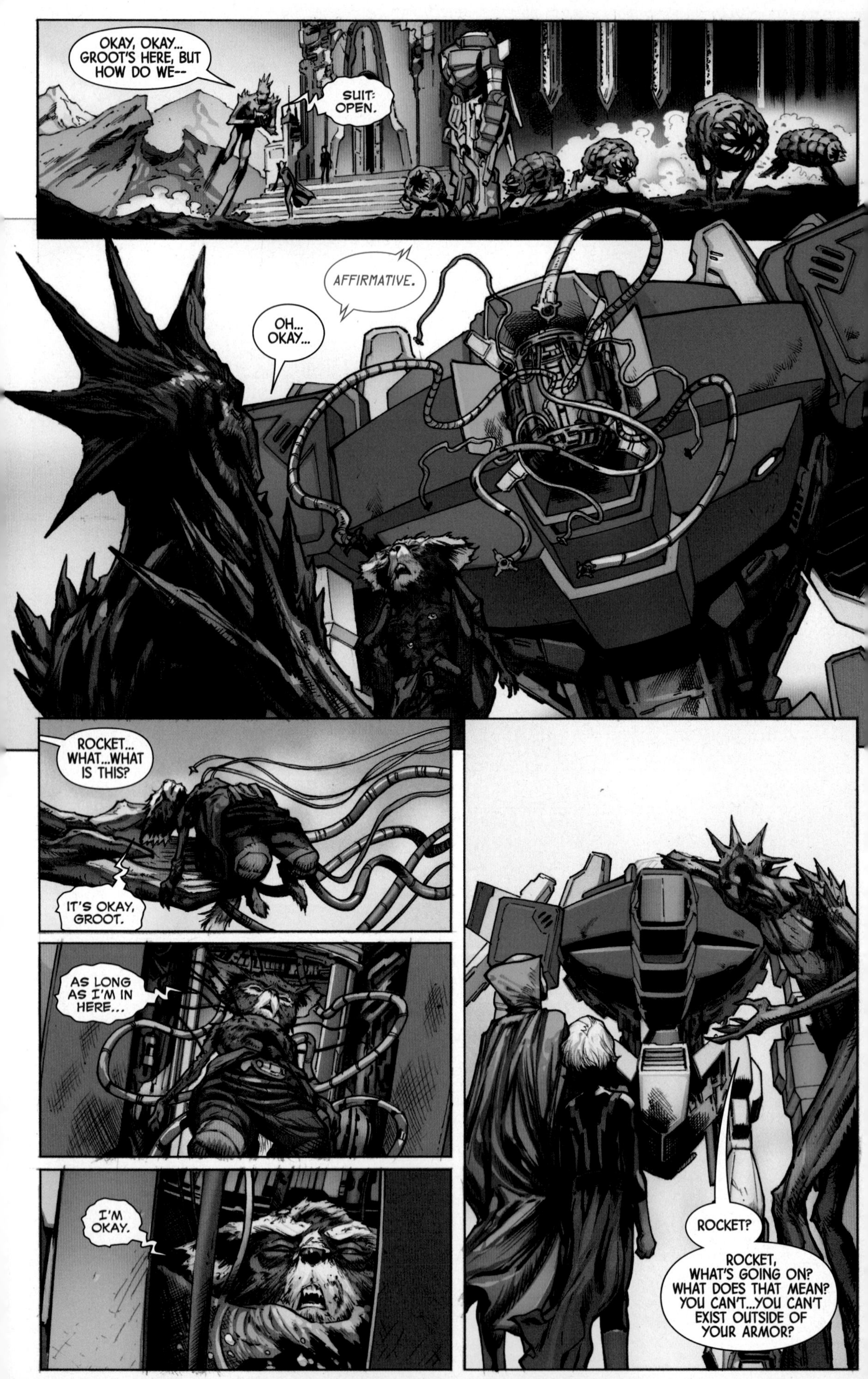
OKAY, OKAY... GROOT'S HERE, BUT HOW DO WE--
SUIT: OPEN.
AFFIRMATIVE.
OH... OKAY...
ROCKET... WHAT...WHAT IS THIS?
IT'S OKAY, GROOT.
AS LONG AS I'M IN HERE...
I'M OKAY.
ROCKET?
ROCKET, WHAT'S GOING ON? WHAT DOES THAT MEAN? YOU CAN'T...YOU CAN'T EXIST OUTSIDE OF YOUR ARMOR?

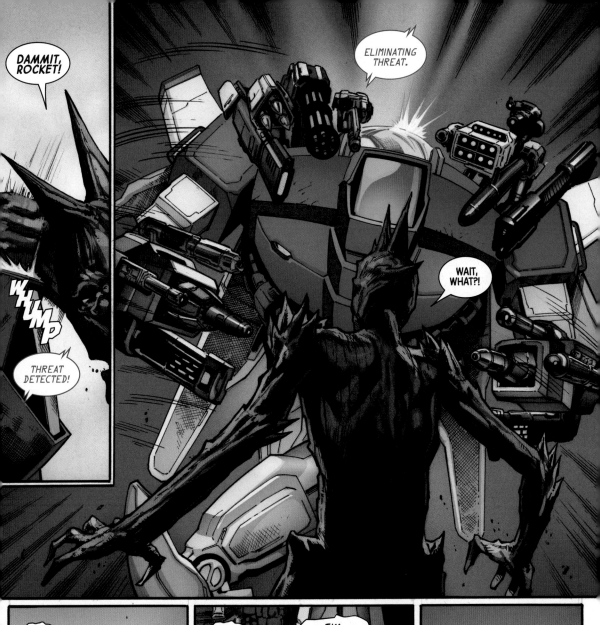

DAMMIT, ROCKET!

ELIMINATING THREAT.

WHUMP

THREAT DETECTED!

WAIT, WHAT?!

HEH. LOOK AT YOU, SHAKING LIKE A...

...WELL, YOU GET IT.

LET'S ROLL.

ROCKET... WAIT. ARE YOU--

I'M FINE, GROOT. NOW HURRY UP. WE GOT A BUNCH OF IDIOTS TO SAVE FROM A DUMB CULT.

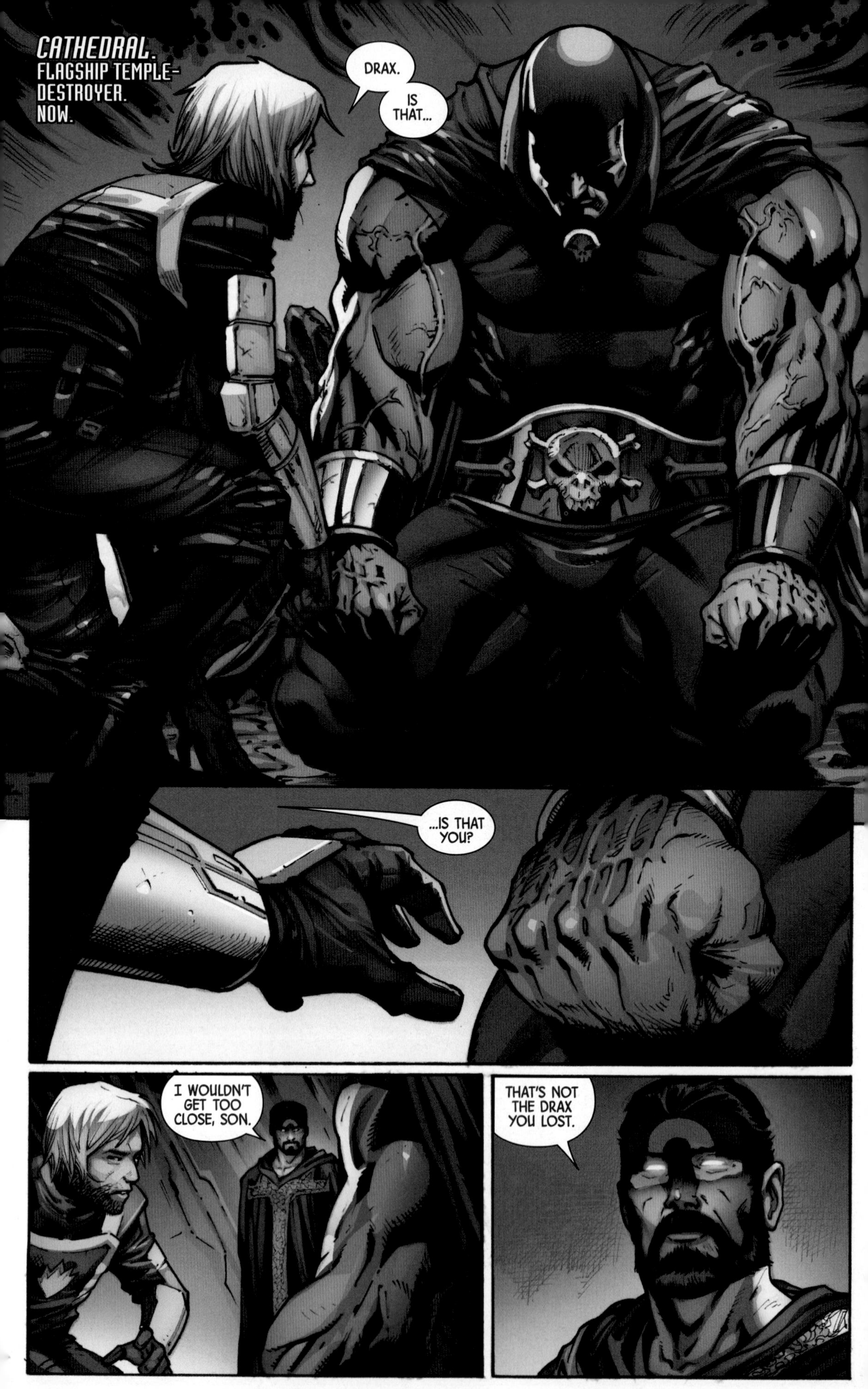
CATHEDRAL.
FLAGSHIP TEMPLE-DESTROYER.
NOW.
DRAX.
IS THAT...
...IS THAT YOU?
I WOULDN'T GET TOO CLOSE, SON.
THAT'S NOT THE DRAX YOU LOST.

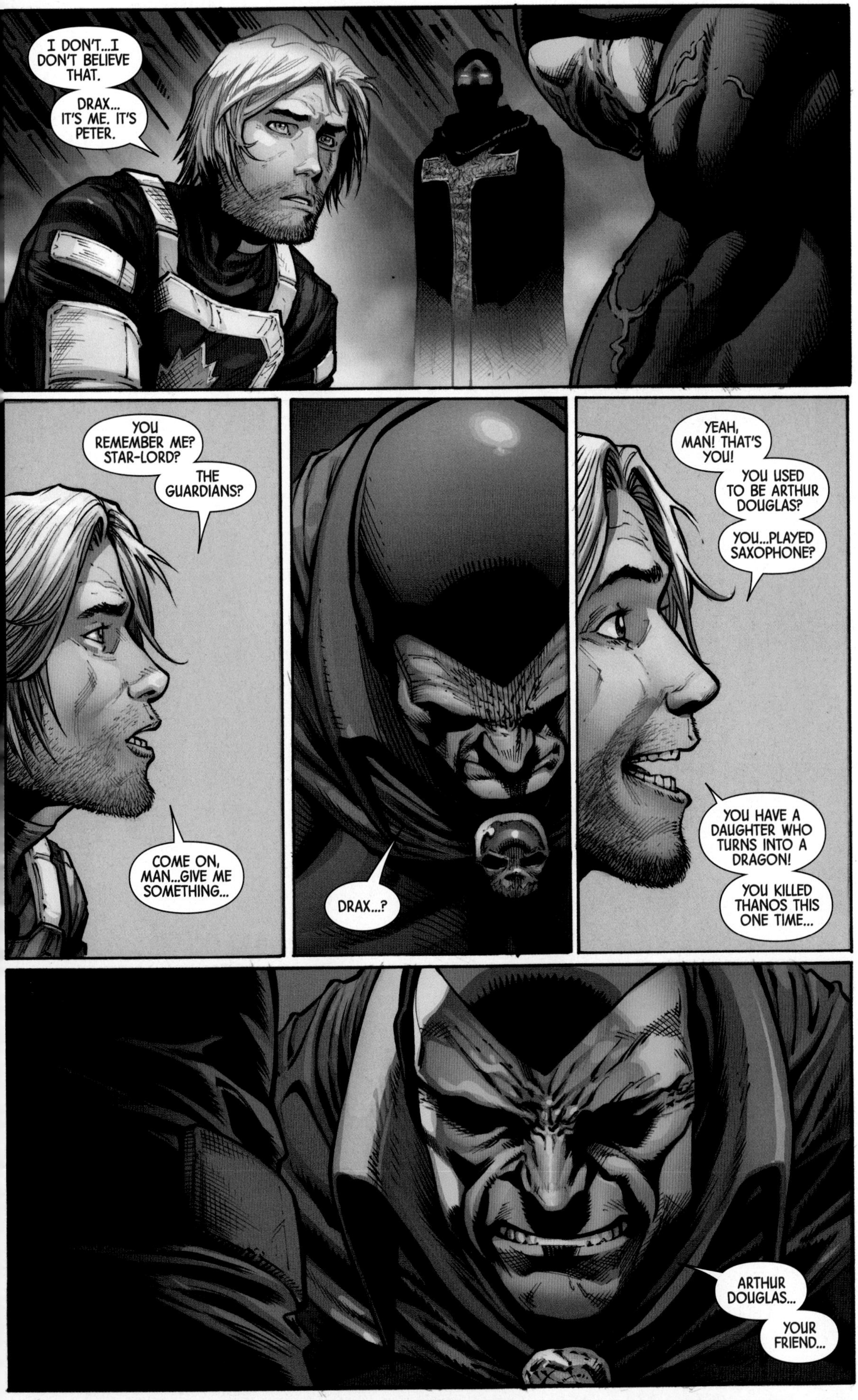
I DON'T...I DON'T BELIEVE THAT.
DRAX... IT'S ME. IT'S PETER.
YOU REMEMBER ME? STAR-LORD?
THE GUARDIANS?
COME ON, MAN...GIVE ME SOMETHING...
DRAX...?
YEAH, MAN! THAT'S YOU!
YOU USED TO BE ARTHUR DOUGLAS?
YOU...PLAYED SAXOPHONE?
YOU HAVE A DAUGHTER WHO TURNS INTO A DRAGON!
YOU KILLED THANOS THIS ONE TIME...
ARTHUR DOUGLAS...
YOUR FRIEND...

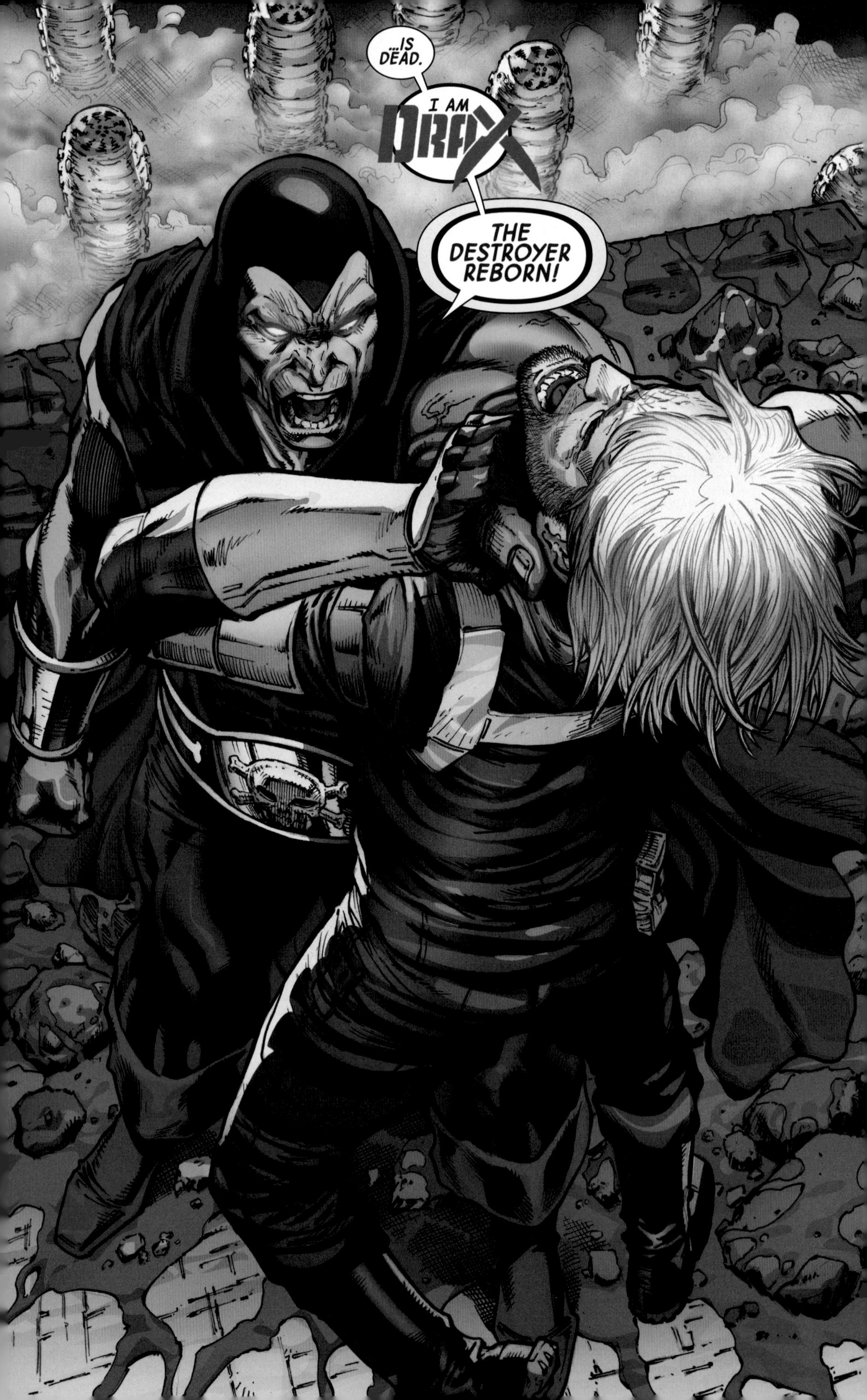
...IS DEAD.
I AM DRAX
THE DESTROYER REBORN!

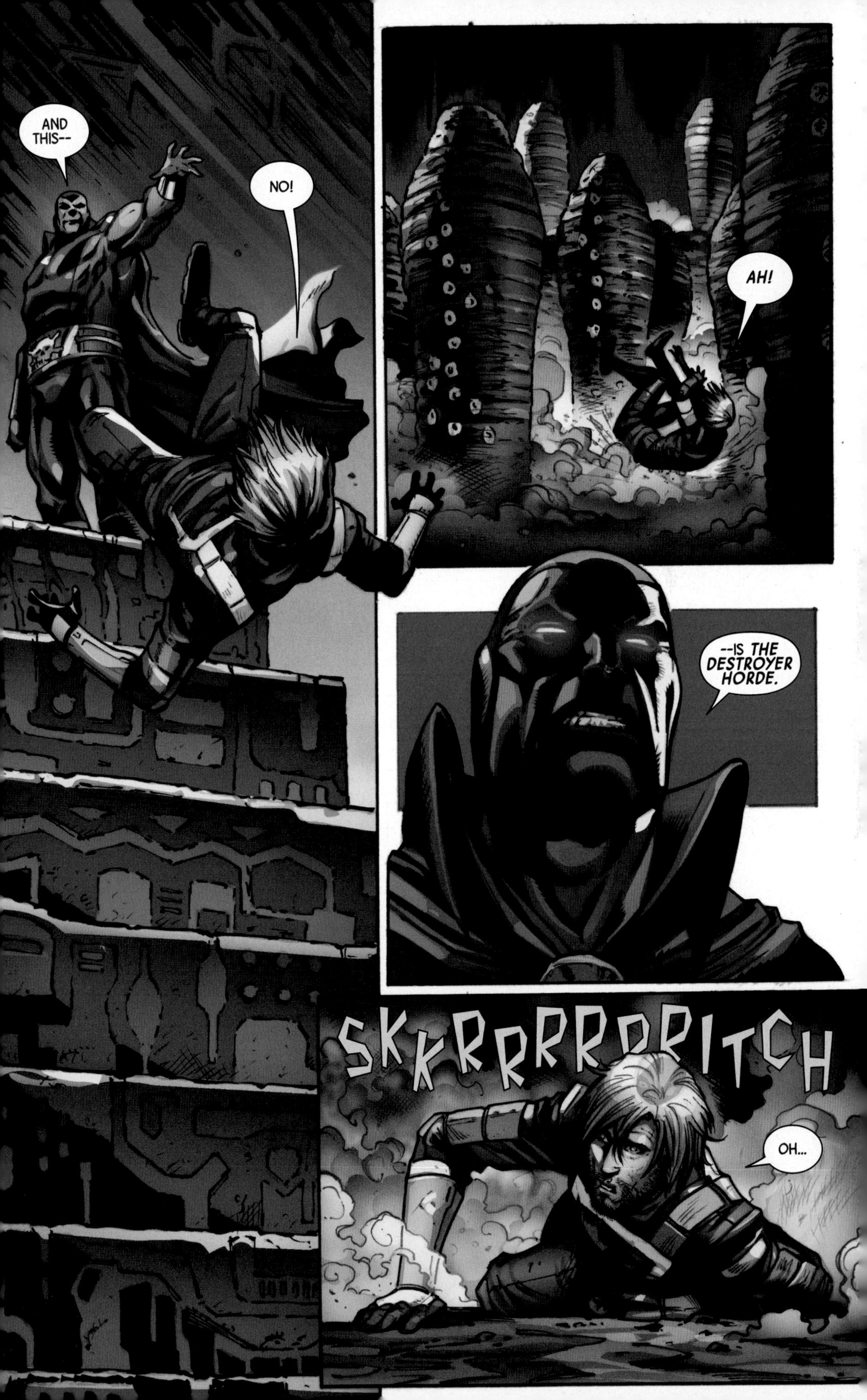
AND THIS--
NO!
AH!
--IS THE DESTROYER HORDE.
SKKRRRRRRITCH
OH...

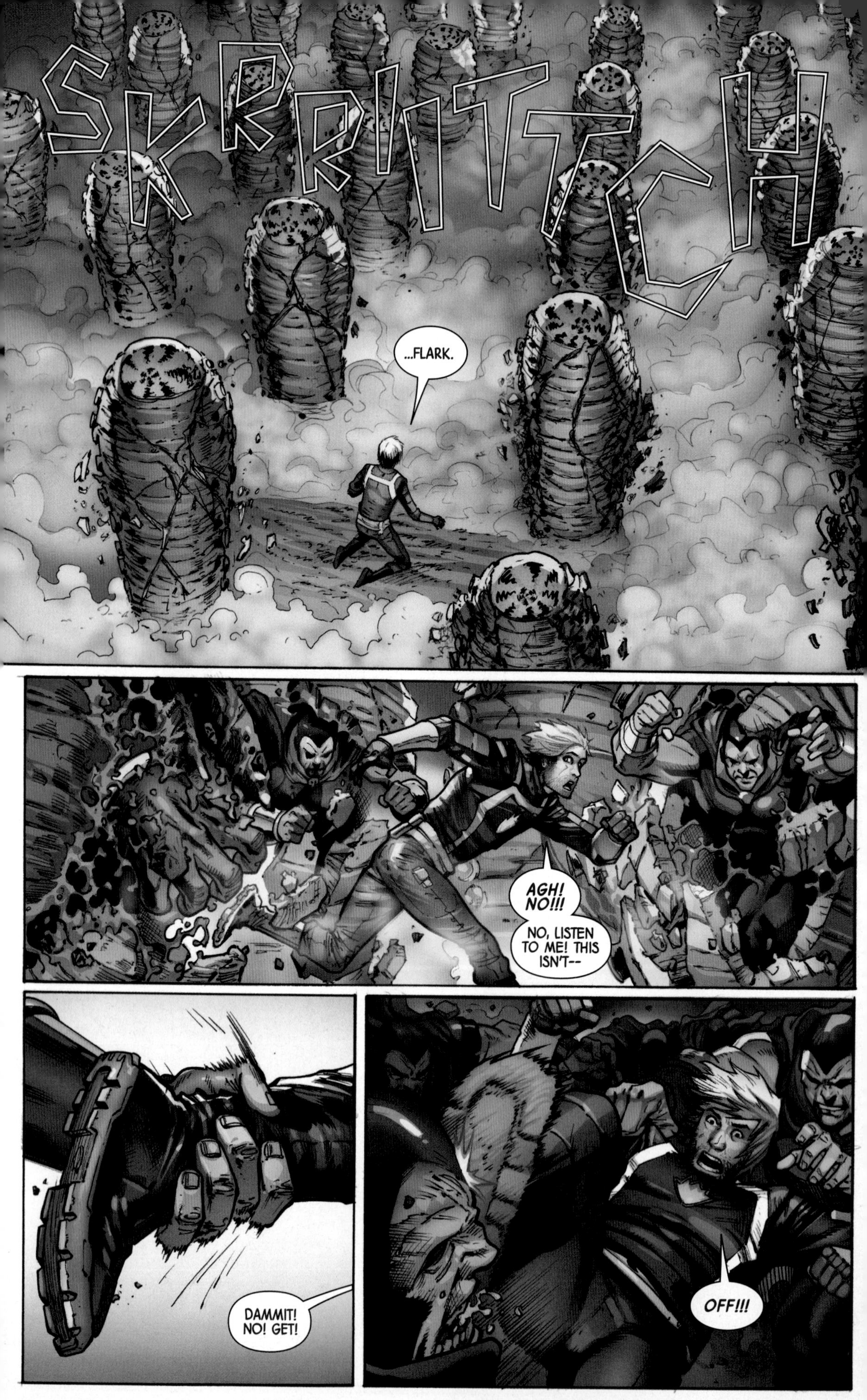
SKRRITTCH
...FLARK.
AGH! NO!!!
NO, LISTEN TO ME! THIS ISN'T--
DAMMIT! NO! GET!
OFF!!!

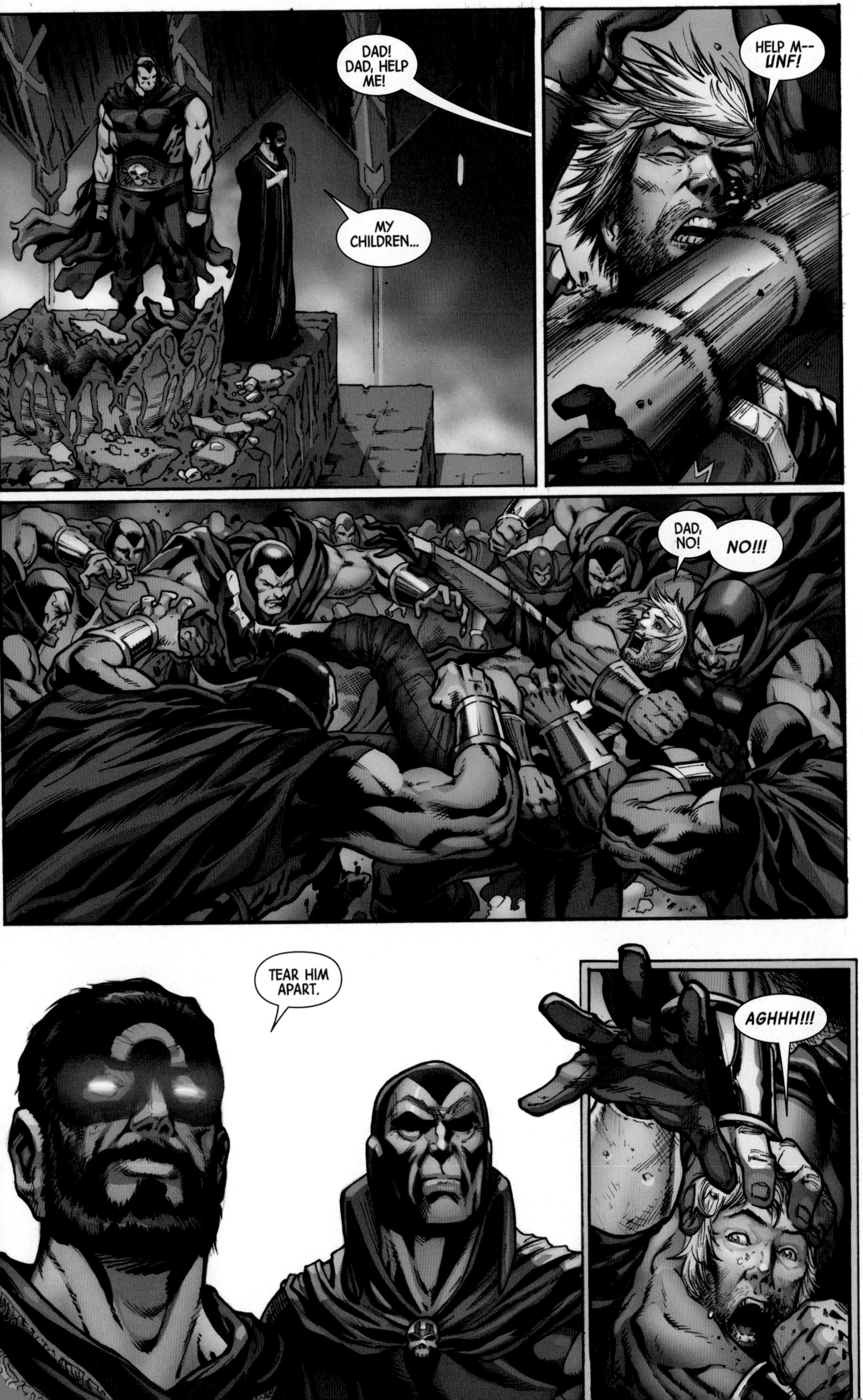
DAD! DAD, HELP ME!
MY CHILDREN...
HELP M-- UNF!
DAD, NO!
NO!!!
TEAR HIM APART.
AGHHH!!!

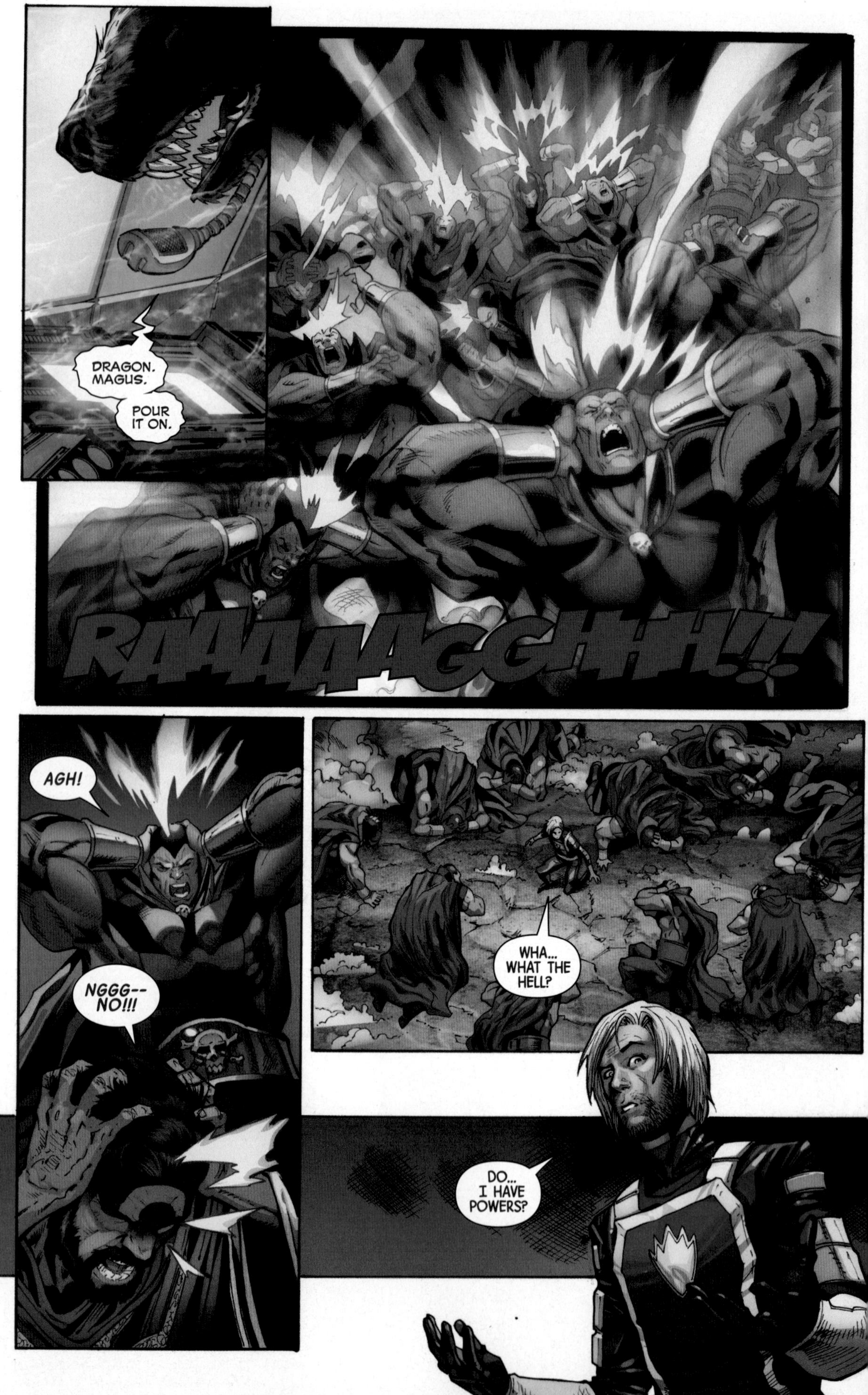
DRAGON. MAGUS.
POUR IT ON.
RAAAAAGGHHH!!!
AGH!
NGGG-- NO!!!
WHA... WHAT THE HELL?
DO... I HAVE POWERS?

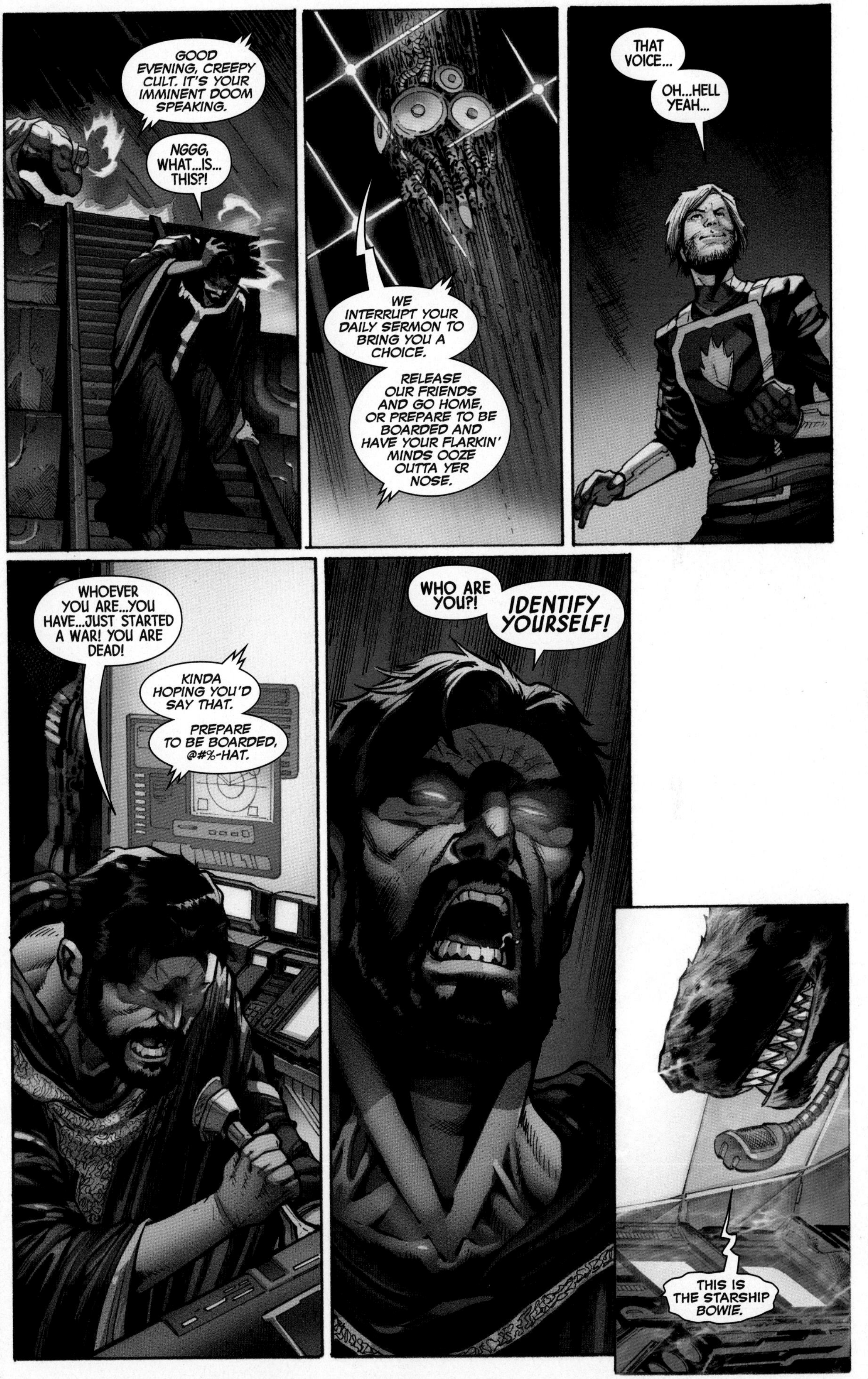
GOOD EVENING, CREEPY CULT. IT'S YOUR IMMINENT DOOM SPEAKING.
NGGG, WHAT...IS... THIS?!
WE INTERRUPT YOUR DAILY SERMON TO BRING YOU A CHOICE.
RELEASE OUR FRIENDS AND GO HOME, OR PREPARE TO BE BOARDED AND HAVE YOUR FLARKIN' MINDS OOZE OUTTA YER NOSE.
THAT VOICE...
OH...HELL YEAH...
WHOEVER YOU ARE...YOU HAVE...JUST STARTED A WAR! YOU ARE DEAD!
KINDA HOPING YOU'D SAY THAT.
PREPARE TO BE BOARDED, @#%-HAT.
WHO ARE YOU?!
IDENTIFY YOURSELF!
THIS IS THE STARSHIP BOWIE.

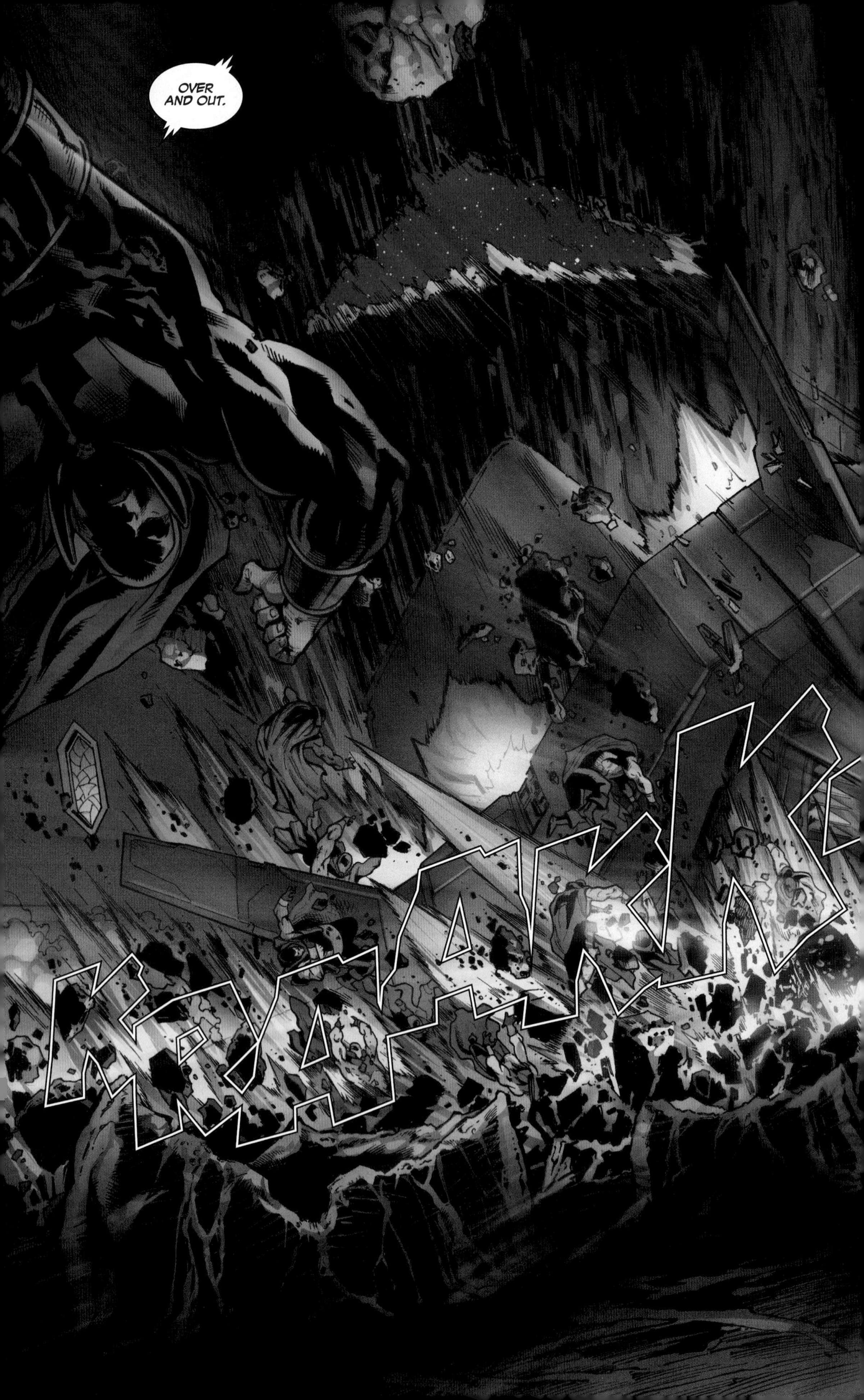
OVER AND OUT.

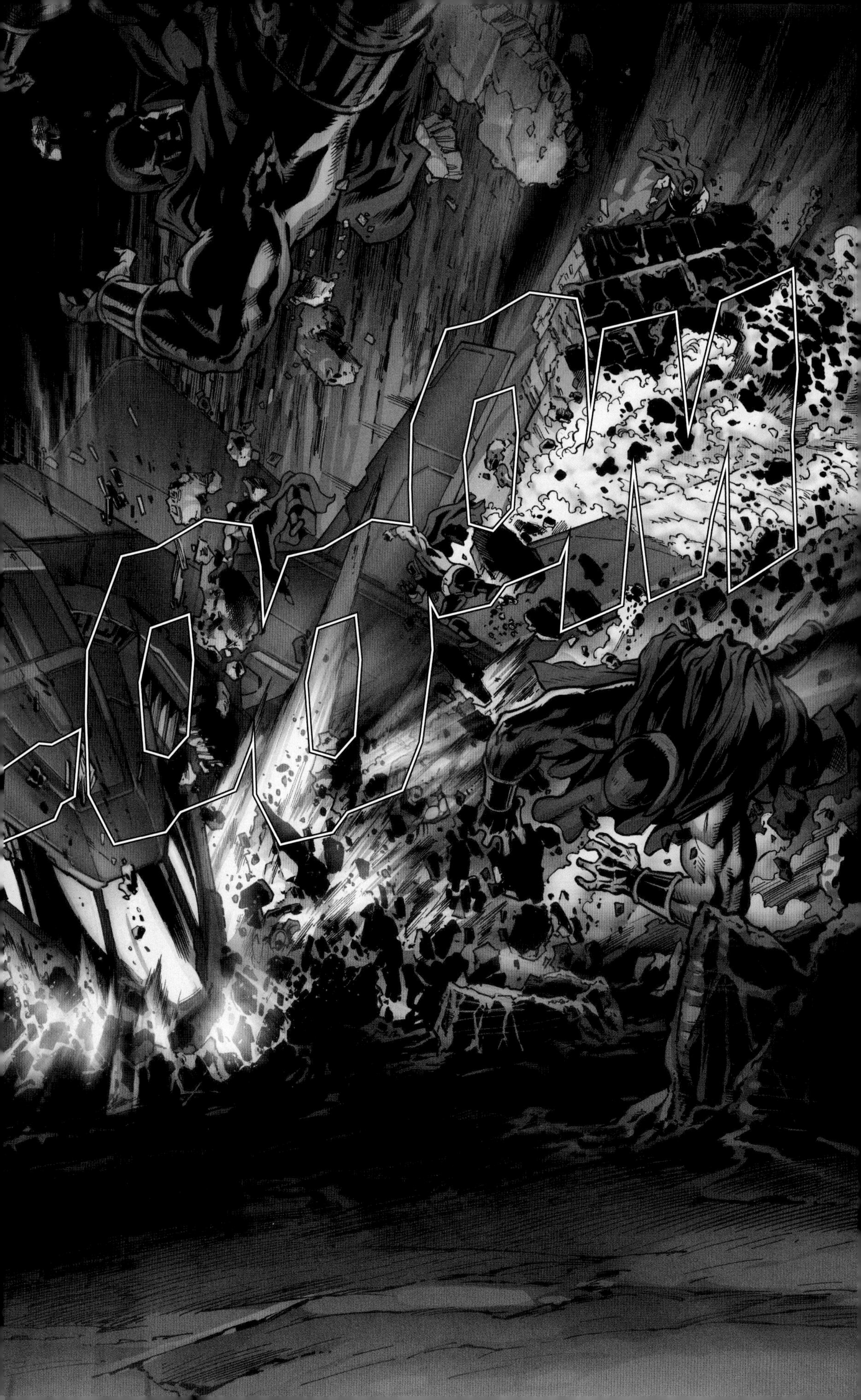
OOOM

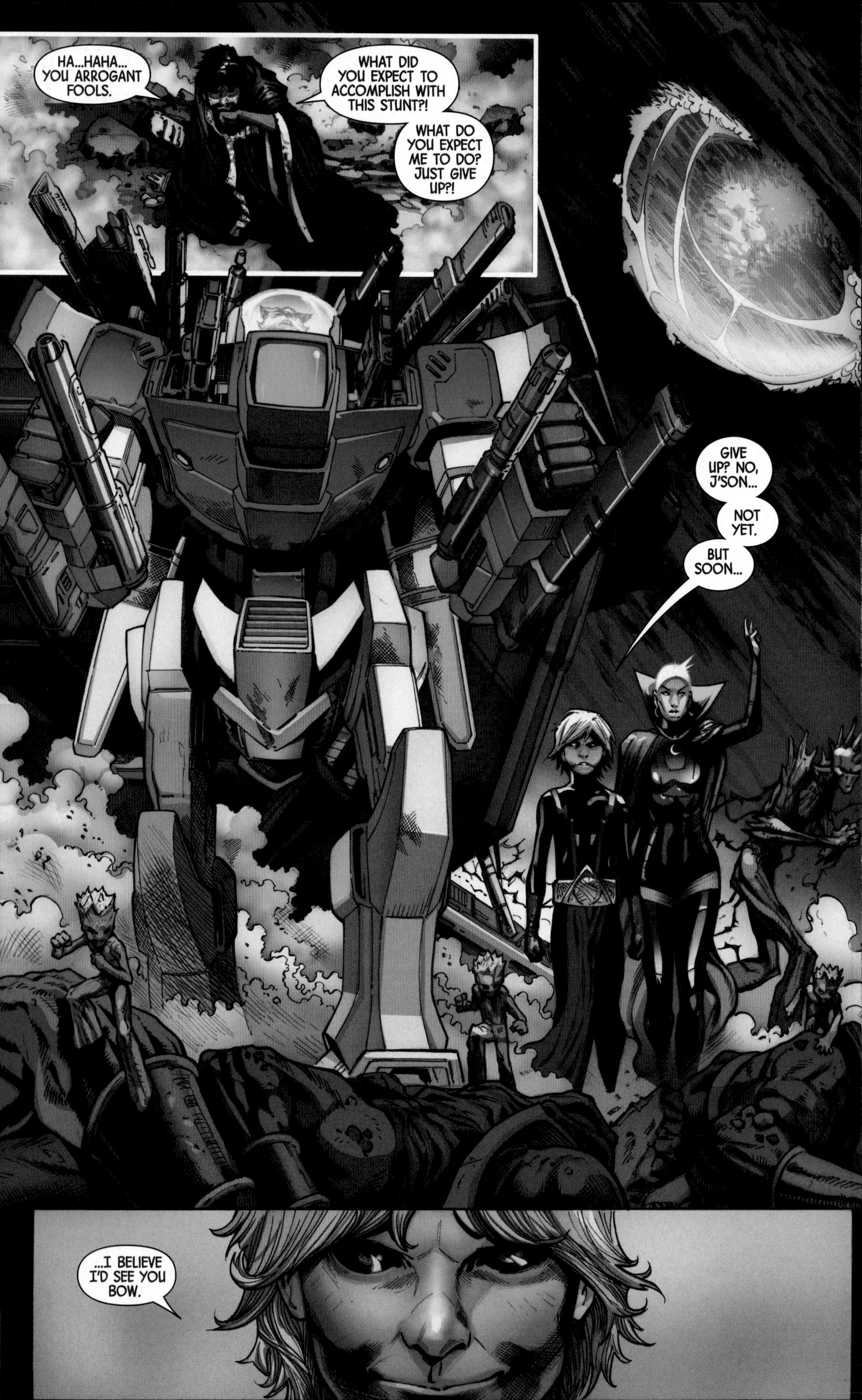
HA...HAHA... YOU ARROGANT FOOLS.
WHAT DID YOU EXPECT TO ACCOMPLISH WITH THIS STUNT?!
WHAT DO YOU EXPECT ME TO DO? JUST GIVE UP?!
GIVE UP? NO, J'SON...
NOT YET.
BUT SOON...
...I BELIEVE I'D SEE YOU BOW.

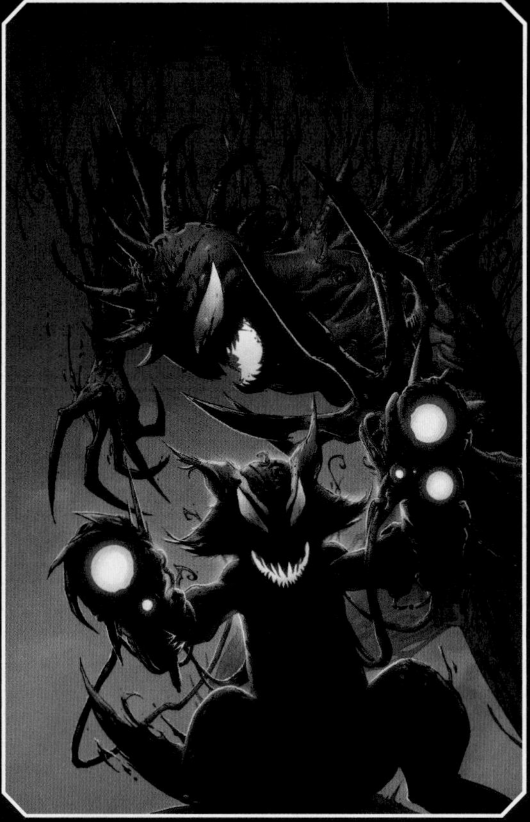

GIUSEPPE CAMUNCOLI &
JEAN-FRANÇOIS BEAULIEU
#7 Carnage-ized variant

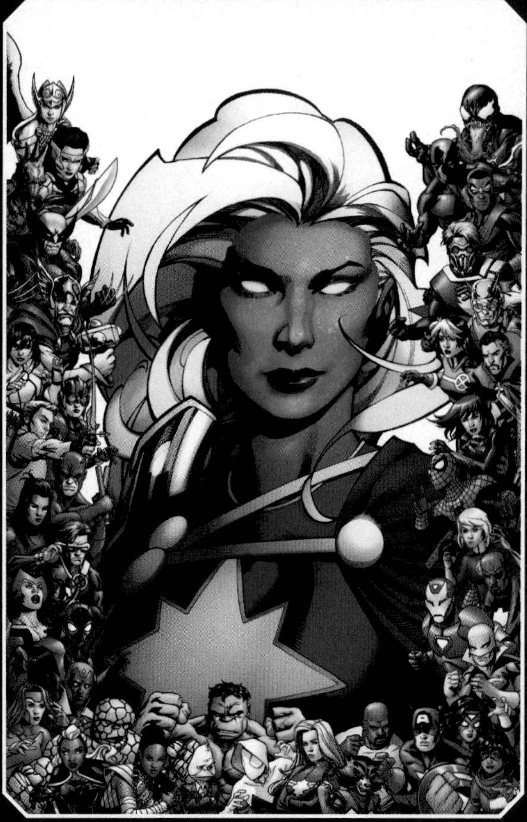

CHRIS STEVENS & JASON KEITH
WITH MIKE McKONE & EDGAR DELGADO
#8 80th Anniversary Frame variant

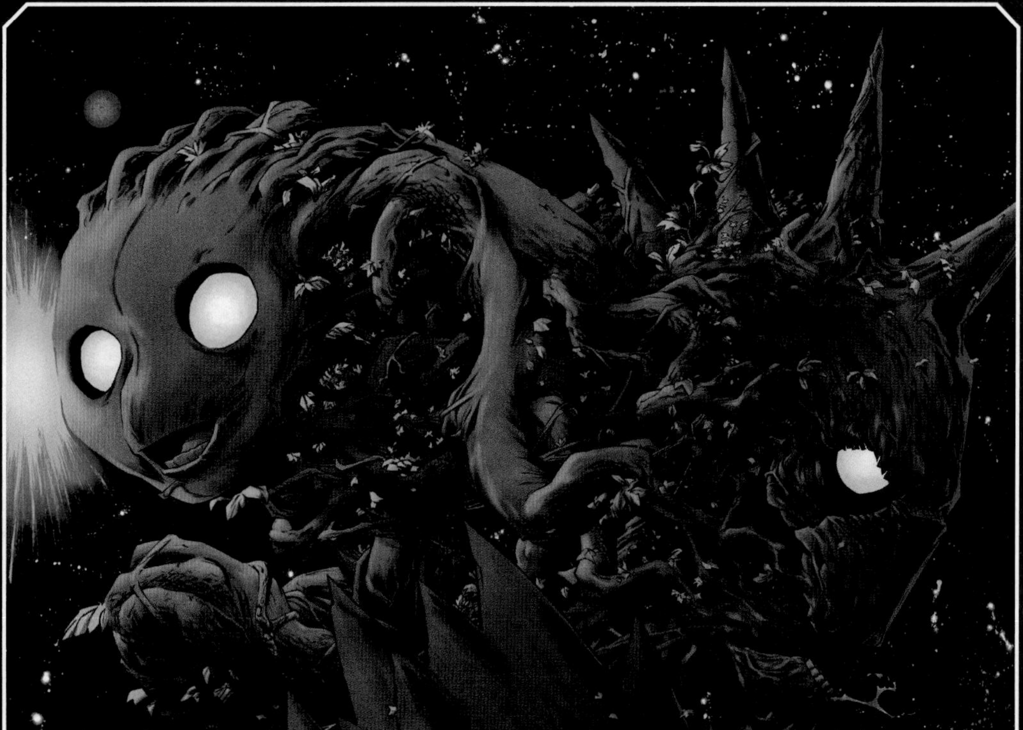

DECLAN SHALVEY
#9 Immortal variant

ELEVEN

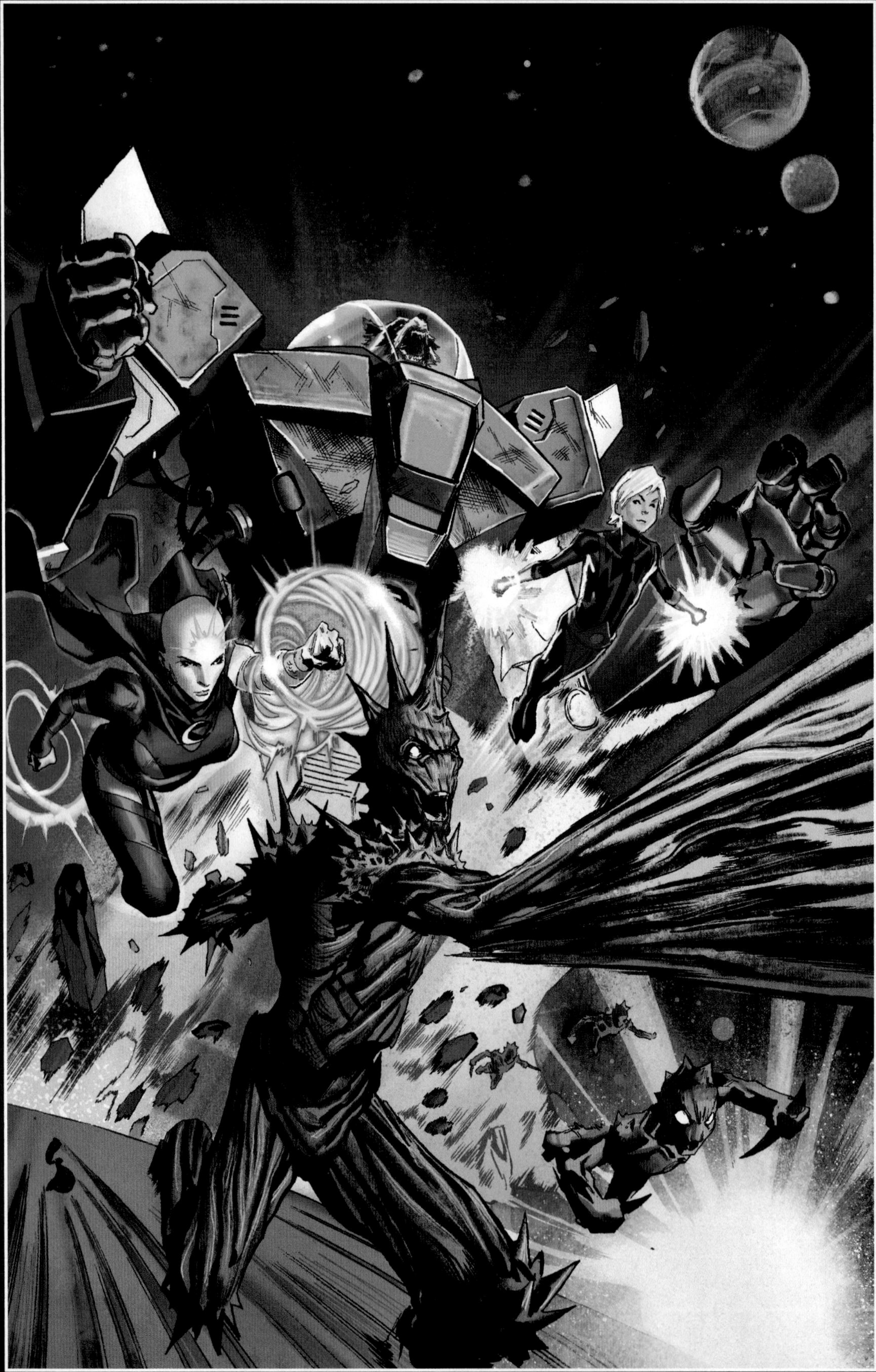

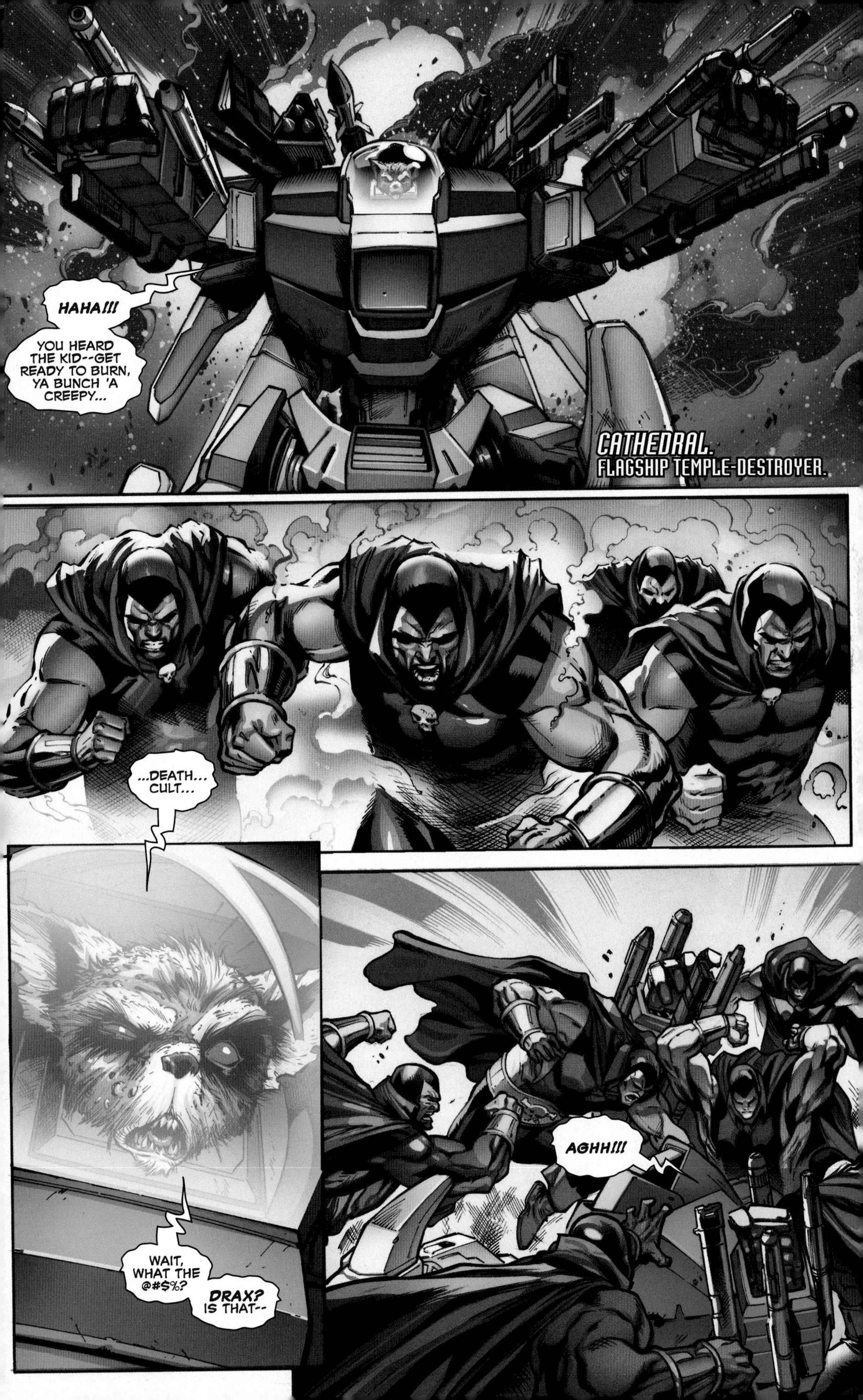
HAHA!!!
YOU HEARD THE KID--GET READY TO BURN, YA BUNCH 'A CREEPY...
CATHEDRAL.
FLAGSHIP TEMPLE-DESTROYER.
...DEATH... CULT...
AGHH!!!
WAIT, WHAT THE @#$%?
DRAX? IS THAT--

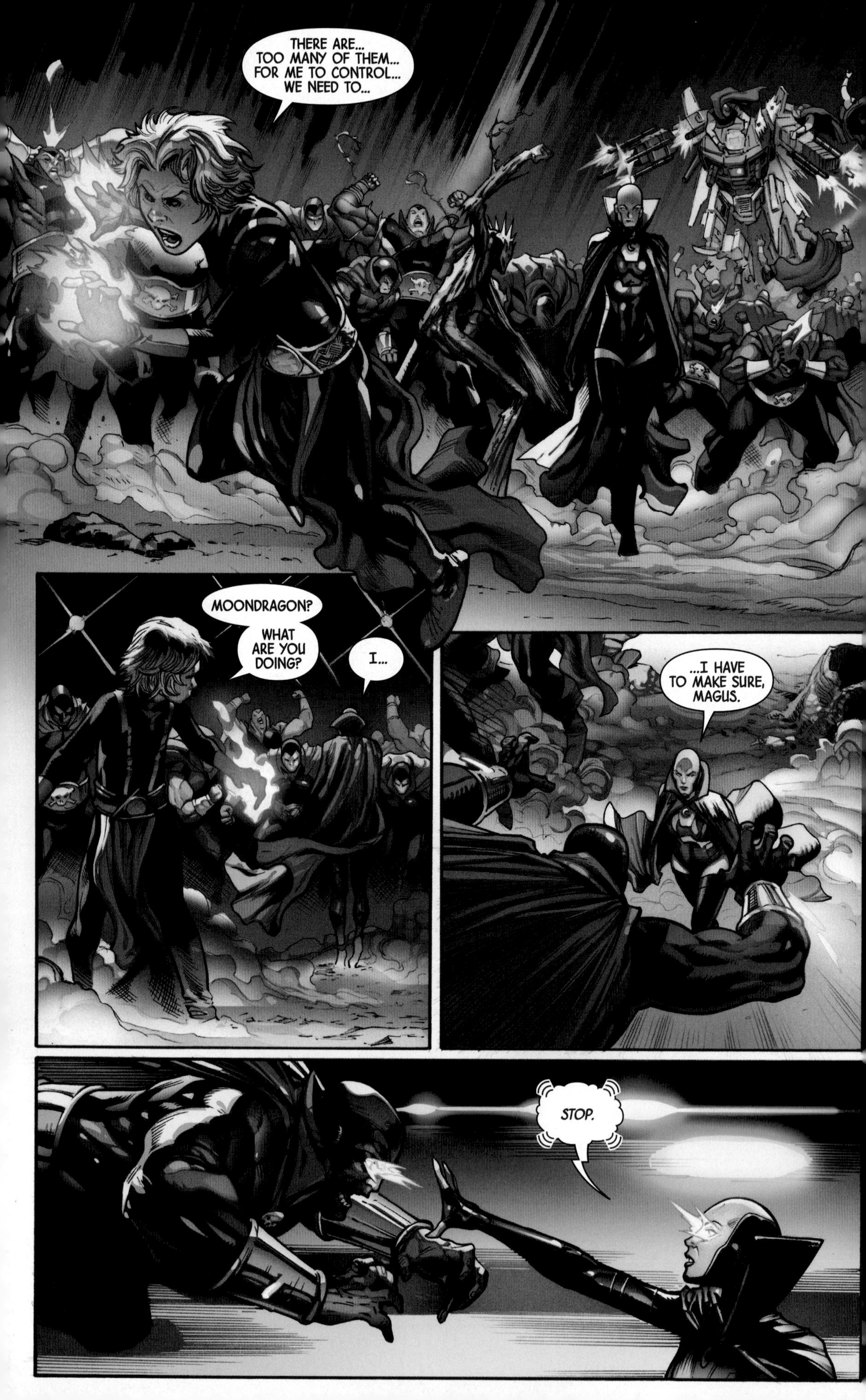
THERE ARE... TOO MANY OF THEM... FOR ME TO CONTROL... WE NEED TO...
MOONDRAGON? WHAT ARE YOU DOING?
I...
...I HAVE TO MAKE SURE, MAGUS.
STOP.

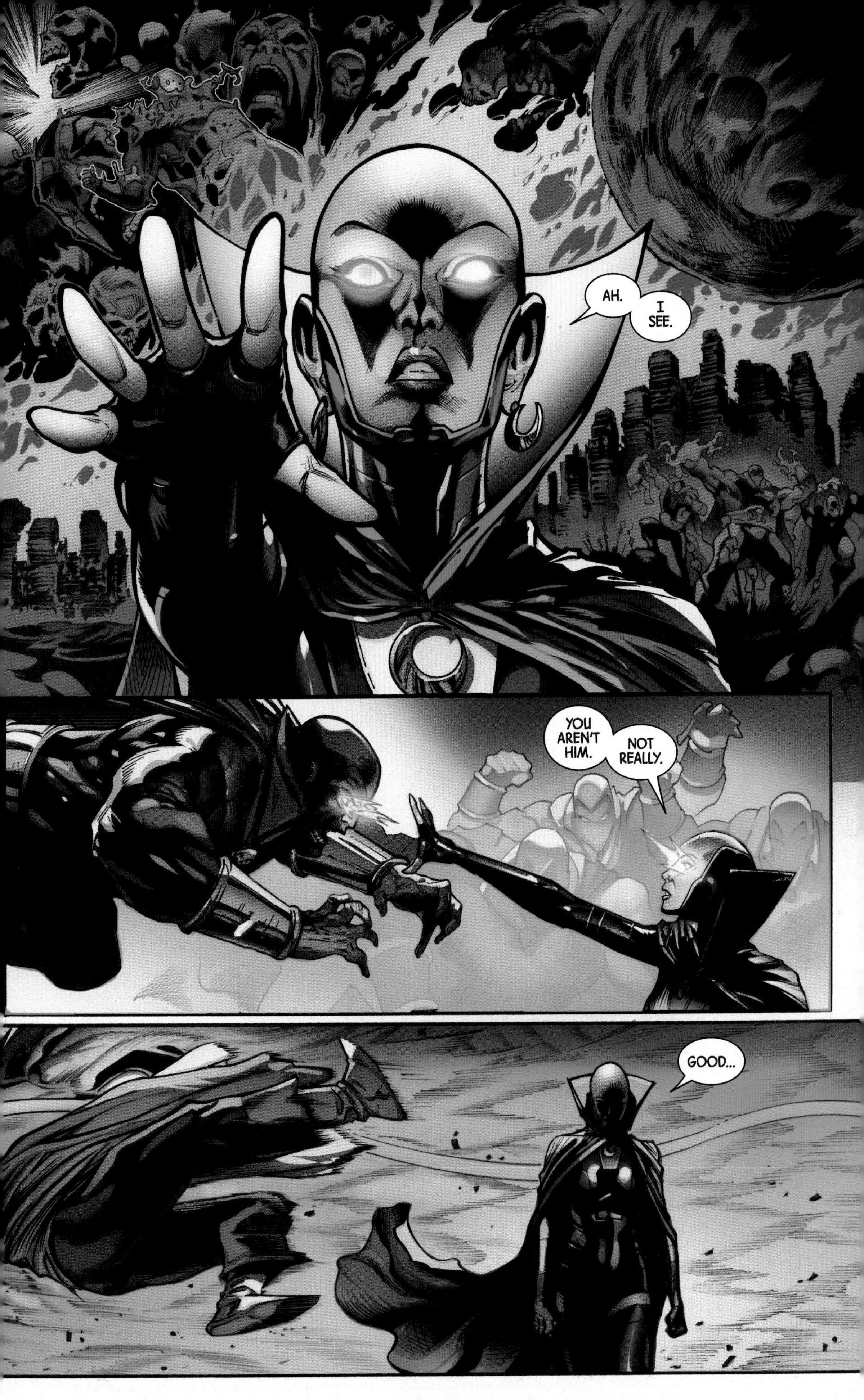
AH.
I SEE.
YOU AREN'T HIM.
NOT REALLY.
GOOD...

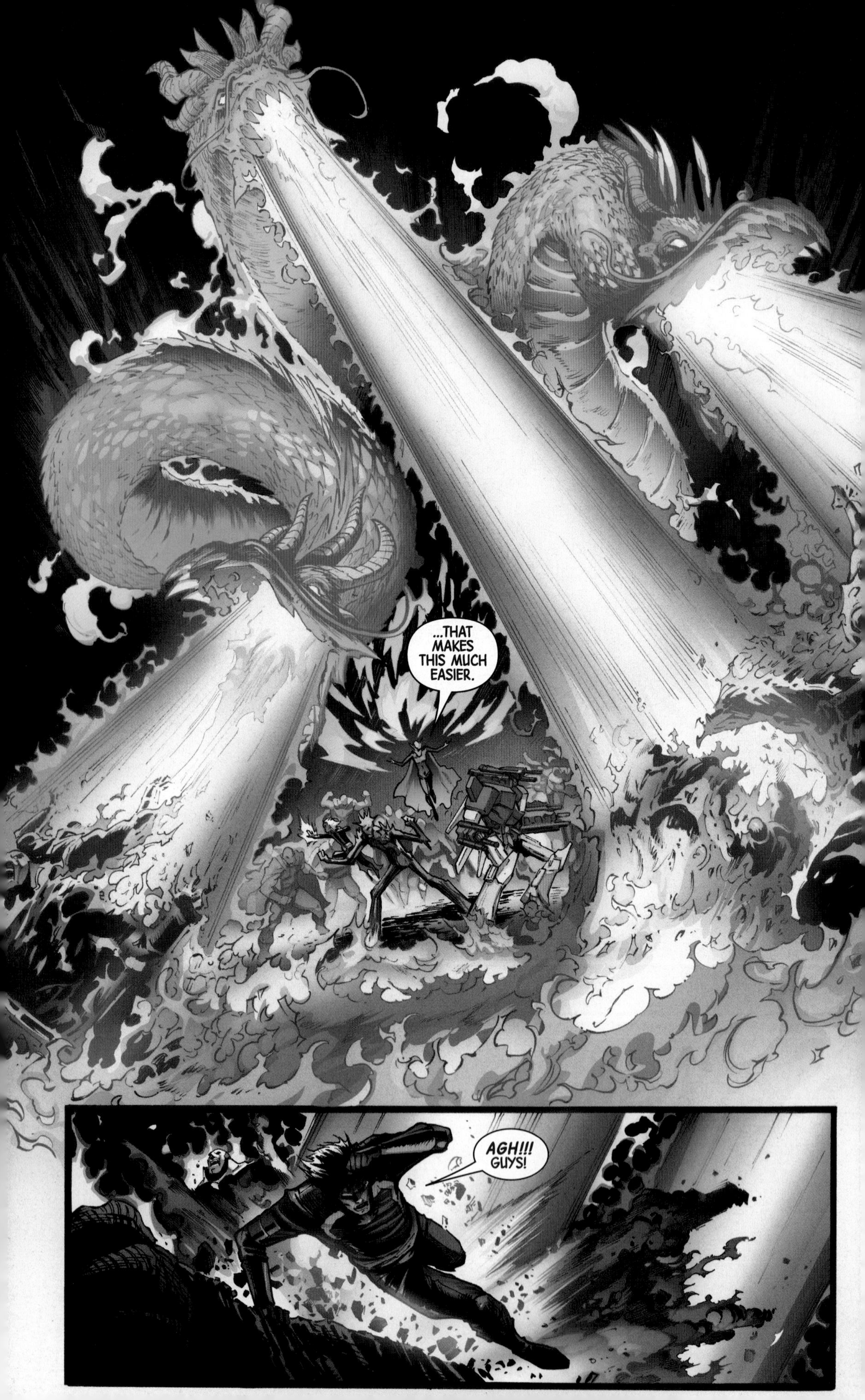
...THAT MAKES THIS MUCH EASIER.
AGH!!! GUYS!

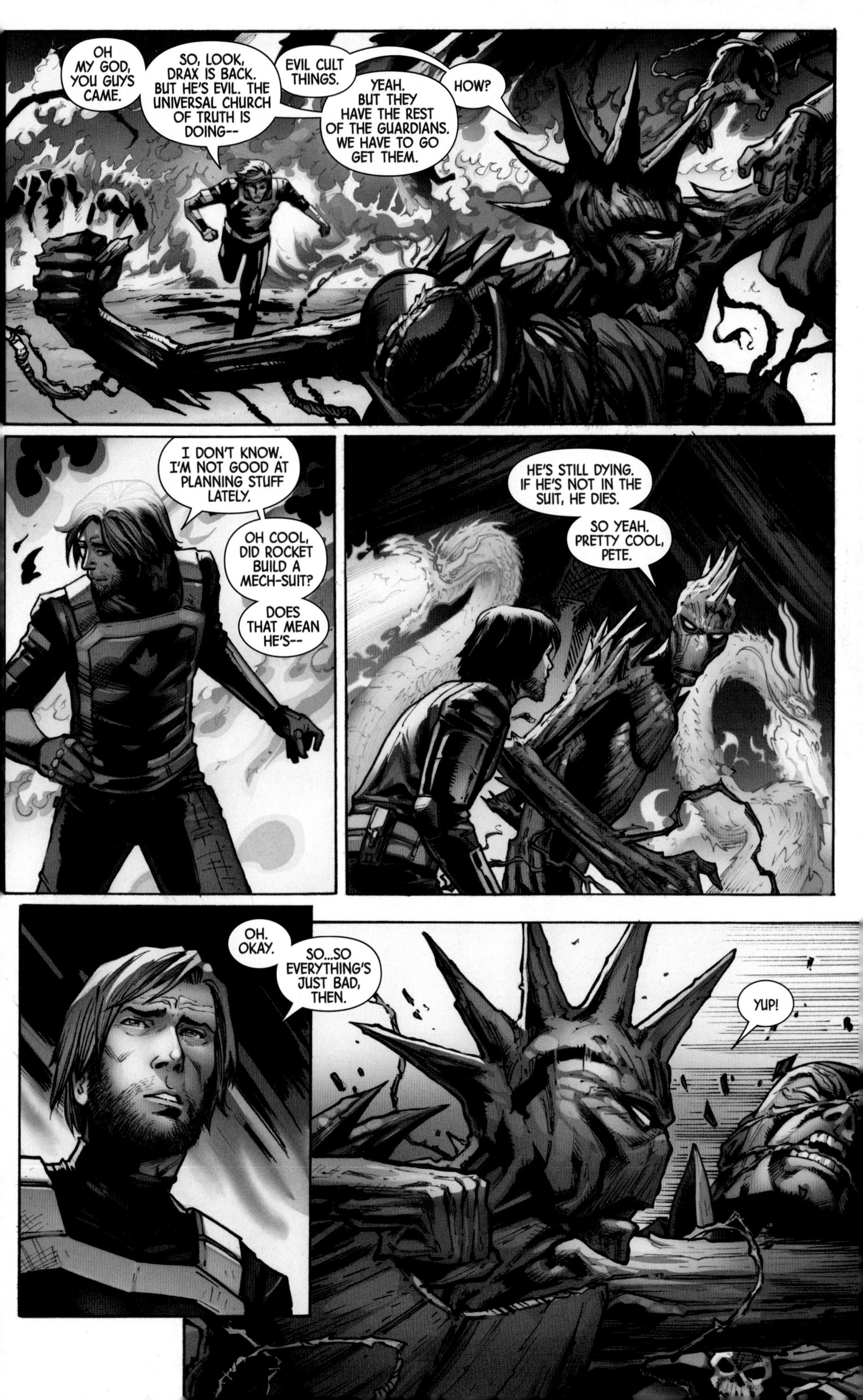
OH MY GOD, YOU GUYS CAME.
SO, LOOK, DRAX IS BACK. BUT HE'S EVIL. THE UNIVERSAL CHURCH OF TRUTH IS DOING--
EVIL CULT THINGS.
HOW?
YEAH. BUT THEY HAVE THE REST OF THE GUARDIANS. WE HAVE TO GO GET THEM.
I DON'T KNOW. I'M NOT GOOD AT PLANNING STUFF LATELY.
OH COOL, DID ROCKET BUILD A MECH-SUIT?
DOES THAT MEAN HE'S--
HE'S STILL DYING. IF HE'S NOT IN THE SUIT, HE DIES.
SO YEAH. PRETTY COOL, PETE.
OH. OKAY.
SO...SO EVERYTHING'S JUST BAD, THEN.
YUP!

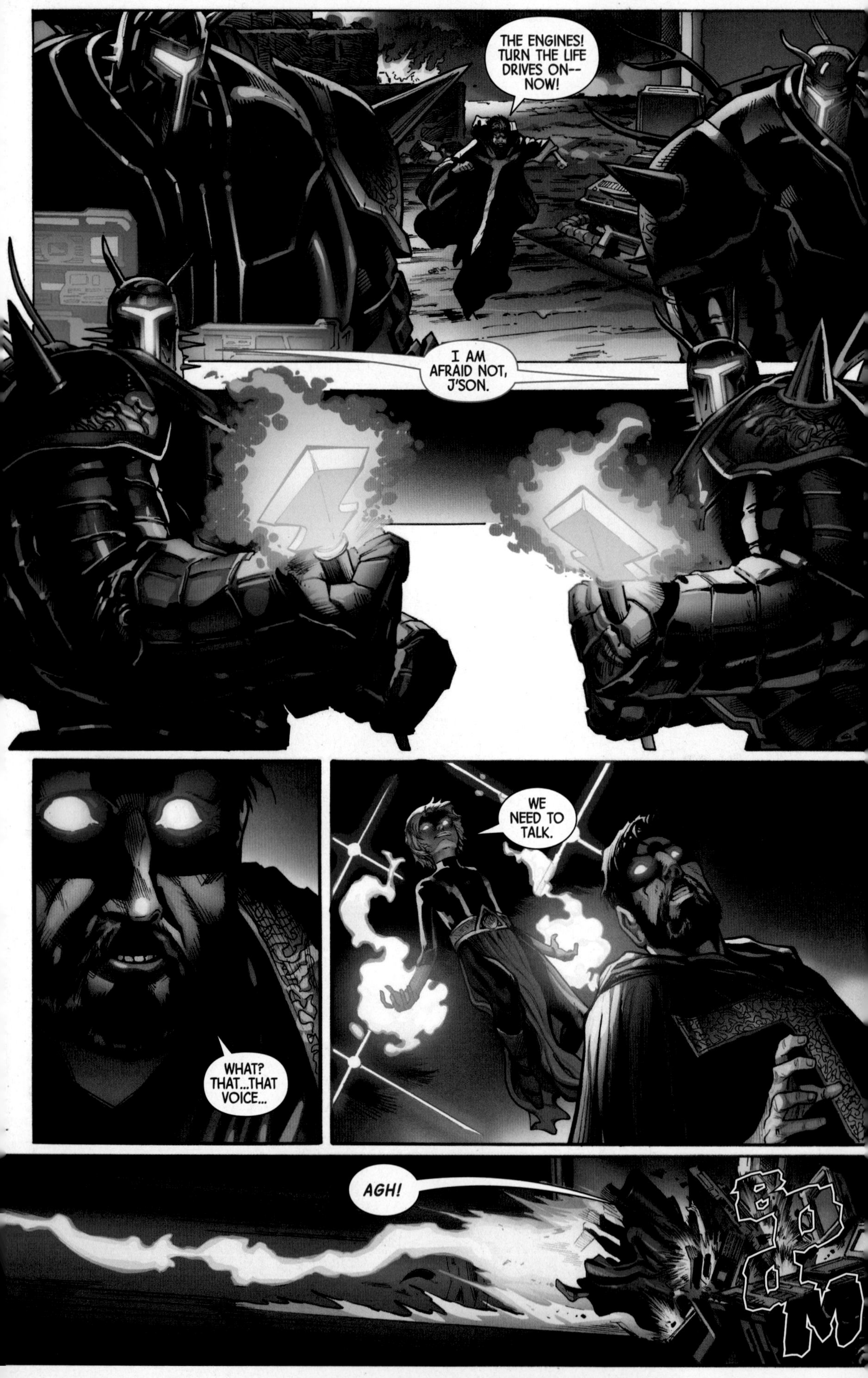
THE ENGINES! TURN THE LIFE DRIVES ON-- NOW!
I AM AFRAID NOT, J'SON.
WHAT? THAT...THAT VOICE...
WE NEED TO TALK.
AGH!
BOOM

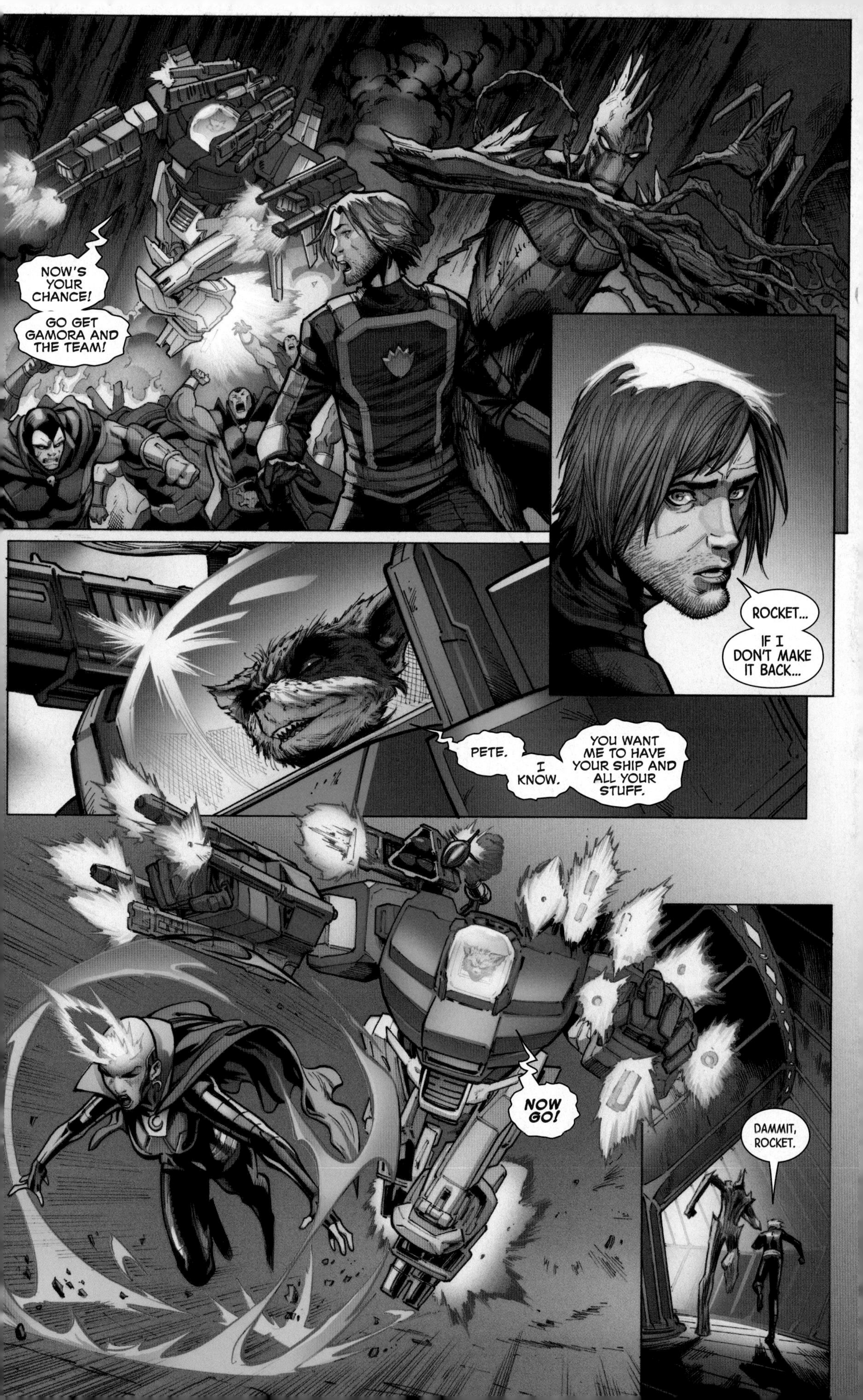
NOW'S YOUR CHANCE!
GO GET GAMORA AND THE TEAM!
ROCKET...
IF I DON'T MAKE IT BACK...
PETE.
I KNOW.
YOU WANT ME TO HAVE YOUR SHIP AND ALL YOUR STUFF.
NOW GO!
DAMMIT, ROCKET.

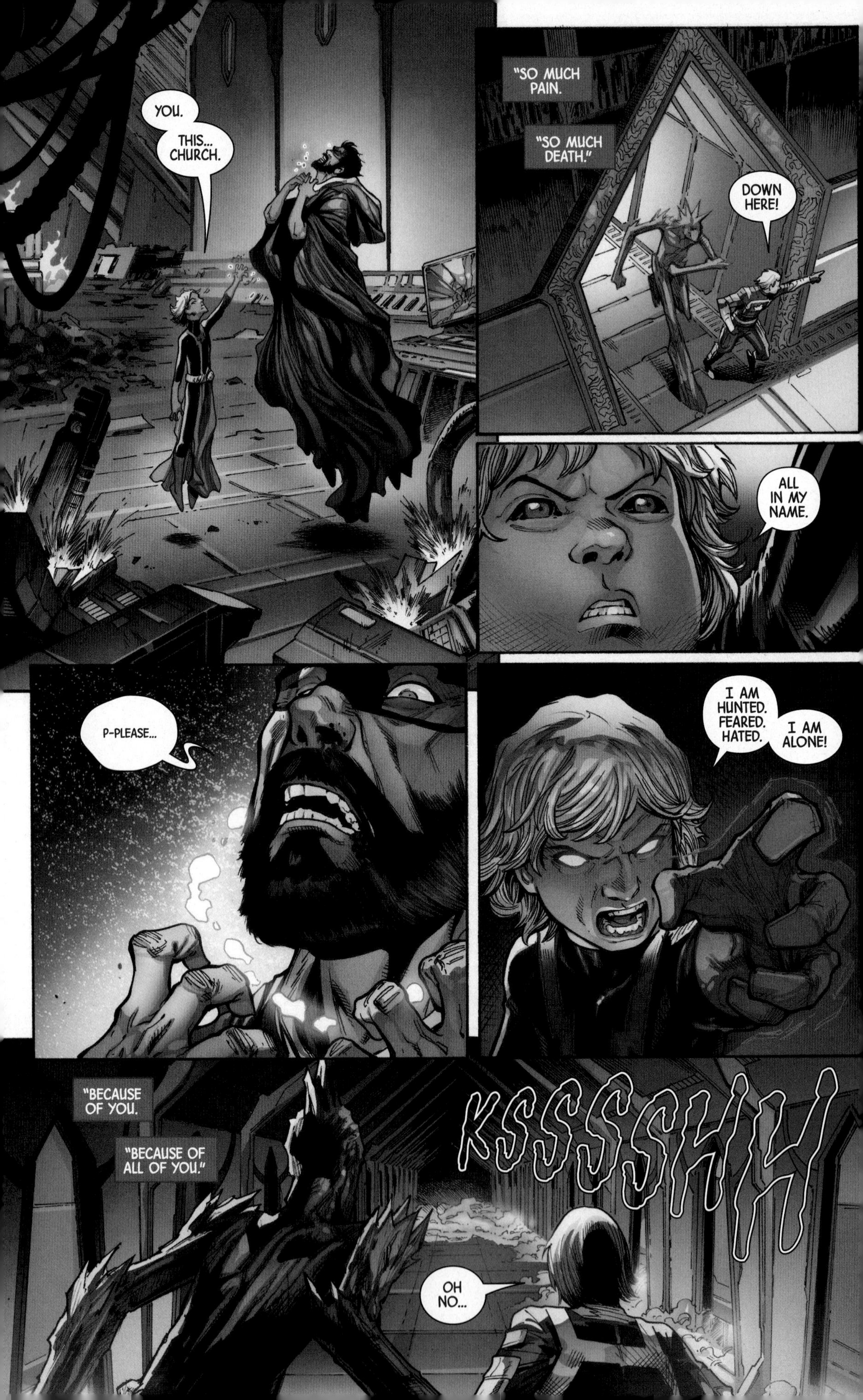
YOU.
THIS... CHURCH.
"SO MUCH PAIN.
"SO MUCH DEATH."
DOWN HERE!
ALL IN MY NAME.
P-PLEASE...
I AM HUNTED. FEARED. HATED.
I AM ALONE!
"BECAUSE OF YOU.
"BECAUSE OF ALL OF YOU."
KSSSSHH
OH NO...

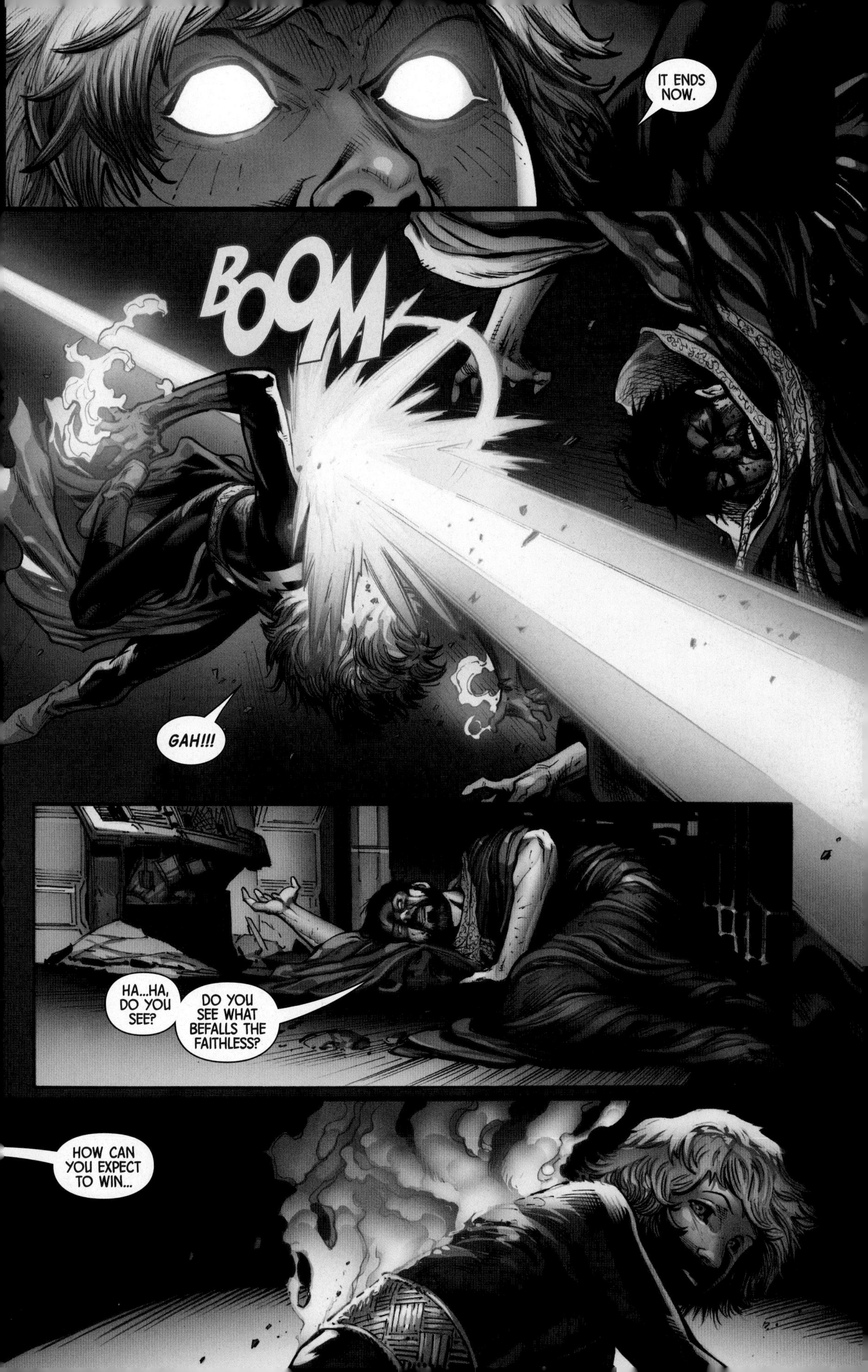
IT ENDS NOW.
BOOM
GAH!!!
HA...HA, DO YOU SEE?
DO YOU SEE WHAT BEFALLS THE FAITHLESS?
HOW CAN YOU EXPECT TO WIN...

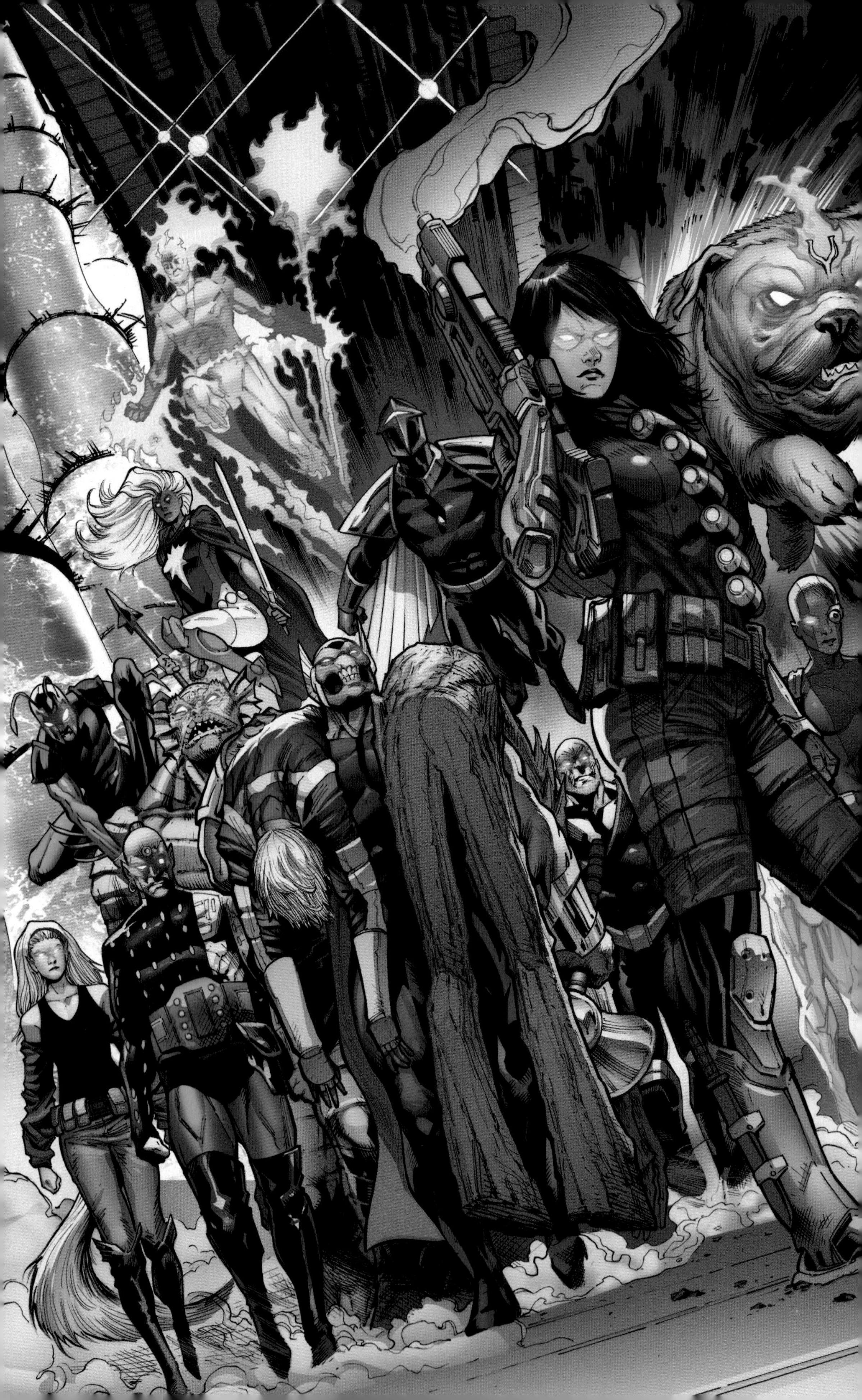

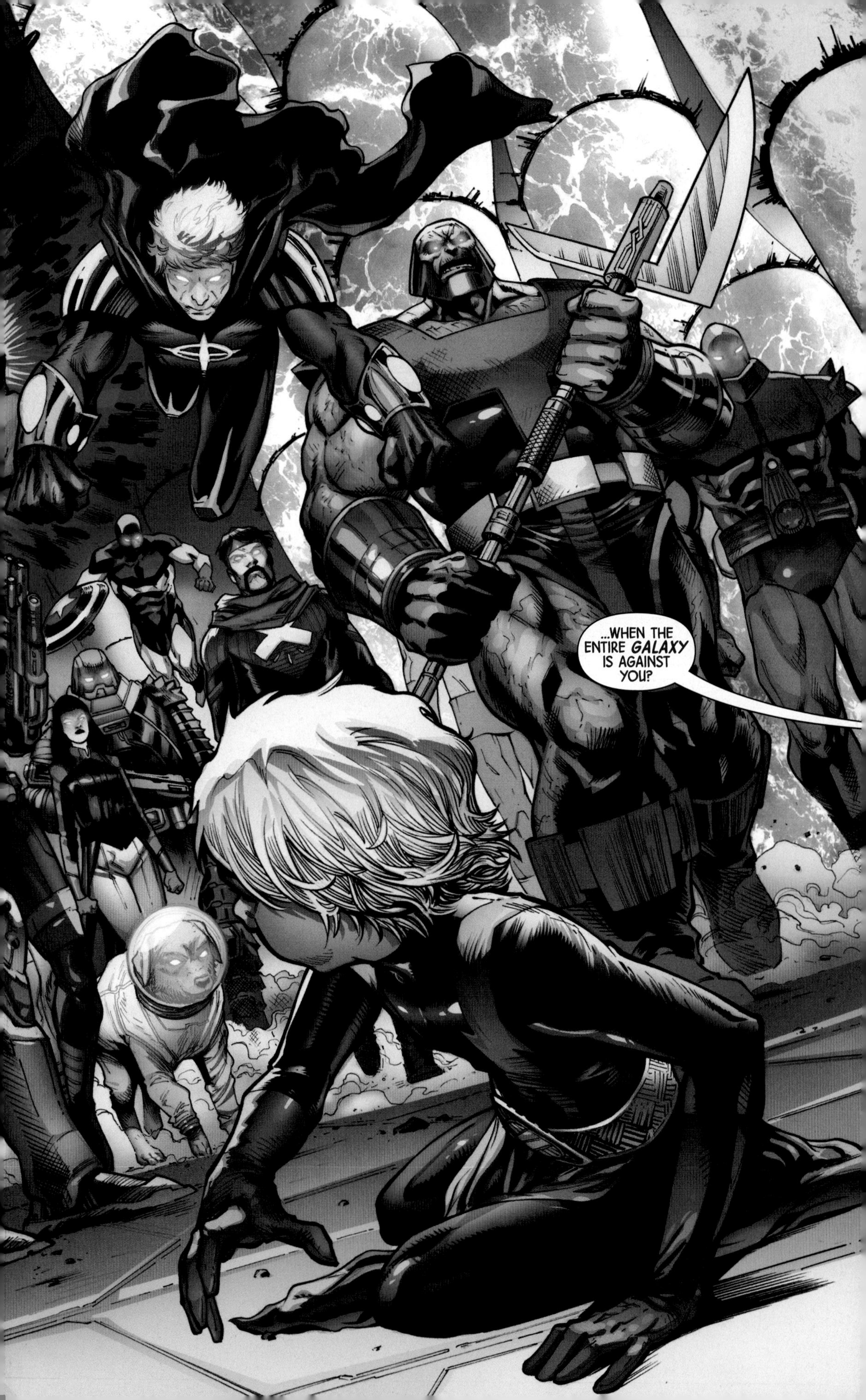
...WHEN THE ENTIRE GALAXY IS AGAINST YOU?

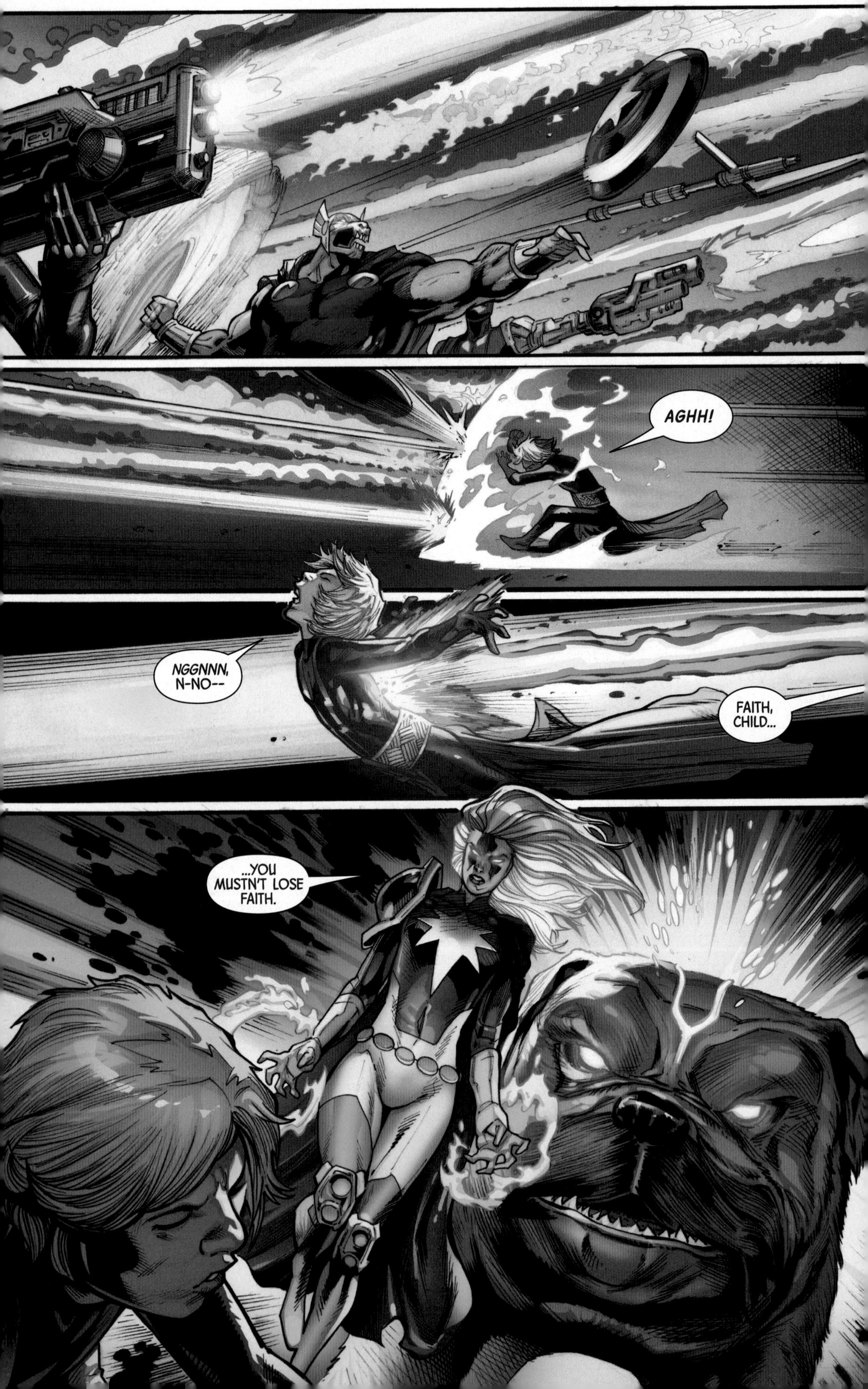
AGHH!
NGGNNN, N-NO--
FAITH, CHILD...
...YOU MUSTN'T LOSE FAITH.

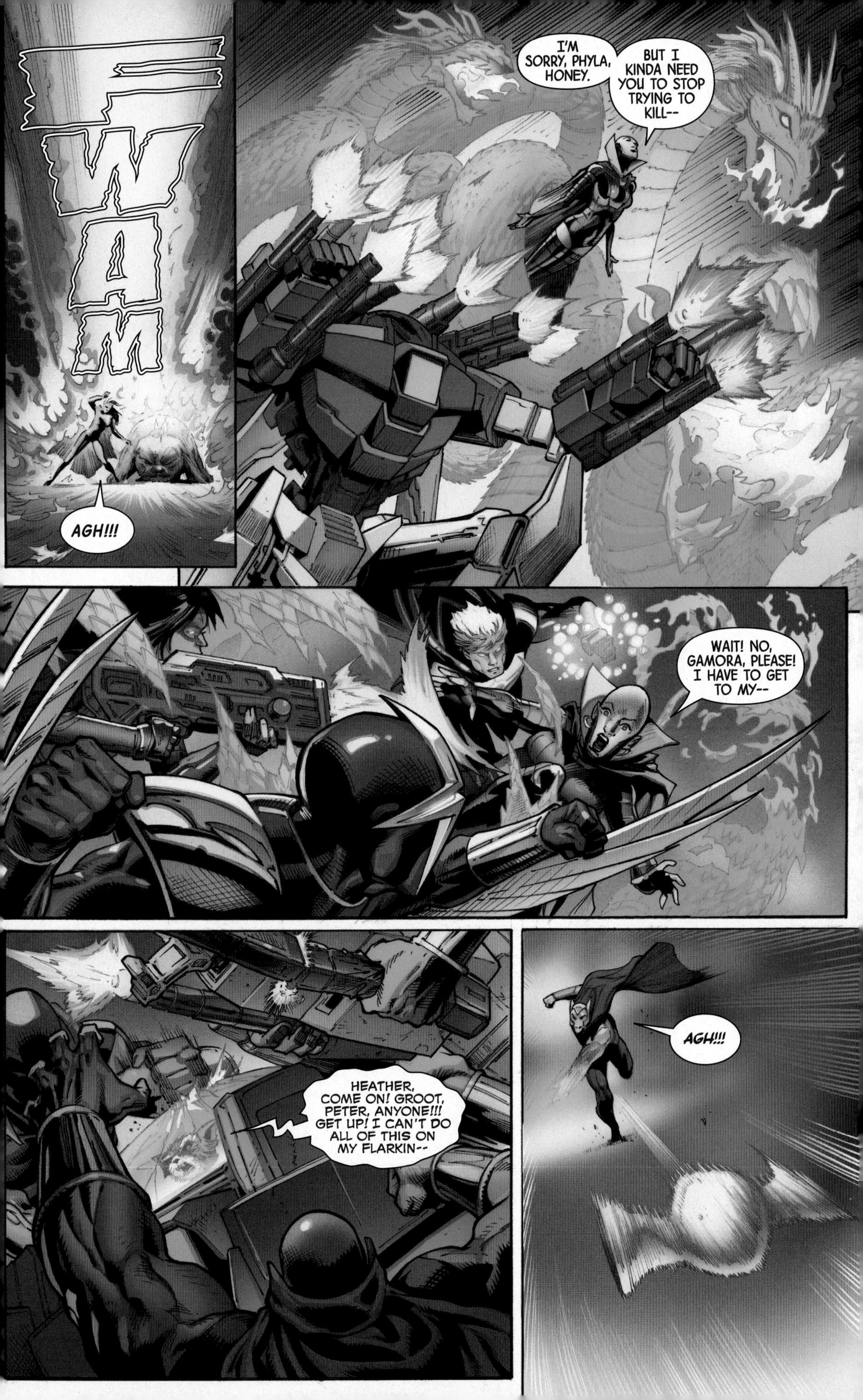
WAM
AGH!!!
I'M SORRY, PHYLA, HONEY.
BUT I KINDA NEED YOU TO STOP TRYING TO KILL--
WAIT! NO, GAMORA, PLEASE! I HAVE TO GET TO MY--
HEATHER, COME ON! GROOT, PETER, ANYONE!!! GET UP! I CAN'T DO ALL OF THIS ON MY FLARKIN--
AGH!!!

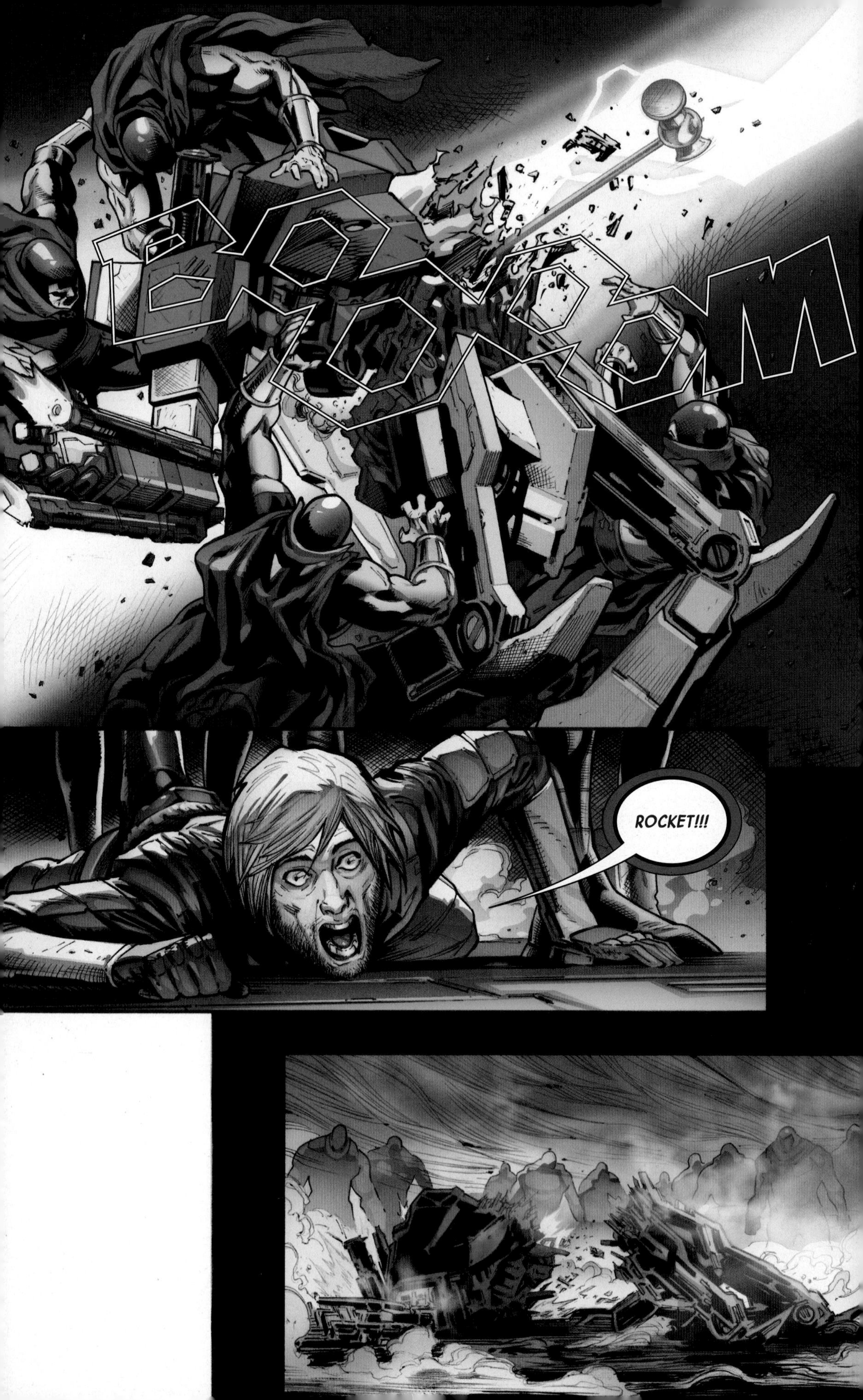
BOOOOM
ROCKET!!!

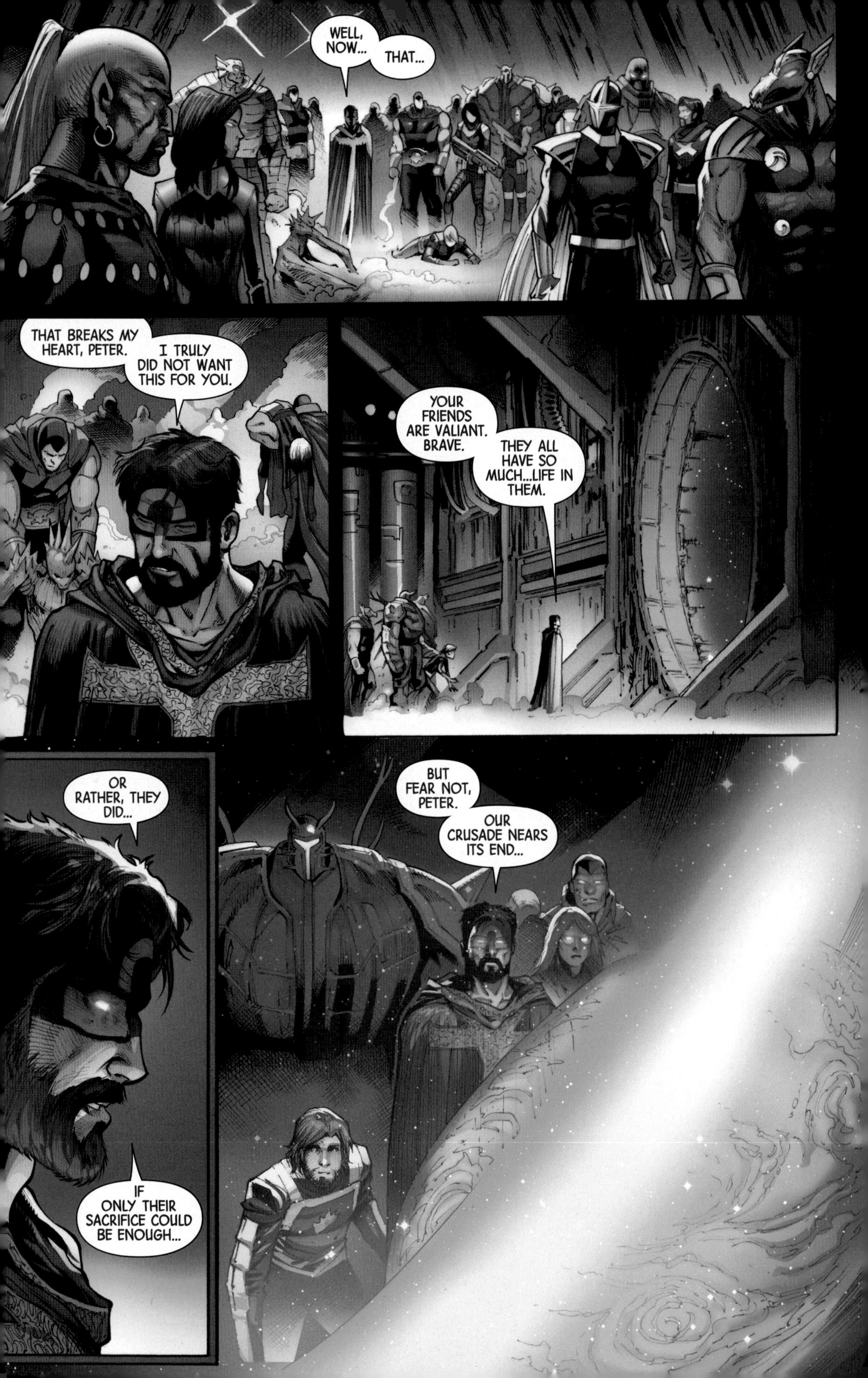

WELL, NOW...
THAT...
THAT BREAKS MY HEART, PETER.
I TRULY DID NOT WANT THIS FOR YOU.
YOUR FRIENDS ARE VALIANT. BRAVE.
THEY ALL HAVE SO MUCH...LIFE IN THEM.
OR RATHER, THEY DID...
IF ONLY THEIR SACRIFICE COULD BE ENOUGH...
BUT FEAR NOT, PETER.
OUR CRUSADE NEARS ITS END...

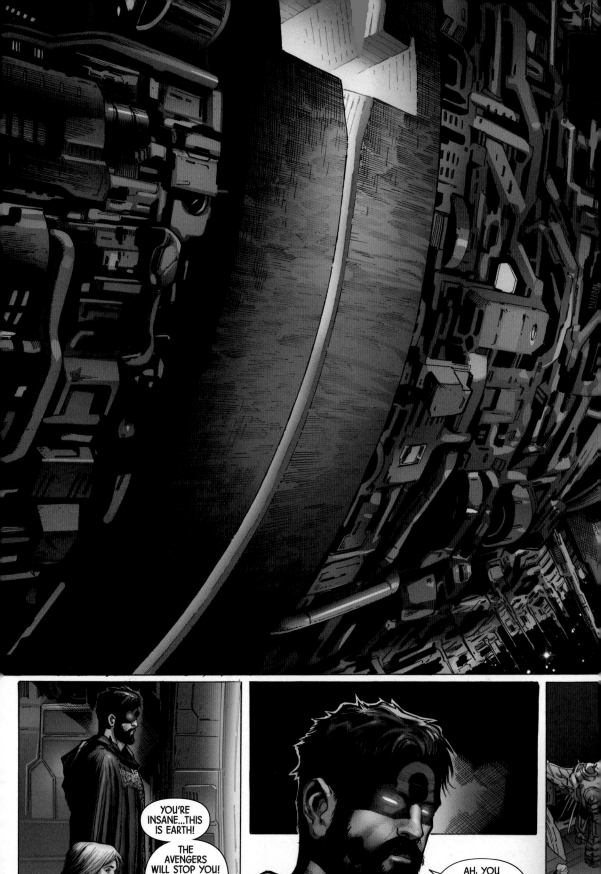

YOU'RE INSANE...THIS IS EARTH!

THE AVENGERS WILL STOP YOU! THE X-MEN, SOMEONE! YOU CAN'T BEAT THEM!

AH, YOU MEAN HOW THE NOVA CORPS OR THE GUARDIANS OF THE GALAXY STOPPED US?

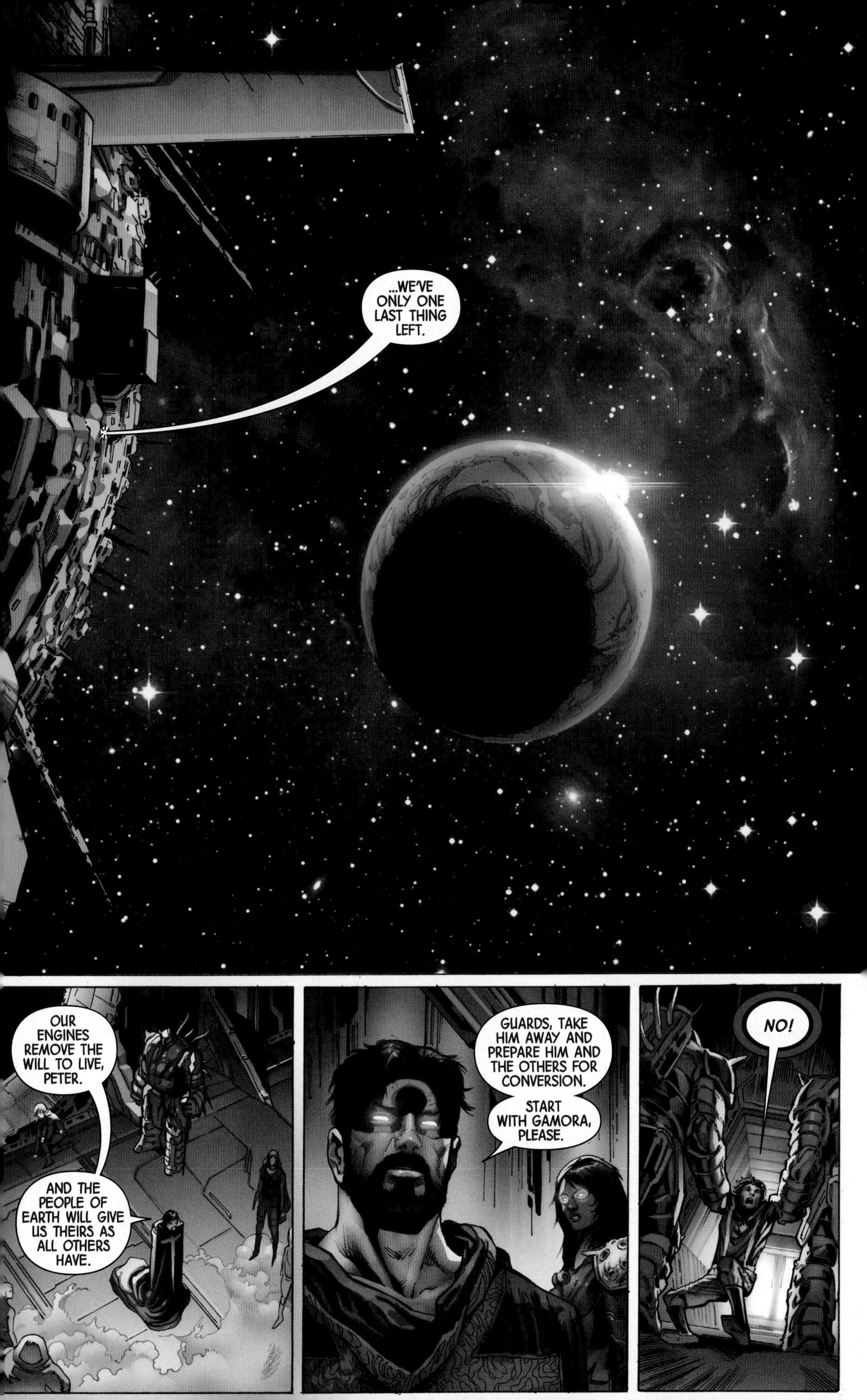
...WE'VE ONLY ONE LAST THING LEFT.
OUR ENGINES REMOVE THE WILL TO LIVE, PETER.
AND THE PEOPLE OF EARTH WILL GIVE US THEIRS AS ALL OTHERS HAVE.
GUARDS, TAKE HIM AWAY AND PREPARE HIM AND THE OTHERS FOR CONVERSION.
START WITH GAMORA, PLEASE.
NO!

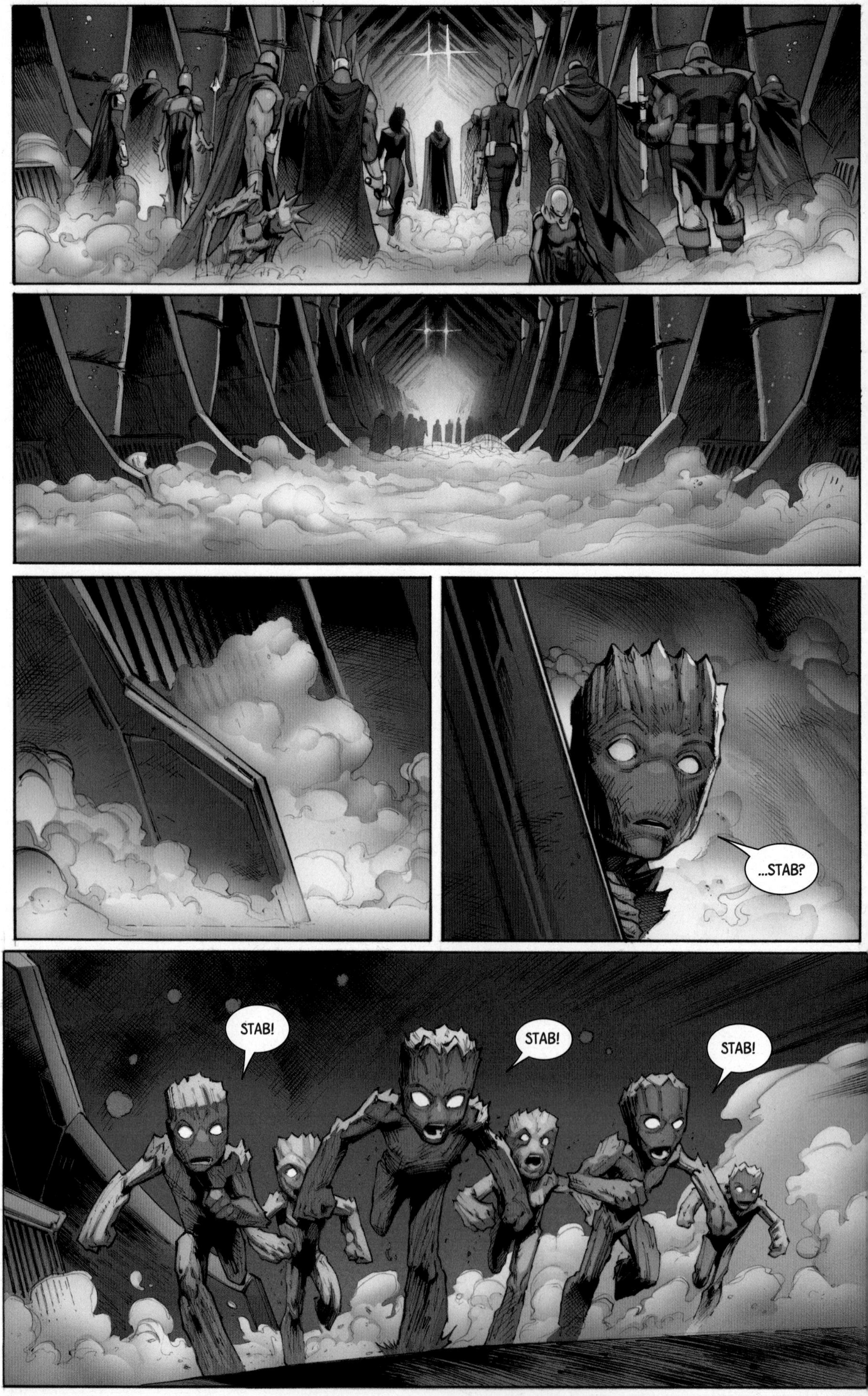
...STAB?
STAB!
STAB!
STAB!

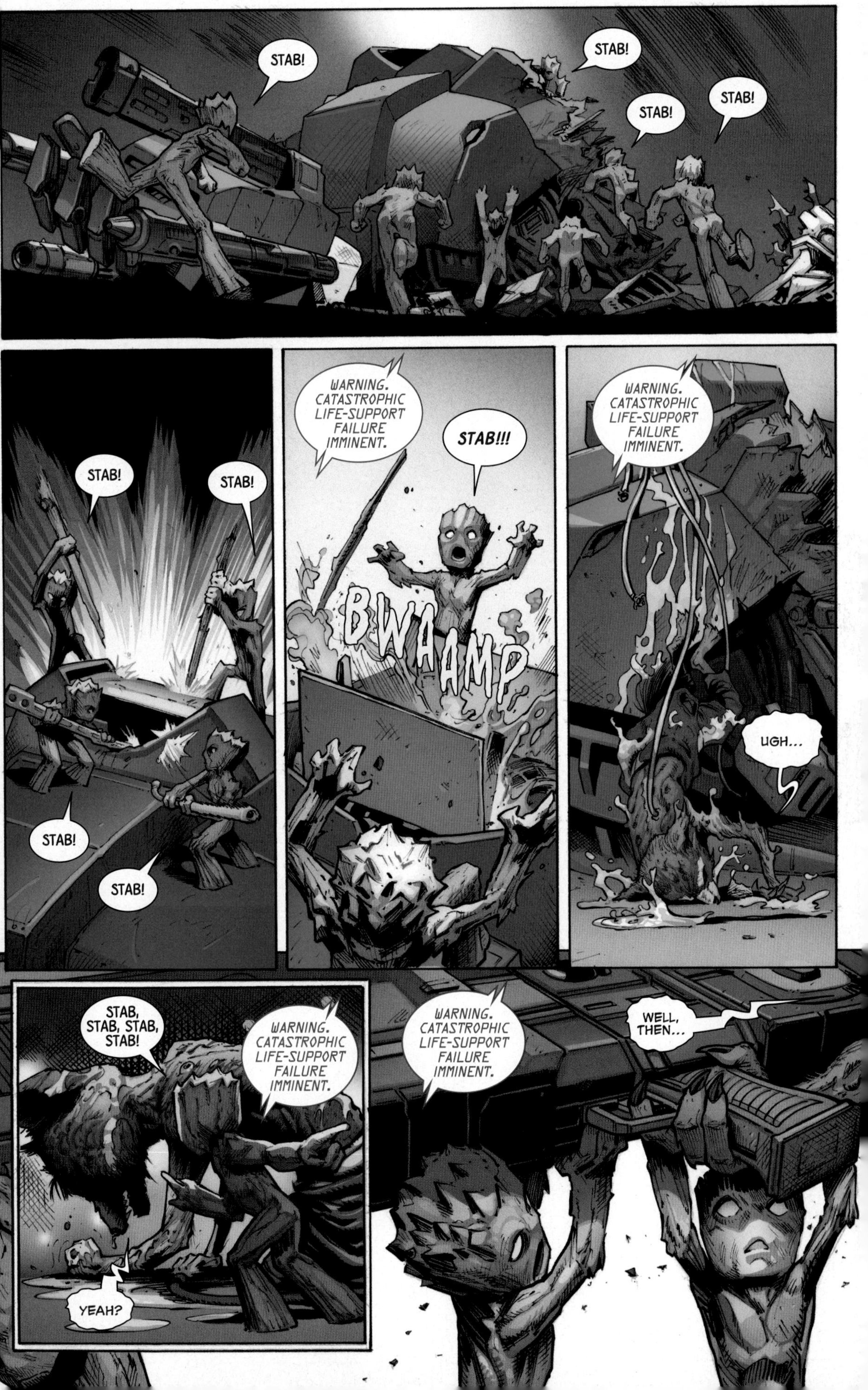
STAB!
STAB!
STAB!
STAB!
STAB!
STAB!
STAB!
STAB!
WARNING. CATASTROPHIC LIFE-SUPPORT FAILURE IMMINENT.
STAB!!!
BWAAMP
WARNING. CATASTROPHIC LIFE-SUPPORT FAILURE IMMINENT.
UGH...
STAB, STAB, STAB, STAB!
WARNING. CATASTROPHIC LIFE-SUPPORT FAILURE IMMINENT.
YEAH?
WARNING. CATASTROPHIC LIFE-SUPPORT FAILURE IMMINENT.
WELL, THEN...

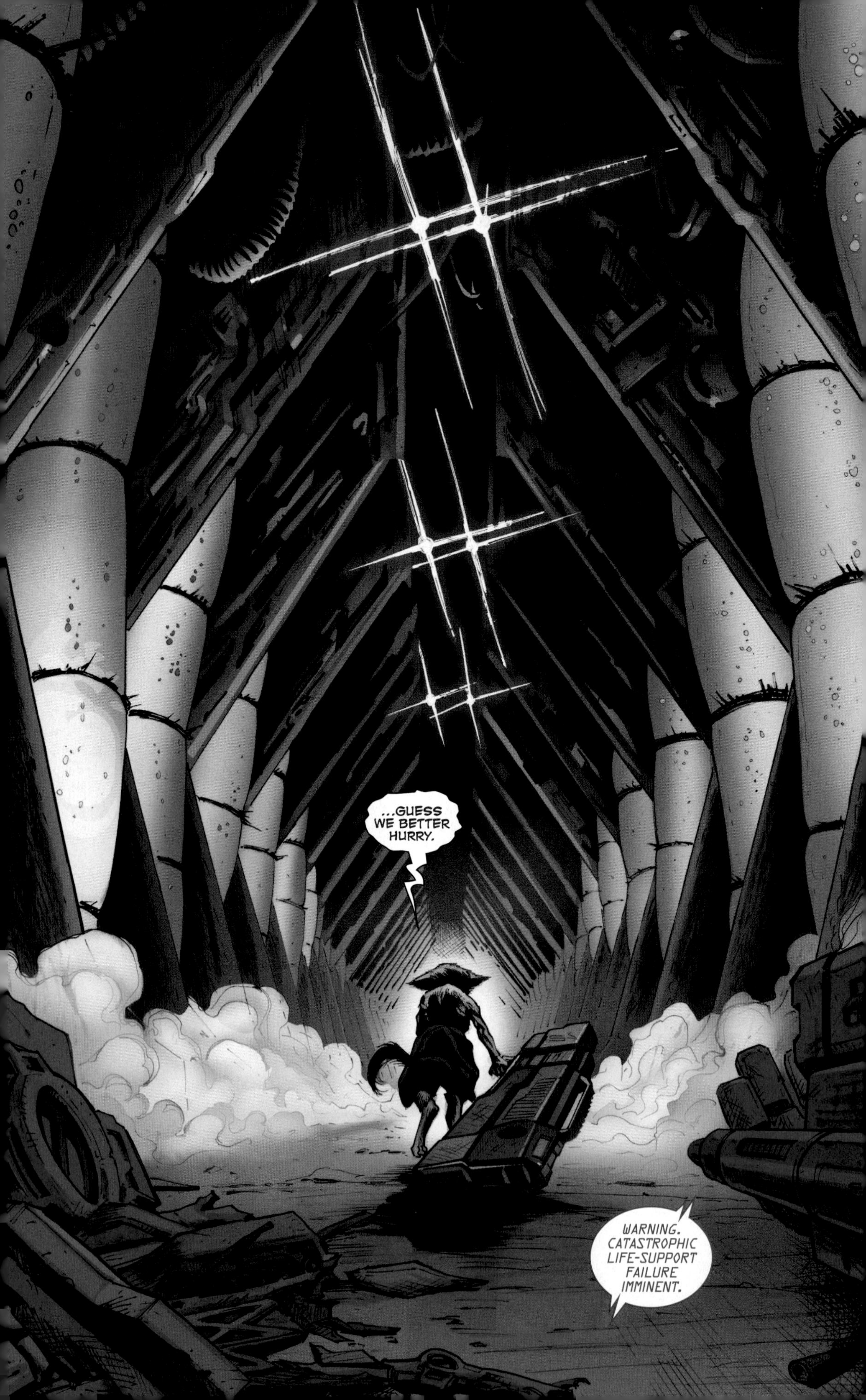
...GUESS WE BETTER HURRY.
WARNING. CATASTROPHIC LIFE-SUPPORT FAILURE IMMINENT.

ARTHUR ADAMS & FEDERICO BLEE
#10 Mary Jane variant

TOM RANEY & CHRIS SOTOMAYOR
#12 2020 variant

TWELVE

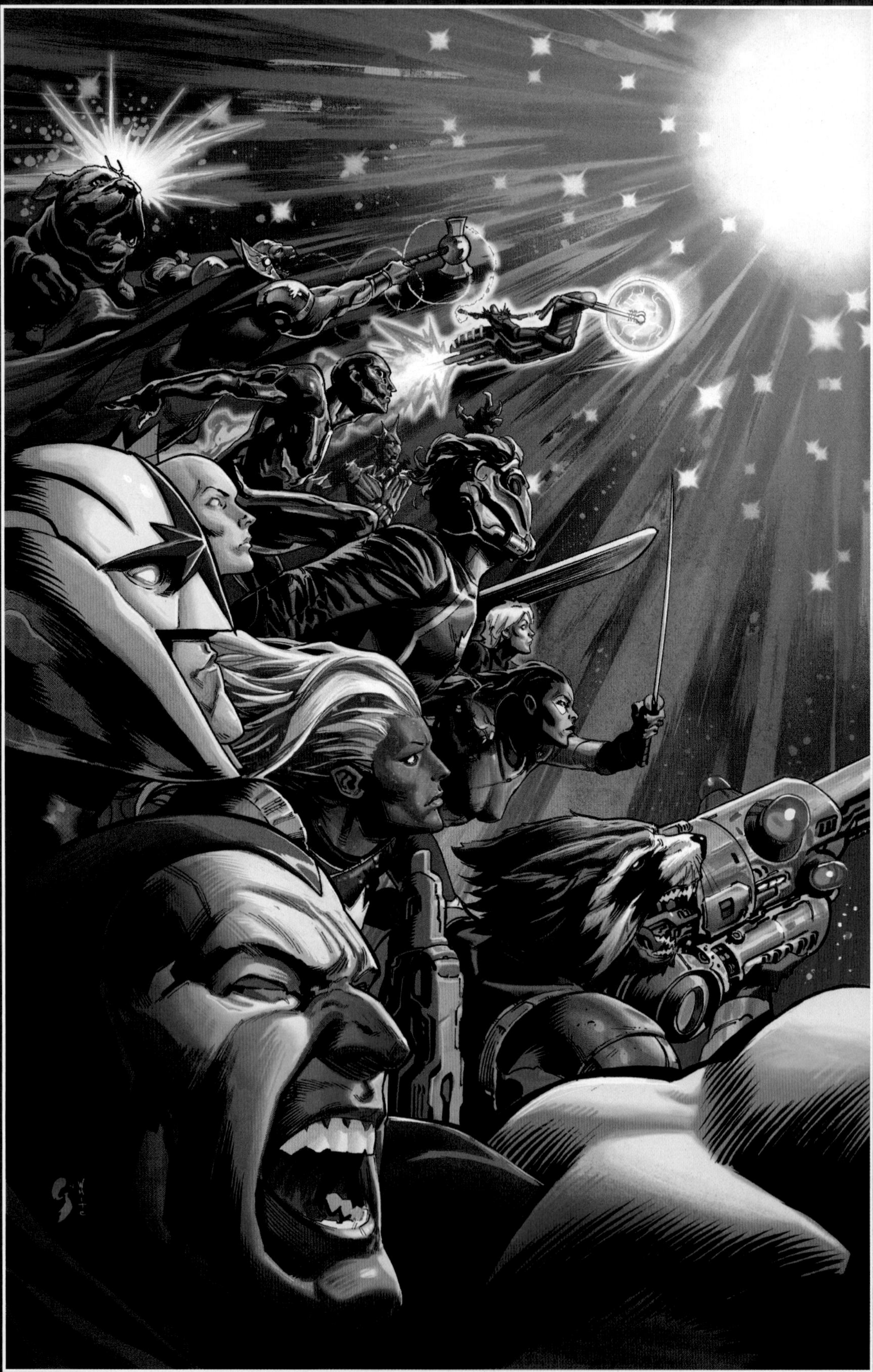

"WE ARE SO CLOSE TO THE END NOW."

WE MUSTN'T WAVER.

"SOON OUR LIFE-FORCE ENGINES WILL BE FILLED, AND WE CAN RETURN TO OUR TIME.

"AND THERE, WITH OUR NEWLY BORN DESTROYER MESSIAH, WE WILL END OUR GREATEST FOE.

"WE WILL KILL *DEATH.*"

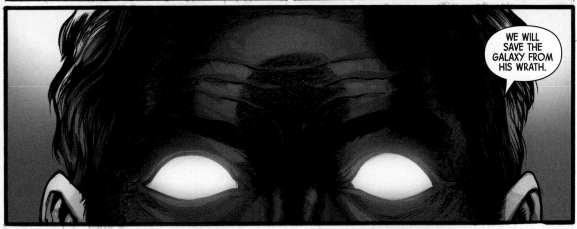

WE WILL SAVE THE GALAXY FROM HIS WRATH.

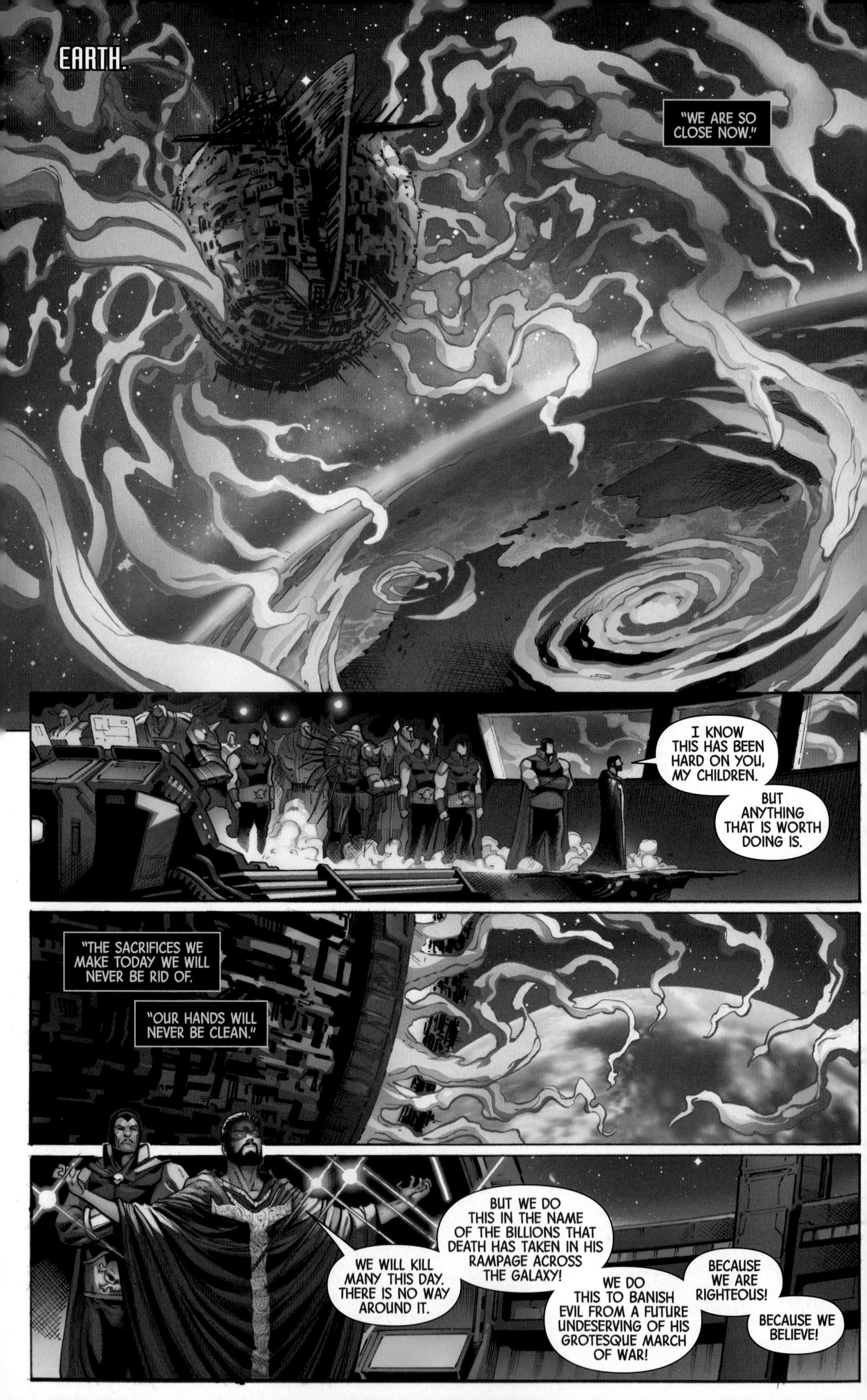
EARTH.
"WE ARE SO CLOSE NOW."
I KNOW THIS HAS BEEN HARD ON YOU, MY CHILDREN.
BUT ANYTHING THAT IS WORTH DOING IS.
"THE SACRIFICES WE MAKE TODAY WE WILL NEVER BE RID OF.
"OUR HANDS WILL NEVER BE CLEAN."
WE WILL KILL MANY THIS DAY. THERE IS NO WAY AROUND IT.
BUT WE DO THIS IN THE NAME OF THE BILLIONS THAT DEATH HAS TAKEN IN HIS RAMPAGE ACROSS THE GALAXY!
WE DO THIS TO BANISH EVIL FROM A FUTURE UNDESERVING OF HIS GROTESQUE MARCH OF WAR!
BECAUSE WE ARE RIGHTEOUS!
BECAUSE WE BELIEVE!

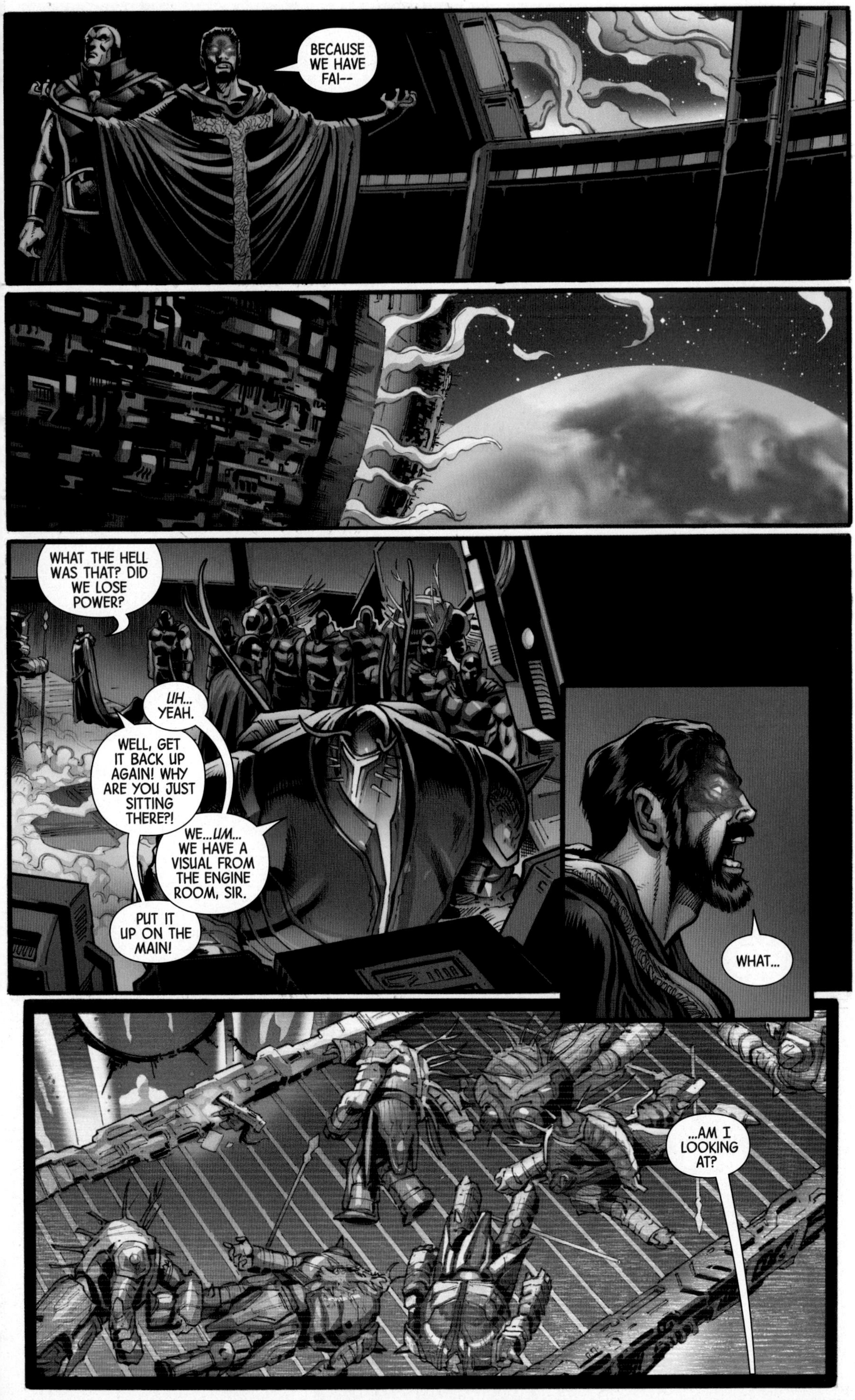
BECAUSE WE HAVE FAI--
WHAT THE HELL WAS THAT? DID WE LOSE POWER?
UH... YEAH.
WELL, GET IT BACK UP AGAIN! WHY ARE YOU JUST SITTING THERE?!
WE...UM... WE HAVE A VISUAL FROM THE ENGINE ROOM, SIR.
PUT IT UP ON THE MAIN!
WHAT...
...AM I LOOKING AT?

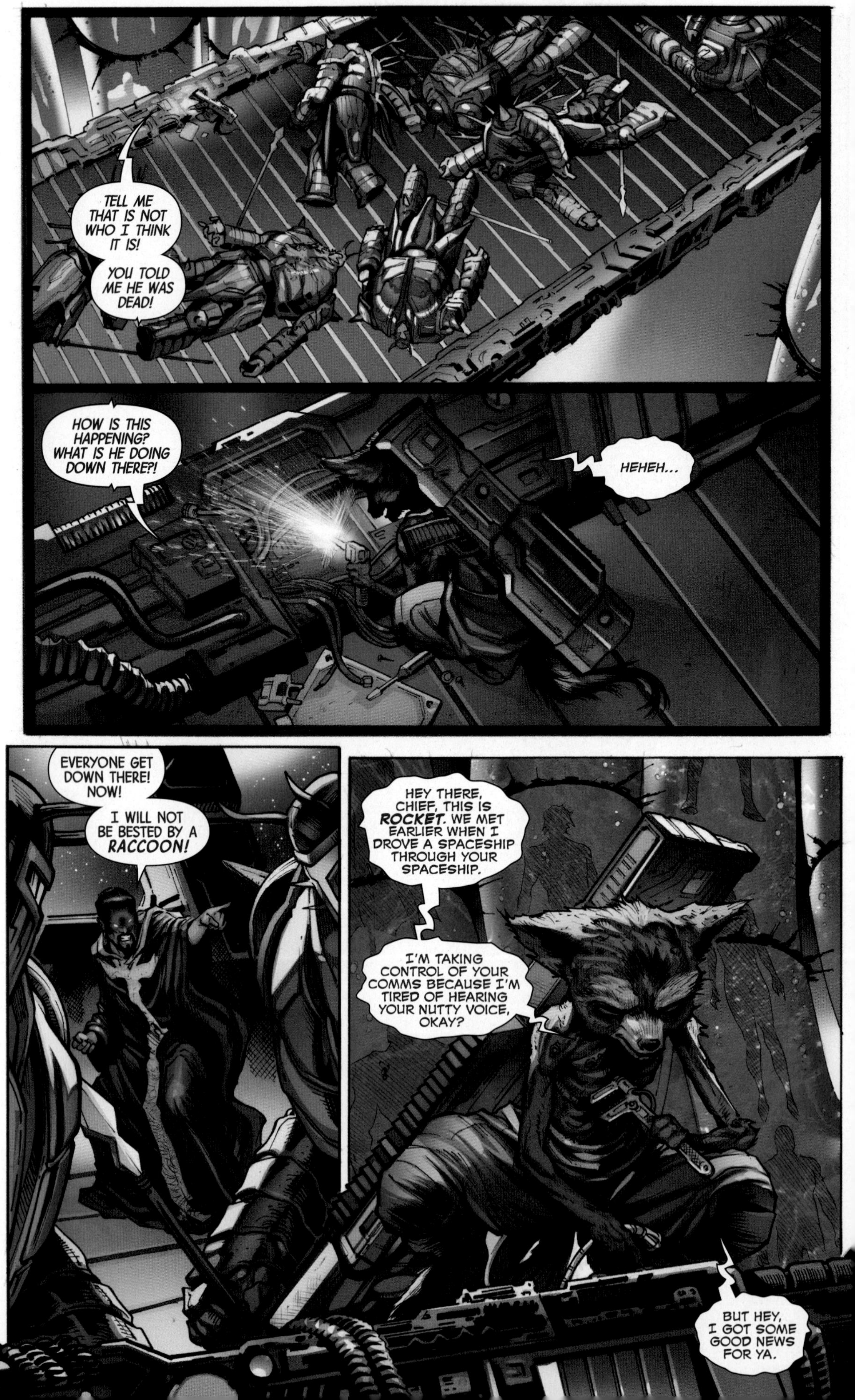
TELL ME THAT IS NOT WHO I THINK IT IS!
YOU TOLD ME HE WAS DEAD!
HOW IS THIS HAPPENING? WHAT IS HE DOING DOWN THERE?!
HEHEH...
EVERYONE GET DOWN THERE! NOW!
I WILL NOT BE BESTED BY A RACCOON!
HEY THERE, CHIEF, THIS IS ROCKET. WE MET EARLIER WHEN I DROVE A SPACESHIP THROUGH YOUR SPACESHIP.
I'M TAKING CONTROL OF YOUR COMMS BECAUSE I'M TIRED OF HEARING YOUR NUTTY VOICE, OKAY?
BUT HEY, I GOT SOME GOOD NEWS FOR YA.

YOU'RE NOT LOSING TO A RACCOON.

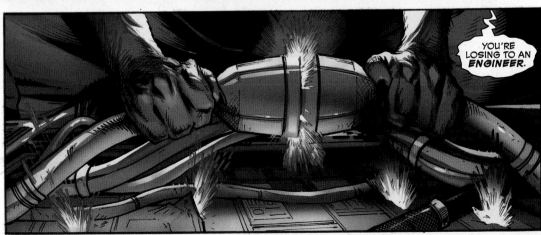

YOU'RE LOSING TO AN ENGINEER.

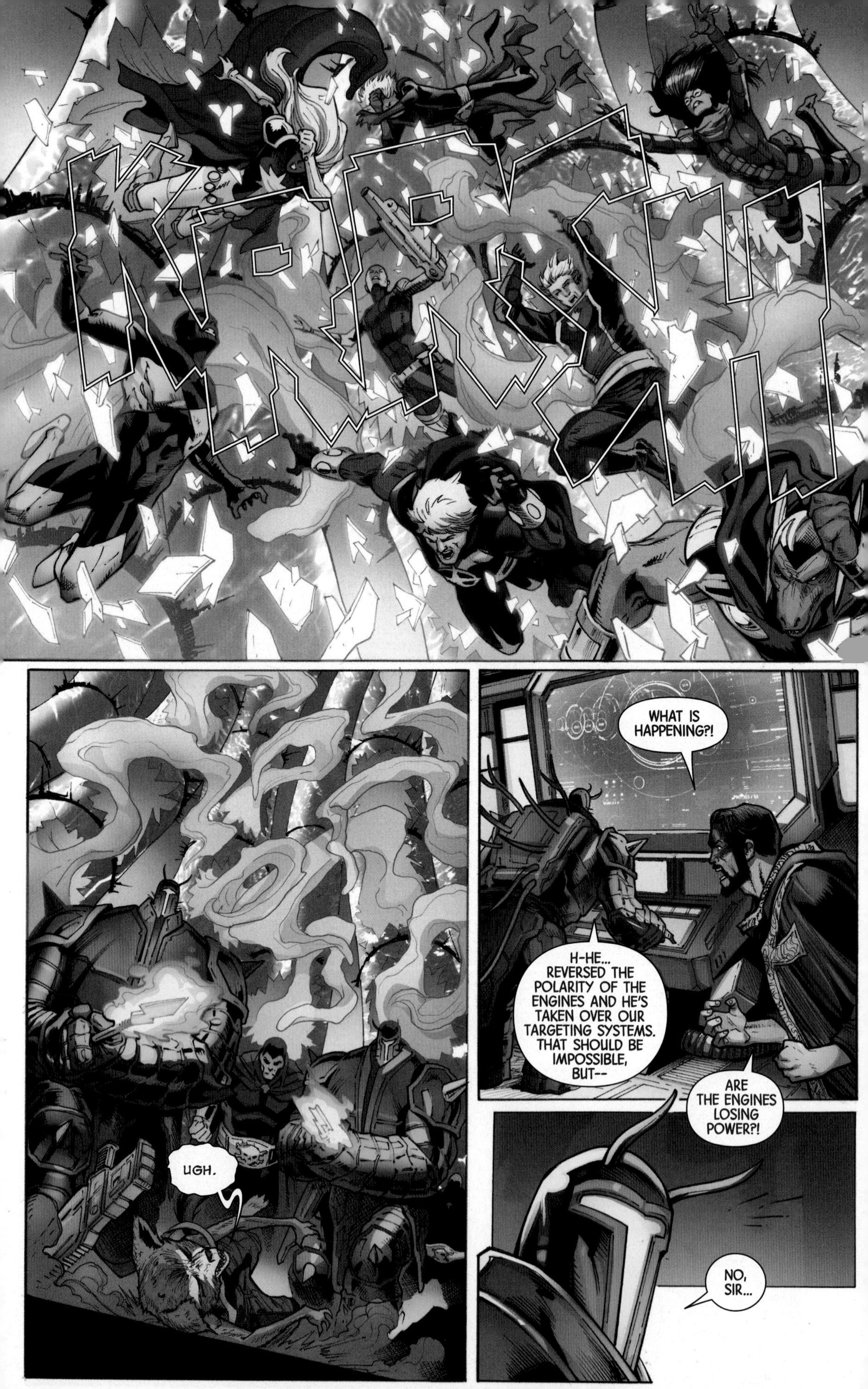
UGH.
WHAT IS HAPPENING?!
H-HE... REVERSED THE POLARITY OF THE ENGINES AND HE'S TAKEN OVER OUR TARGETING SYSTEMS. THAT SHOULD BE IMPOSSIBLE, BUT--
ARE THE ENGINES LOSING POWER?!
NO, SIR...

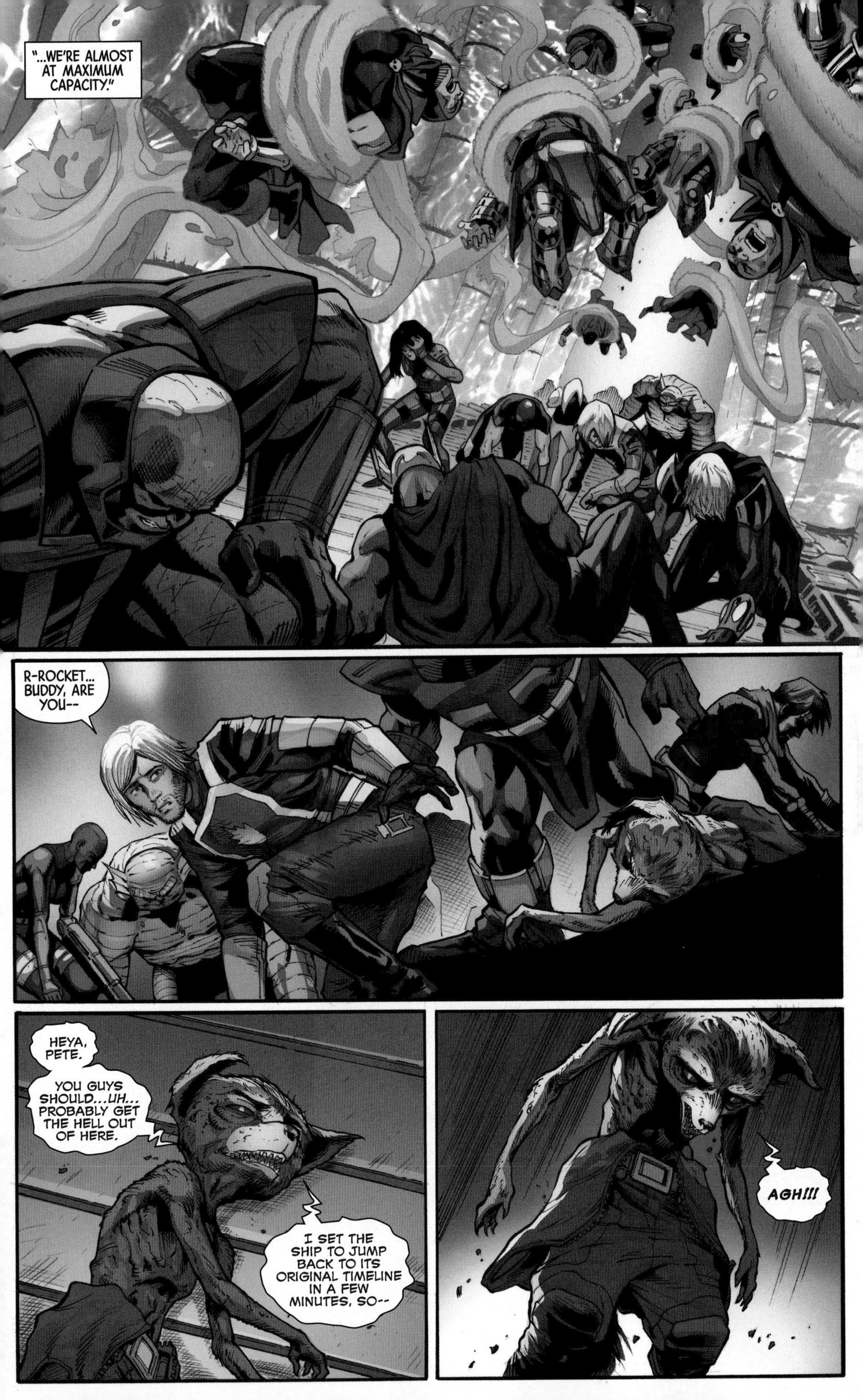
"...WE'RE ALMOST AT MAXIMUM CAPACITY."
R-ROCKET... BUDDY, ARE YOU--
HEYA, PETE.
YOU GUYS SHOULD...UH... PROBABLY GET THE HELL OUT OF HERE.
I SET THE SHIP TO JUMP BACK TO ITS ORIGINAL TIMELINE IN A FEW MINUTES, SO--
AGH!!!

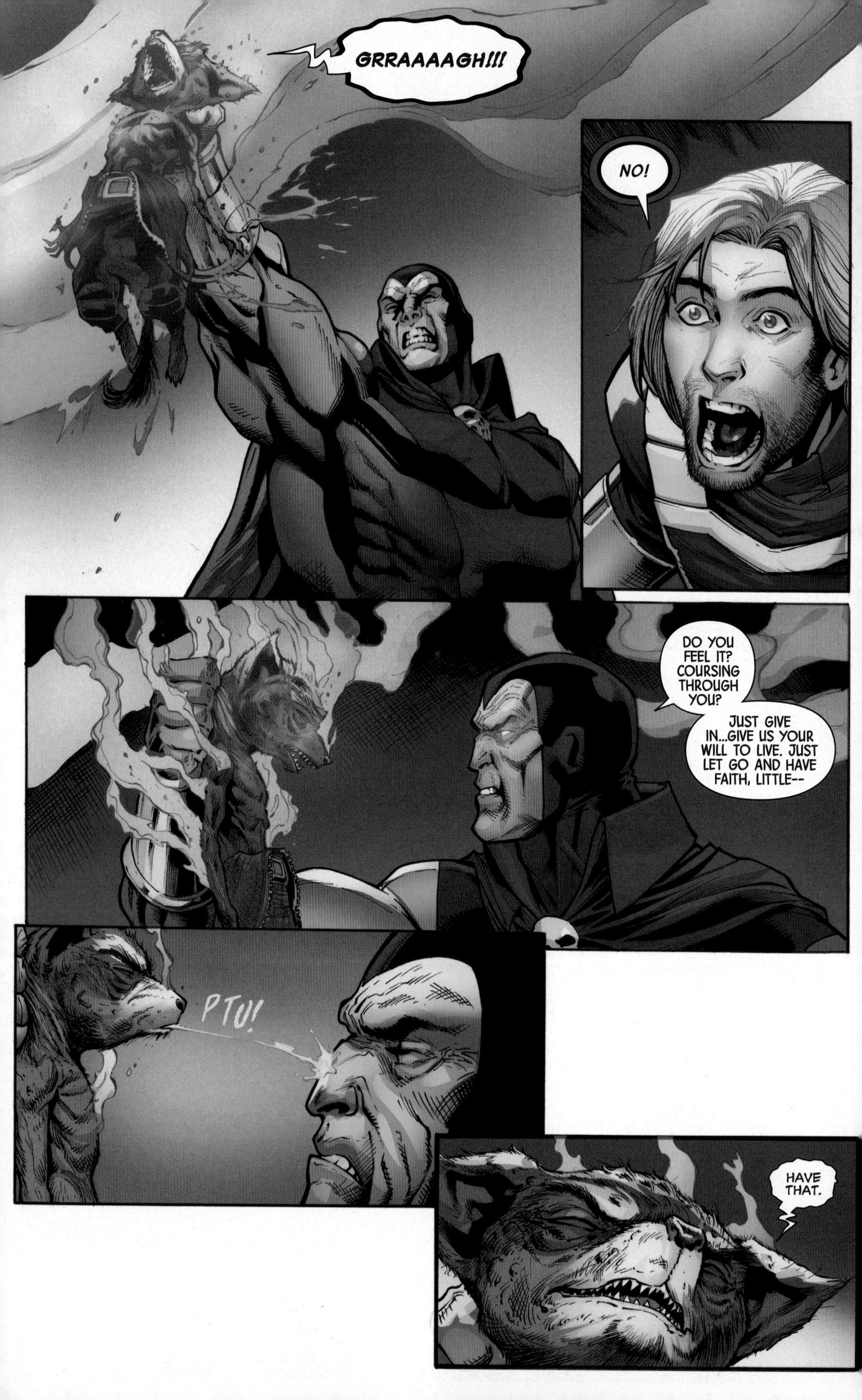
GRRAAAAGH!!!
NO!
DO YOU FEEL IT? COURSING THROUGH YOU?
JUST GIVE IN...GIVE US YOUR WILL TO LIVE. JUST LET GO AND HAVE FAITH, LITTLE--
PTU!
HAVE THAT.

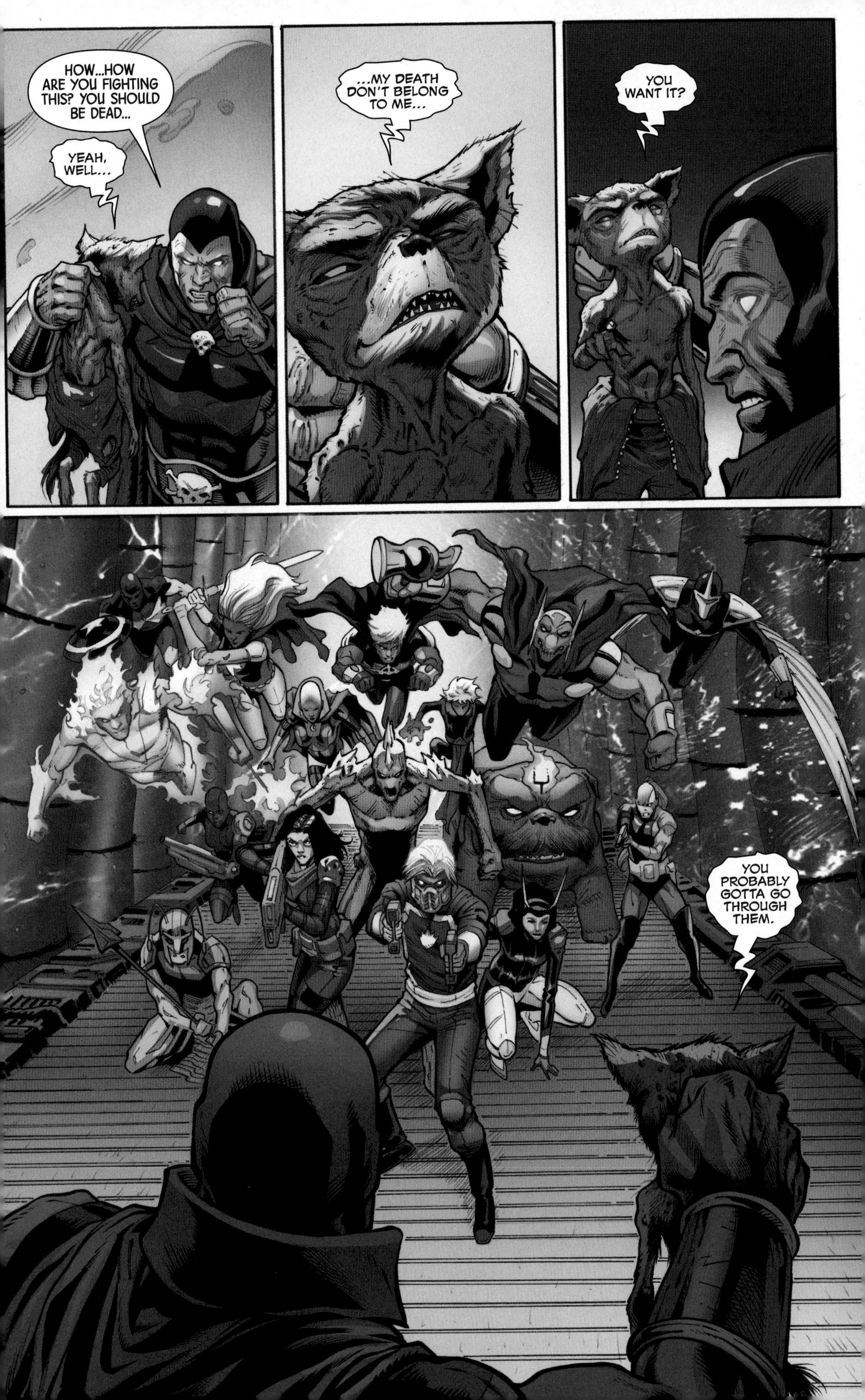
HOW...HOW ARE YOU FIGHTING THIS? YOU SHOULD BE DEAD...
YEAH, WELL...
...MY DEATH DON'T BELONG TO ME...
YOU WANT IT?
YOU PROBABLY GOTTA GO THROUGH THEM.

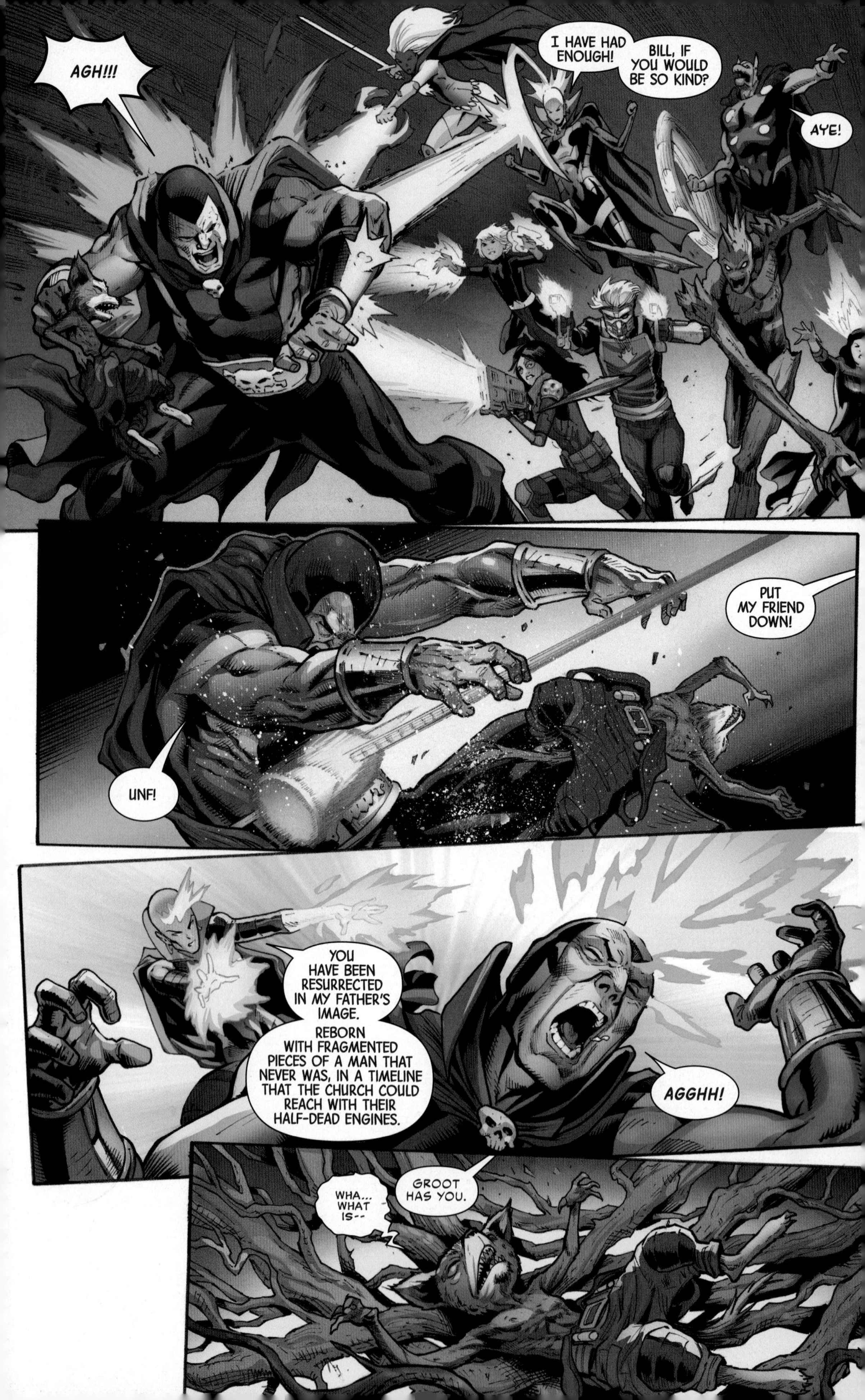
AGH!!!
I HAVE HAD ENOUGH!
BILL, IF YOU WOULD BE SO KIND?
AYE!
PUT MY FRIEND DOWN!
UNF!
YOU HAVE BEEN RESURRECTED IN MY FATHER'S IMAGE.
REBORN WITH FRAGMENTED PIECES OF A MAN THAT NEVER WAS, IN A TIMELINE THAT THE CHURCH COULD REACH WITH THEIR HALF-DEAD ENGINES.
AGGHH!
WHA... WHAT IS--
GROOT HAS YOU.

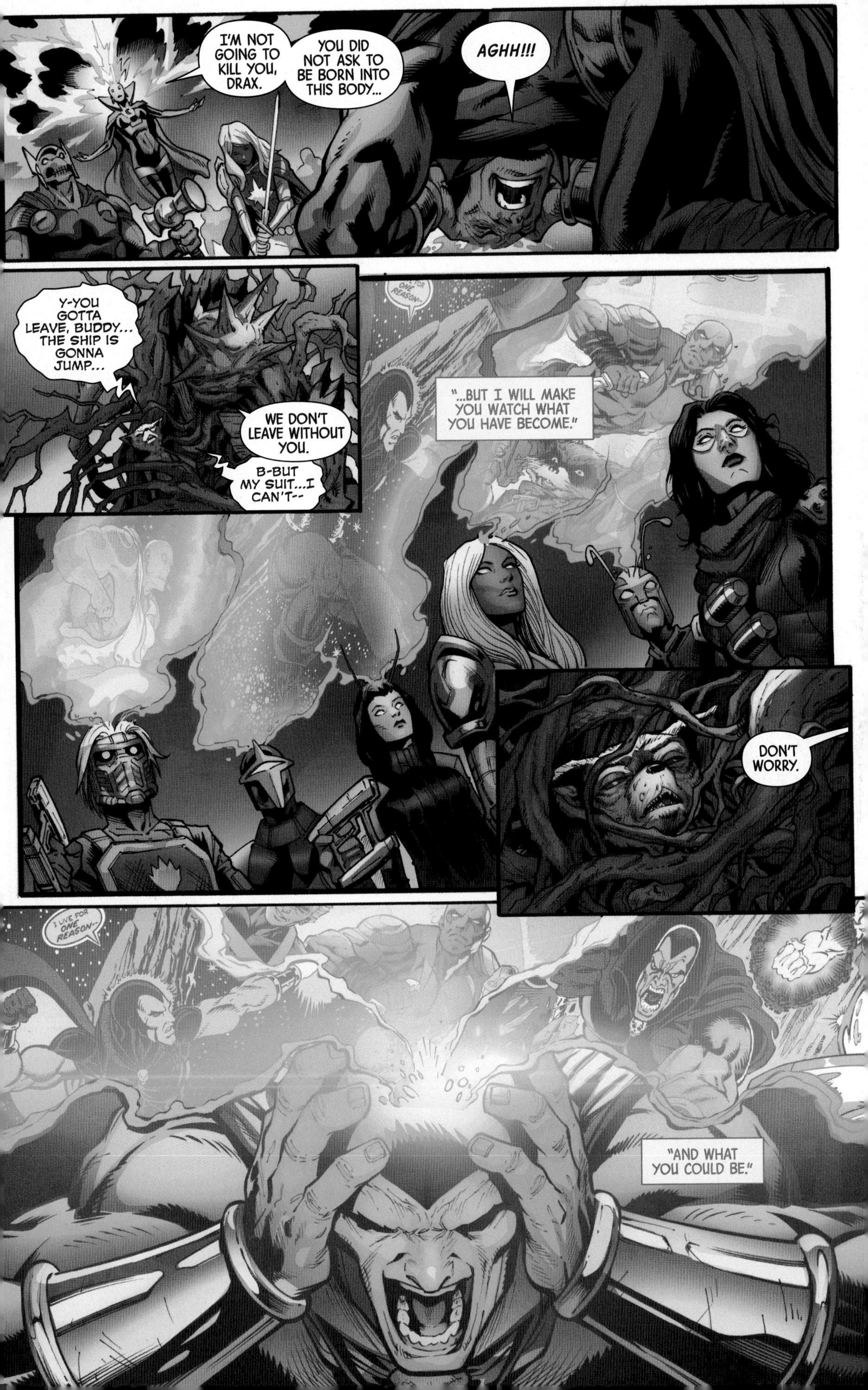
I'M NOT GOING TO KILL YOU, DRAX.
YOU DID NOT ASK TO BE BORN INTO THIS BODY...
AGHH!!!
Y-YOU GOTTA LEAVE, BUDDY... THE SHIP IS GONNA JUMP...
WE DON'T LEAVE WITHOUT YOU.
B-BUT MY SUIT...I CAN'T--
"...BUT I WILL MAKE YOU WATCH WHAT YOU HAVE BECOME."
DON'T WORRY.
I LIVE FOR ONE REASON--
"AND WHAT YOU COULD BE."

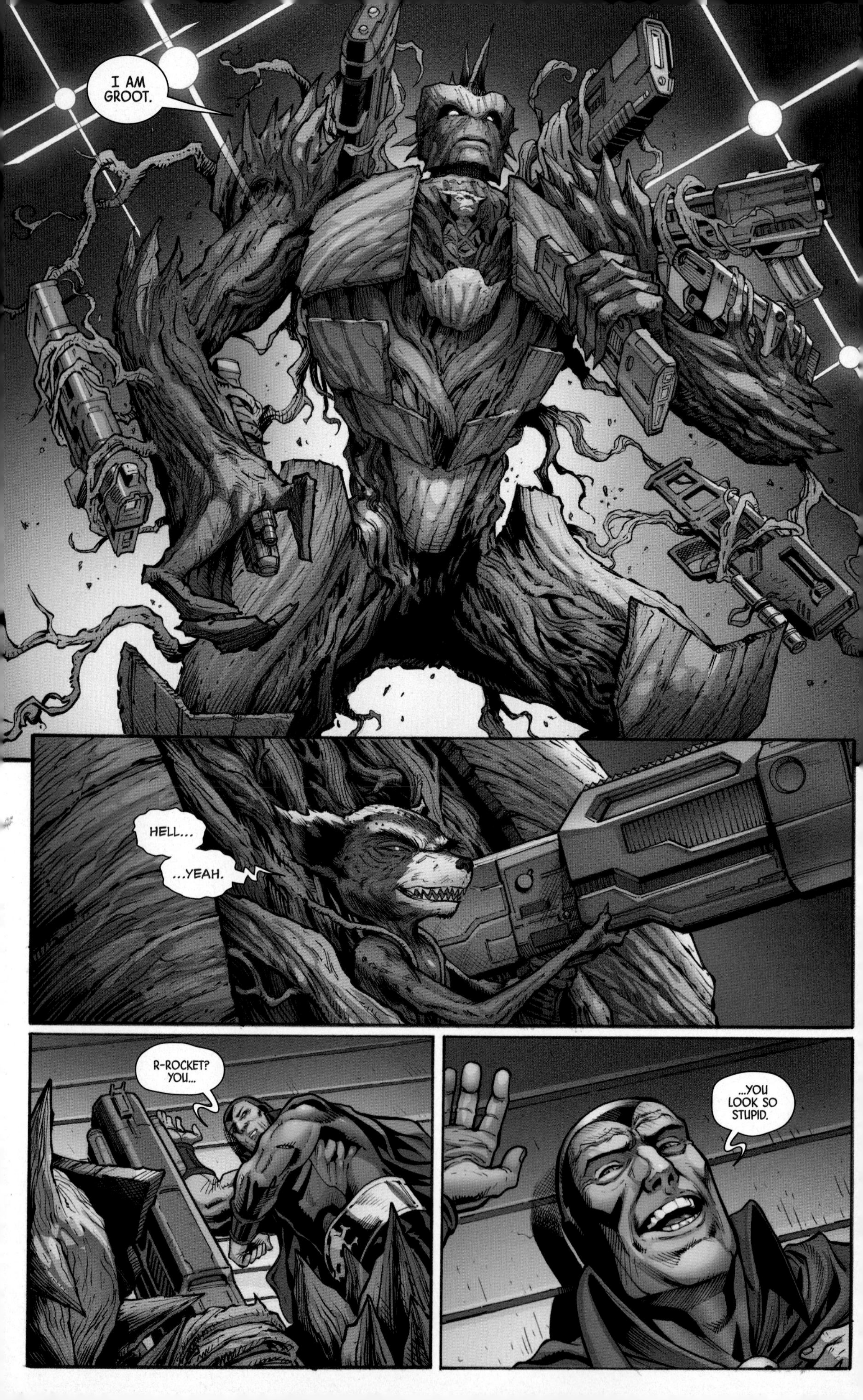
I AM GROOT.
HELL...
...YEAH.
R-ROCKET? YOU...
...YOU LOOK SO STUPID.

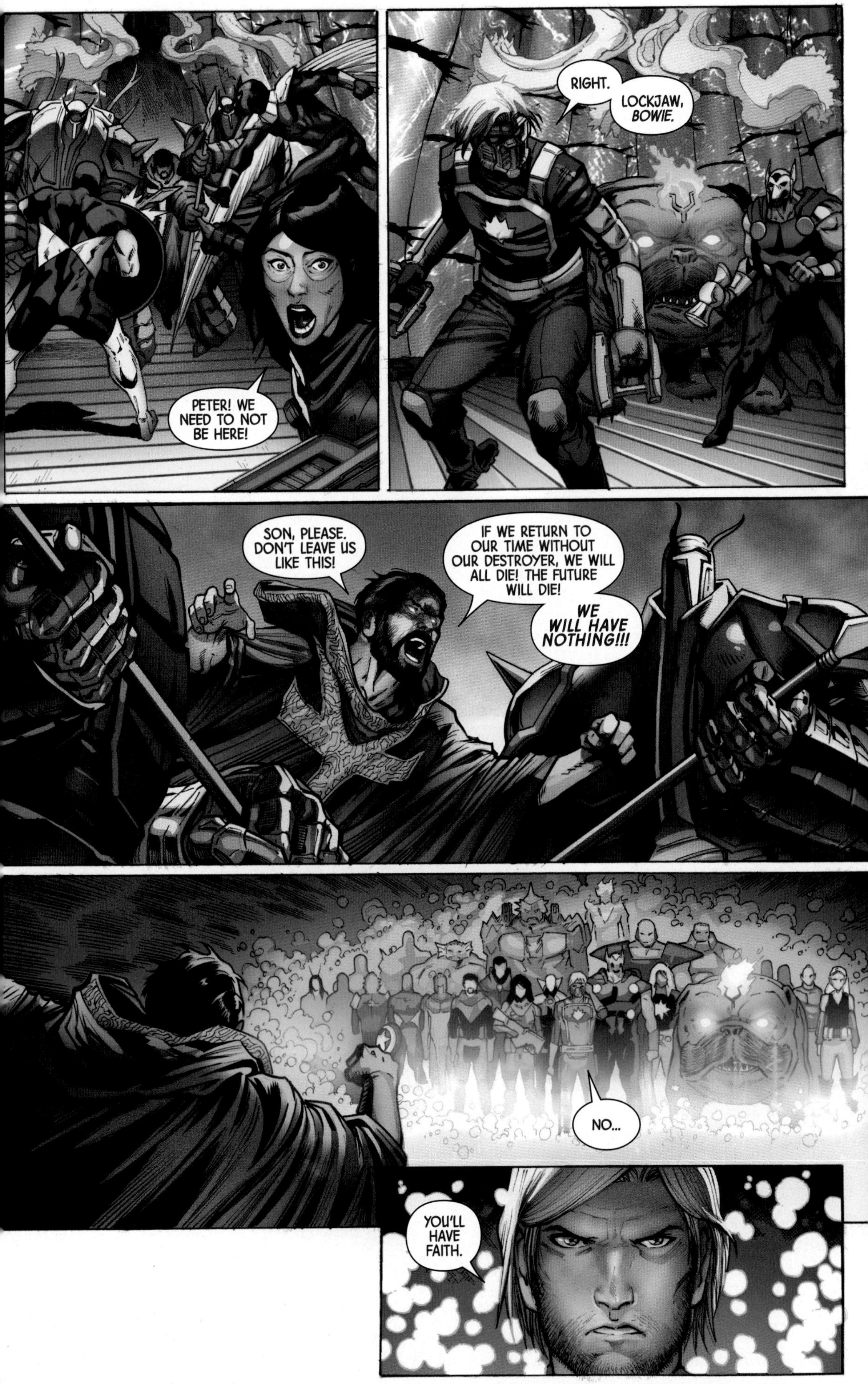
PETER! WE NEED TO NOT BE HERE!
RIGHT.
LOCKJAW, BOWIE.
SON, PLEASE. DON'T LEAVE US LIKE THIS!
IF WE RETURN TO OUR TIME WITHOUT OUR DESTROYER, WE WILL ALL DIE! THE FUTURE WILL DIE!
WE WILL HAVE NOTHING!!!
NO...
YOU'LL HAVE FAITH.

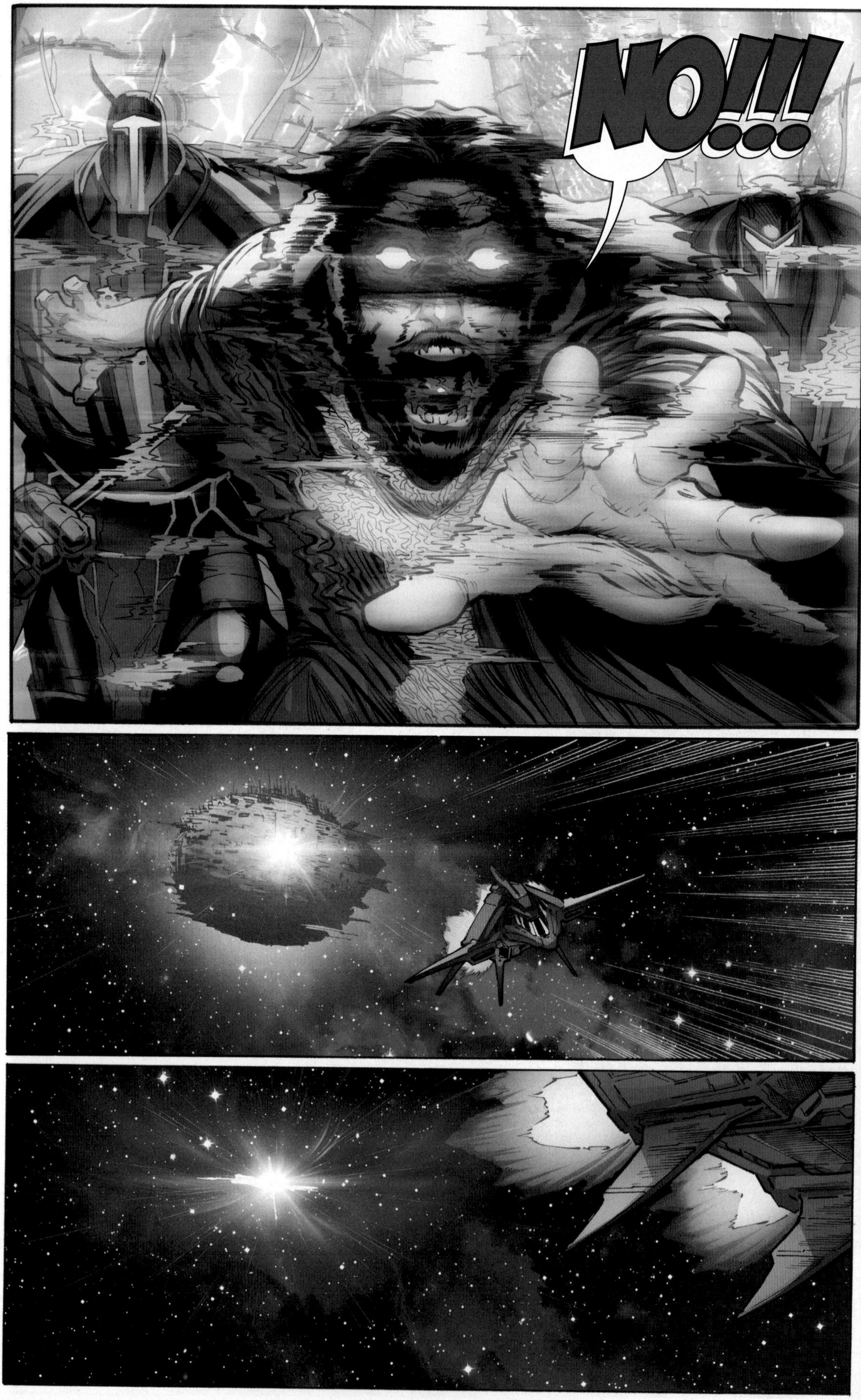
NO!!!....

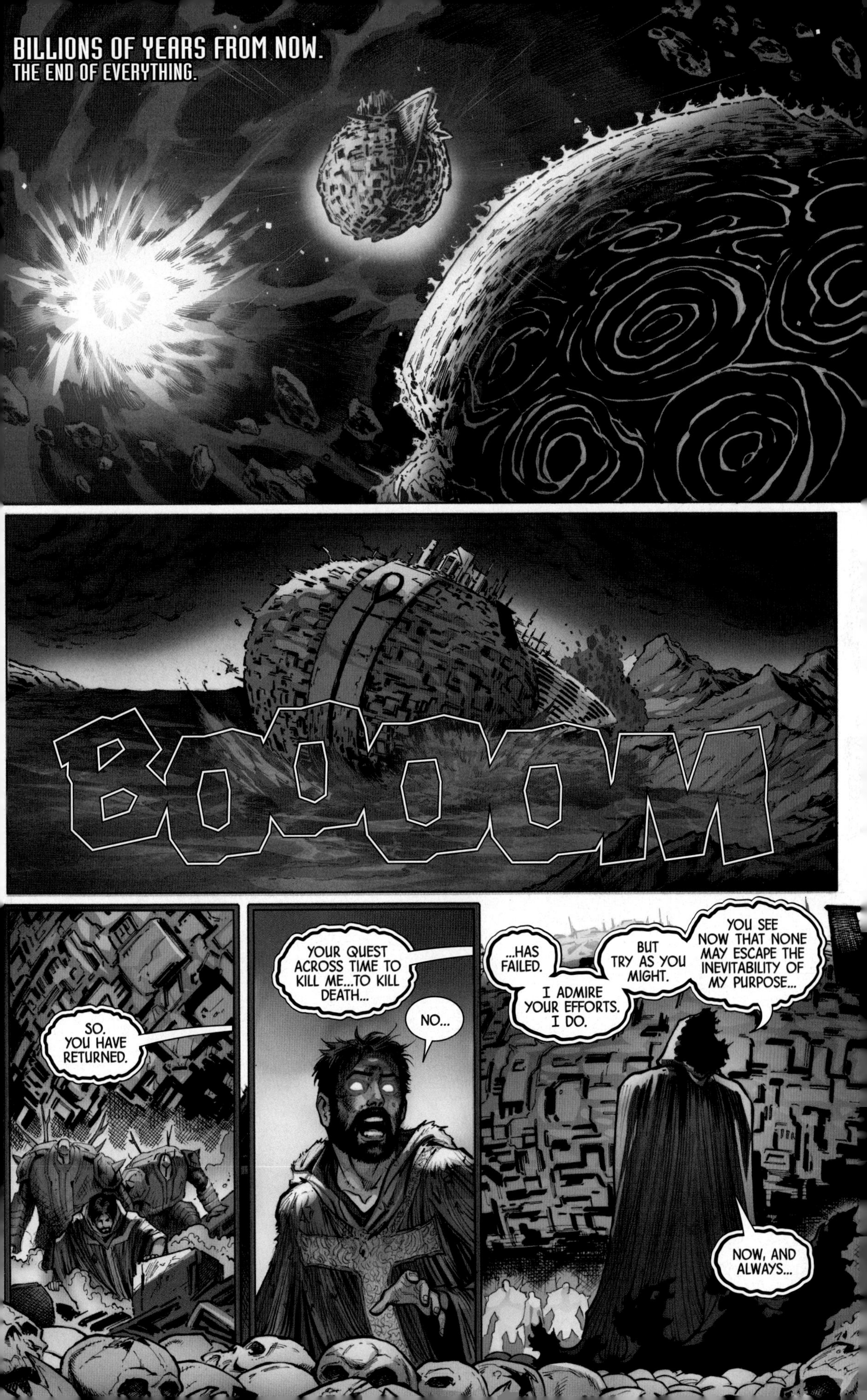
BILLIONS OF YEARS FROM NOW.
THE END OF EVERYTHING.
BOOOOM
SO. YOU HAVE RETURNED.
YOUR QUEST ACROSS TIME TO KILL ME...TO KILL DEATH...
NO...
...HAS FAILED.
I ADMIRE YOUR EFFORTS. I DO.
BUT TRY AS YOU MIGHT.
YOU SEE NOW THAT NONE MAY ESCAPE THE INEVITABILITY OF MY PURPOSE...
NOW, AND ALWAYS...

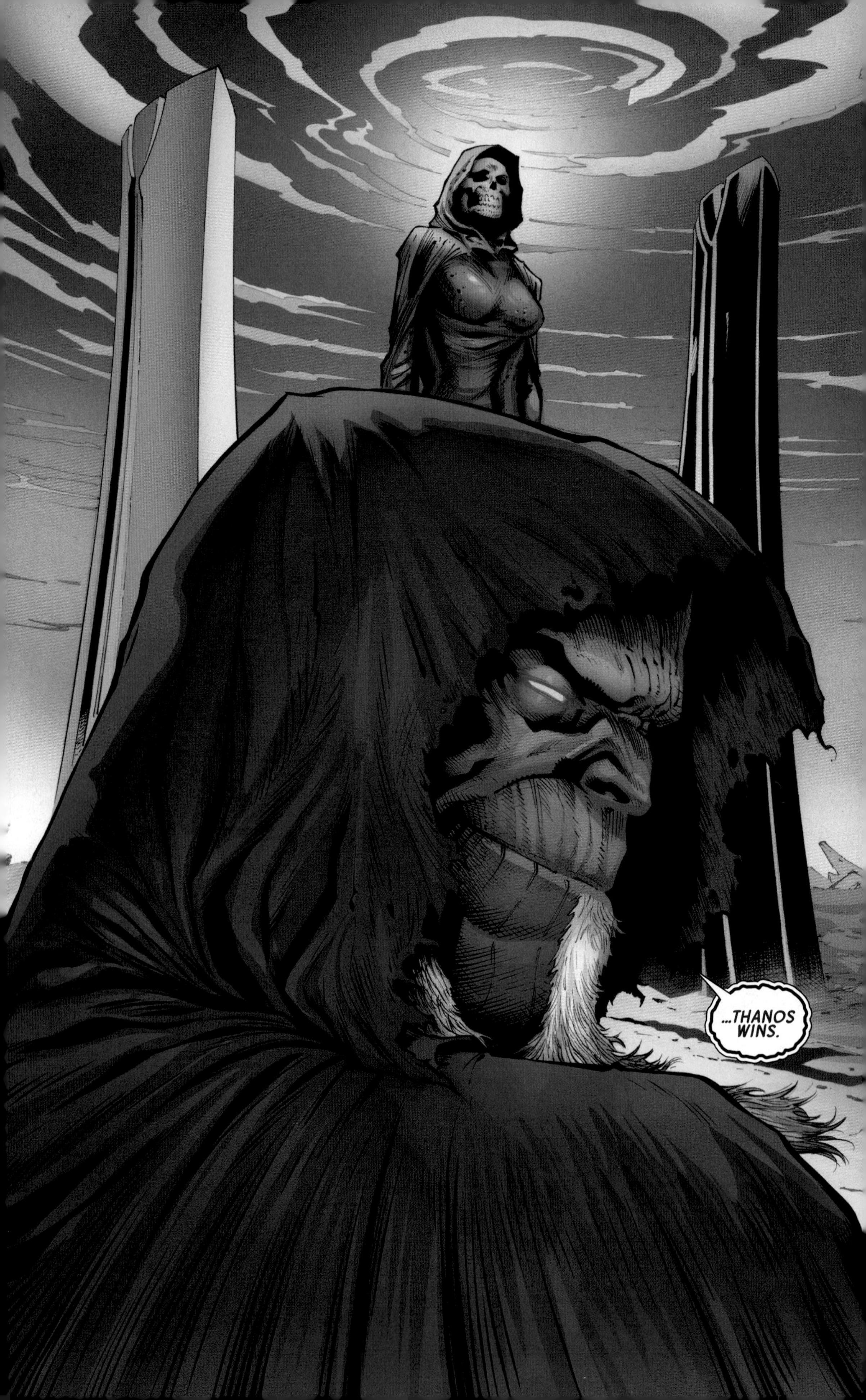
...THANOS WINS.

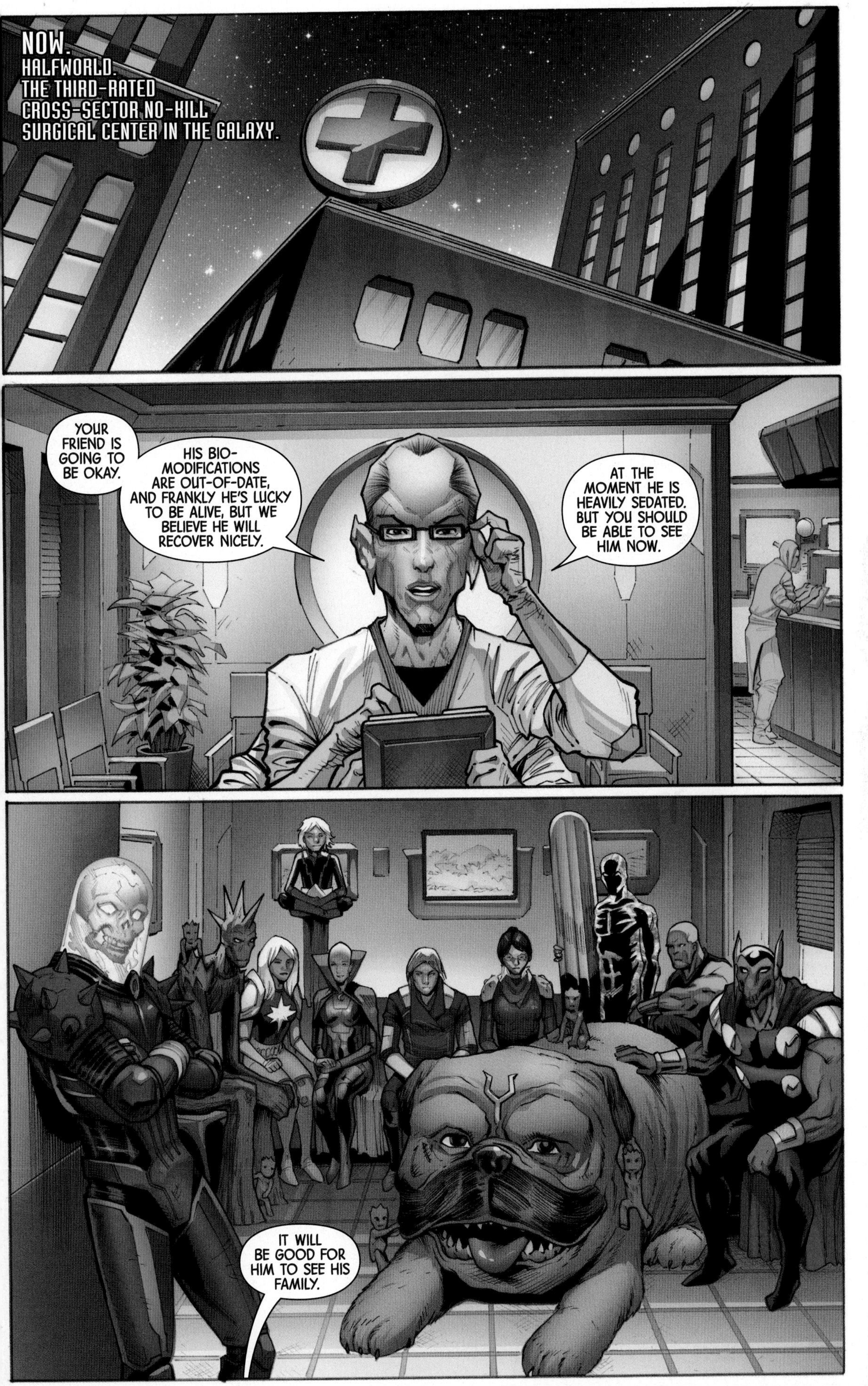
NOW.
HALFWORLD.
THE THIRD-RATED
CROSS-SECTOR NO-KILL
SURGICAL CENTER IN THE GALAXY.
YOUR FRIEND IS GOING TO BE OKAY.
HIS BIO-MODIFICATIONS ARE OUT-OF-DATE, AND FRANKLY HE'S LUCKY TO BE ALIVE, BUT WE BELIEVE HE WILL RECOVER NICELY.
AT THE MOMENT HE IS HEAVILY SEDATED. BUT YOU SHOULD BE ABLE TO SEE HIM NOW.
IT WILL BE GOOD FOR HIM TO SEE HIS FAMILY.

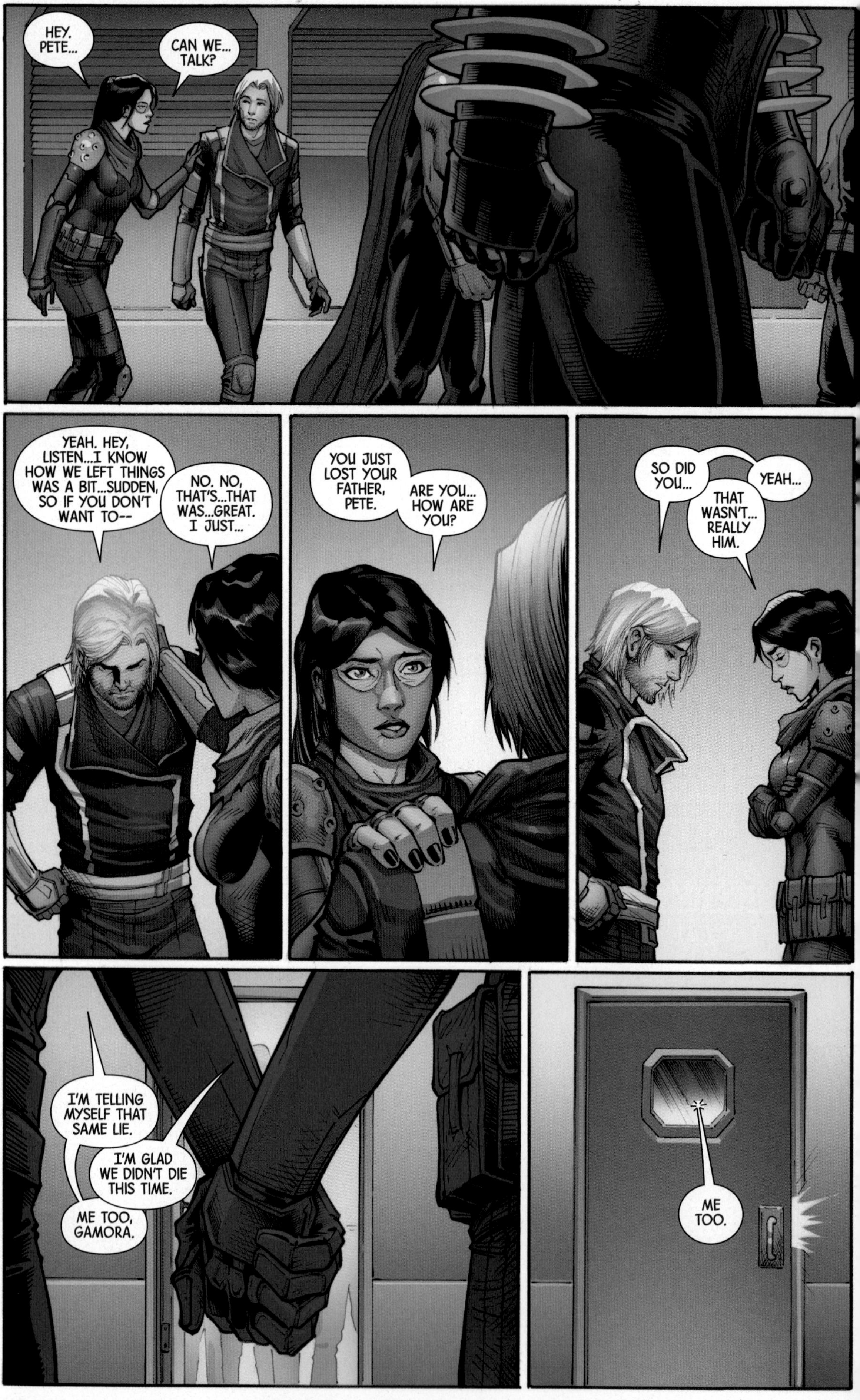
HEY. PETE...
CAN WE... TALK?
YEAH. HEY, LISTEN...I KNOW HOW WE LEFT THINGS WAS A BIT...SUDDEN, SO IF YOU DON'T WANT TO--
NO. NO, THAT'S...THAT WAS...GREAT. I JUST...
YOU JUST LOST YOUR FATHER, PETE.
ARE YOU... HOW ARE YOU?
SO DID YOU...
YEAH...
THAT WASN'T... REALLY HIM.
I'M TELLING MYSELF THAT SAME LIE.
I'M GLAD WE DIDN'T DIE THIS TIME.
ME TOO, GAMORA.
ME TOO.

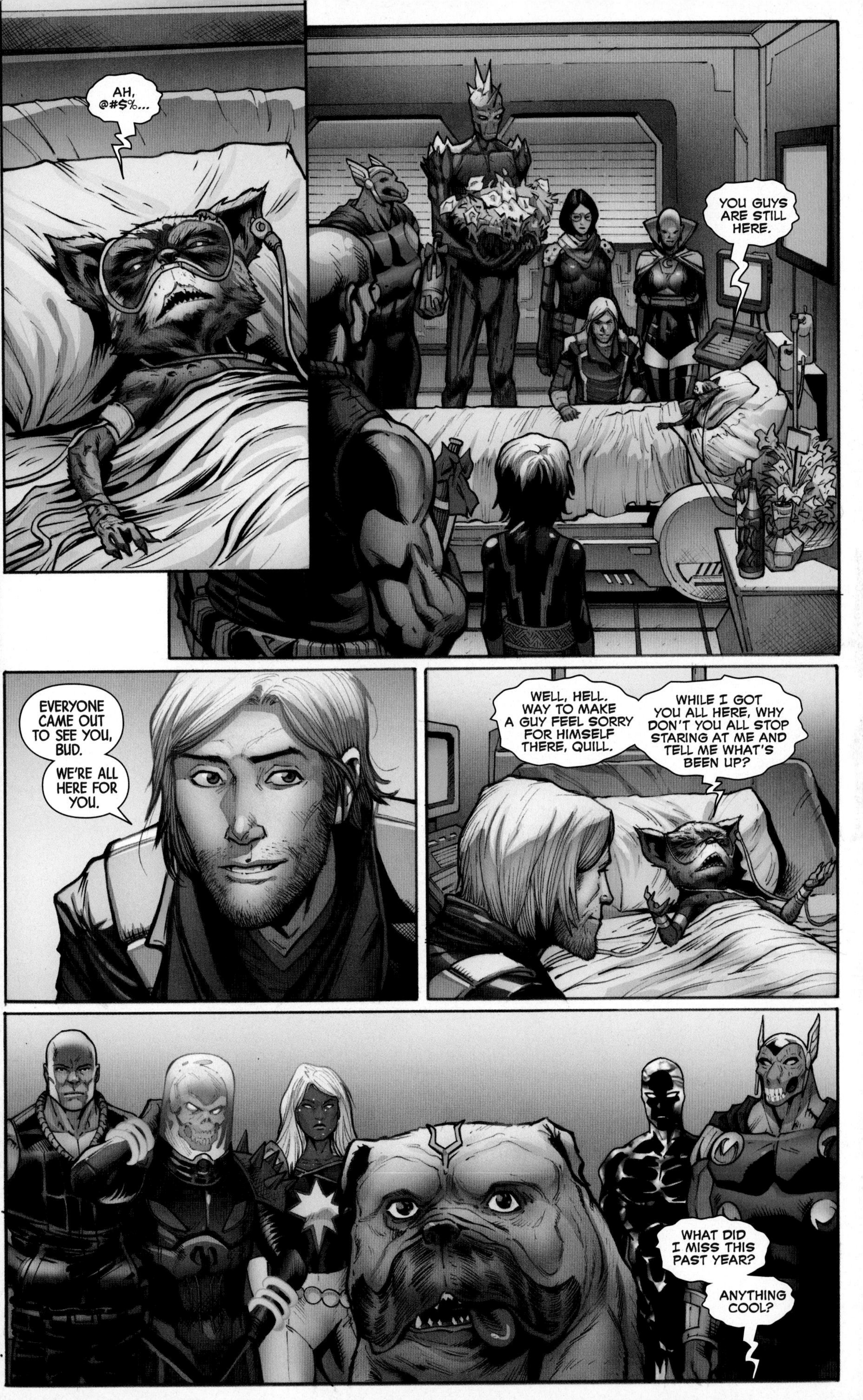
AH, @#$%...
YOU GUYS ARE STILL HERE.
EVERYONE CAME OUT TO SEE YOU, BUD.
WE'RE ALL HERE FOR YOU.
WELL, HELL. WAY TO MAKE A GUY FEEL SORRY FOR HIMSELF THERE, QUILL.
WHILE I GOT YOU ALL HERE, WHY DON'T YOU ALL STOP STARING AT ME AND TELL ME WHAT'S BEEN UP?
WHAT DID I MISS THIS PAST YEAR?
ANYTHING COOL?

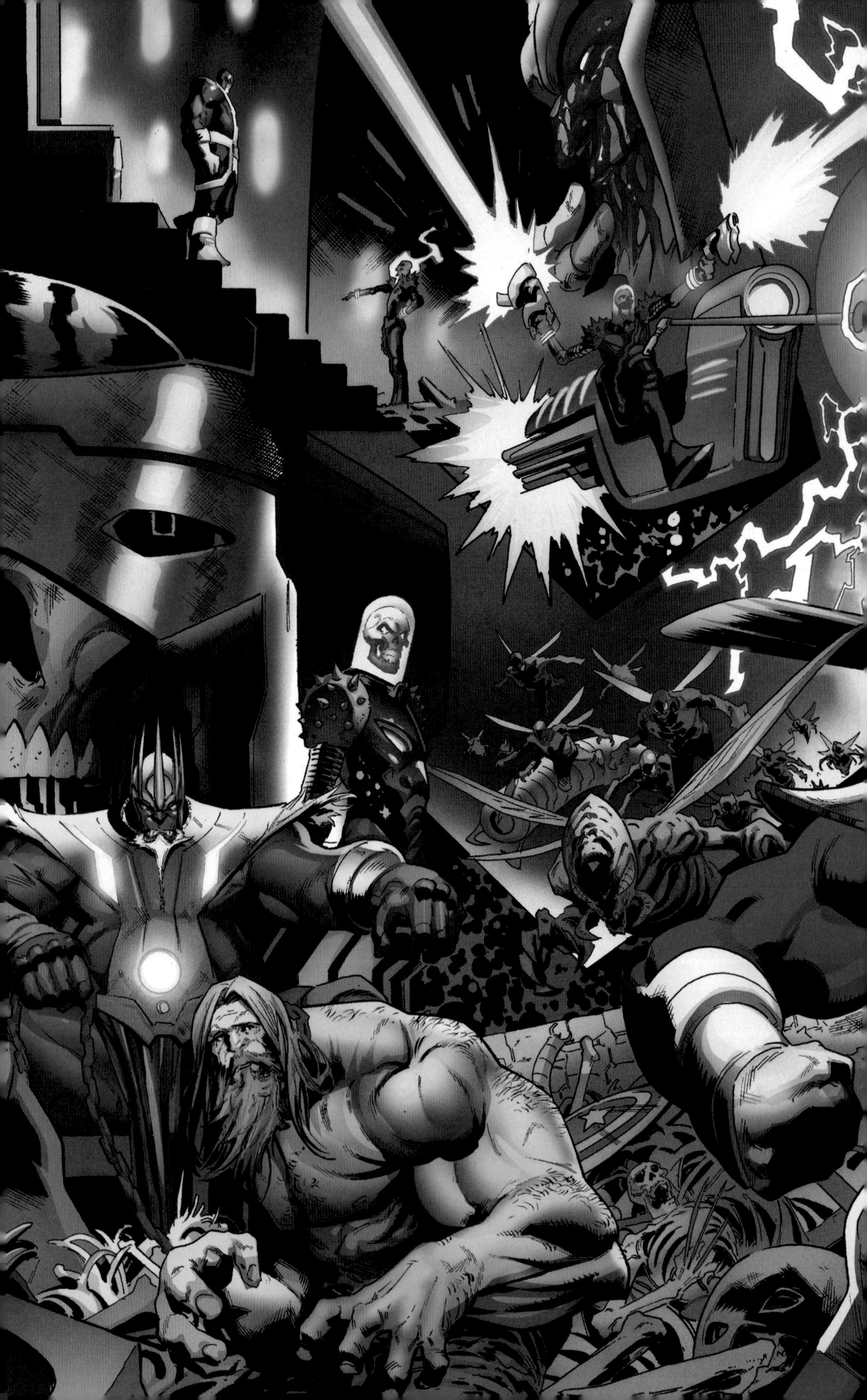

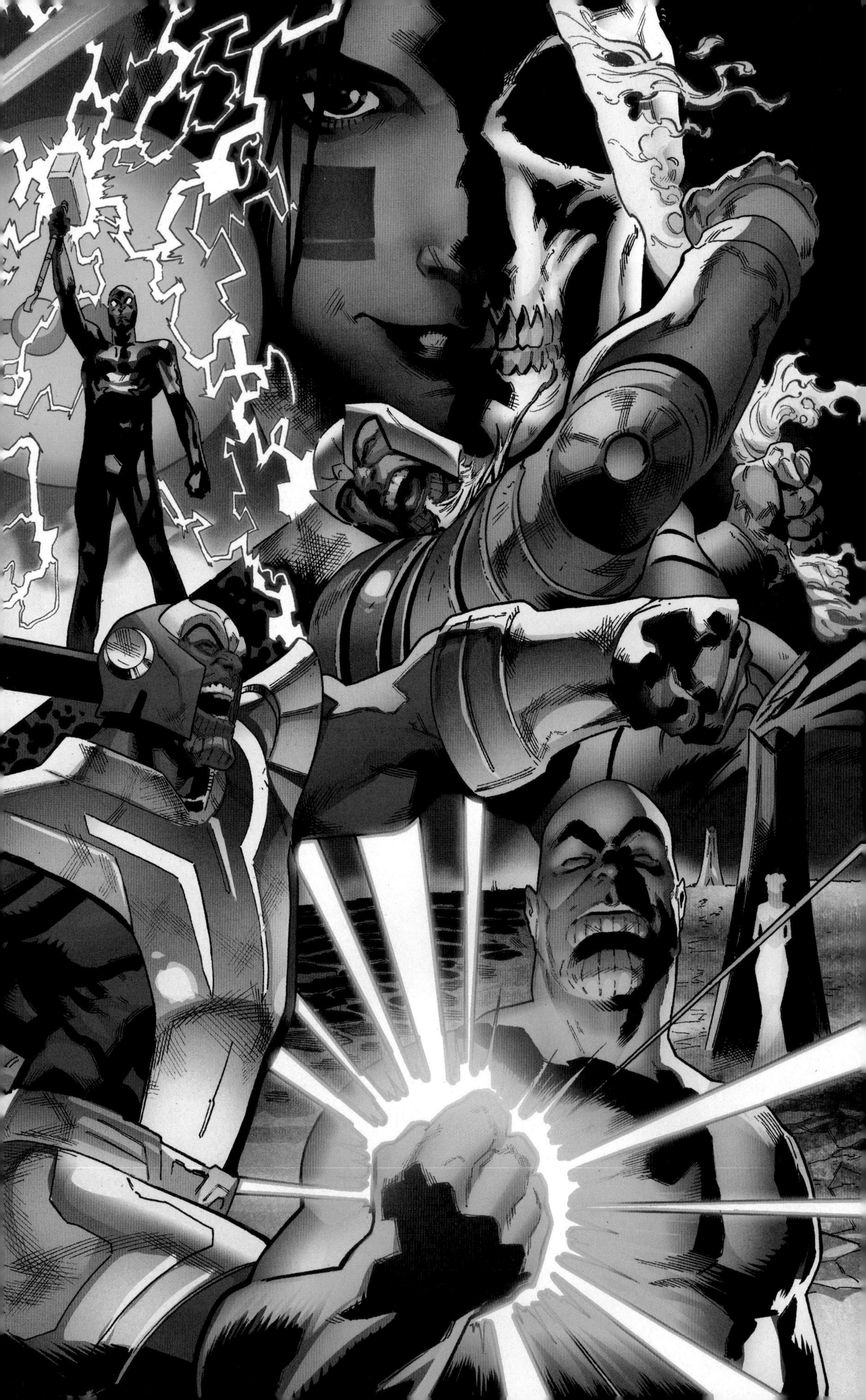

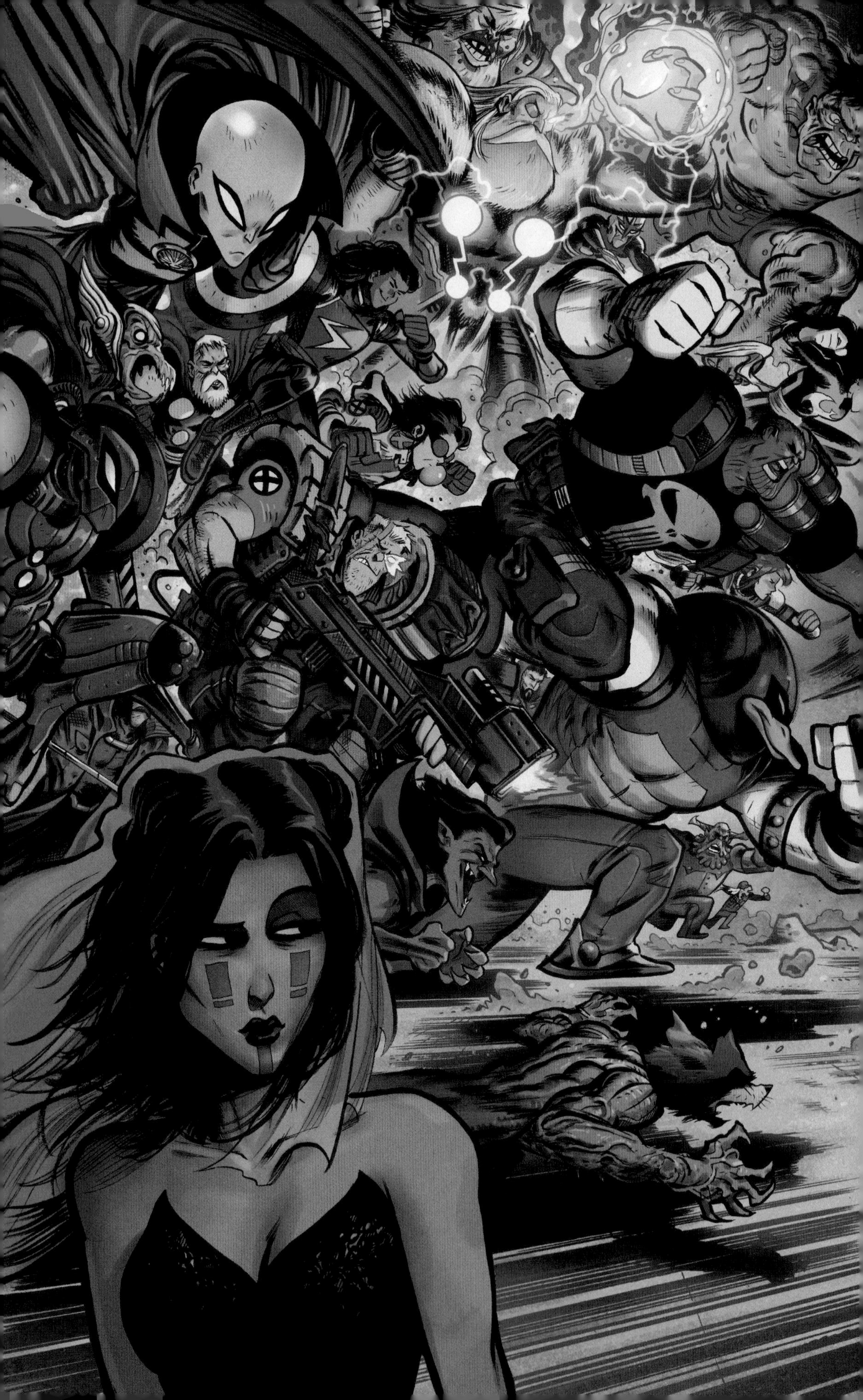

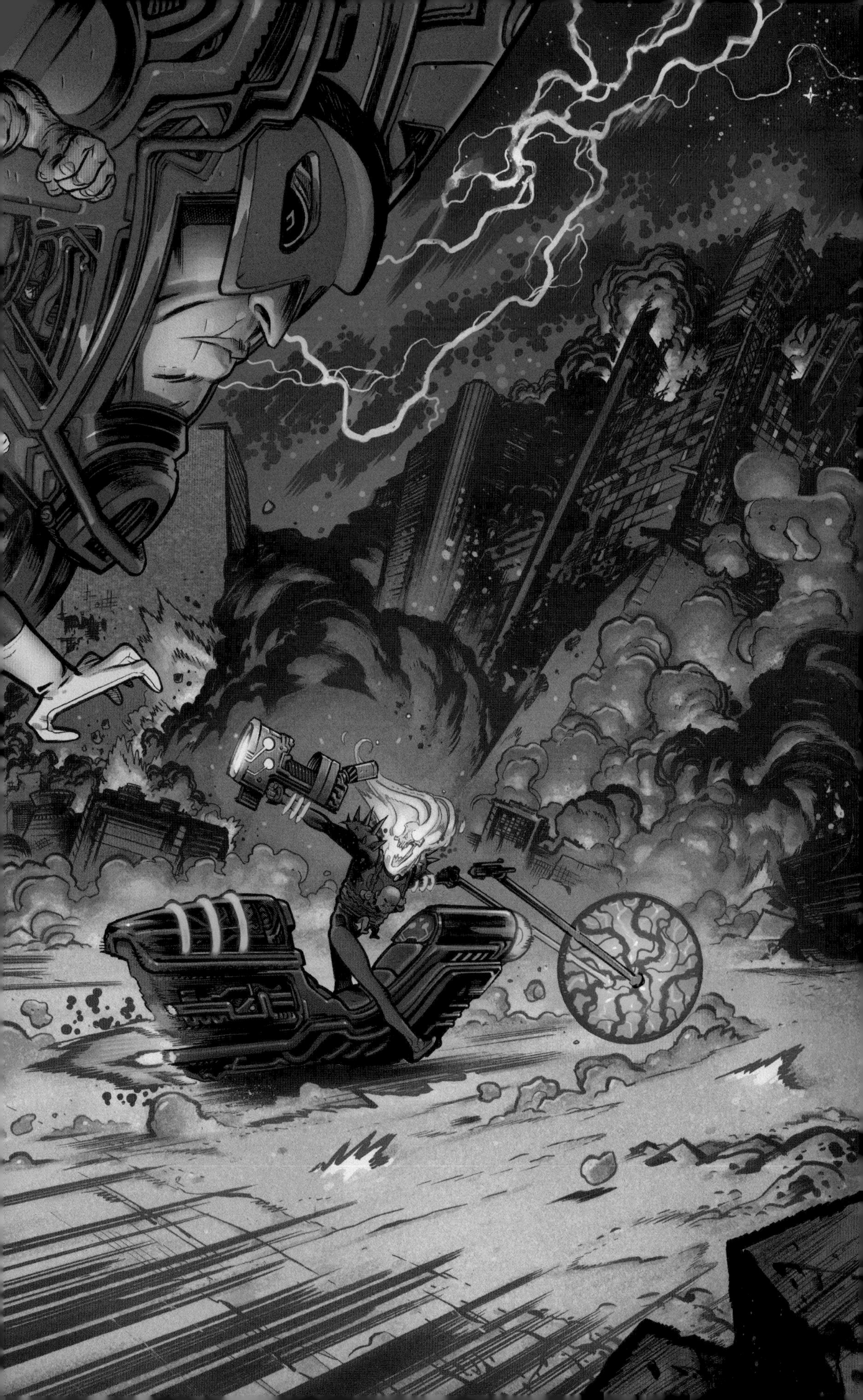

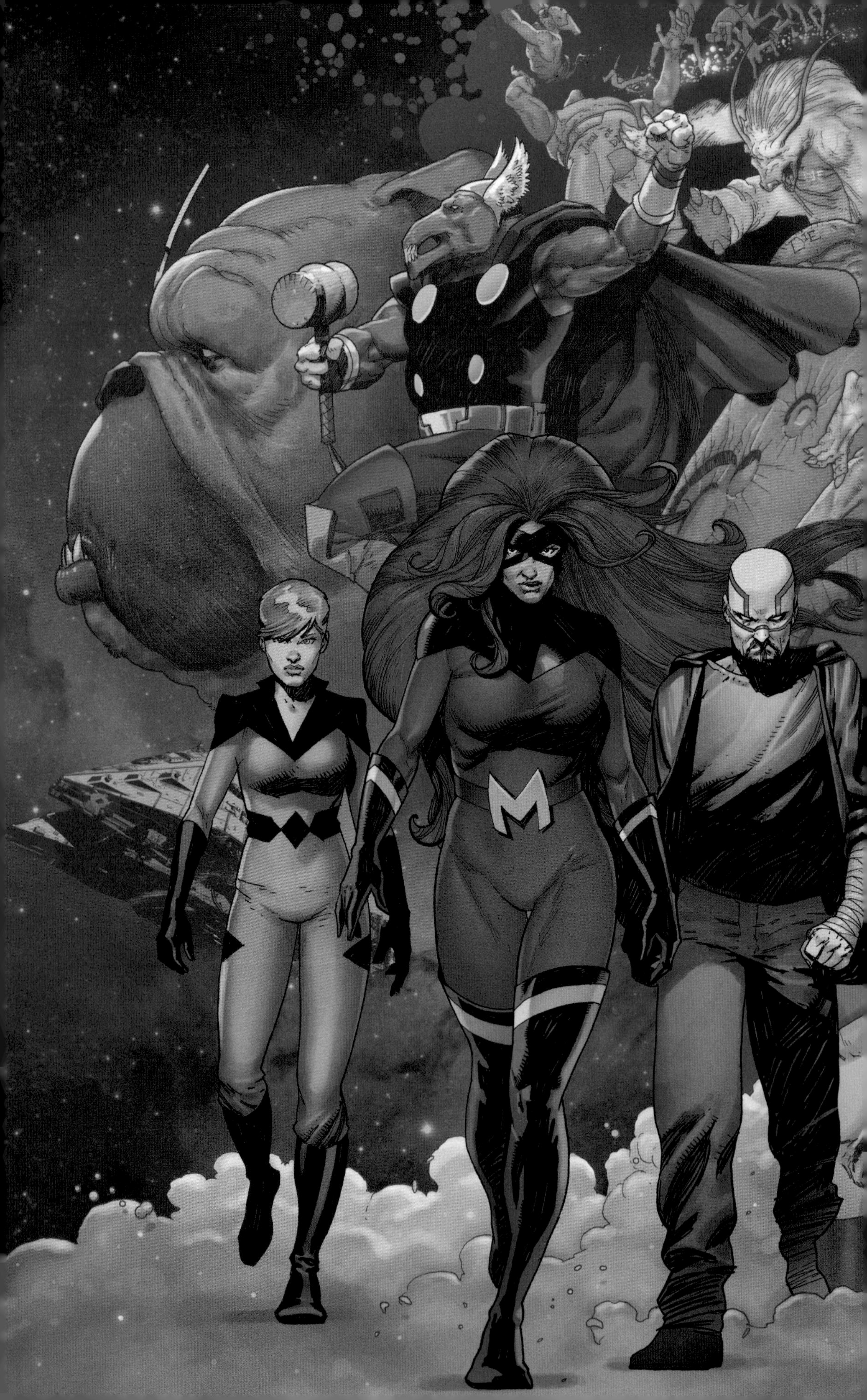

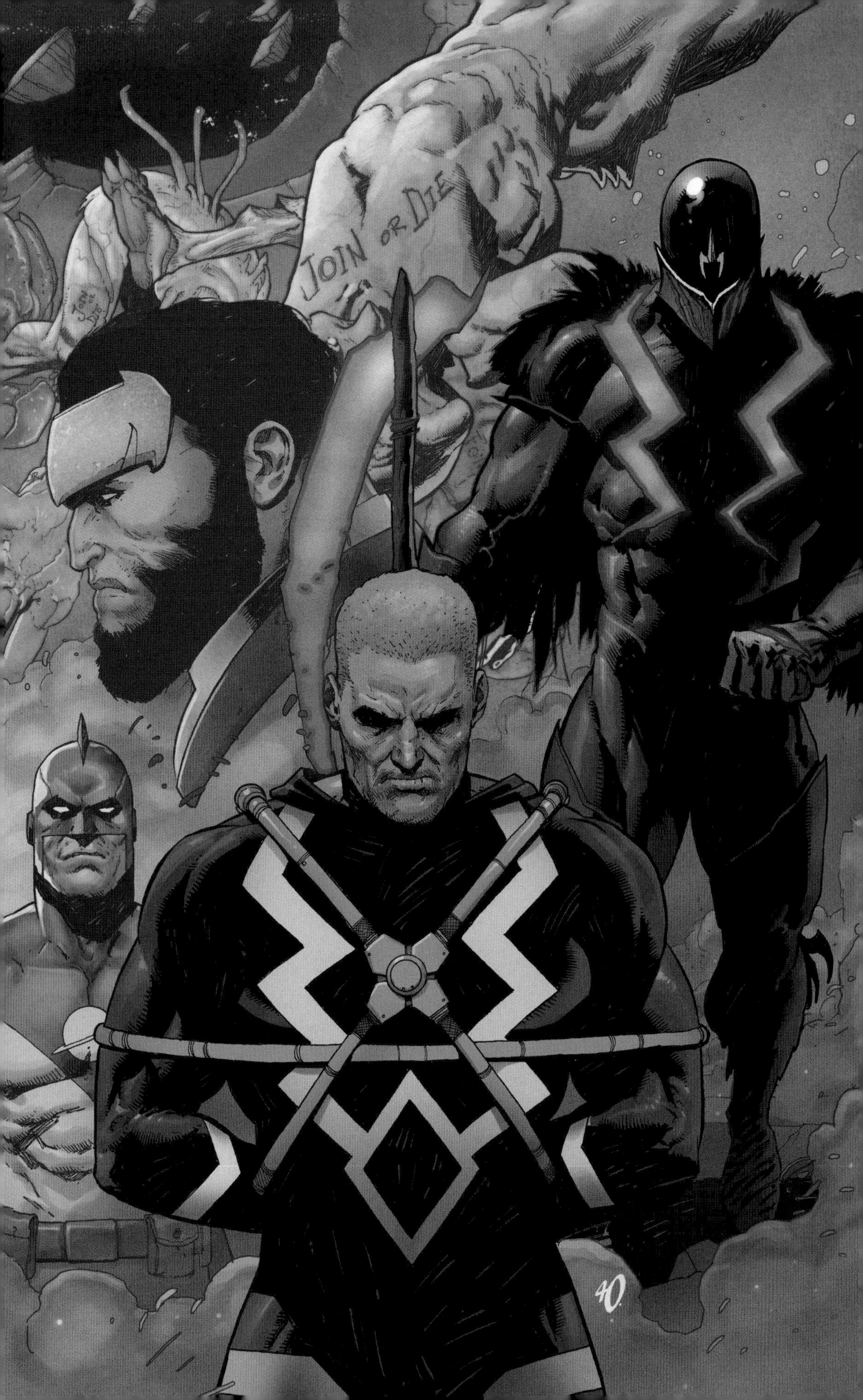
JOIN OR DIE

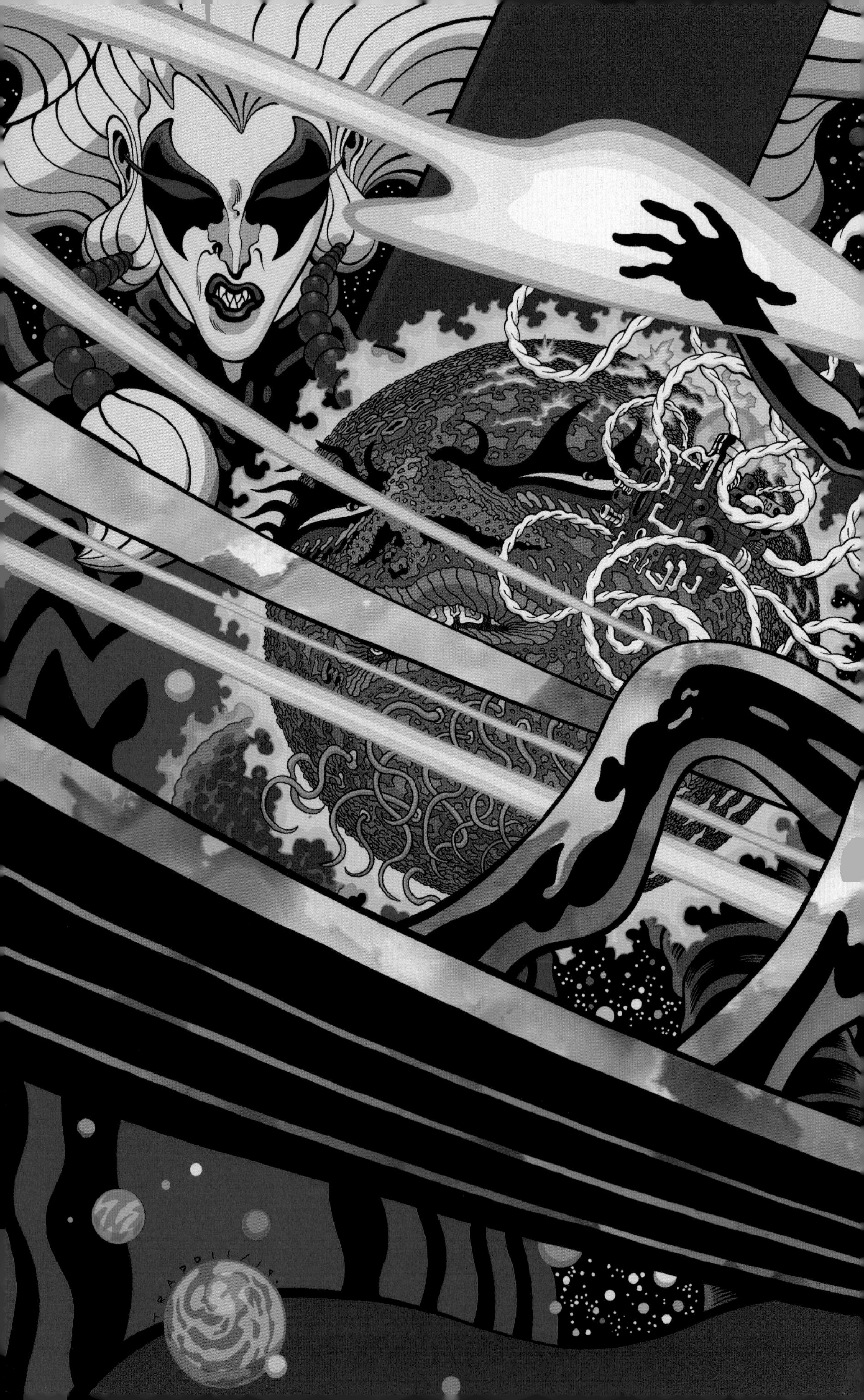

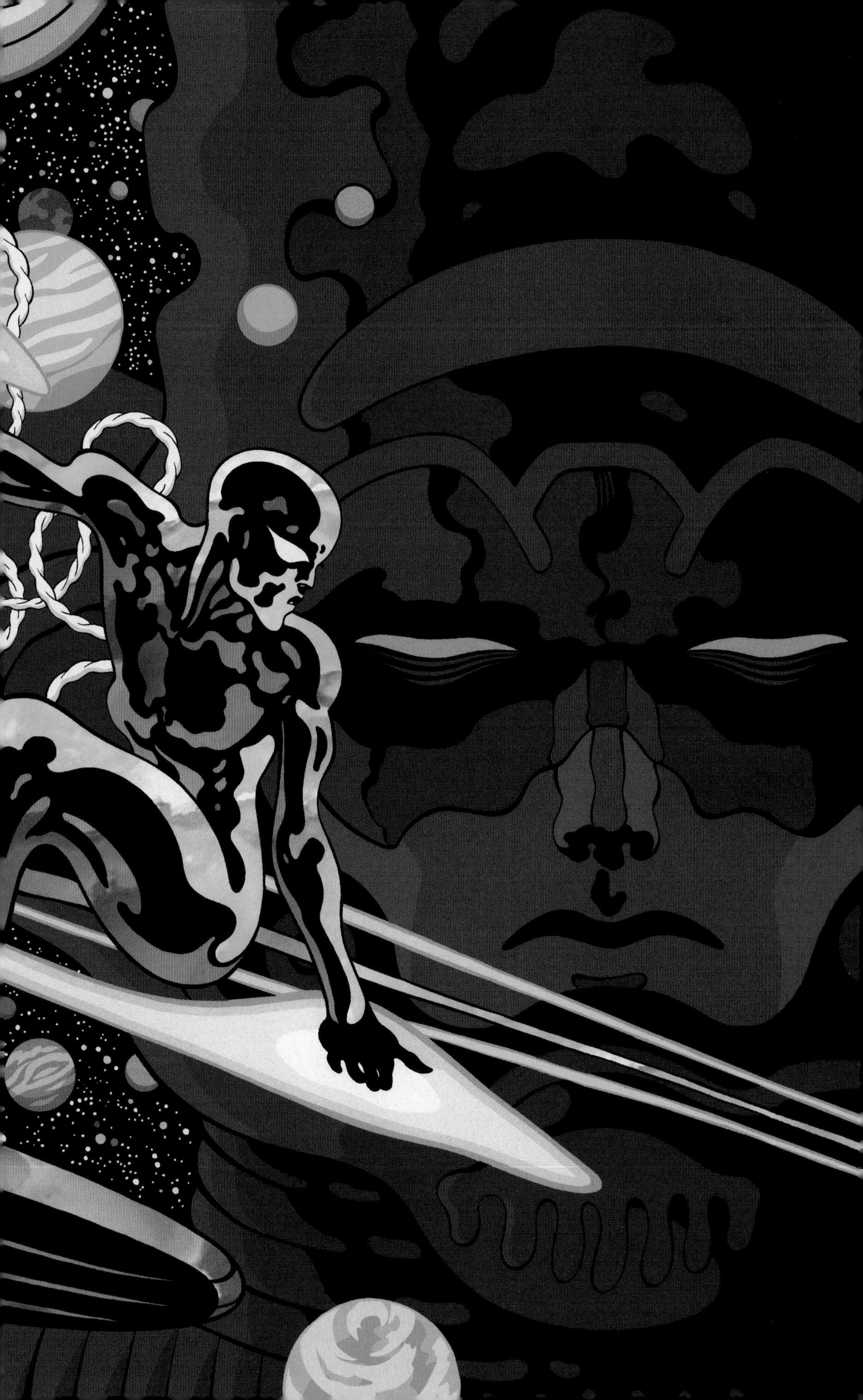

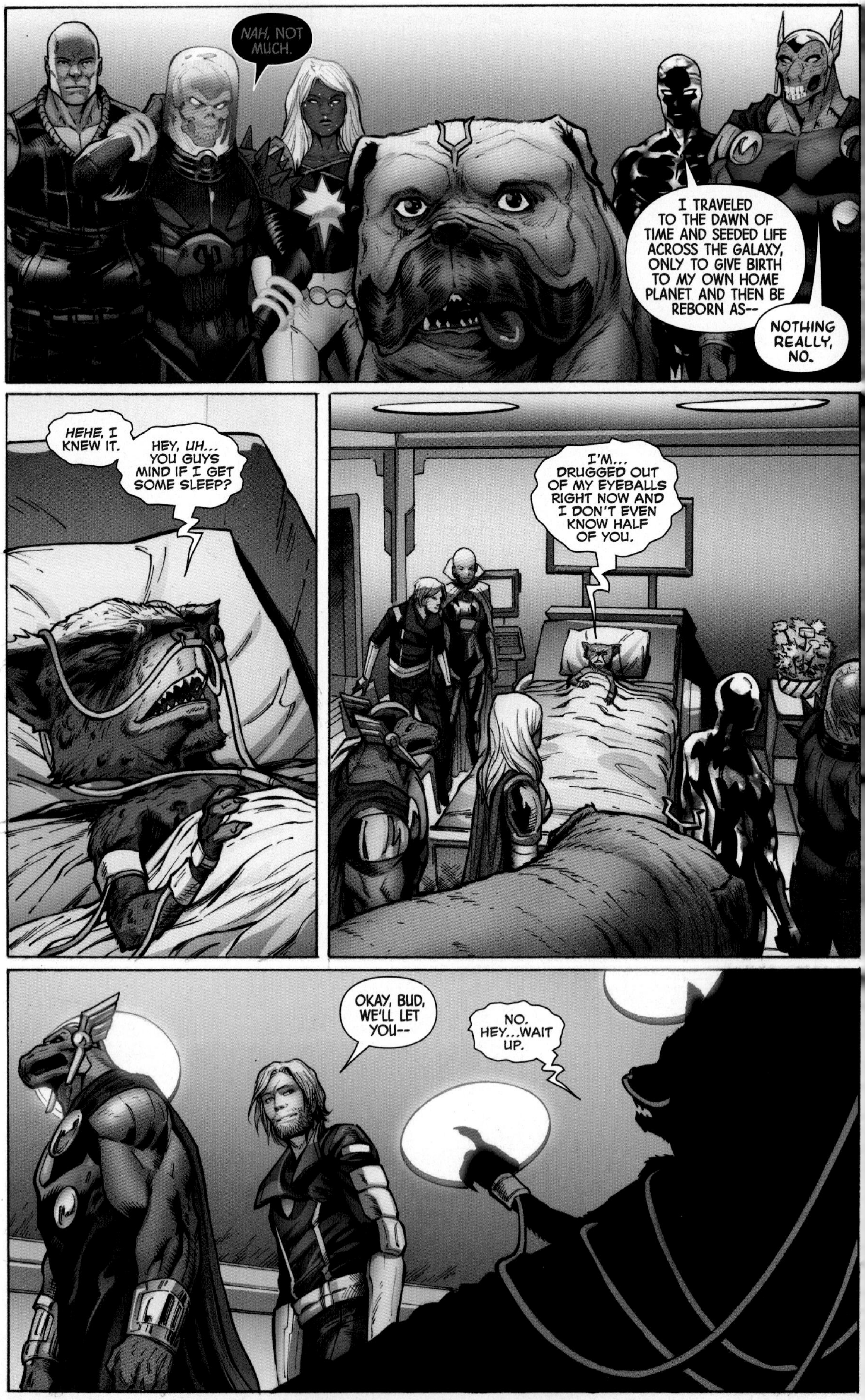
NAH, NOT MUCH.
I TRAVELED TO THE DAWN OF TIME AND SEEDED LIFE ACROSS THE GALAXY, ONLY TO GIVE BIRTH TO MY OWN HOME PLANET AND THEN BE REBORN AS--
NOTHING REALLY, NO.
HEHE, I KNEW IT.
HEY, UH... YOU GUYS MIND IF I GET SOME SLEEP?
I'M... DRUGGED OUT OF MY EYEBALLS RIGHT NOW AND I DON'T EVEN KNOW HALF OF YOU.
OKAY, BUD, WE'LL LET YOU--
NO. HEY...WAIT UP.

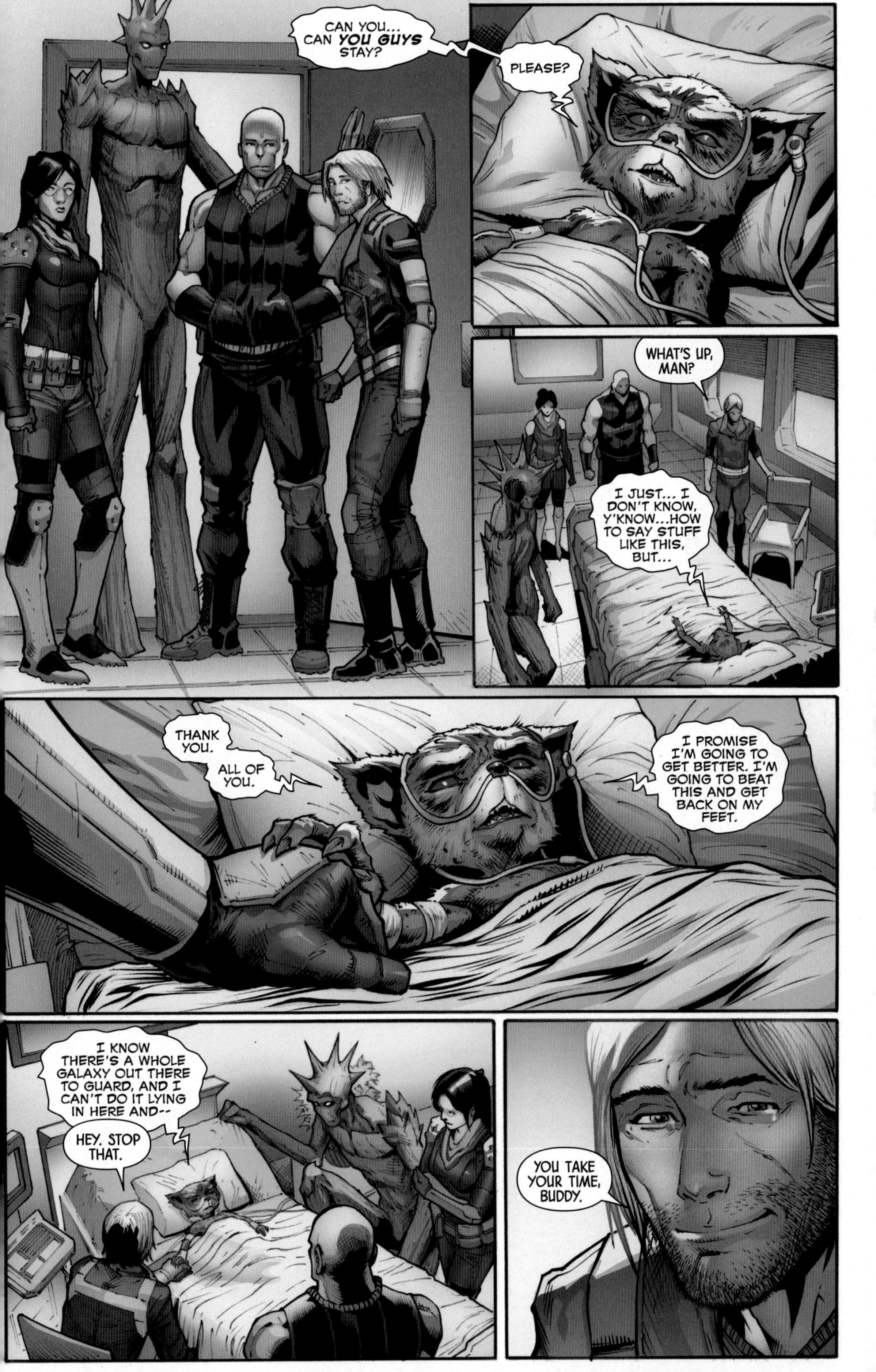
CAN YOU... CAN YOU GUYS STAY?
PLEASE?
WHAT'S UP, MAN?
I JUST... I DON'T KNOW, Y'KNOW...HOW TO SAY STUFF LIKE THIS, BUT...
THANK YOU.
ALL OF YOU.
I PROMISE I'M GOING TO GET BETTER. I'M GOING TO BEAT THIS AND GET BACK ON MY FEET.
I KNOW THERE'S A WHOLE GALAXY OUT THERE TO GUARD, AND I CAN'T DO IT LYING IN HERE AND--
HEY. STOP THAT.
YOU TAKE YOUR TIME, BUDDY.

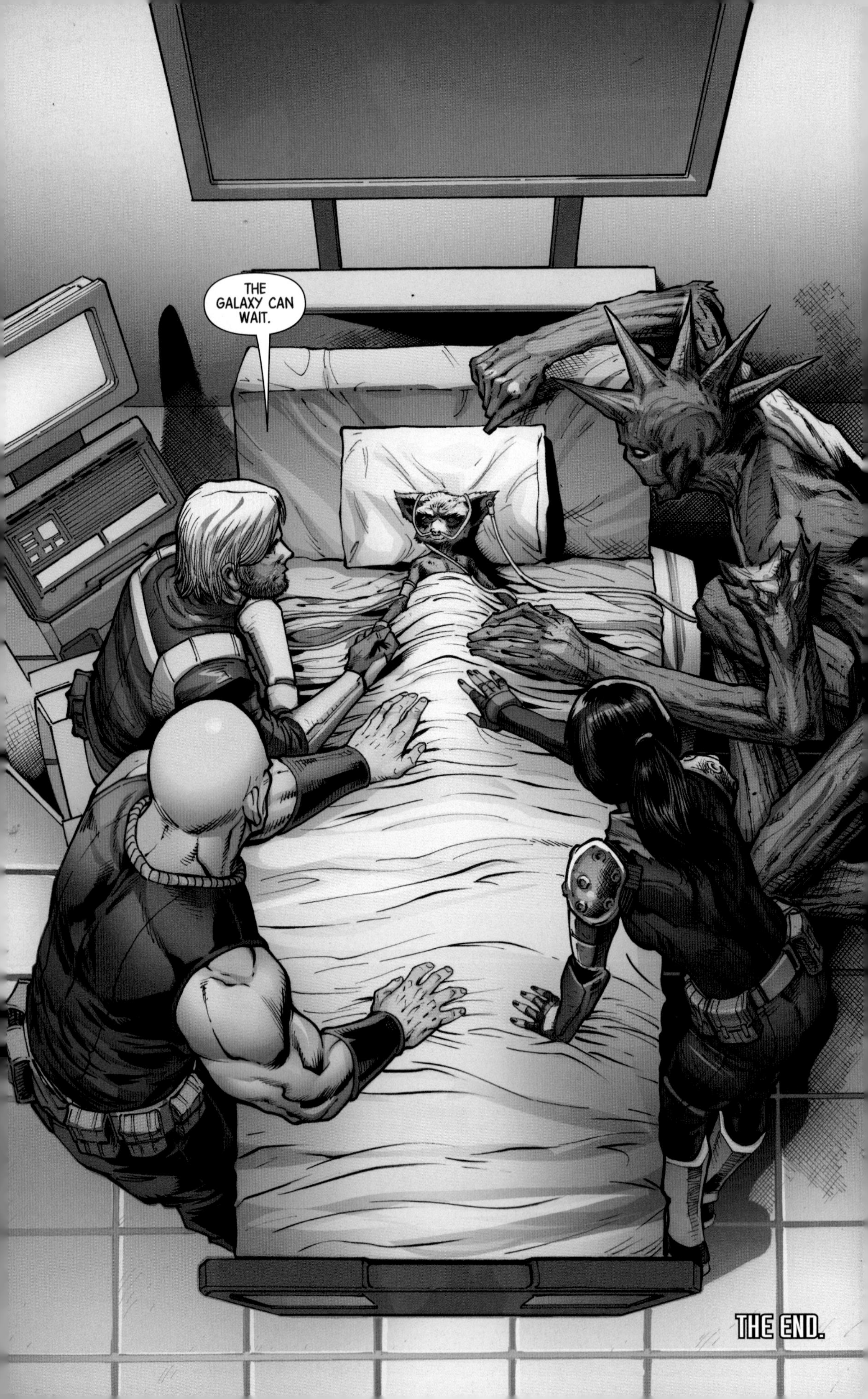
THE GALAXY CAN WAIT.
THE END.

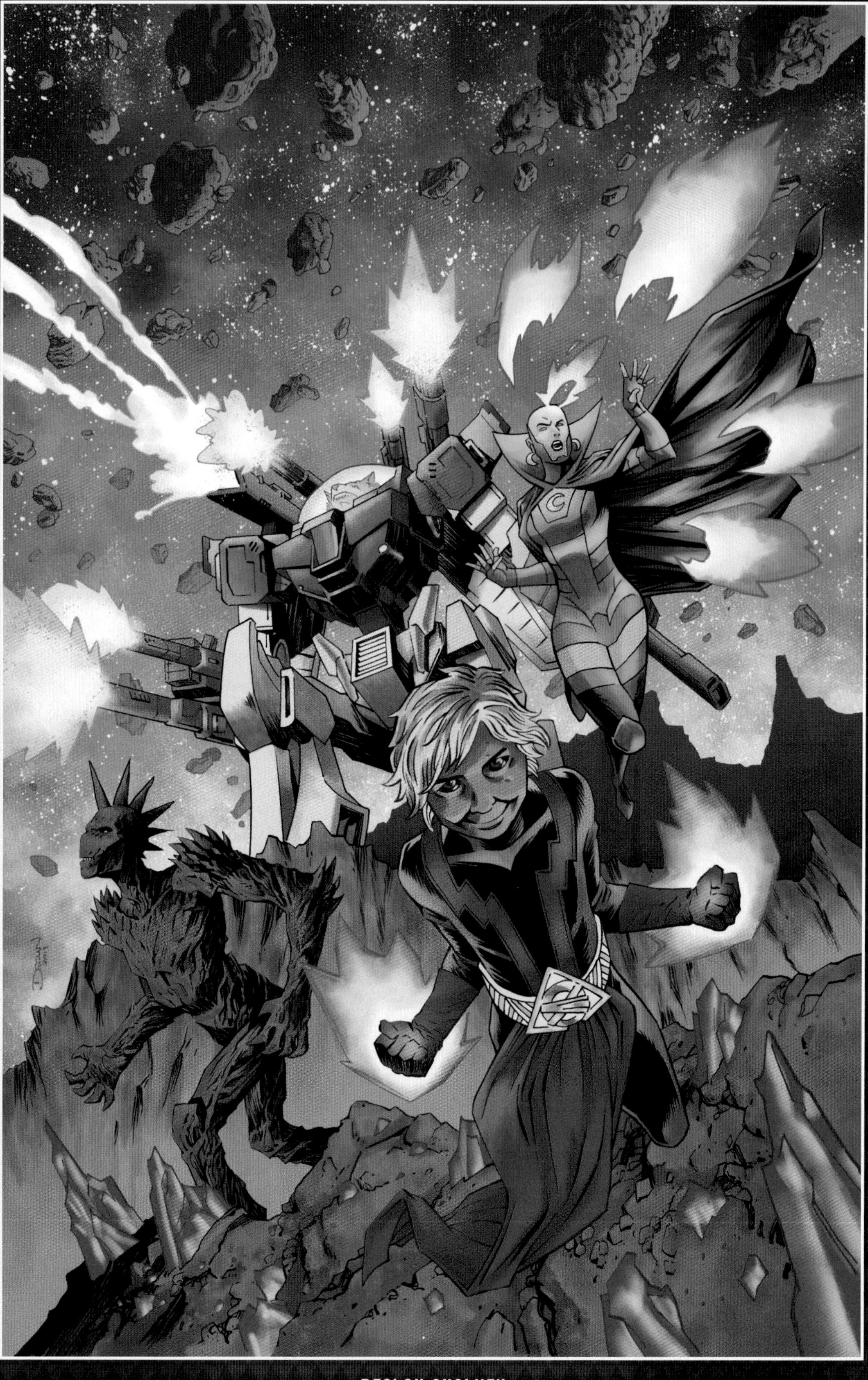

DECLAN SHALVEY
#12 variant

CORY SMITH & ROMULO FAJARDO JR.
ANNUAL #1 variant

RON LIM & ISRAEL SILVA
ANNUAL #1 variant

JOHN TYLER CHRISTOPHER
ANNUAL #1 variant